PIZZA NAPOLI
PIZZA NAPOLI
PIZZA PILGRIMS
ALESSANDRO BARASCHINO PIZZA FRITTA P.227
PIZZA FRITTA ISABELLA DE CHAM P.237
SANITA
ATTANAS
P.296
POGGIOREALE
VIA FORIA
GINO & TOTO SORBILLO P.48
SALVATORE CAPPARELLI BABA P.288
VIA DEI TRIBUNALI
VIA DEI TRIBUNALI
CENTRO STORICO
PIAZZA GARIBALDI
NAPOLI CENTRALE
VIA TOLEDO
FRITTO MISTO P.252
ZINZI SALUMERIA P.278
DA MICHELE P.26
CAPUTO MILL
NENNELLA P.260
DAVIDE RUOTOLO P.216
CORSO UMBERTO UNO
VIA NUOVA MARINA
QUARTIERI SPAGNOLI
GENOVESE RISTORANTE EUROPEO MATTOZZI P.272
PORTO
LELLO SPRITZ P.310
DAVIDE CIVITIELLO P.194
VINCENZO CAPUANO PIZZA P.124
TUNNEL DELLA VITTORIA
MT. VESUVIO
ERRICO PORZIO P.170
CASTEL DELL'OVO

CW01237183

PIZZA NAPOLI

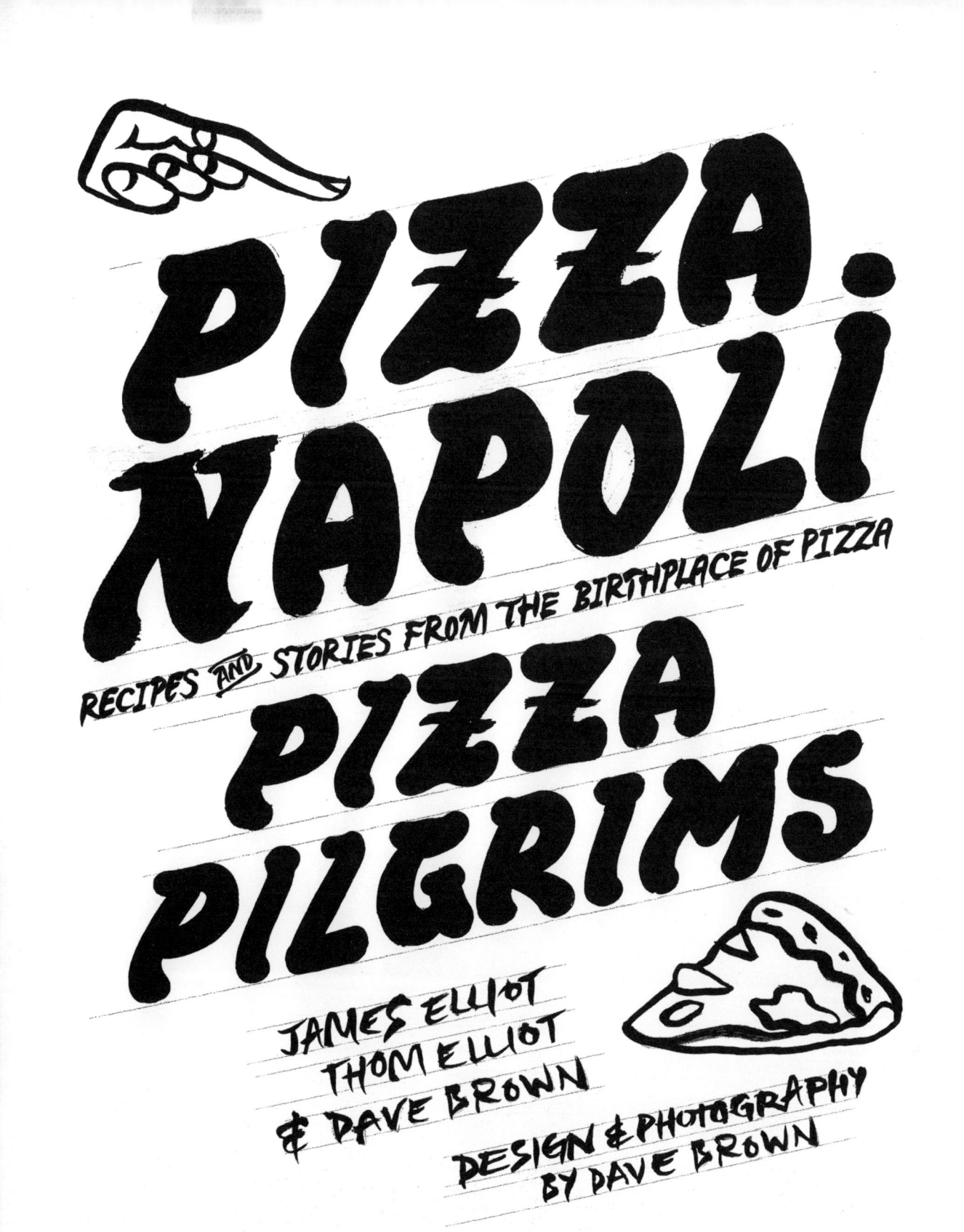

RECIPES AND STORIES FROM THE BIRTHPLACE OF PIZZA

PIZZA PILGRIMS

JAMES ELLIOT
THOM ELLIOT
& DAVE BROWN

DESIGN & PHOTOGRAPHY
BY DAVE BROWN

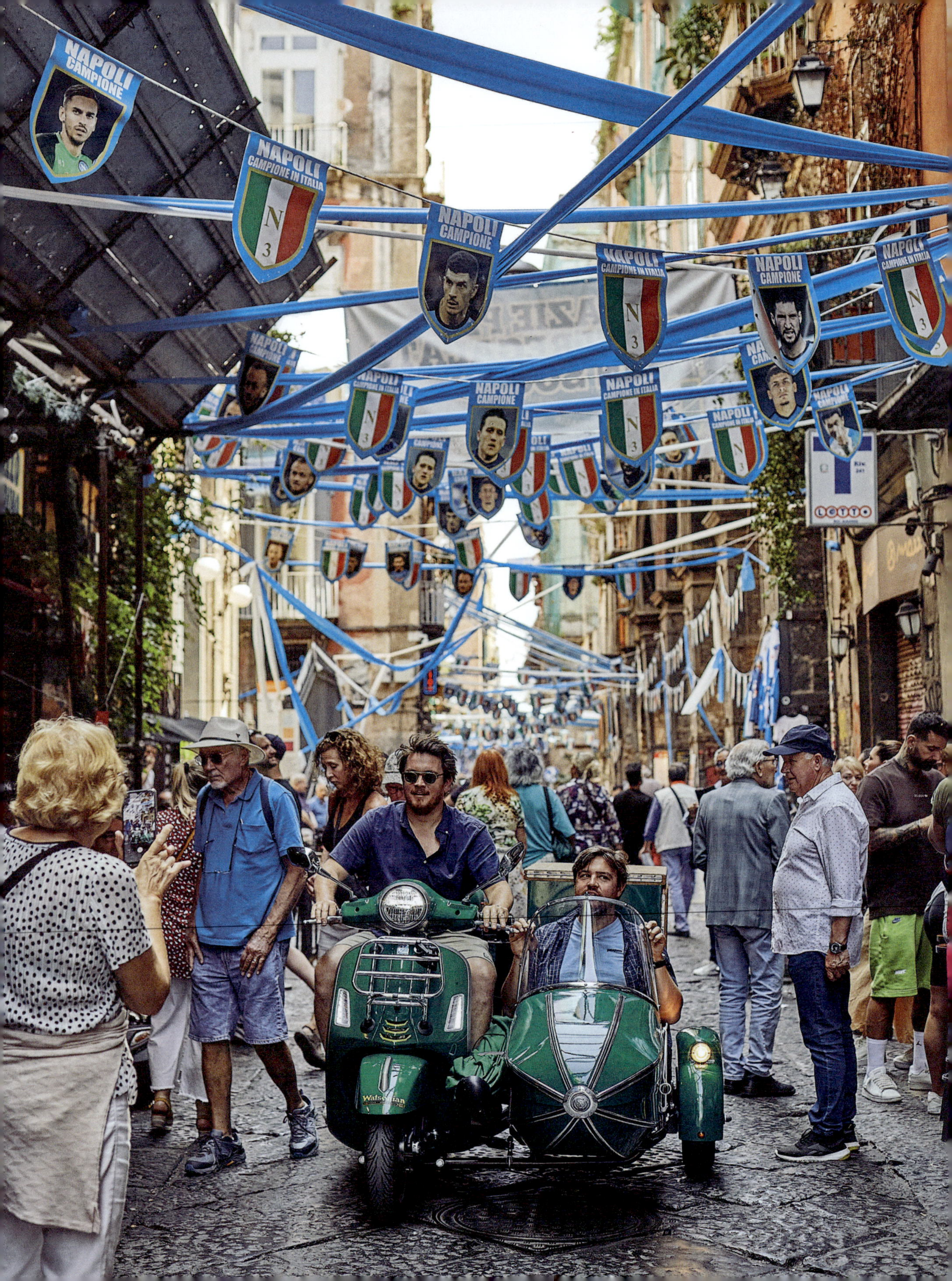
NAPOLI CAMPIONE
NAPOLI CAMPIONE IN ITALIA
LOTTO

PIZZA
PILGRIMS
DAL 2013 LONDON

A3 NAPOLI
E 45 A1 ROMA
TORRE
ANNUNZIATA sud
BOSCOREALE
90
70
A1
28

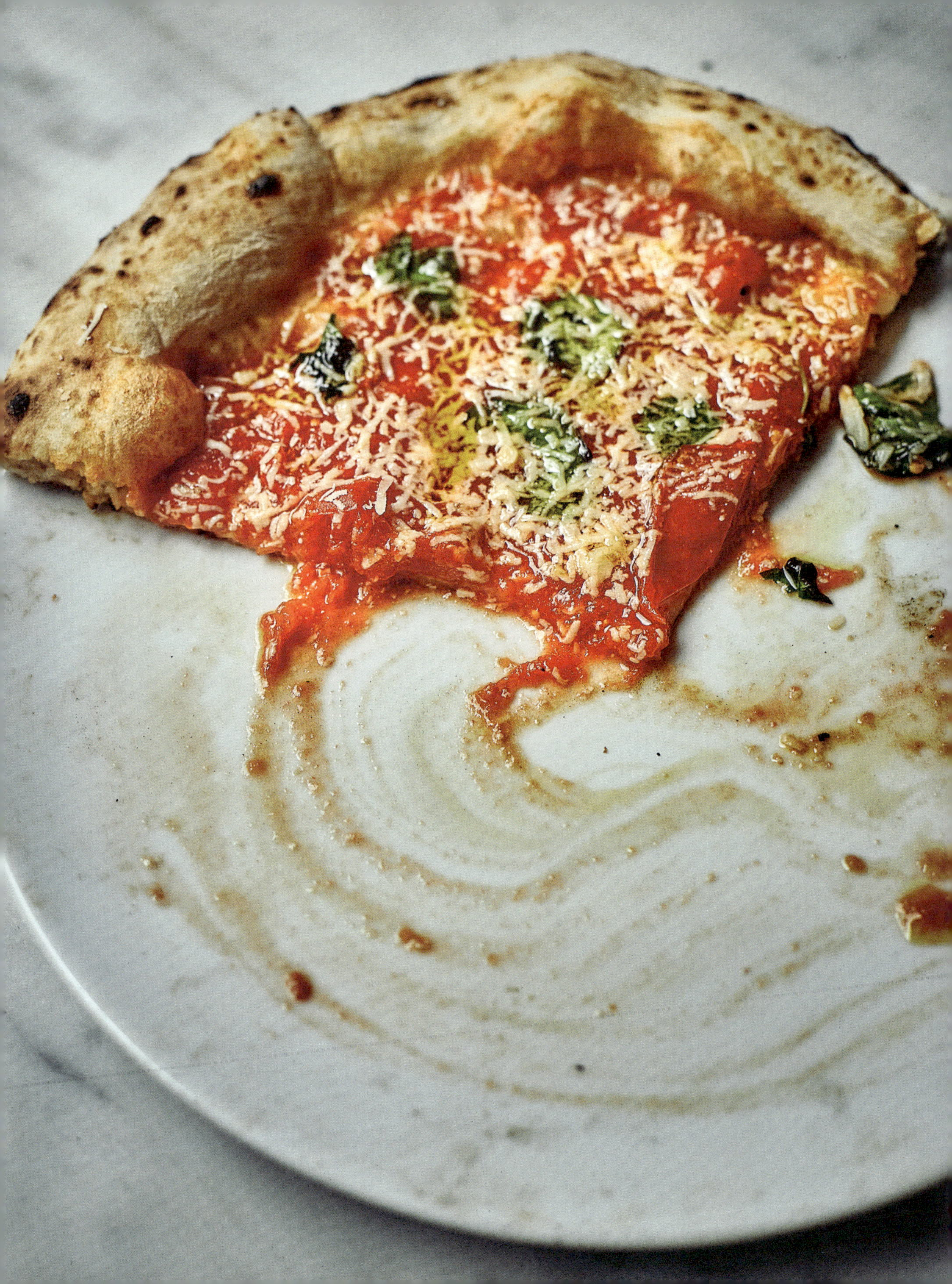

INTRODUCTION 8
PIZZA PRODUCE 44
PIZZA & DOUGH 86
PIZZA LEGENDS 110
PIZZA FRITTA 224
NAPOLI CUCINA 242
COFFEE & DOLCI 280
GRAZIE 312
INDEX 314

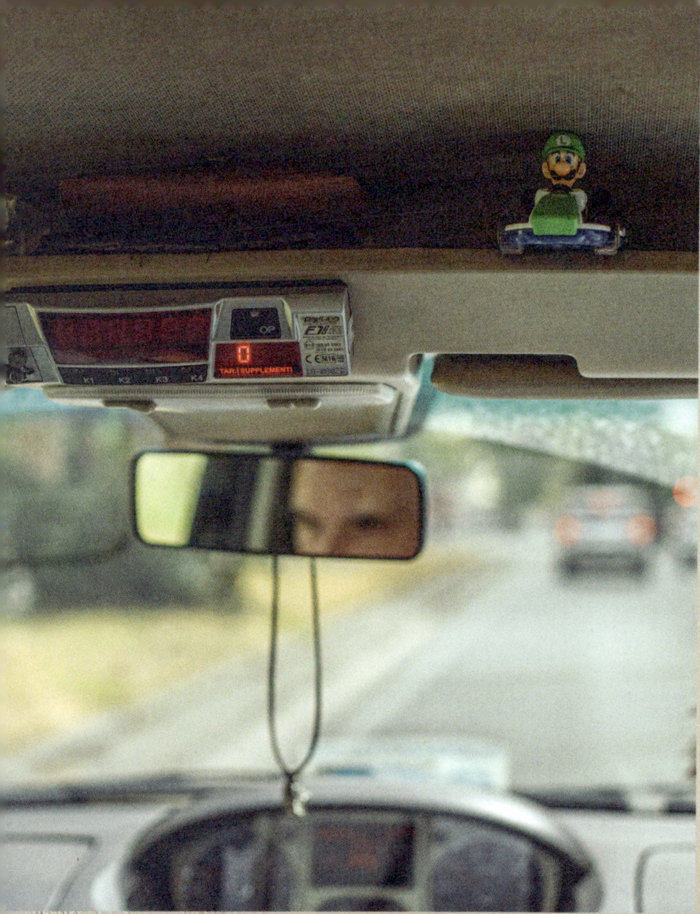
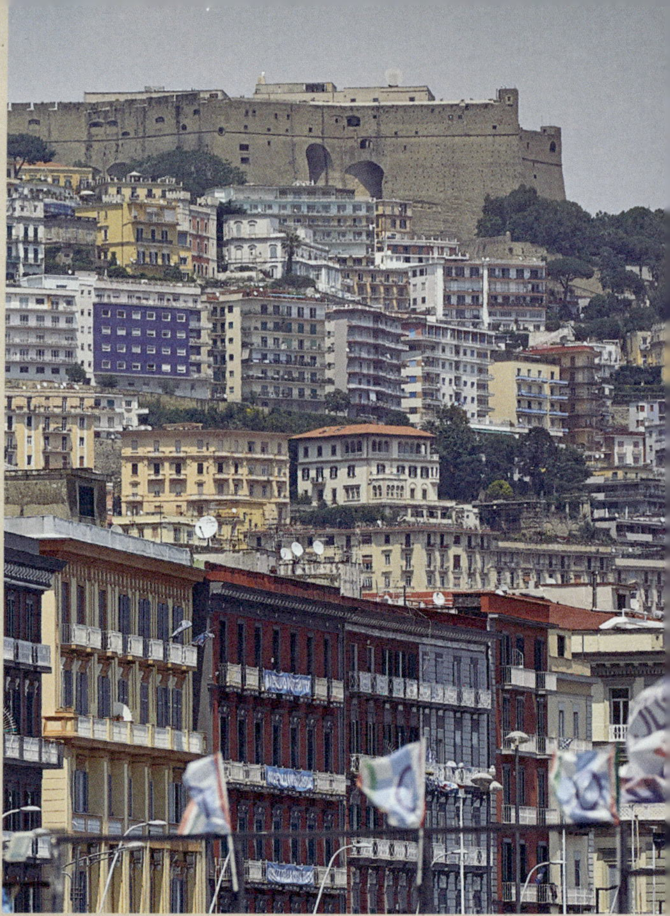
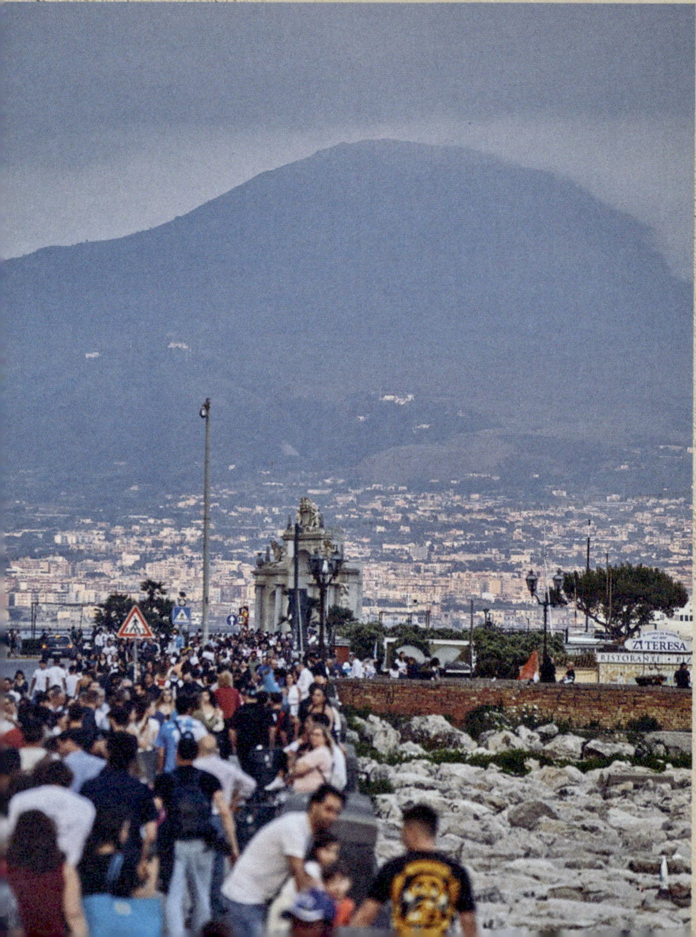
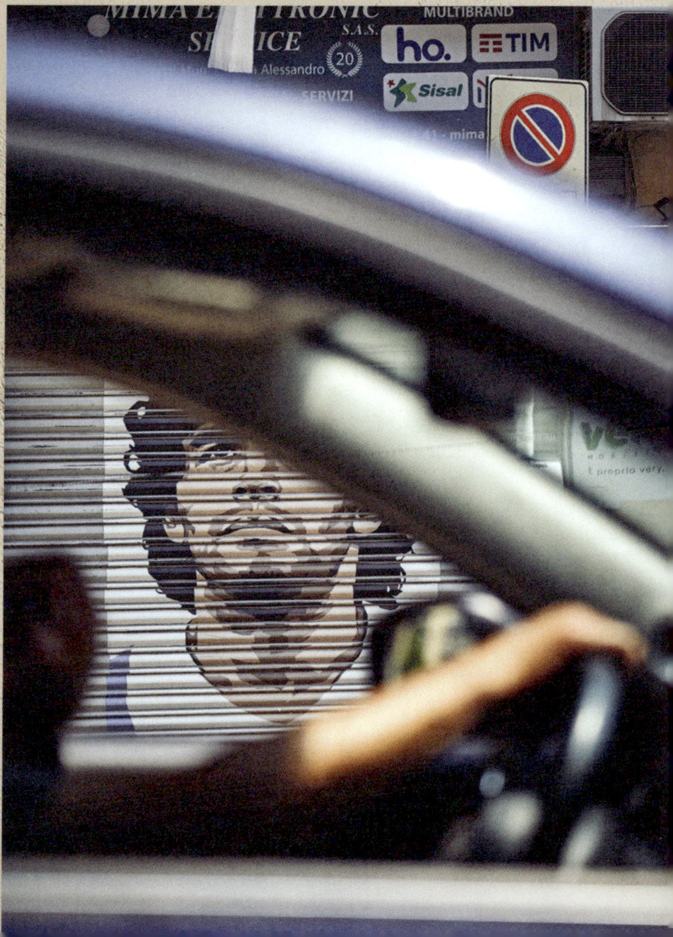
MULTIBRAND
ho.
TIM
Sisal
SERVIZI

A Flavour of Napoli

Napoli is, for lack of any other word, special.

There is no other city in Italy like Napoli. In fact, there is no other European city that matches the unique energy, passion and chaos of Napoli. It has the feeling of a pan always just about to boil over – and every so often, of course, it does. We have always found it totally infectious.

running of any other European city. That nearly a million people can co-exist in this 'shoot first ask questions later' environment is as inspiring as it is beguiling.

There is obviously a well-publicized dark side to all of this. But, in all our visits to Napoli, either through naivety or being constantly on the move, we have not seen direct evidence of this.

NAPOLI, TI AMO

One potential explanation for Napoli being so Neapolitan is its location – it is built in the foothills of Mount Vesuvius, an alarmingly active volcano. It is the only volcano in Europe to have erupted in the last 100 years, and with 3 million people living in its vicinity it is the most densely populated volcanic region in the world! Let's also not forget that Vesuvius has form – she wiped out Pompeii in AD 79. So you can imagine, having Vesuvius as your neighbour might cause you to have a slightly escalated world view: live your life to the full at all times, don't worry so much about the little things. We could all potentially learn something from that kind of thinking.

This manifests itself in a place living on the edge. Where the next fender bender is literally only 3 centimetres away, and is shrugged off when it happens (who needs the paperwork?). A place where whatever you do, you do with immense pride and dedication. A place where food, love and football rule supreme – and matter more than the bureaucracy and rule following that are seemingly essential to the

We have never felt threatened or intimidated, or ever so much as had a phone stolen off us (well, apart from that one time…).

What we have seen much, much more of is the warmth of the people – albeit with one eye on a commercial opportunity at all times. They are keen to tell you what they do, and why it is the best version of that. They are delighted that you are interested in their culture, from mozzarella to Pino Daniele, and will defend their local produce and art to the end.

Over the course of these pages we really hope to capture a slice of what this pride and passion looks like in this beautiful and unique city. We are a long way from the Trevi fountain here; the most stunning buildings are usually covered with graffiti. But that's Napoli in all its eccentric glory. We wouldn't want it any other way.

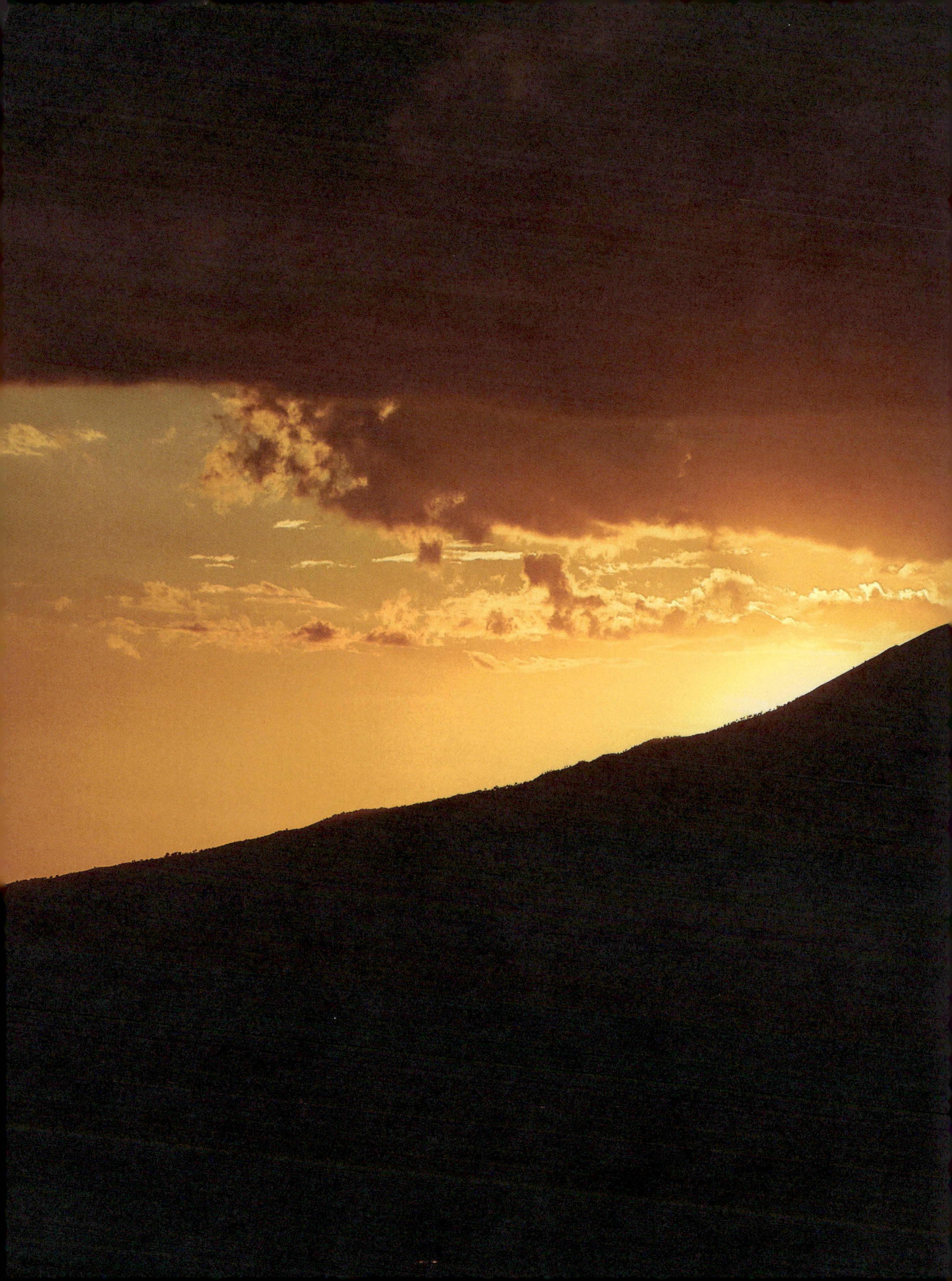

Whatever you think of Napoli, it will always be one thing to most people: the birthplace of pizza.

There are plenty of stories out there that relate to some kind of pre-pizza missing link existing before pizza as we know it was born in Napoli. Lots of bread topped with fruit – that kind of thing. In 2023, archaeologists uncovered an almost 2,000-year-old fresco, buried by ash from the Vesuvius eruption, that clearly shows something anyone would identify as a pizza, minus the mozzarella. You really need to understand the definition you want to accept for pizza before you start to set your heart on when or where it was invented.

We think that if we are true to ourselves, then what we know as pizza today was born in Napoli in the late 1800s. And whether you like it or not, the people of Napoli have definitely taken that as the truth, and have run with it.

From our point of view, it is really the invention of the Margherita pizza that marks the beginning (and many would say still the high point) of the history of pizza. The classic story goes that the dish was created in 1889 by a young chef called Raffaele Esposito in the establishment known as Brandi (which is still open to visit today in the centre of Napoli, just behind Piazza Plebiscito). He had been tasked with coming up with a dish for the visit of Queen Margherita of Savoy, who had expressed that she was fed up with the rich French food she had been subjected to on her recent tour.

Raffaele was a dedicated chap, so he tried three different pizzas for the Queen to get her approval. The first two (essentially a Marinara with tomato, oil and garlic, and a Napoletana with anchovies and capers) were met with disdain. Refusing to be disheartened, and working with the classic 'third time lucky' approach, he combined crushed tomatoes, fresh mozzarella and basil on top of a bread base, inspired by the colours of the newly formed Italian states flag: basil for the green, tomato for the red and mozzarella for the white.

PIZZA AND NAPOLI

Finally, the Queen was said to be delighted with the simplicity of this dish, and wrote to the chef after her visit to say how much she had enjoyed her experience. The Margherita was named after her, and so cemented its place in history. You can still see a copy of the letter on the wall in Pizzeria Brandi if you don't believe us.

Turns out, some people don't believe us. The letter's veracity has been repeatedly questioned. To be fair, there are plenty of references to a very Margherita-type product dating from the 1830s, and it has been pointed

"JULIA RO
CON LA M
PIZZ
NELLE SALE CINEM
DAL 17 SETTEMBRE 201
MANGIA PR
MANGIA PREGA AMA
L'antica Pizzeria

> **NAPOLI HAS AN ESTIMATED 8,200 PIZZERIAS, AND NEAPOLITAN PIZZA HAS BEEN EMBRACED BY THE WORLD; EVERY MAJOR CITY ON EARTH IN 2025 WILL HAVE A NEAPOLITAN PIZZERIA.**

out that this Queen of Savoy narrative was not reported at the time and instead first reared its head in the 1930s. But we think, why mess with a great story...?

Cut to today, and it is fair to say Neapolitan pizza is thriving. Napoli has an estimated 8,200 pizzerias, and Neapolitan pizza has been embraced by the world; every major city on Earth has a Neapolitan pizzeria. The product itself has been protected by UNESCO to 'intangible cultural heritage' status – the same as yoga in India. The Associazione Verace Pizza Napoletana (AVPN) was established almost 40 years ago to protect the core elements of Neapolitan pizza; they have set the definition of Neapolitan pizza and they mean to defend it.

Despite all this protectionism, however, the most notable development in the pizza of Napoli has been its evolution. Over the last decade, the once ruthlessly traditionalist position of the city's great pizza makers has given way to a new generation of chefs looking to move pizza forward. Everywhere you look in and around Napoli, you now see people testing the AVPN fences – from the Instagram-friendly puffed up crusts of canotto pizza at Vincenzo Capuano, to the finishing stations and complex flavour combinations of Concettina ai Tre Santi or Palazzo Petrucci. Franco Pepe – often cited as the best pizza maker in the world – even had the audacity to mess with the revered Margherita. His 'Margherita sbagliata' (translation: 'Margherita gone wrong') is cooked with cheese only, before fresh tomato and basil-reduction flourishes are added. Sacrilege! Delicious, delicious sacrilege!

We have all the time in the world for the tradition and cannot deny that maybe our favourite pizza experience in Napoli is a Margherita from Pizzeria da Michele. However, it is actually this inventiveness and evolution that ensures Napoli stays synonymous with pizza the world over. If the city was going to stay as the global capital of pizza, then they had to translate their dedication and passion into developing the art form. It's fantastic to see that happening now and, what's more, being embraced by the city itself.

Throughout the course of writing this book, as well as over our many trips to Napoli while growing our own pizza business, we have had the opportunity to meet with the most revered pizza chefs there. We have aimed to share in these pages many of their unique philosophies, along with their own signature pizza recipes and some of the secrets of their craft. We hope that their efforts and dedication can inspire your own pizza efforts, and take your home pizza making to the next level.

WHITE
GRAPPA

MARGHERITA
MARINARA
100 ORE IN AULA
STAGE IN PIZZERIA

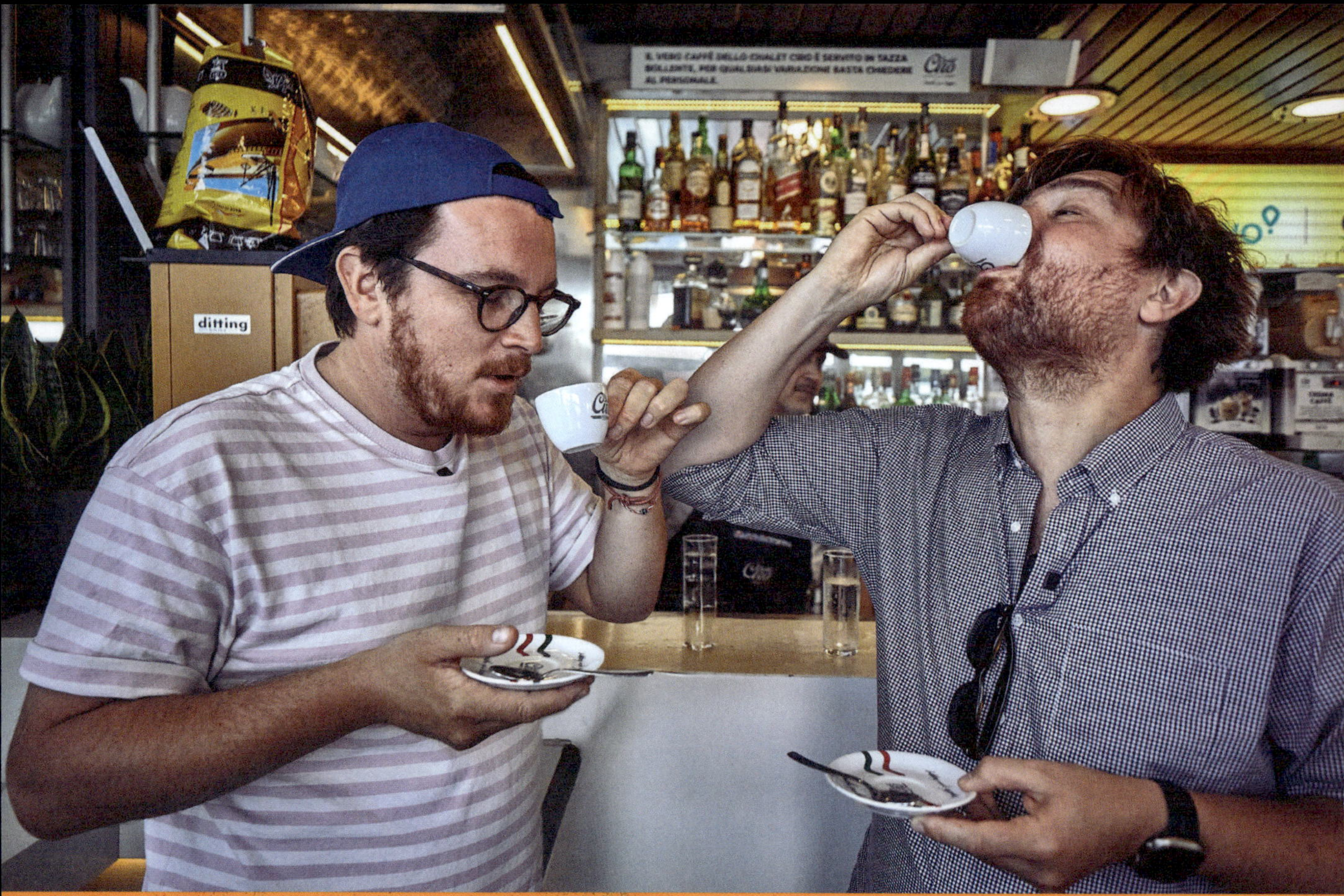
ditting

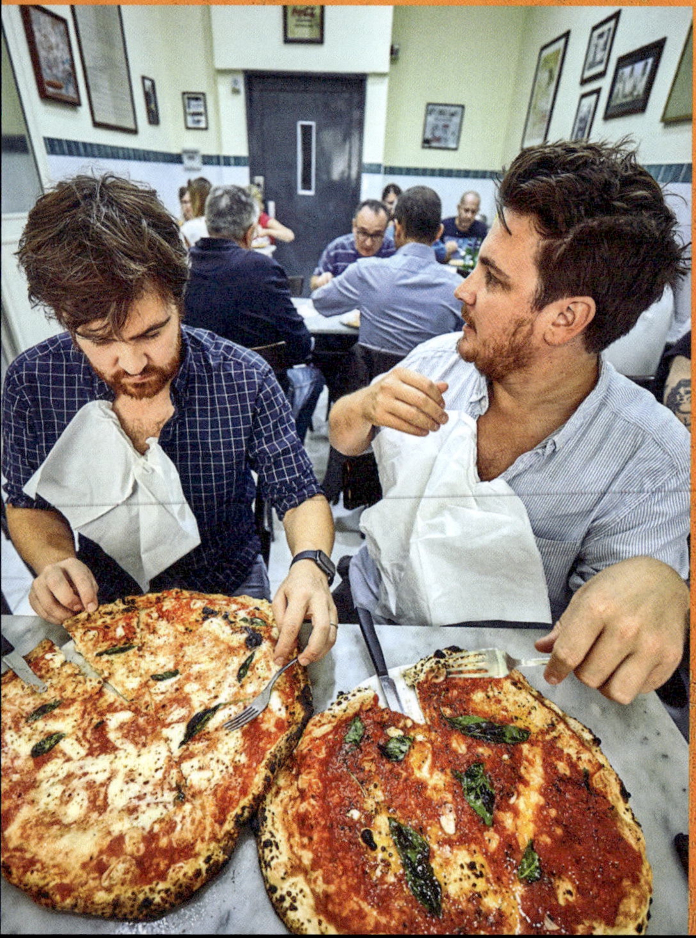

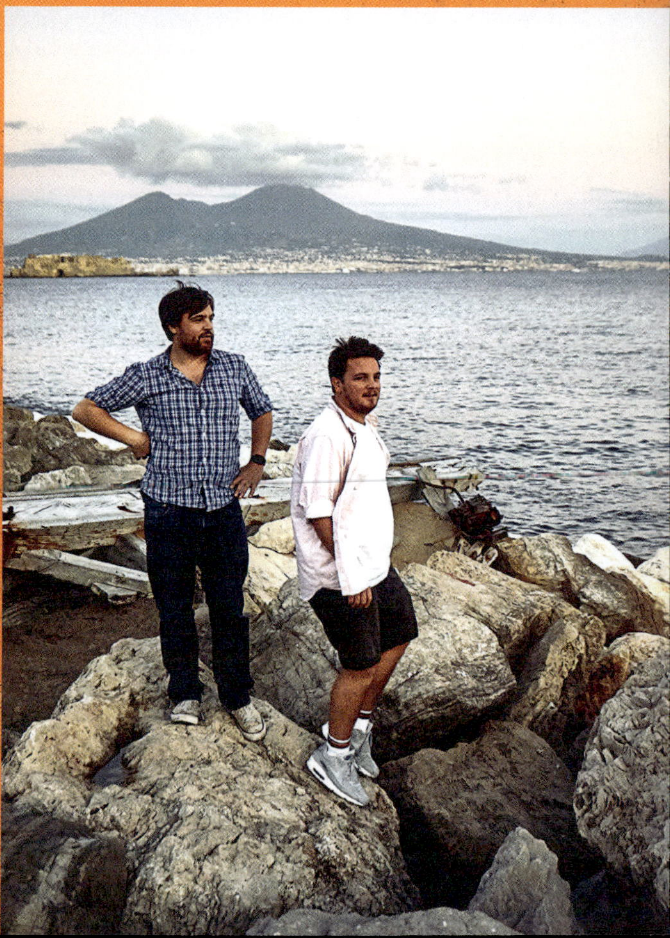

65 Trips and Counting

Pizza Pilgrims had very inauspicious beginnings. We knew nothing about pizza at all when we started out back in 2011 and, looking back, our first ever pizza event was a celebration of amateurishness. We had a rolling pin in our logo (a big Neapolitan pizza no-no) and the wood we used in the oven looked like it came off a building site!

PIZZA PILGRIMS & NAPOLI

It was clear from the off that we had some serious learning to do, and where better to learn about pizza than Italy? The idea for the pizza pilgrimage was born, and we duly set off to Calabria to collect our brand-new Piaggio Ape van and start our quest for pizza knowledge.

We didn't even know at this stage that Napoli was the place where our perspective on pizza would change. On 19 October 2011 we walked into Da Michele for a Margherita. It is fair to say that our view on pizza would never be the same again.

Since that first ever visit, we have worked out that we have been to Napoli over 65 times between us in the 12 years we have been running Pizza Pilgrims. We take all of our managers and head chefs for all the pizzerias twice a year, and we have been on countless inspiration trips and supplier visits on top of that. And we can genuinely say that we have always come home from those trips with more ideas, more inspiration, more little tips for making our pizza better.

The really amazing thing is that, during that time, we have seen Napoli and its attitude to pizza change. When we first visited, it was before the global explosion of Neapolitan pizza; the Napoli scene was very old fashioned and centred on tradition – almost protectionism. The focus was on consistency and no deviating from old methods to make very specific kinds of pizza.

However, since the world (including ourselves) discovered Neapolitan pizza in a big way in the early 2010s, the scene in Napoli itself has changed. There has been a new wave of pizzaioli searching for something new, bringing their own style and ideas to the medium. This has led to much more inventive toppings and recipes and whole new styles of dough designed to look great on Instagram (see Vincenzo Capuano's contemporary pizza on page 124). The traditional pizza and pizzerias absolutely remain, but there has been a concerted effort from the city to remain world leaders when it comes to pizza. And we think we can all agree that benefits all of us.

> **WE HAVE WORKED OUT THAT WE HAVE BEEN TO NAPOLI OVER 65 TIMES BETWEEN US IN THE 12 YEARS WE HAVE BEEN RUNNING PIZZA PILGRIMS.**

Pizza Pilgrims, the Neapolitan pizza business that we run, is named after a trip we undertook in 2011 through Italy with a view to improving our pizza knowledge (as well as to bring back our beloved Conchetta, which was the vehicle we used to house our pizza oven on the market stall in Soho, in London, and at events across the UK).

The original pilgrimage really was born of necessity on a number of fronts. We had realized we needed

so slow, in fact, that she was not allowed to drive on the autostrada at all, and we even have footage of us being overtaken up a hill by a jogger.

Undeterred, we soldiered on. We had lined up a number of pizza-adjacent trips over the weeks we had planned in Italy – from basil farms in Genova to mozzarella in Caserta, focaccia in Recco to red wine in Montepulciano. There was a lot to cover.

THE ORIGINAL PILGRIMAGE

a vehicle to transport the oven (so we could take it home after each event!) and we had fallen in love with the idea of the vehicle being a Piaggio Ape – the beloved three-wheeled Italian vehicle so synonymous with rural Italy. Developed by Piaggio after World War II in order to 'rebuild the country', the Ape is essentially a Vespa with a van on the back (*ape* is Italian for 'bee', which is of course the working version of a *vespa*, which means 'wasp').

So, we had fallen in love with this amazing vehicle but couldn't quite afford to buy one with our meagre savings. But we soon realized that we could save some money by flying to Italy to buy one there. This plan quickly developed to make the trip a tour of Italy, with a view to learning about pizza and developing our burgeoning dough skills. The pizza pilgrimage was born.

So we did the deal for the van, to be collected on the very tip of the toe of Italy in Reggio Calabria. We lined up a selection of places to visit on our way home and said goodbye to our 'proper' jobs to pursue a life of pizza.

As we pulled out of the dealership in our new vehicle we were excited to hit the open road in search of our pizza dreams. However, we quickly hit a snag when we realized the top speed of the vehicle we had just bought was about 18 miles per hour... and with just under 1,800 miles to drive back to the UK, it was quite the discovery. She was

All of this was blown out of the water when we arrived in Napoli in mid-October 2011. We vaguely knew that pizza was a big deal here, but we had no idea how much our lives were about to change.

The Napoli trip was like a bomb going off in our heads. We tasted San Marzano tomatoes in the foothills of Mount Vesuvius, we tried mozzarella that was still warm from being made just minutes earlier; we even milked a buffalo! We spent time with some amazing pizza celebrities – from Antimo Caputo (page 48), the flour king of Napoli, to Antonino Esposito (page 93), who helped us cook our first ever pizza in a wood-fired oven.

But none of this compares to our first experience of a Neapolitan pizza in a pizzeria. We had selected Da Michele – the same pizzeria where Julia Roberts first tastes Neapolitan pizza in the film *Eat, Pray, Love*, and one of the true giants of the city of Napoli. They only served two pizzas – a Margherita or a Marinara – and from the first bite we were truly blown away. The Da Michele Margherita is still a thing of beauty: the softness of the dough, the fresh acidity of the mozzarella, the sweetness of the tomato. It honestly is a taste combo that will never be beaten for us, but we have been trying our best to do so in our pizzerias since that moment.

But it wasn't just about the pizza. The energy of Da Michele also grabbed us on that day. There is such

Pizza Oven in the back

PIZZA PILGRIMS

PIZZA

a sense of anticipation from every guest, many of whom have queued in a rather haphazard way for this moment and never fully knew when they were due to get their pizza fix. The service is slightly surly, but with a sense of pride, and safe in the knowledge that the pizza they are serving will always win the guest over. The pizzaioli team is a well-oiled machine, turning out perfect pizza after perfect pizza. The decoration is simplicity itself, from marble tables and floors to strip lighting and wooden chairs. The walls are adorned with little pieces of Neapolitan pizza history, including a large portrait of Michele Condurro himself (a large number of the team are members of the Condurro family).

All in all, it was an experience we will never forget, not least as we got the opportunity to get in the kitchen and watch Luigi Condurro (Michele's grandson) make a pizza for us up close. We were hooked. And from that moment on, we have thought about little else but Neapolitan pizza...

"THE DA MICHELE MARGHERITA IS STILL A THING OF BEAUTY: THE SOFTNESS OF THE DOUGH, THE FRESH ACIDITY OF THE MOZZARELLA, THE SWEETNESS OF THE TOMATO.

The 10 Year Anniversary Vespa Pilgrimage

In 2023 we were celebrating 10 years since we opened our first pizzeria in London's Soho. We wanted to mark this moment in style – not with a 10% money-off offer, or some balloons in the shape of 10 (although there were a few of those). We wanted to do something that reflected our history and reminded our customers (and ourselves) about what had got us into this mess in the first place. And very quickly the answer became clear. It was going to have to be another pilgrimage. Through Italy. On an even more ridiculous vehicle than we had used in the first instance.

The Pizza Vespa was born… albeit only in sketch form.

The idea was simple, really. Take a Vespa (the sister vehicle of our original Piaggio Ape), add a side car and also a fold-out pizza kitchen (including a Gozney Roccbox oven). It was set to become our very own pizza kitchen transformer. Eat that, Michael Bay.

A cursory Google told us that the number-one place in the country for making side cars was Watsonian in Gloucestershire, so we quickly got in touch with them to see if they were up for the challenge. And, of course, they totally were (they had already made side cars for Hagrid in *Harry Potter* and the *Two Fat Ladies* cookery TV show).

So while they got on with bringing our ropey sketch to life, we started to think about what kind of pilgrimage we should do, and very quickly we realized there was only one city we wanted to go to: Napoli!

The plan quickly took shape. Take our newly created 'Pizzeria on a Vespa' to Napoli. Embark on a 10-day tour in and around the city, showing off our amazing new vehicle and meeting the best pizza chefs, suppliers and pizza fans in order to inspire new items for our pizzeria menu. What could possibly go wrong? Before we knew it, we were driving out of the Watsonian workshop on what we can only assume was the world's smallest pizzeria. The second pizza pilgrimage had begun…

We didn't really know what to expect once we got to Napoli. Would people love our creation, or bemoan us messing with a design classic? Was pizza too serious a deal here to be shown the lack of respect of being made by the roadside, without the bells and whistles of a pizzeria? Would Napoli accept two non-Neapolitans coming up with this idea?

Well, we can safely say that Napoli LOVES the Pizza Vespa. The Neapolitans are an effusive bunch at the best of times, but the number of smiles, high fives, head turns and 'throw myself into the street to show my appreciation' we got from the people of that city was truly heart-warming.

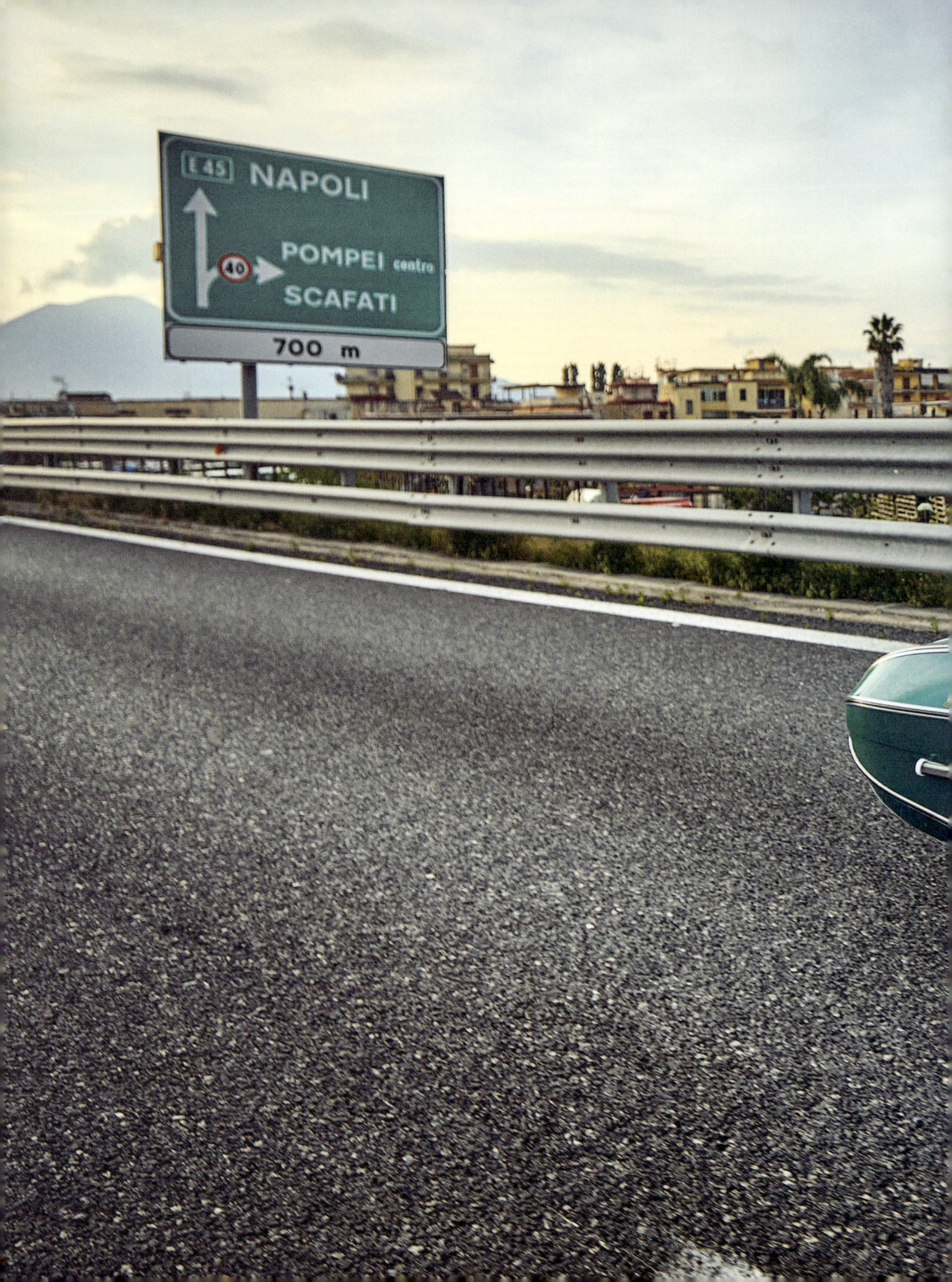
E 45
NAPOLI
40
POMPEI centro
SCAFATI
700 m

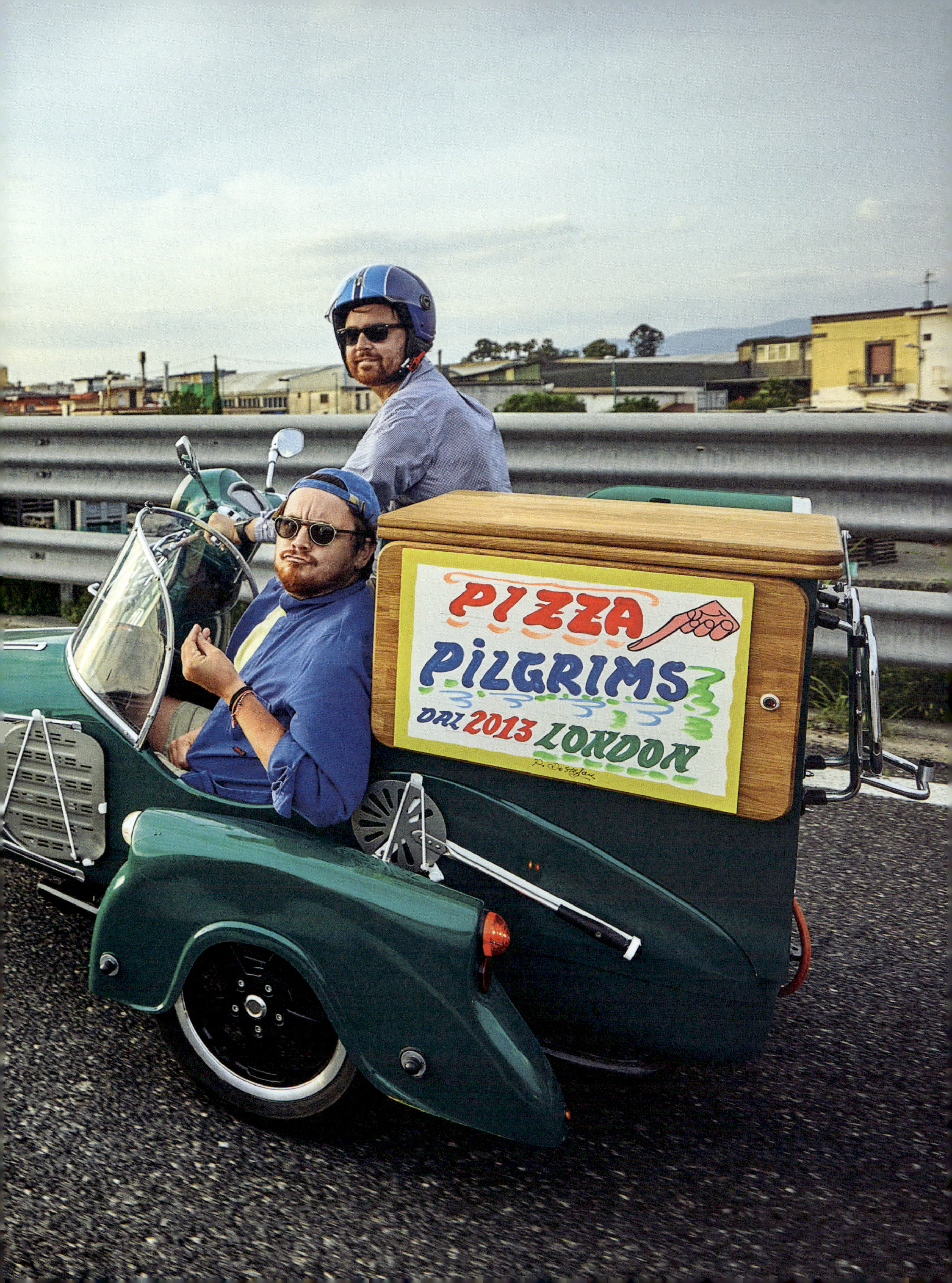
PIZZA
PILGRIMS
DAL 2013 LONDON

Over and above the bike itself, it was fantastic to spend time with the movers and shakers of Napoli's pizza and food scene, learning from them, sharing ideas both ways and deepening our understanding of both Napoli and its rich pizza history. We have distilled what we learned, and much more, into the pages of this book in the hope that you too can bring the energy and passion of the Napoli pizza scene to your home.

The highlight of the trip was undoubtedly on the last day. Back in 2011, we had eaten our first ever Neapolitan pizza in the famed pizzeria Da Michele – the true start of our Neapolitan pizza journey. Over the years we have become good friends with Alessandro Condurro, who is the fifth generation Condurro to run Da Michele. We have spent many hours with him and his team over multiple trips to Napoli and pizza events around the world. As such, to mark our 10th anniversary trip we took a punt and decided to ask them if Da Michele would allow us to celebrate the wrap party for the trip in their renowned pizzeria. We were absolutely knocked for six when they agreed!

We had the most amazing evening we could have imagined. They allowed us to park the Vespa outside (next to their never-ending queue) and put our Pizza Pilgrims brand banner next to theirs. We invited all the suppliers we had been with for the week into the pizzeria for a private party. We toured the place and had the chance to interview Alessandro about the significance of Da Michele in the history of pizza, and we even got in the historic kitchen to make pizza for their customers and our guests! At the end of the evening, we swapped Da Michele and Pizza Pilgrims shirts like Bobby Moore and Pele (well, sort of like that). It was a sensational end to an amazing week – and an emotional and historic moment for us to cap 10 years of drawing inspiration from the amazing city of Napoli.

Here is a summary of the visits we did during the summer of 2023 Vespa Trip, and where you can find them in the book.

Day 1: Developing the Margherita Extra Extra with Toto Sorbillo (page 155)
Day 2: A deep dive into Italian snacks and drinks at local kiosks (page 244)
Day 3: Signwriting with Pasquale de Stefano (page 38)
Day 4: Spritz culture with the team from Lello Spritz in the Spanish Quarter (page 308)
Day 5: Pistachio affogato at Chalet Ciro (page 292)
Day 6: Football culture and friends – Napoli win the league for the 3rd time! (page 30)
Day 7: Day trip to Amalfi to make limoncello (page 302)
Day 8: The Americana: the Italian favourite that no one believes is real (page 127)
Day 9: Pizza of the gods with Franco Pepe, at Pepe in Grani (page 158)
Day 10: The future of flour with Antimo Caputo (page 48)
Day 11: Deep-fried smoked mozzarella bites with our friends at Latteria Sorrentina (page 82)
Day 12: Da Michele x Pizza Pilgrims pop-up wrap party (overleaf)!

Watsonian
SIDECARS · SINCE 1912

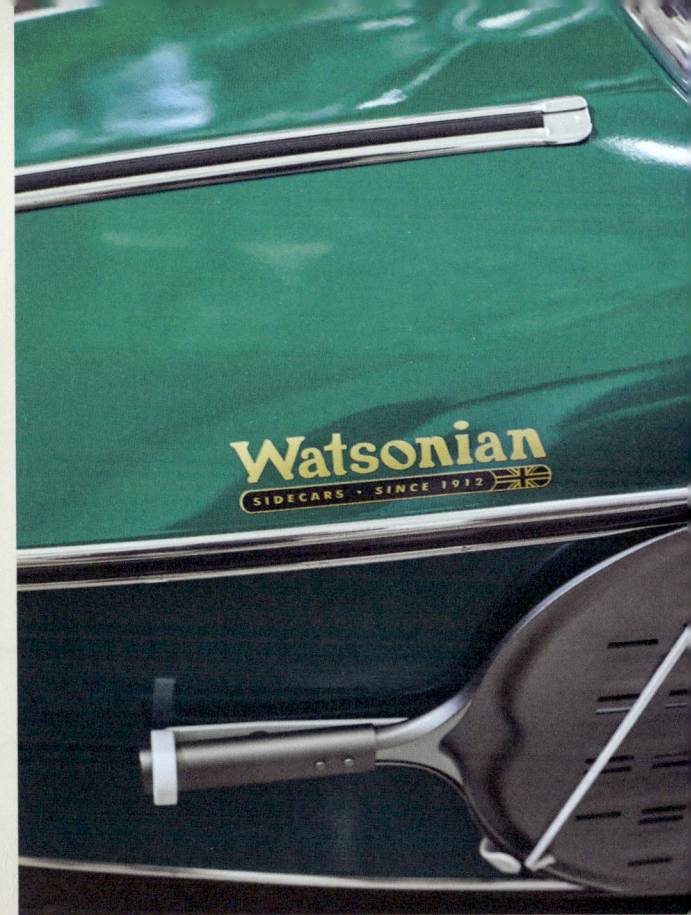

PIZZA PILGRIMS · GOZNEY

DA MICHELE PIZZA VESPA POP-UP

On our very first trip to Napoli in our little green Ape we did what all pizza fans do and got in line at Pizzeria da Michele to take pizza communion at this legendary Napoli temple. Da Michele has been in business since 1906, serving up some of the most traditional, simple, delicious pizzas in the city. The menu is brutally short. Four pizzas. Margherita, Marinara, Cossaca and Marita (which is just half and half of the first two!). They only serve water, coke and beer in plastic cups and you can't book. OLD. SCHOOL. We sat in the same seat that Julia Roberts sat in in the movie that sky-rocketed the pizzeria to international fame and tasted our first bite of proper Neapolitan pizza. Not to get emotional about it, but it was a bit of a lightning bolt moment for the both of us and it led us on a 12-year adventure (so far) into the amazing world of Neapolitan Pizza. Over the years, we have got to know Alessandro Condurro, the 5th-generation custodian of Da Michele. It was at the 50 Top Pizza Awards in Madrid, after a few *tinto de veranas*, that we hatched a plan to host a Pizza Pilgrims pop-up in his legendary pizzeria. So, on the last day of our Vespa pilgrimage through Napoli, we got the chance to take over the kitchen with our team and cook some pizzas for a party of friends, suppliers, producers and pizza chefs from Napoli. It was such an amazing honour. We got to work side by side with their pizzaioli and say thank you to all the people that have helped us make Pizza Pilgrims what it is today. It was a genuinely surreal moment that neither of us will forget, and felt like the pizza world of Napoli was somehow ordaining us into the Neapolitan Church of pizza. OK, we're getting over the top, but if you had told us 10 years ago that we would be taking over Napoli's most famous pizzeria for the day we would have said *vaffanculo*!

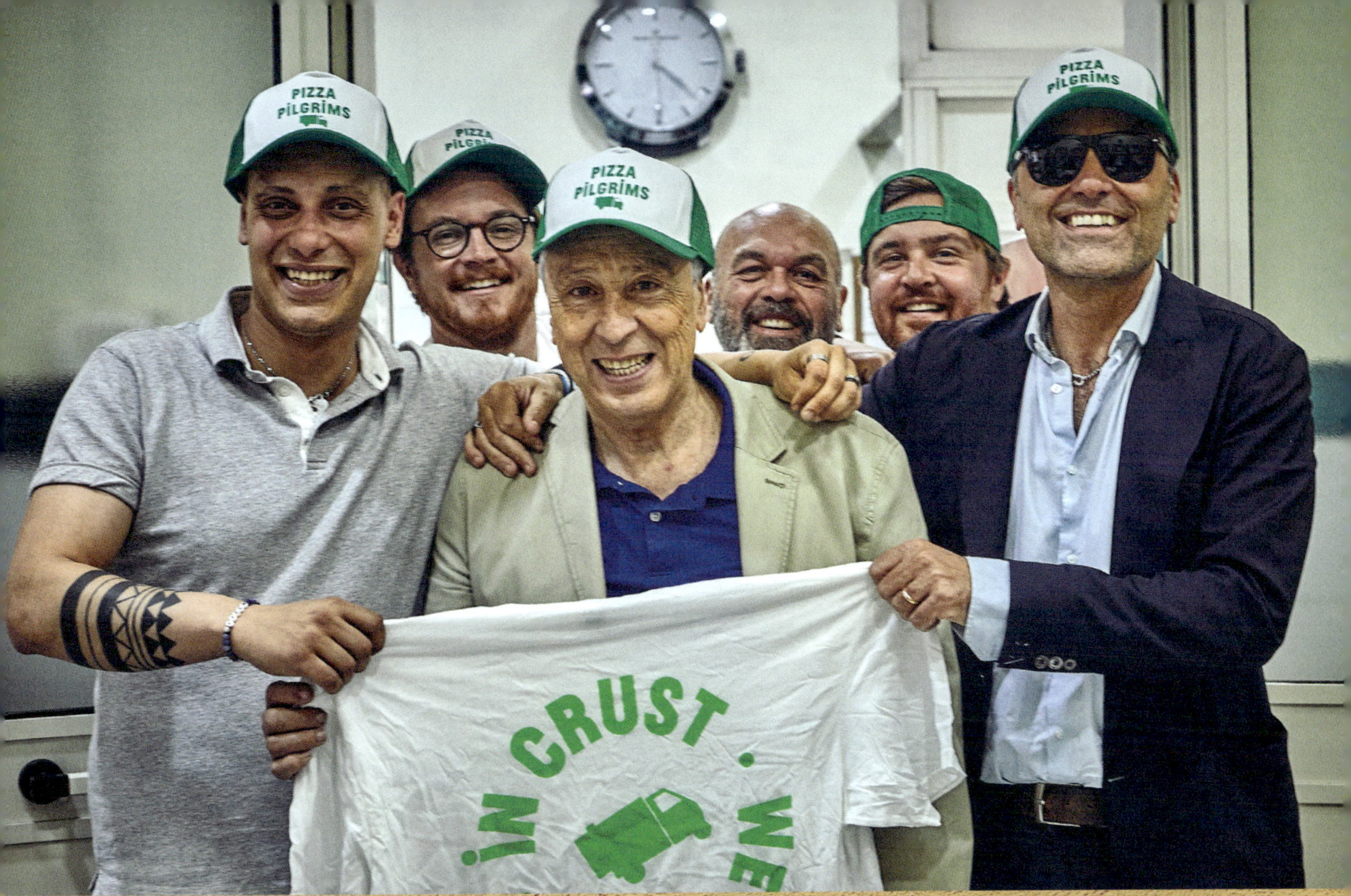
PIZZA PILGRIMS
IN CRUST

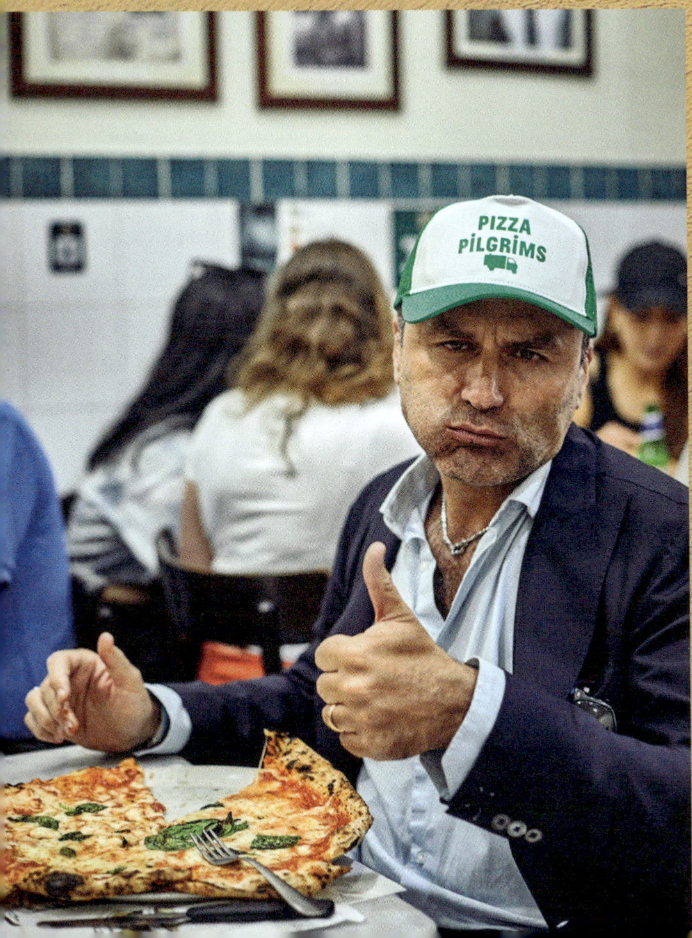
PIZZA PILGRIMS

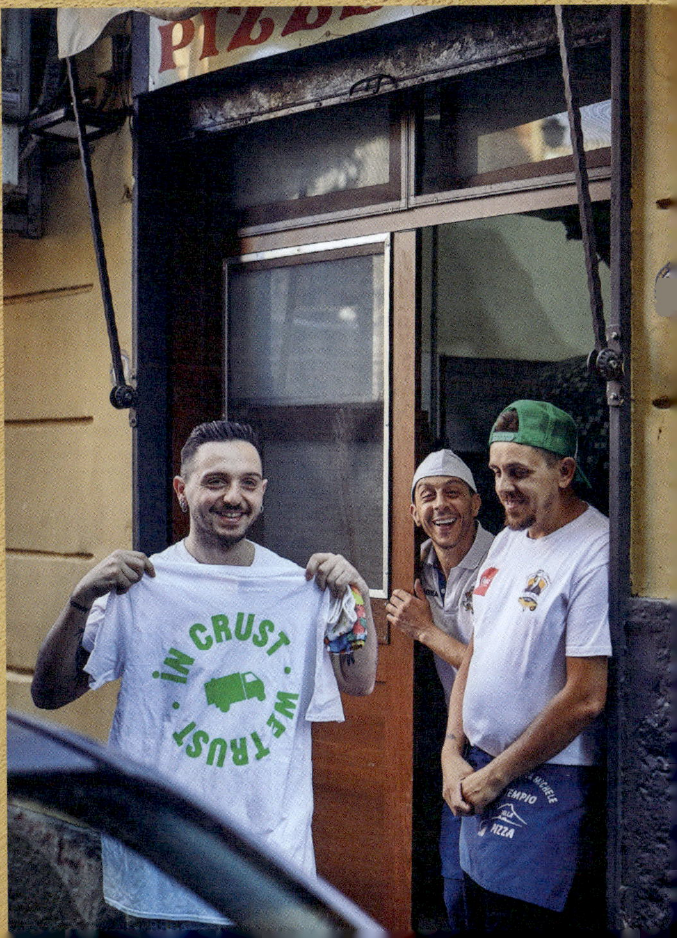
IN CRUST WE TRUST

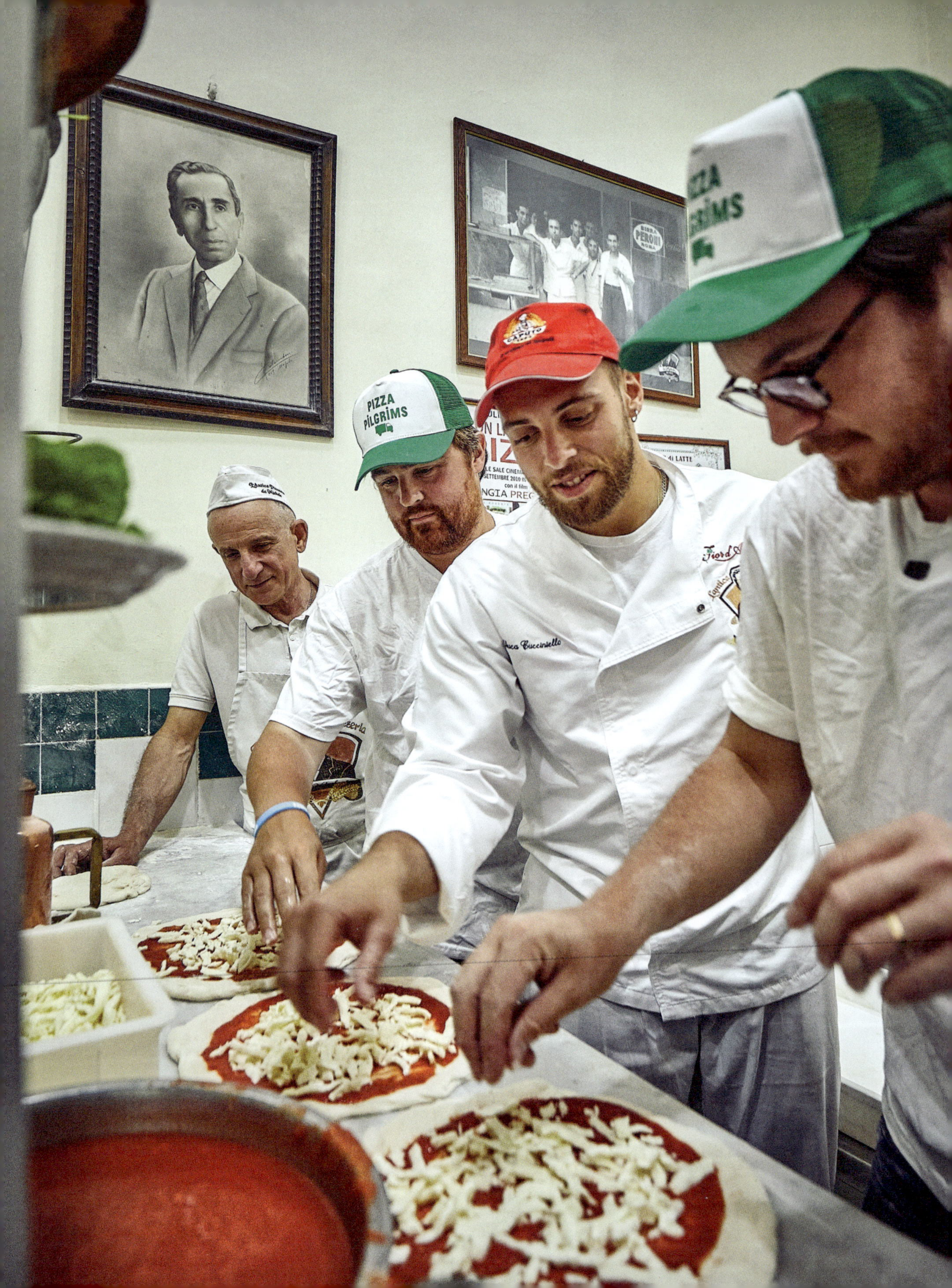
PIZZA PILGRIMS
PIZZA PILGRIMS

antica Pizzeria "da Michele"
PIZZERIA
da MICHELE
L'ANTICA
PIZZA PILGRIMS
PIZZA PILGRIMS
DAL 2013 LONDON

PIZZA PILGRIMS
L'Antica Pizzeria
DA MICHELE
a Napoli
CON LA NOSTRA
PIZZA
ANTONIO ABATE

FOOTBALL IN NAPOLI

Winning the League

Napoli FC has the fourth biggest fan base of any team in the Italian league, but what makes it unique in its relationship with its home is that it is the only club in the city. Unlike Rome, Turin, Milan and Genoa, which all have multiple support and a split fan base, everyone who follows football in and around Napoli will support Napoli FC. This is what makes the colour of the club throughout the city so omnipresent – combined of course with the natural passion and exuberance of the locals.

In 2023, on our Pizza Vespa tour of Napoli, we were lucky enough to be spending the day in the city centre when the football team won the league for only the third time in their existence.

The city was absolutely electric – every street was decorated in the famous light blue, and the number 3 (representing the third league win) was literally everywhere. It felt like there was no happier place on the entire planet!

The streets were packed with people with banners, flags and blue flares – even the kids had flares!

We had created a collaboration beer with Camden Brewery to celebrate the league win (the beer was called Campiones). We decided it would be fun to set up in the main square of Napoli and give away a free can to anyone who could do five keepie-uppies with a lemon!

They showed the final game of the season on huge screens in the main square.

The atmosphere was incredible – they had to stop the game a couple of times as the flares got out of hand. What was amazing for us was how many people who either did work or had worked at Pizza Pilgrims were there on the day – we must have ended up watching the match with a group of 20 people, all of whom we had worked with! Got to love Napoli for that!

FORZA NAPOLI!

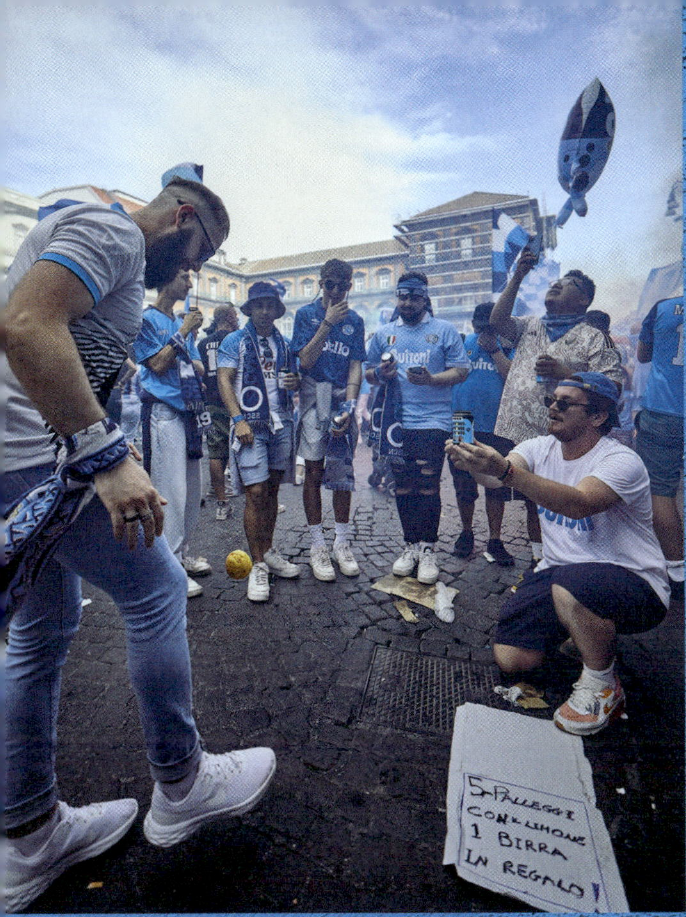
5 PALLEGGI
CON LIMONE
1 BIRRA
IN REGALO

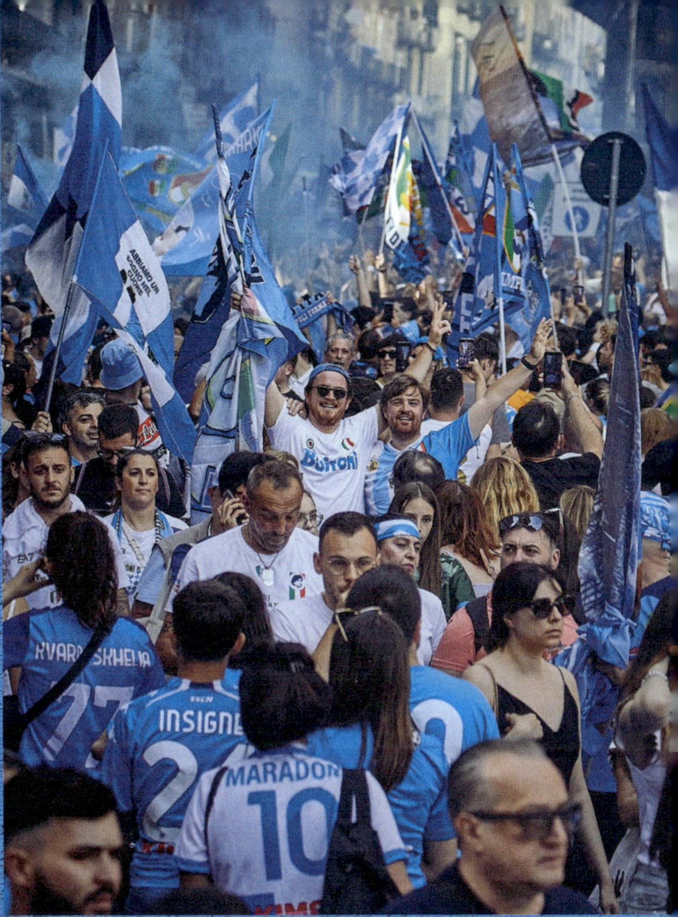
INSIGNE
MARADON
10

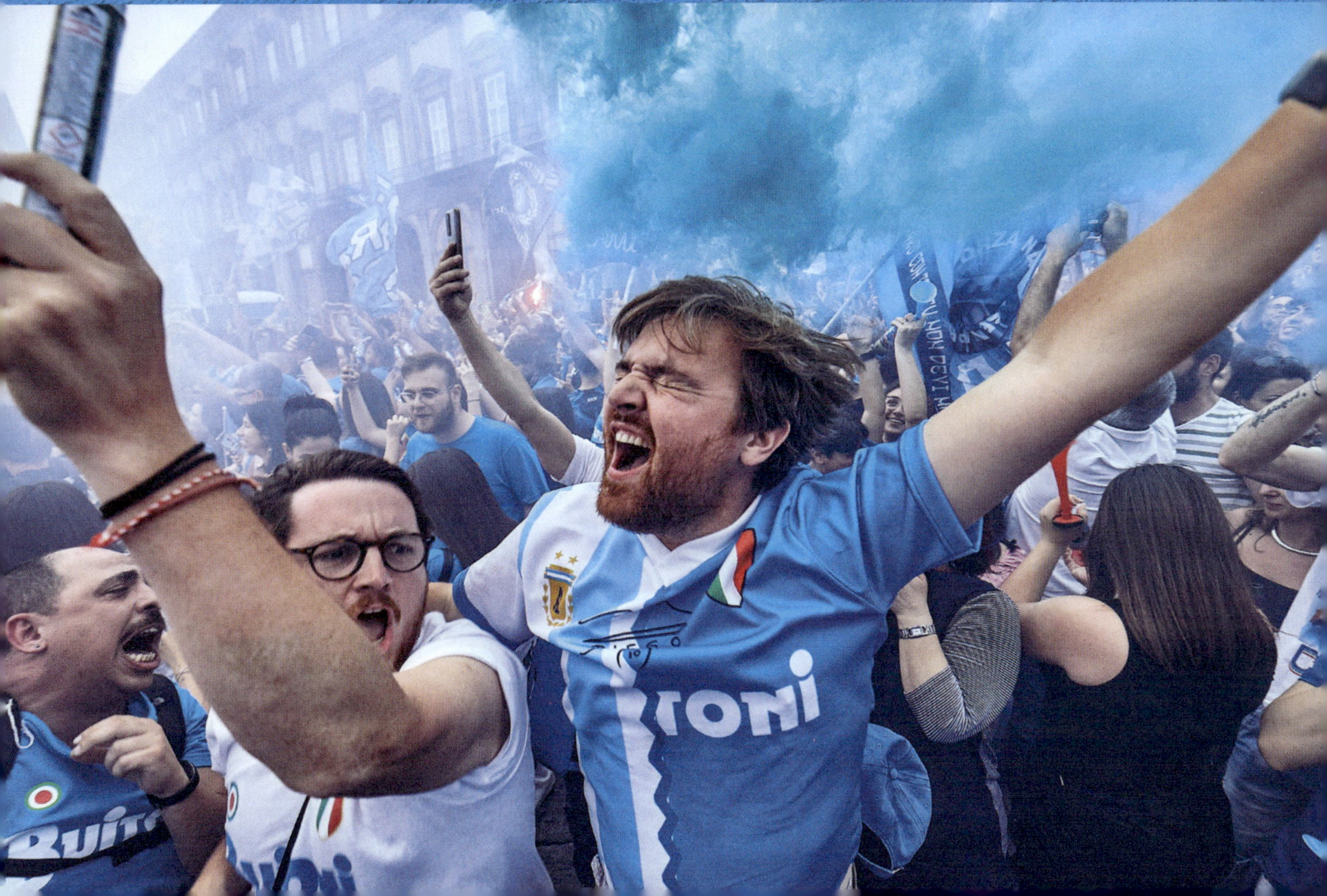

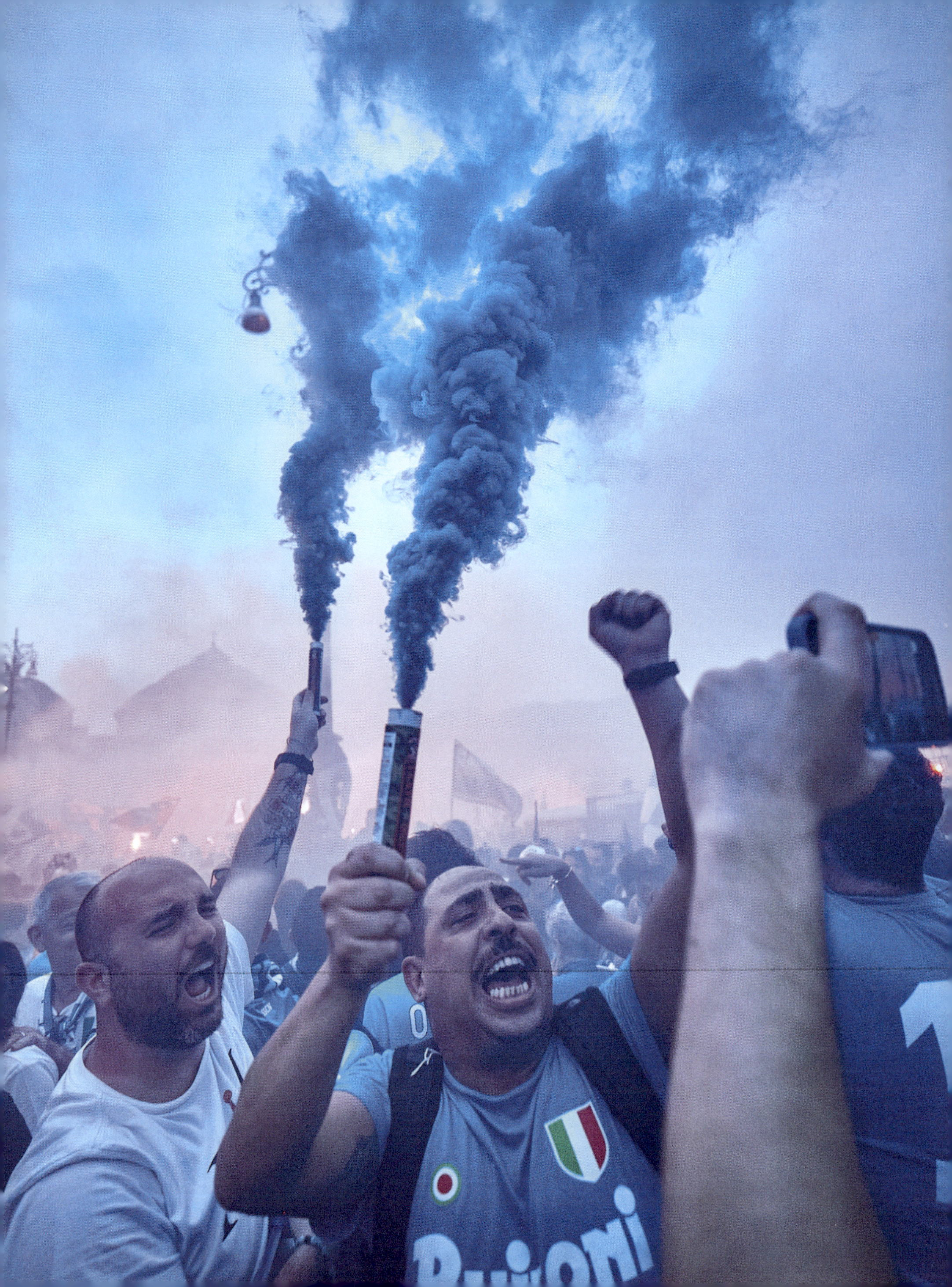

JUVE MERDA

'Un giorno all'improvviso
Mi innamorai di te
E il cuore mi batteva
Non chiedermi il perché
Di tempo ne è passato
Ma siamo ancora qua
Ed oggi come allora
Difendo la città'

'One day all of a sudden
I fell in love with you
My heart was beating
Don't ask me why
Now time has passed
But we are still here
And today, as then,
I defend the city'

This is the chant you will hear on the on the famous Curva B terraces of the Diego Maradona stadium in the centre of Napoli: an expression of the love of the city, even more than that of the football team.

What is worth noting is that the tune stems from a classic 1980s Italo Disco tune... written by a Juventus fan!

DIEGO MARADONA

No one in Napoli comes closer to a god-like status than Diego Armando Maradona. The Argentine's face is everywhere – pictures of him in every shop, restaurant and bar. His shirt adorns the stalls of every street seller. His mural in the Spanish Quarter is one of the main tourist attractions in Napoli.

They even renamed the stadium after him when he died in 2020. Back in London, many of the Neapolitan pizza chefs we work with were in tears; they described his passing as like losing a family member. Truly, Napoli is Maradona's city.

Maradona signed for Napoli from Barcelona in 1984 and, at the last minute, Barcelona requested an additional £500,000 on his transfer fee. The people of Napoli clubbed together – making collections in the streets – in order to make up the extra and get the deal over the line. Ever since that moment, Maradona has literally belonged to the city of Napoli.

The impact Maradona had on Napoli FC is hard to overstate. Just weeks before he signed, the club had narrowly avoided relegation (having equally narrowly dodged the same fate the year before). Traditionally the much poorer part of Italy, no club from the south had ever won the league.

Both Maradona's on-field exploits and the sheer enormity of his signing, inspiring other world-class players to join Napoli, meant that just three years later Napoli were lifting the Scudetto for the first time – a truly remarkable turnaround. And it is the sheer flair that Maradona brought to the game that made him such a perfect match for Napoli the city. If you haven't already, search for his pre-game warm-up in the UEFA Cup semi-final against Bayern Munich is 1989. It is otherworldly. And it highlights why so many great players are adamant that Maradona is, and always will be, the most naturally talented footballer of all time.

> ## 'THE THINGS I COULD DO WITH A FOOTBALL, HE COULD DO WITH AN ORANGE.'
>
> **Michel Platini**

There was an undoubtly dark side to Maradona in Napoli, and the city allowed him (and protected him) to follow some of his less wholesome pursuits off the field. There was the protracted paternity suit which took decades to resolve, and the many drug-related incidents. The latter would ultimately prove to be his downfall in Italy, after he tested positive for cocaine after a Serie A match and was banned for an unprecedented 15 matches.

Despite this, Napoli continued to love Maradona. One of the most powerful moments came in the 1990 World Cup. The tournament hosts, Italy were due to play against Maradona's Argentina in the semi-finals, and some genius decided it would be a good idea to host that game in Napoli. What resulted was, we think, unprecedented in world football: the Neapolitans supported Argentina and Maradona over their native Italy! Argentina won the game, and the nation went into absolute uproar! To this day, many in the city of Napoli identify more closely with Argentina than they do with Italy. 'Napoli Is Not Italy' stickers can still be found all over the city.

All in all, the relationship between Maradona and Napoli is more intense, more passionate, more appropriate than any other we can think of between a single footballer and a club. The love is real, and you cannot escape it anywhere in the city. San Gennaro himself is less present – and that truly is saying something.

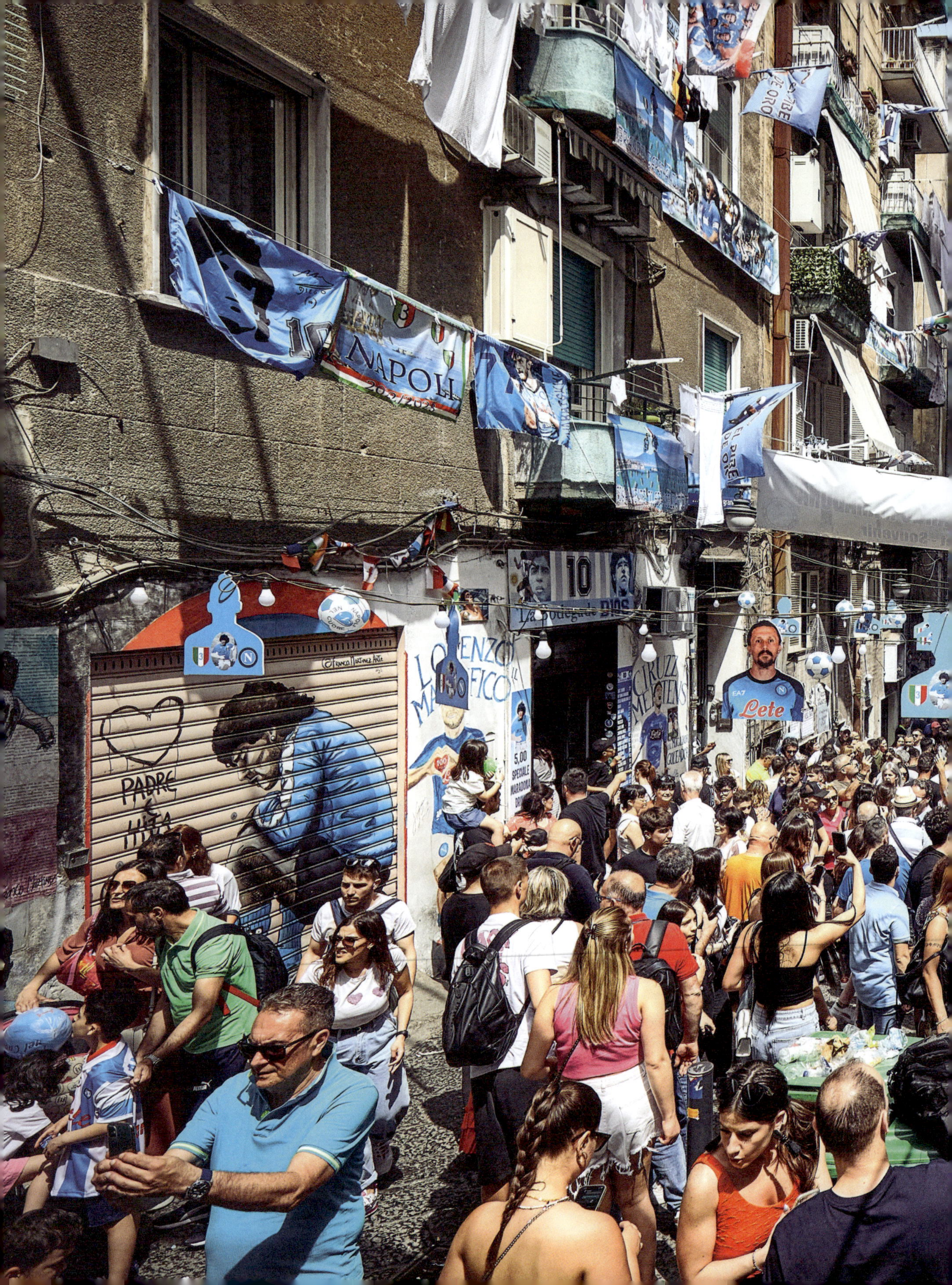
NAPOLI
10
Lete

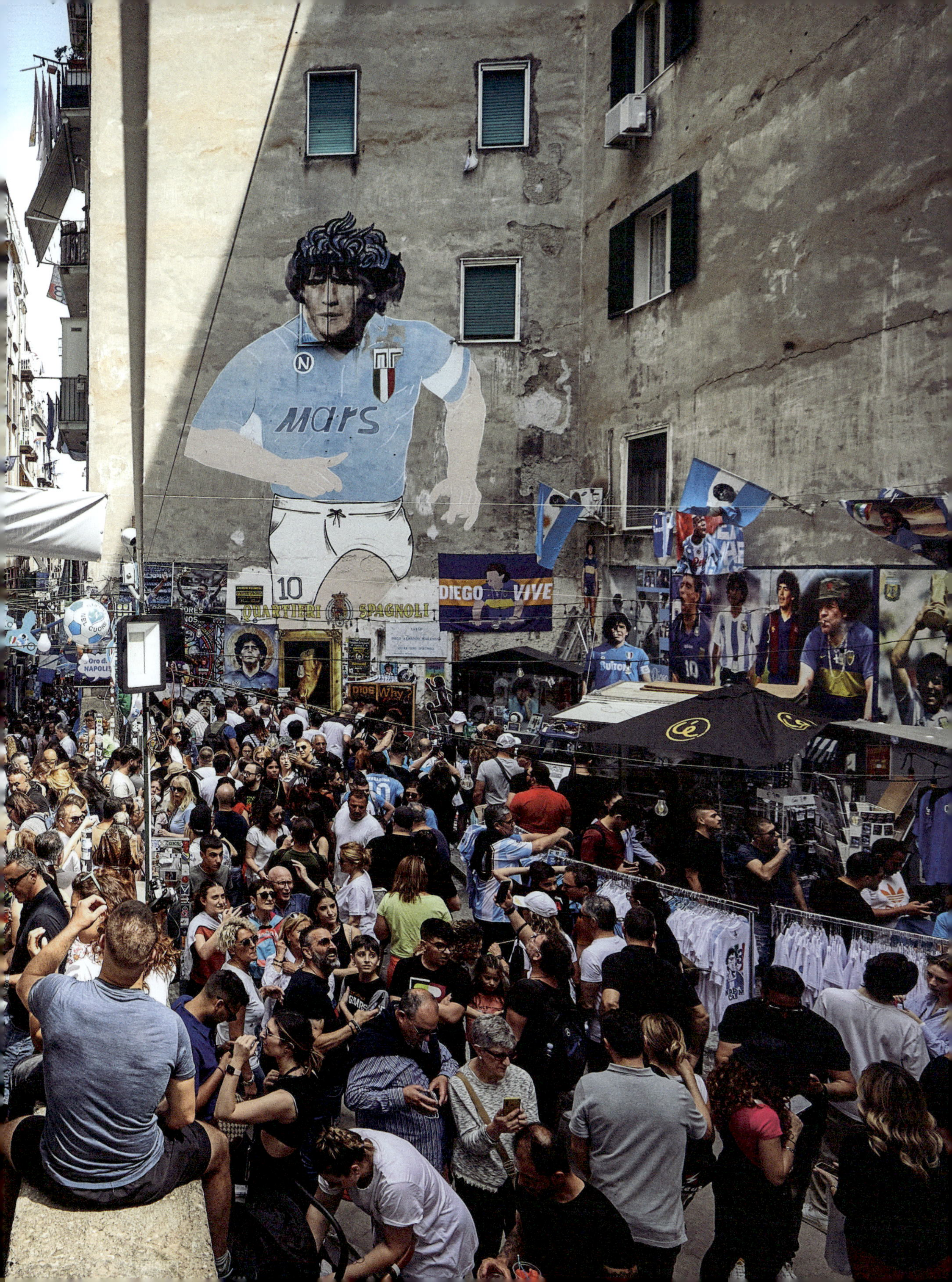
Mars
10
QUARTIERI SPAGNOLI
DIEGO VIVE

PASQUALE

DE STEFANO

> # HE IS LOVINGLY KNOWN AS 'O NUMMARARO' ('THE NUMBER MAN')

There must only be a few people who can lay claim to encapsulating the spirit of Napoli. Maradona. Sofia Loren. The guy in his Speedos with 'Tutto Passa' tattooed across his chest. All good candidates. But for us, it has to be Pasquale de Stefano.

We went to meet our contact and good friend of Pizza Pilgrims, Giovanni from Latteria Sorrentina, producers of the best mozzarella in Napoli. He was our 'in'. 'You can't just turn up at this place, it's not on the map, it's difficult to find and if you are not introduced by a local Neapolitan, you've no chance of meeting him.' Giovanni was taking us to meet the legend that is lovingly known as 'o nummararo ('the number man'), and his job for the past 65 years has been to hand paint all the incredible vibrant signage that adorns the shop fronts, fruit stalls and veg markets of the city. He is the last of eight brothers still continuing the tradition that their father taught them. When he dies, so too will this amazing tradition. Despite a handful of poor imitators, he is the last in line of a family business that has produced pretty much every one of the stunning hand-painted signs across the whole of Napoli.

His work is a Neapolitan institution woven into the visual fabric of the city – if Napoli had brand guidelines, this would be the typography section. The blue, yellow, red and occasionally green type; a yellow or a blue frame border; two font styles – the thick, chunky, almost bubble headline font and the looser hand brush script supporting style; along with the occasional naive illustration of an eye, or his signature long, pointing finger.

We go to visit him at his studio behind the general chaos that is the Via Sant'Antonio Abate daily market. As with being taken to an infamous crime lord, we were told to be low key on our way to meet Pasquale – inconspicuous and discreet. A left at the fishmongers, a right at the baker, around the corner behind a stall selling Maradona underpants, and we found ourselves in a very tight, typically Neapolitan alley – drying laundry hanging above us, the distant sound of a football match blending into some operatic music playing from a balcony somewhere above us.

We crawl the Vespa down the narrow street (picking up a Napoli FC flag en route, of course, in true 'low key' style...) and park up outside a – hilariously – unmarked door. Could there be anything more Napoli than being a sign writer and not having a sign over your door?

Stepping inside, you instantly get the feeling that Pasquale has not changed his set-up in the studio for decades. He sits in his one chair, surrounded by his artworks. His pots of paint are on the floor next to him, with incredible paint brushes that have developed stalactite-esque paint growths that are the result of years of use and layer upon layer of paint.

Pasquale was exactly as we'd imagined him. It was almost as if Scorsese had built sets and gone through rounds of castings to find the right-looking, slightly moody, intimidating character with paint-covered, leathery hands and a face full of wisdom and stories, and maybe just a little thunder.

While we are there, two students pop by in need of a big sign for a party they are having that night, showing the rules for a drinking game they want to play. They hand over the words, Pasquale hand-cuts a wooden board

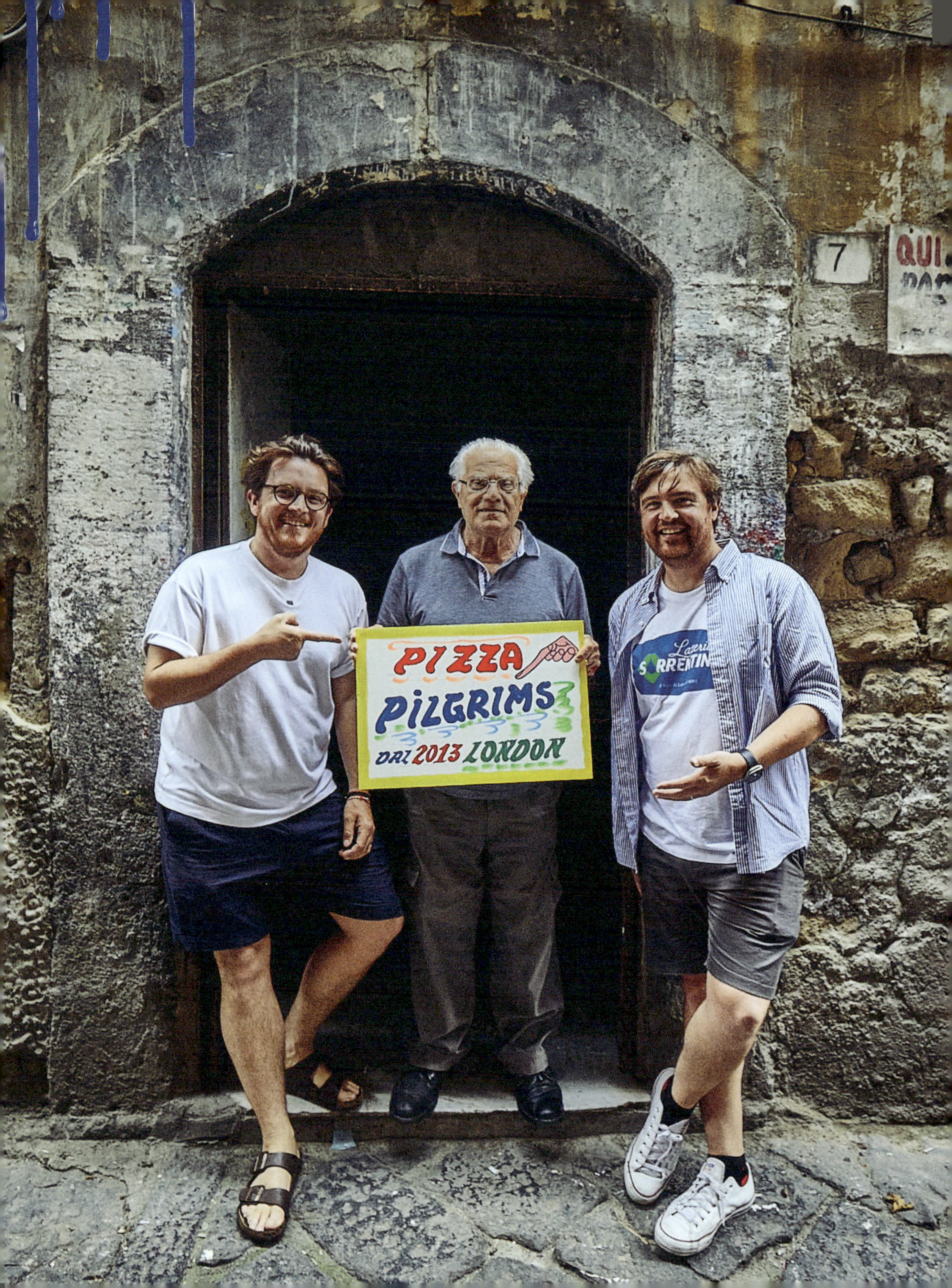
PIZZA
PILGRIMS
DAL 2013 LONDON
7

to size, whitewashes it and gets to work. No sketch, no template; he just starts making the curves of the letters with his thick brush that seems both so naive and also so incredibly precise. Five minutes later and the sign is done, with only a couple of minutes leaning up against the electric heater for the paint to dry. The boys hand over 20 euros and that's that. Probably the same way he's being doing it for 65 years.

This is something that really strikes us about Napoli: how it lives by the ethos of 'if it ain't broke, don't fix it'. There are so many ways that they could modernize and become more efficient, more logical. But the city seems to us to have a deep understanding that to do that would steamroll through all the beautiful, idiosyncratic crafts and livelihoods sustained by them. It's why the city is bursting with character, and why sometimes people from other parts of the world can't understand it. But as with so many things in Napoli, Pasquale's signs do their job today just as well as they did when he started 65 years ago, so why change? Go have a pizza and a glass of wine instead!

We talk to Pasquale about the book we are writing and he gives us his blessing for us to pay tribute to his work. He then whips out another board and, without missing a beat, deftly knocks out what you now see on the cover of this book. Dipping the red brush that looks about 30 years old with layer upon layer of dry red paint, making a lump about the size of his thumb on the handle, into the red paint pot, repeating with each colour, and he's done. It's so incredibly special that he was happy to do this for us, and we are absolutely in love with a cover that represents the passion, colour and can-do attitude of Napoli... pencil lines and all.

He waves us goodbye and a very special mission is complete.

> **"HIS WORK IS A NEAPOLITAN INSTITUTION WOVEN INTO THE VISUAL FABRIC OF THE CITY.**

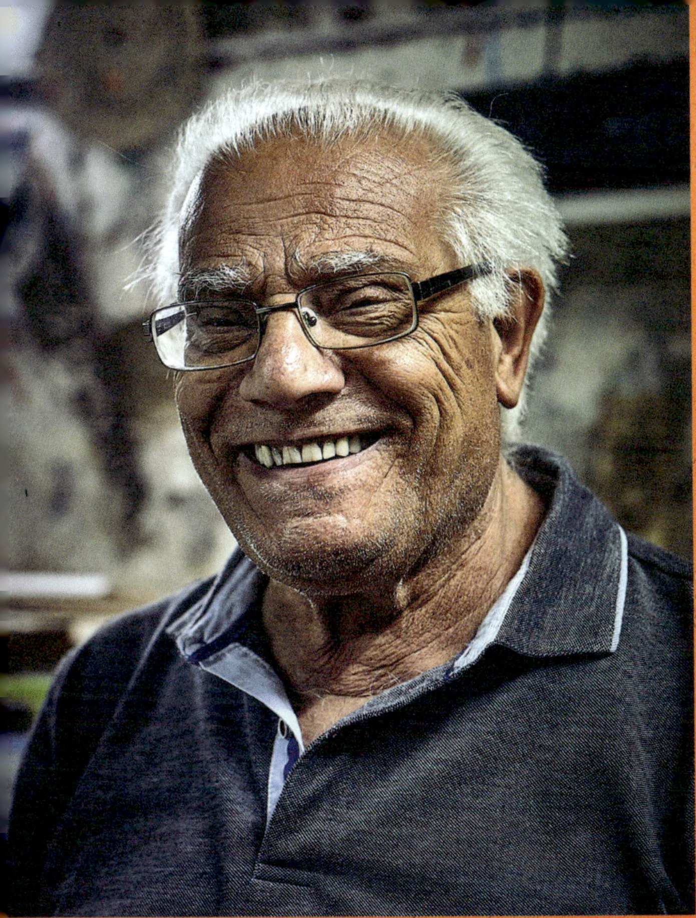

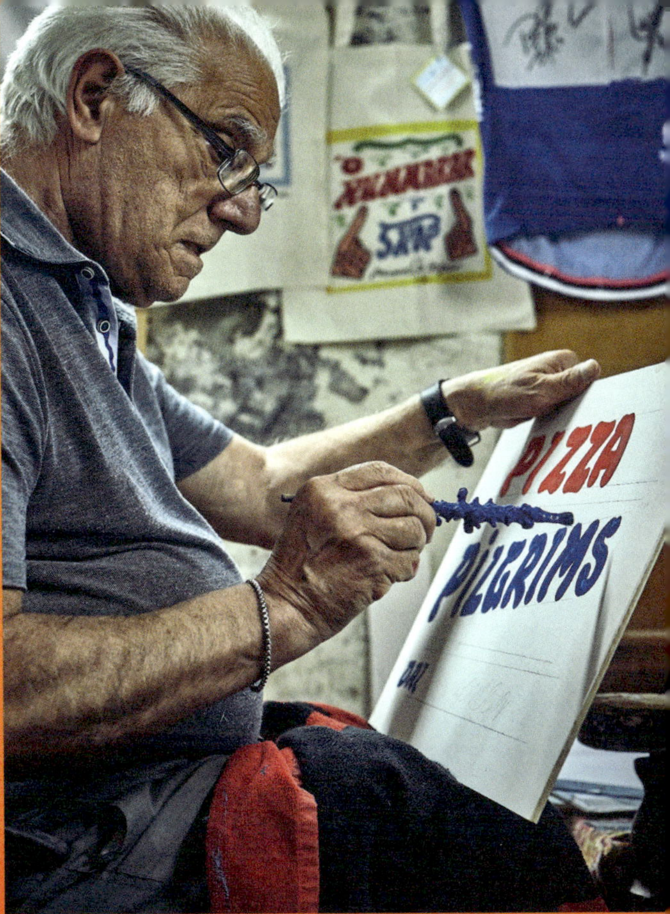
PIZZA
PILGRIMS

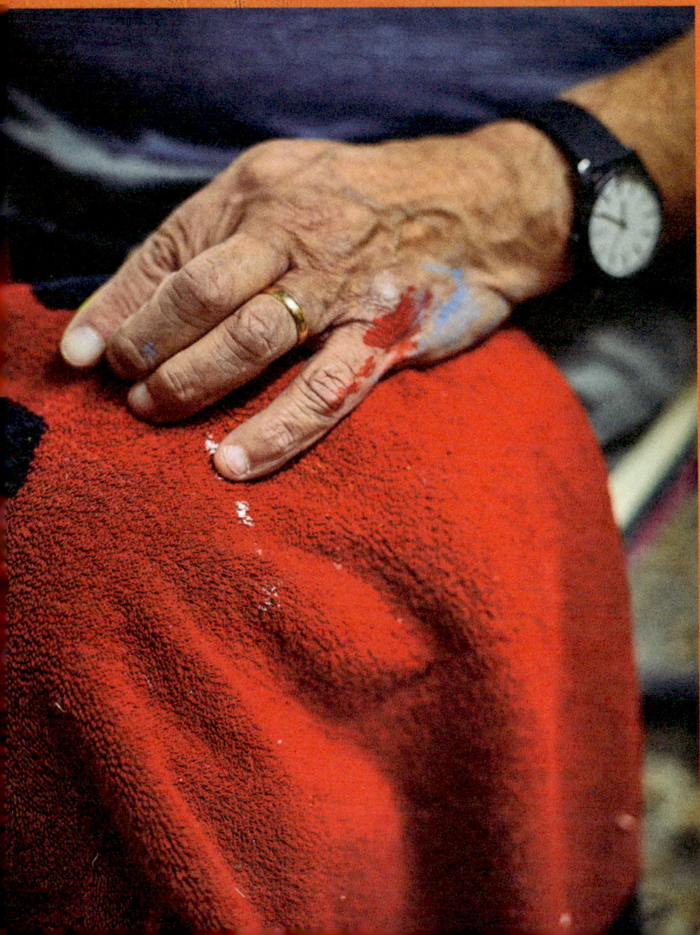

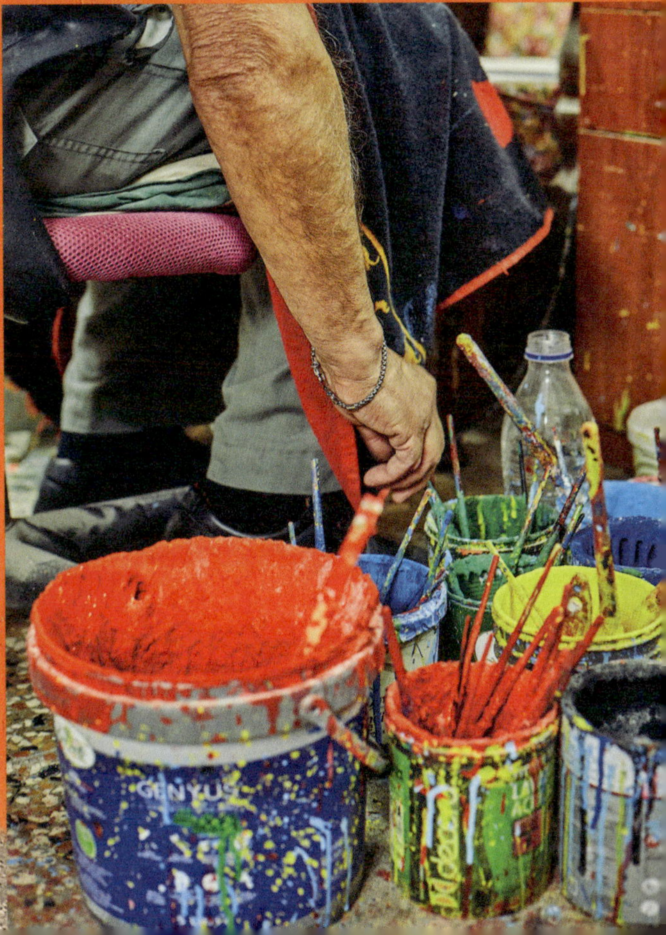
GENYUS

PIZZA

PRODUCE

CAPUTO

FLOUR

Il mulino di Napoli - 1924

100 ANNI

1924 • 2024

CAPUTO
CAPUTO
CAPUTO
CAPUTO
CAPUTO
CAPUTO
1924
Il mulino di Napoli

IF NAPOLI IS A CITY OF PIZZA, THEN FLOUR HAS TO THE BE ITS LIFE BLOOD. EVERYWHERE YOU LOOK IN NAPOLI YOU SEEM TO SEE FLOUR BEING TRANSPORTED AROUND THE CITY – ON TRUCKS, ON VESPAS, EVEN ON HEADS!

And what you quickly realize is that you are only really seeing one brand, distinctive with its bright bags in primary colours of red and blue. Caputo is almost as synonymous with Neapolitan pizza as tomato sauce or mozzarella, and their dominance of the pizza market in Napoli (and the world of Neapolitan pizza) is truly astounding.

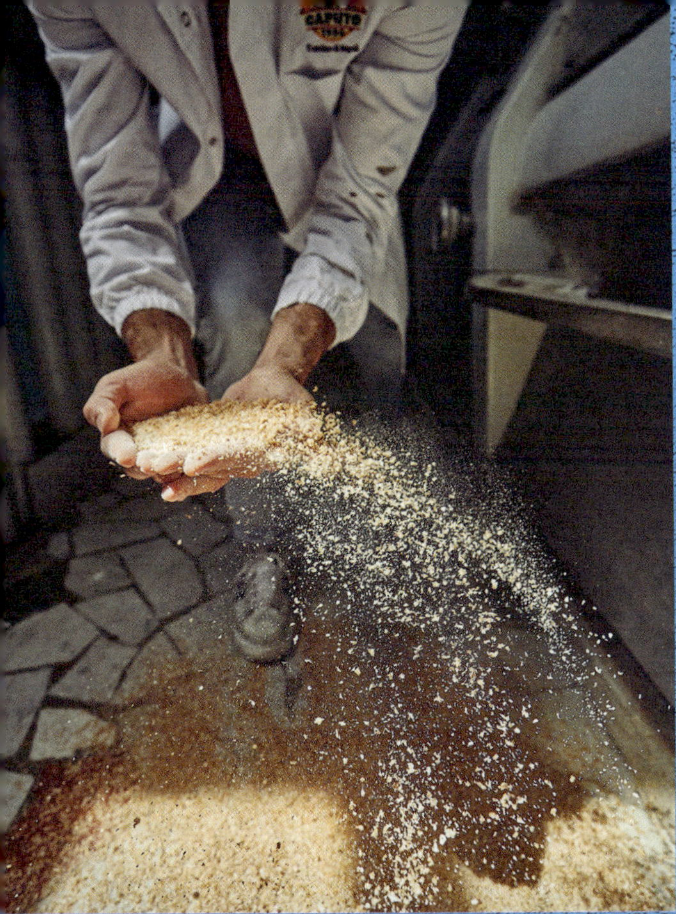
CAPUTO

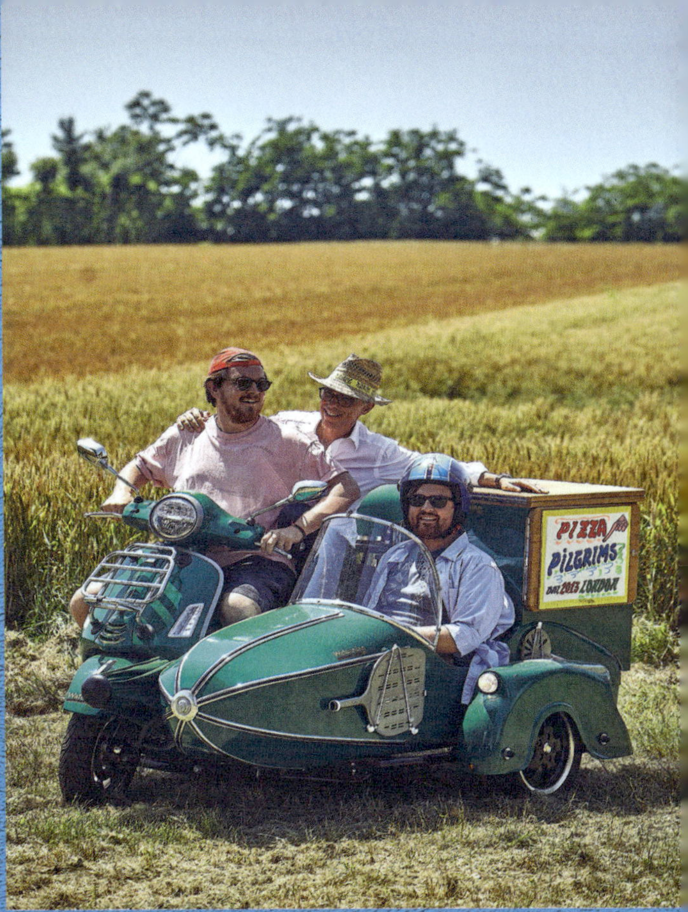
PIZZA
PILGRIMS

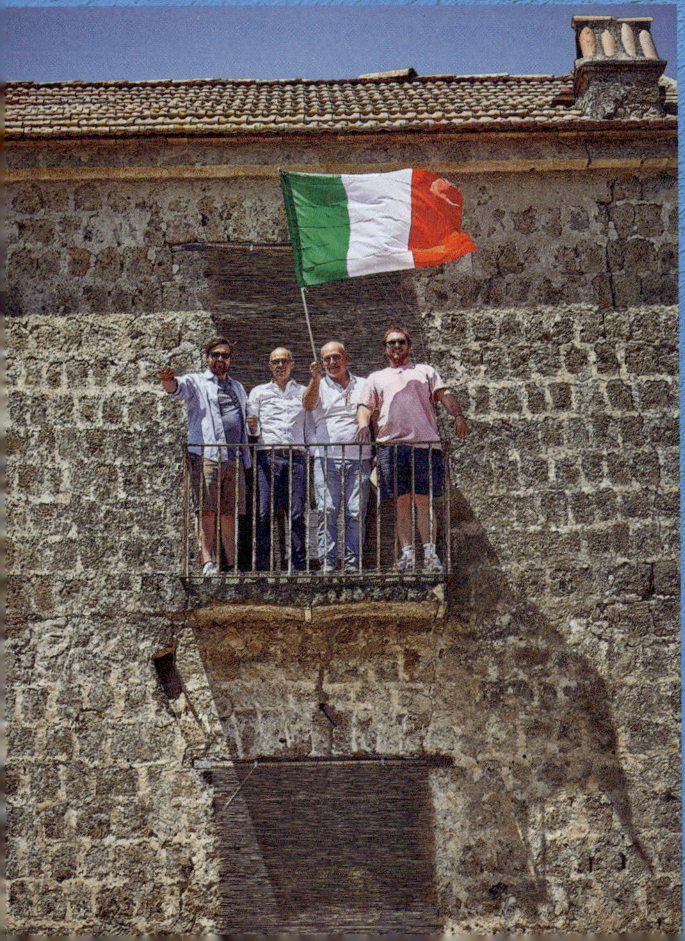

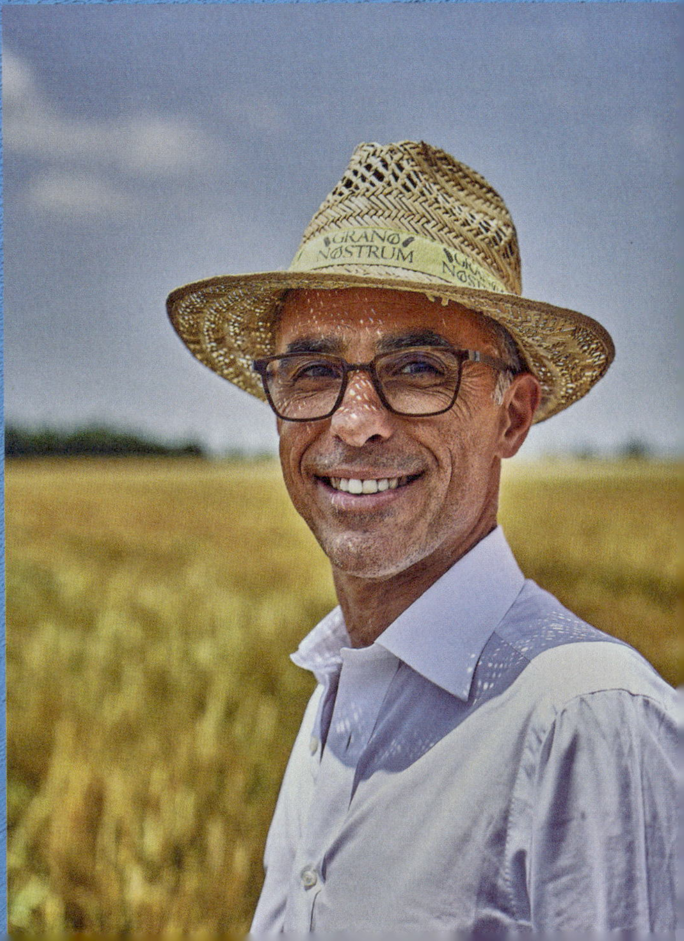
GRANO NOSTRUM

The world-famous Mulino Caputo is still housed near the centre of Napoli, and is weirdly nondescript from the street outside. Inside, however, is a genuinely Willy Wonka-esque celebration of flour. There are huge machines in rows, milling, sifting and bagging flour – a truly hypnotic process. There is a lab dedicated to analysing the grain as it comes through – ensuring that the protein levels and hydration are fully understood for each batch, to allow the master blenders to do their thing. Flour making, it turns out, is really the art of blending different grains from all over the world with different properties, strengths and weaknesses in order to create a flour with specific properties to match the task at hand. That means a totally different blend for cakes, pastries and, of course, many different varieties used to make pizza.

We were lucky enough to meet Antimo Caputo in 2011 when we went on our original pizza pilgrimage to Napoli. We think he was a little bemused when he first met us; we had travelled all the way from London, driving a little Ape van across the country. This was before the global explosion of Neapolitan pizza, so our pilgrimage was not as usual as it is now!

Antimo is, in many ways, the pizza king of Napoli, being directly responsible for the product that powers the vast majority of the greatest pizza shops the world over. However, more than that, he has always been so kind to us and has supported our business from the beginning – from storing our Pizza Vespa in 2023, to letting us bring literally hundreds of Pilgrims managers and head chefs to be immersed in the Mulino over the years (thanks to Mauro Caputo for his amazing Mulino tour that somehow got more passionate each time!). It is an honour to call him a friend. We have shared slices of pizza with him all over the world, from London, to Paris, to Vegas!

In 2023, when we visited Napoli on our Pizza Vespa to celebrate our 10th anniversary (page 20), Antimo took us to Campo Caputo on the outskirts of Napoli. Here, Caputo grow a number of wheat varieties in order to understand what can be done in future to reduce fertilizer use and increase the sustainability of their product. Working with a local university, it is a fantastic operation and a demonstration of their commitment to the future of flour production. We have had many chats about this over the years, and it is clear that Antimo and the team are dedicated to making a big difference, while never compromising on quality.

> **" ANTIMO IS, IN MANY WAYS, THE PIZZA KING OF NAPOLI, BEING DIRECTLY RESPONSIBLE FOR THE PRODUCT THAT POWERS THE VAST MAJORITY OF THE GREATEST PIZZA SHOPS THE WORLD OVER.**

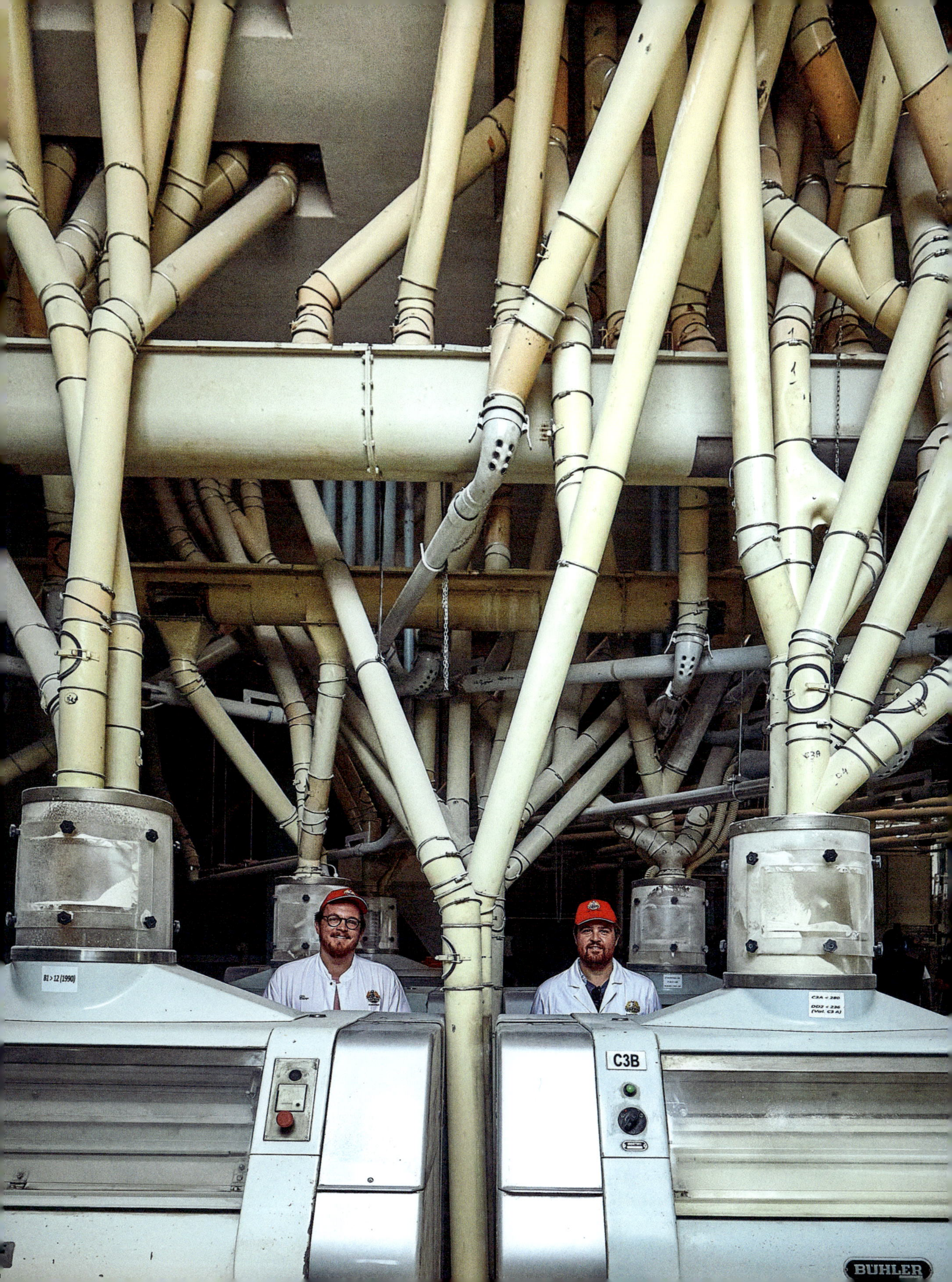
C3B
BUHLER

PIZZA FLOUR

What could be simpler than pizza dough? It's just flour, water, salt and yeast. Well, as it turns out, the devil is in the detail, and the ingredient that gives rise to the most heated debate is flour. Mulino Caputo have been at the heart of that debate now for over 100 years. Caputo is the longest running and (we think) best flour mill in Napoli. The mill itself is right in the heart of the city. You step through a tiny arched door on a terraced street down by the port in San Giovanni a Teduccio and unexpectedly enter a world of grain stores, giant vibrating mills and flour sacking machines.

The Caputo family have helped shape the story of Neapolitan pizza more than most. The mill is now run by Antimo Caputo, the great-grandson of Carmine Caputo, who founded the mill in 1924. Over the years, the Caputos have grown the operation from supplying local bakeries in Napoli to becoming a global exporter, sending their specialist flours to over 90 countries.

If you want to make proper Neapolitan pizza, then in our opinion you have to be using Caputo flour. Here are four of their best varieties to try out on your pizza-making journey.

Pizzeria (aka The Blue Bag)

This is probably Caputo's most popular flour – you'll see the blue bags stacked high in the windows of Neapolitan pizzerias all over the world. It's a great flour for pizza because it is 00 with a good gluten percentage. It works best proved for 24 hours or less, so is perfect for most pizzerias and home pizza chefs.

Type: 00

Protein: 12.5%

W index: W260/270

Elasticity: P/L 0.50/0.60

Saccorosso (aka The Red Bag)

Another very popular flour for pizza, Saccorosso is very similar to 'the blue bag', except you will see it has a higher protein percentage, meaning the W index is higher. This allows for longer proving times of 48–72 hours, as well as allowing for double fermentations and biga processes (page 93). This is now the flour that we use at our Pizza Pilgrims restaurants.

Type: 00

Protein: 13%

W index: W300/320

Elasticity: P/L 0.50/0.60

Nuvola (aka The Purple Bag)

This flour was developed specifically for contemporanea doughs (page 93) that require a light and puffy crust. Nuvola translates directly as 'cloud' in Italian and you will see that the W index is high, allowing for higher-hydration doughs that spring in the oven and create incredibly fluffy crusts. A lot of pizzaioli will cut their flour mix with 10–30% of this flour to give their dough some extra life.

Type: 0

Protein: 12.5%

W index: W260/270

Elasticity: P/L 0.50/0.60

Tipo 1 (aka The Green Bag)

This flour has the most amount of the wholegrain or bran in it so it is an excellent flour for boosting the flavour and aroma of your pizza dough. It has a high protein percentage, meaning it can withstand long proving times, but it is best to blend it with a finer flour to ensure you get a good crust that is not too dense.

Type: 1

Protein: 13%

W index: W260/270

Elasticity: P/L 0.45/0.55

AUSTRIACO
CAMPO CAPUTO
GRANO NOSTRUM LAZIO
CAMPO CAPUTO
GRANO NOSTRUM CAMPANIA

CAPUTO

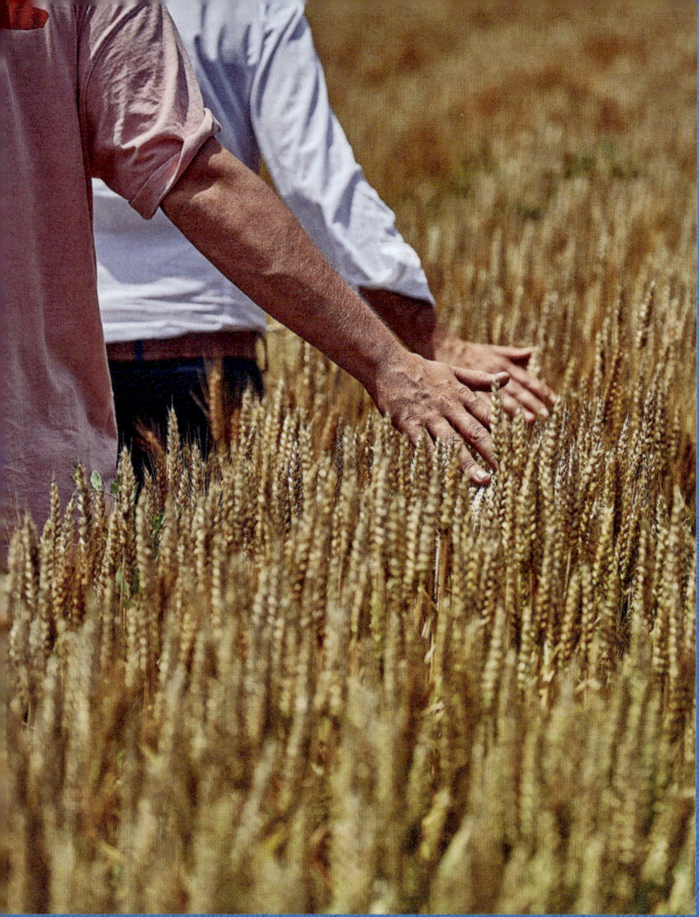

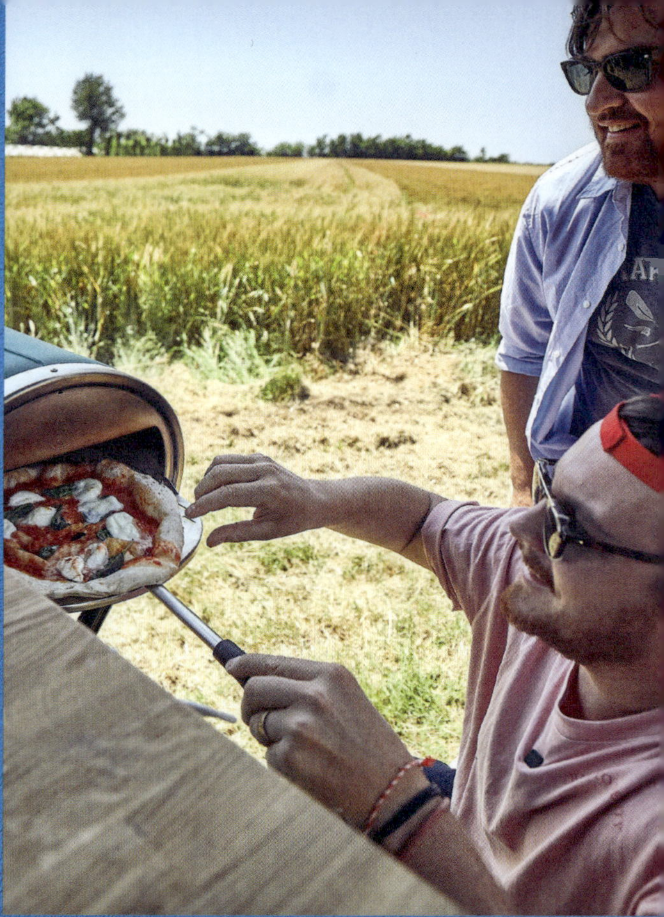

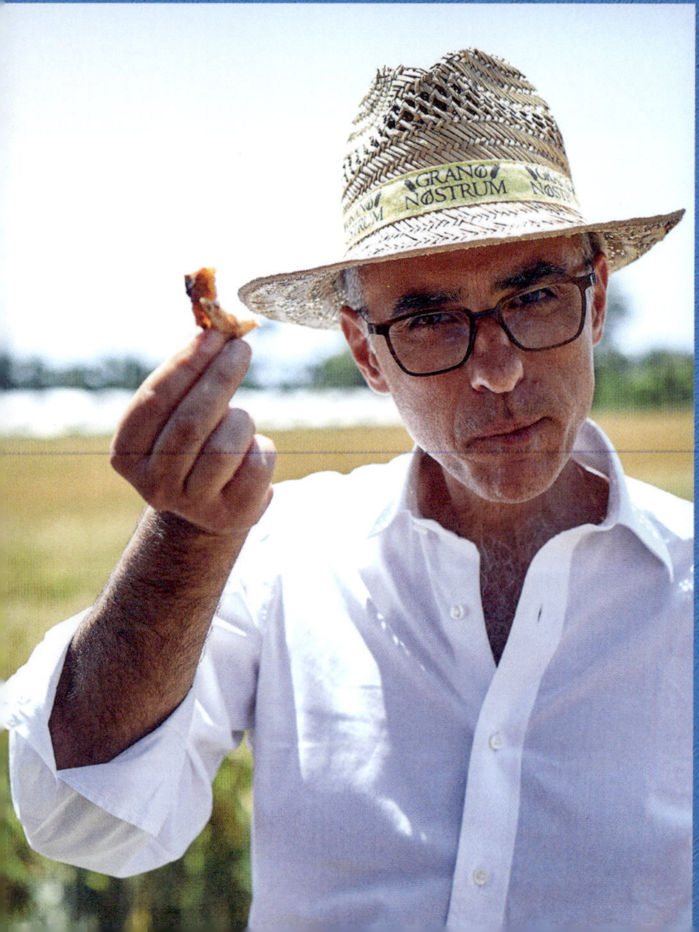
GRANO NOSTRUM

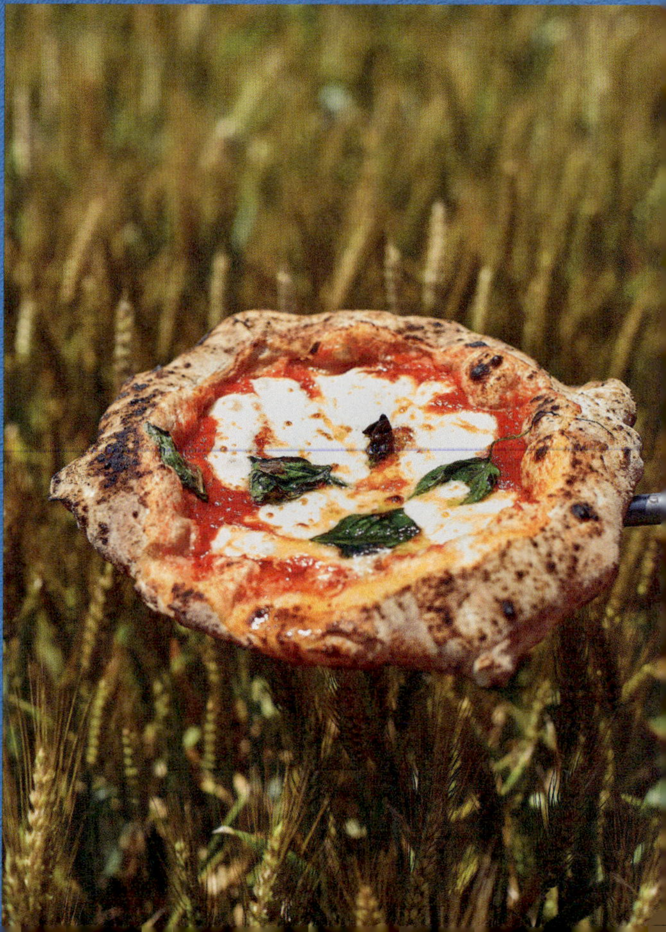

Even if you're looking further afield for your flour, or can't get hold of Caputo flours, here are the four key components to look out for when choosing which pizza flour to buy:

Type

The type, or 'tipo', of flour refers to how finely the flour has been milled. You will probably be aware of tipo 00. This is the most common type of flour used for pizza and pasta making and is the finest milled flour you can get. A 00 flour has been so finely milled that all the flour will contain is the pure white starch of the wheat grain. This creates a super silky dough that allows really strong gluten development and a very clean-tasting finished dish. As you go up through the types from 00 you get 0, 1, 2 and then wholegrain. The further up the scale you go, the courser the milling, meaning you get more of the wholegrain or bran in the mix. More wholegrain adds more flavour, but it also reduces the gluten's ability to develop, meaning less structure to your dough. Quite often, pizzaioli will blend different types of flour to create a dough that has great gluten development but complex flavour.

Gluten (aka protein)

Gluten is a strand of protein that, when it comes into contact with water, begins to connect together to make longer and longer chains and create an elastic structure. Pizza chefs will often talk about protein percentages with great passion. Most pizza flours will range between 9 and 15% protein. The more protein you have in your flour, the more structure your dough will have. This means that it will withstand longer proving times, developing flavour and creating a chewier texture. Flours with a lower protein percentage are used for shorter fermentations and a softer dough, resulting in a lighter pizza.

Strength (aka the 'W index')

When you start talking about the 'W index' then you know you've moved onto the big leagues. At the Caputo mill they have a small lab where they test the flours – it's full of machinery and gadgets and the same two guys in white coats that have been there every time we've visited for the last 12 years. One of the machines, appropriately called the Farinograph, measures the 'W index'. A small puck of dough is placed on a plate and slotted into the machine. The dough is then slowly inflated like a piece of bubblegum until it pops and deflates. This test is to confirm the strength of the dough. The biggest contributing factor to strength is the protein percentage (see 'Gluten', left). A flour with a 'W index' under 250 isn't ideal for making Neapolitan pizza (better for cakes and pastries), whereas a flour with a 'W index' over 300 is incredibly strong and the best for long-fermentation pizza doughs.

Hydration (aka elasticity)

This isn't important when buying your flour, but it's crucial to know when working with dough. In recent years pizza dough hydration has become a hot topic. When contemporanea dough (page 93) appeared, it became very cool to have a high-hydration pizza dough. More hydration in your dough creates a crust that is light and puffy with a soft texture. Conversely, a low-hydration dough will create a chewy crust that has a tighter texture. Hydration is discussed as a percentage. So, if you have 1kg (35oz) of flour and you use 600g (21oz) water, that creates a 60% hydration dough. Neapolitan pizza doughs traditionally sit between 60% and 65% hydration, but it's fun to experiment with 70%, 80% or even 90% doughs to see if you can attain an incredibly light crust. Watch out though – super high hydration doughs are very hard to work with as they lose their elasticity and can feel like you are attempting to stretch soup!

Solania

TOMATOES

POMODORI PELATI ITALIANI

GROWN AND PACKED IN

SAN MARZANO ITALY

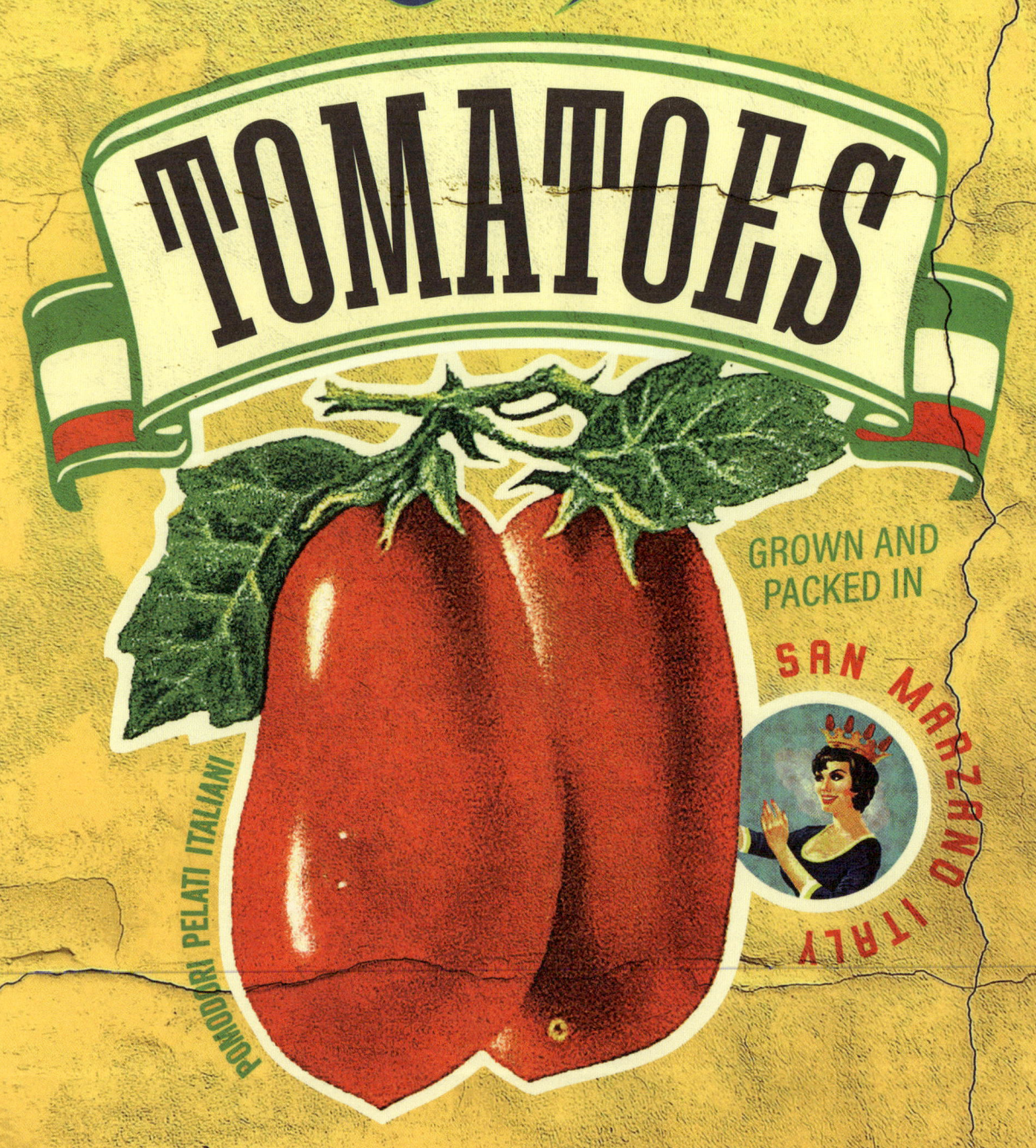

NET WEIGHT
2LBS. 3OZS.

CONDFEZ. SECONDO LE NORME VIGENTI

PESO NETTO
GR. 3050

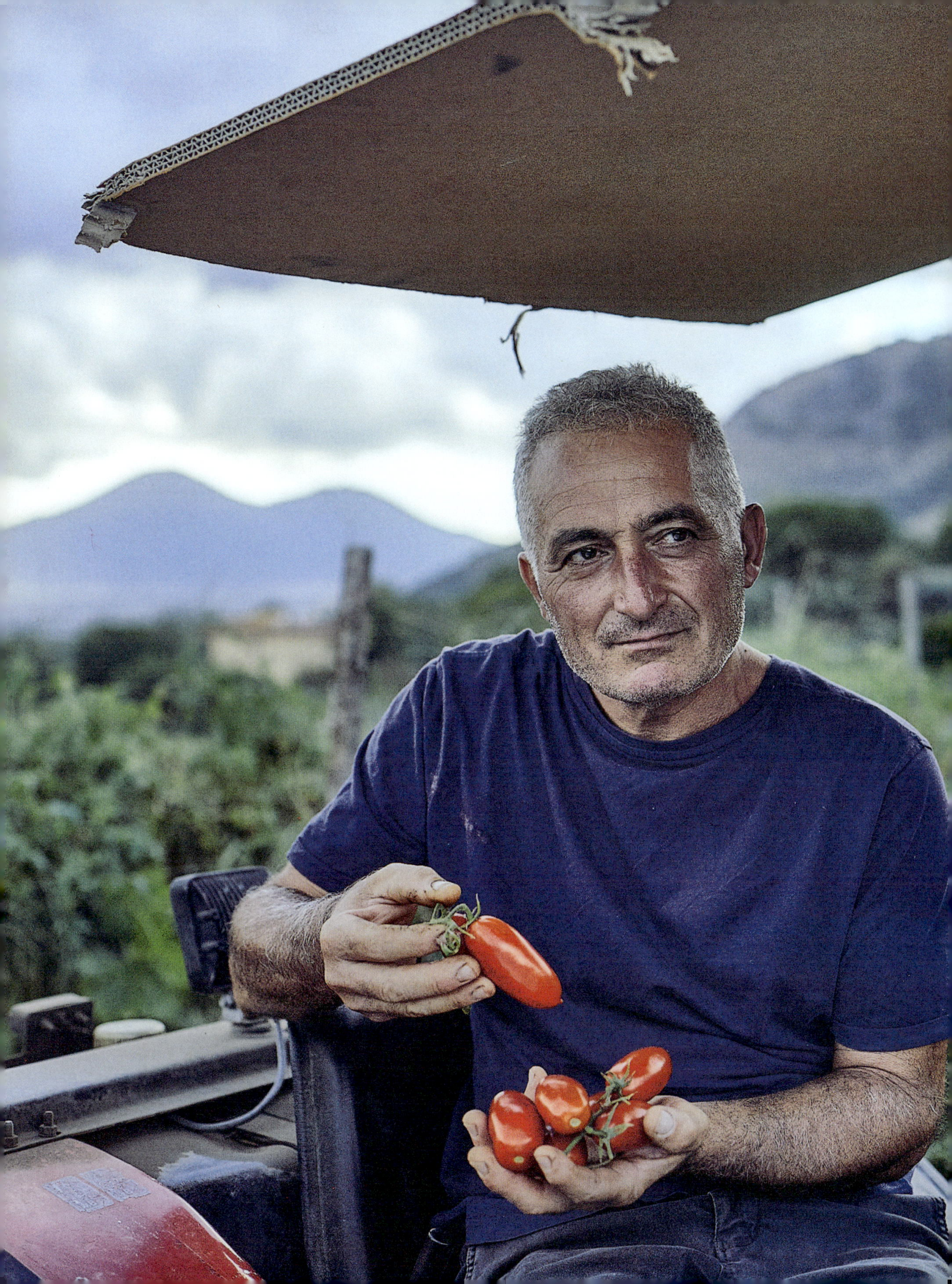

AHHH... GOLDEN APPLES, AS THE ITALIANS CALL TOMATOES (THE DIRECT TRANSLATION OF 'POMODORO'). IMAGINE LOVING A FRUIT THAT MUCH? GOD, WE LOVE ITALY.

Back in 1544, the Spanish conquistadors brought tomatoes back from the Americas and the Italians quickly got their hands on them. They then spent a couple of hundred years growing them as ornaments (odd choice) before someone decided it would be a good idea to knock up a sauce. Now Italy produces some of the best tomatoes in the world, and Campania might just have the best of the best (sorry Sicily and Liguria…). For me, there are two main types that stand out in Campania and they both feature heavily on every pizza menu in Napoli: San Marzano and Piennolo. They both have different flavours and uses. Let's get into it.

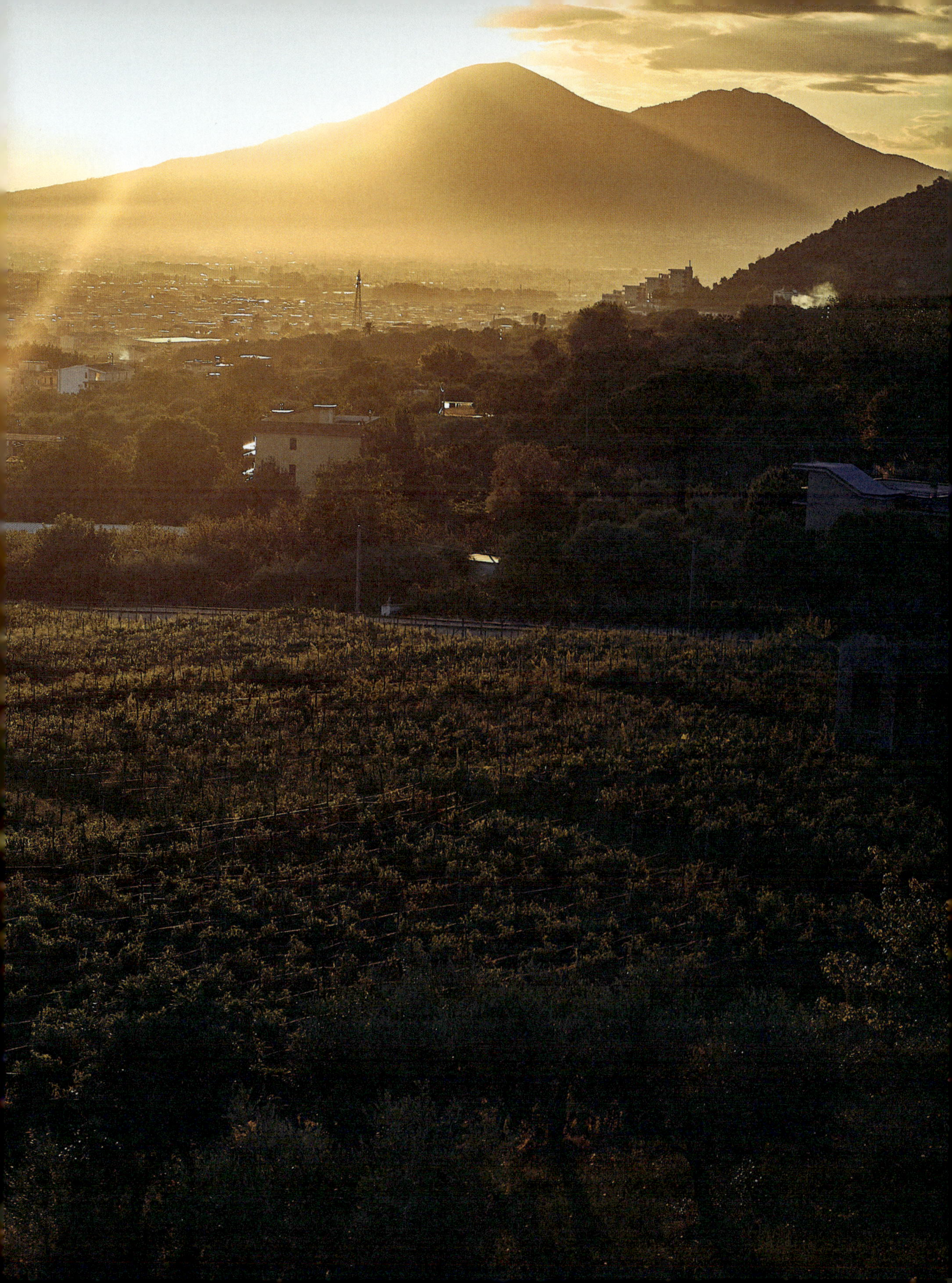

SAN MARZANO

Probably Campania's most famous tomato export, San Marzanos are sold all over the world, prized for their sauce-making prowess. Long and cylindrical, they grow fantastically in the flat, soft, volcanic soils around Mount Vesuvius, most famously from the town of Sarno. They are delicious just off the vine and we got to spend the afternoon with Aniello, a tomato farmer from Sarno, who might just have the most picturesque office in the world. He tells us that San Marzanos are the best because of their sweet, dense flesh, thin skins and lack of seeds. Aniello sends all his tomatoes to our tomato supplier, Solania, run by the inimitable Pepe, who constantly has a cigarillo hanging out of his mouth.

'San Marzano number one!' he shouts as he walks into his factory, where an incredible team of local women are sorting every tomato by hand. The San Marzano harvest is short – just two months – and they work round the clock to process the whole crop. Canning tomatoes is an incredible way to lock in the flavour and means you get tomatoes all year round.

The tomatoes are first washed and blast-steamed before the skins are blown off using a machine we can only imagine is called the TomBlaster 3000. The tomatoes then drop down to The Tomato Ladies, who check each tomato as it passes. The whole tomatoes go straight to canning and the broken ones are picked out to be blended to sauce. The sauce is simple. Fresh basil is washed and a small handful put in the bottom of each can with a pinch of salt. The tomatoes are then pumped in, the lid sealed and the can pasteurized in hot water to cook the sauce; the flavour of the tomato remains intact. This process has always been done in Italy to preserve the tomatoes for the winter months, and was a family tradition normally carried out by the nonnas and nonnos.

At the end of the production line, we get to open a can and taste the tomatoes still hot from cooking. The flavour is, well, incredibly tomatoey. Canned foods get a bad rep, but when it's done like this it allows you to get that sunshine taste all year round.

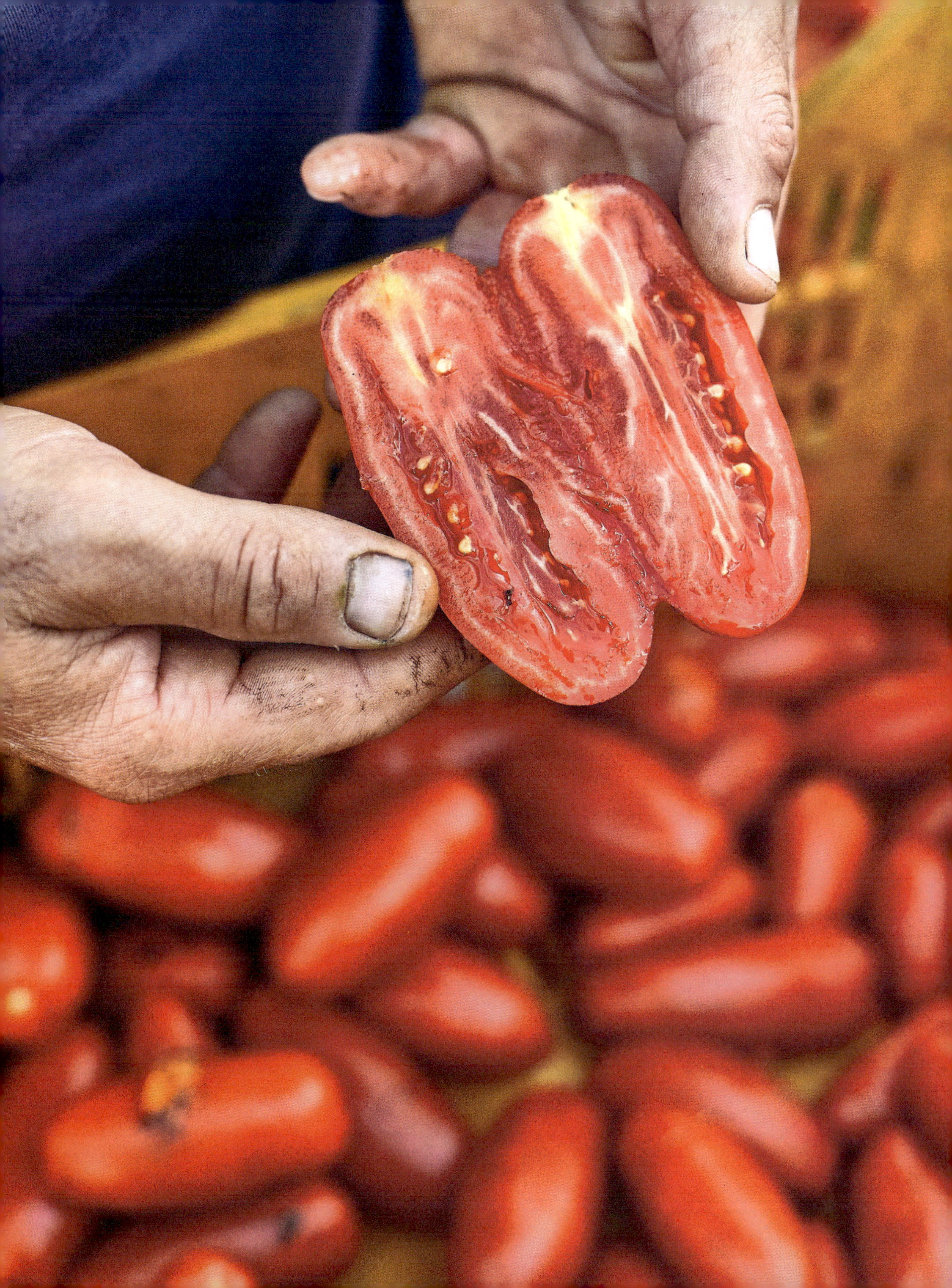

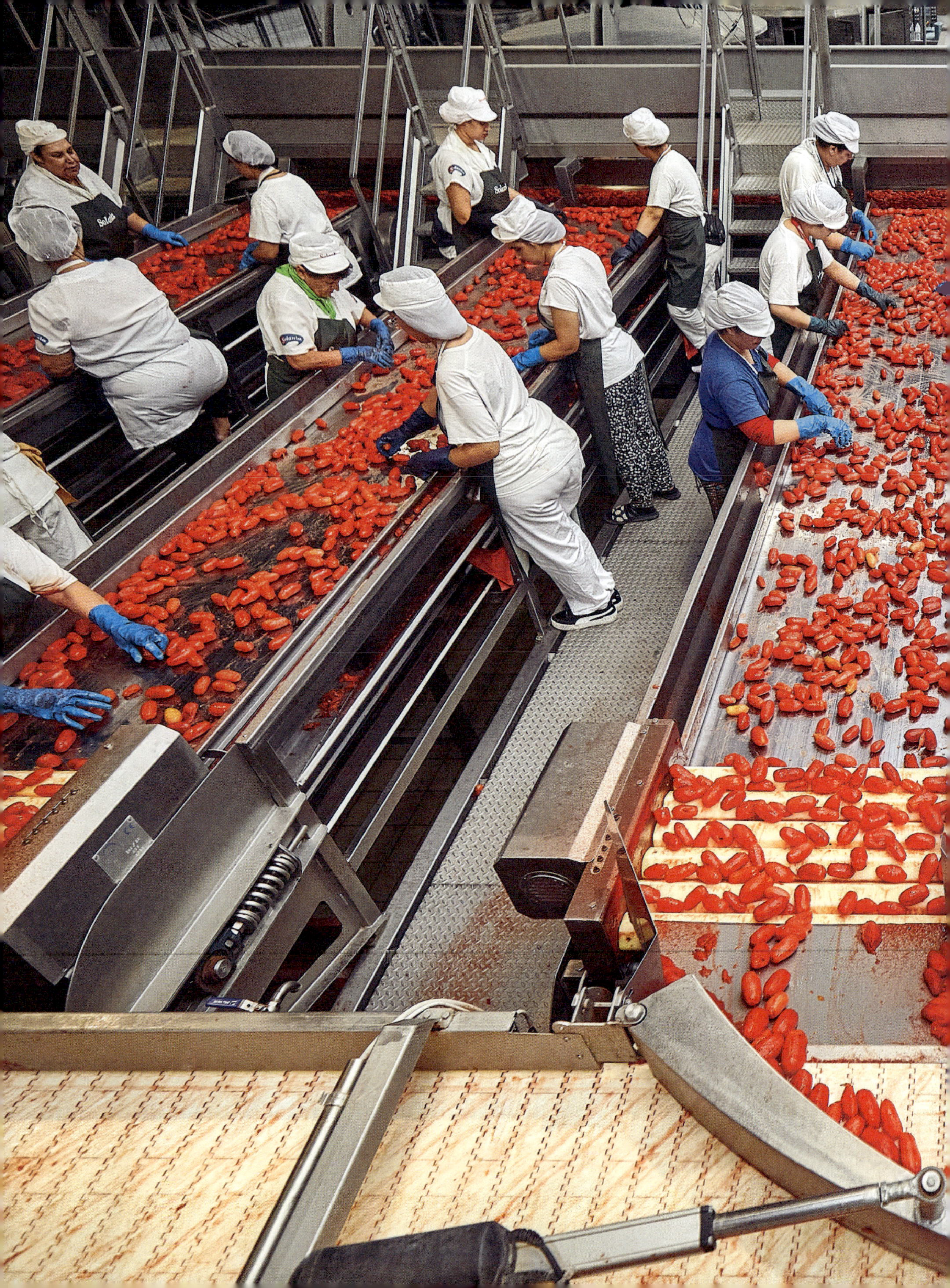

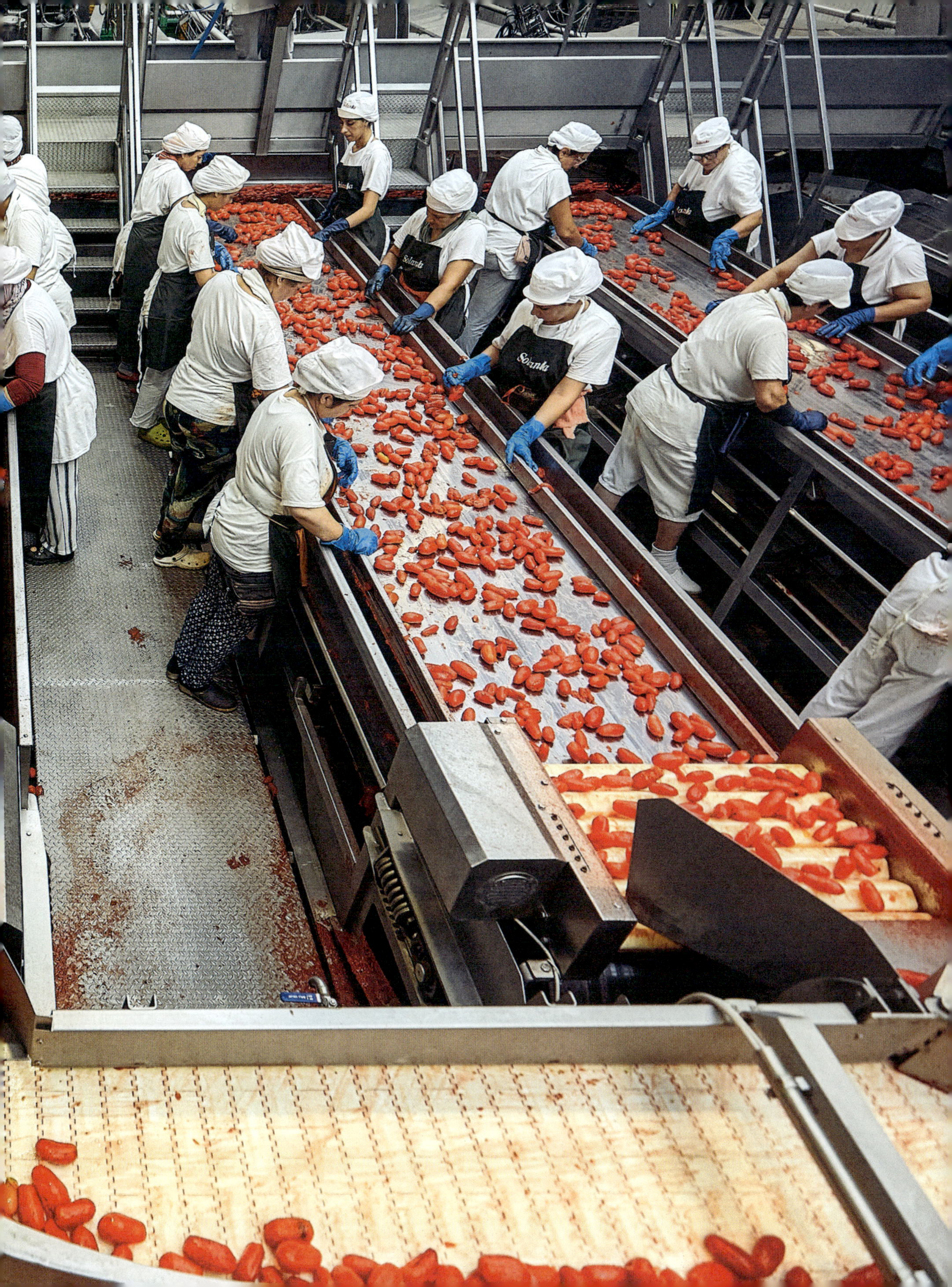

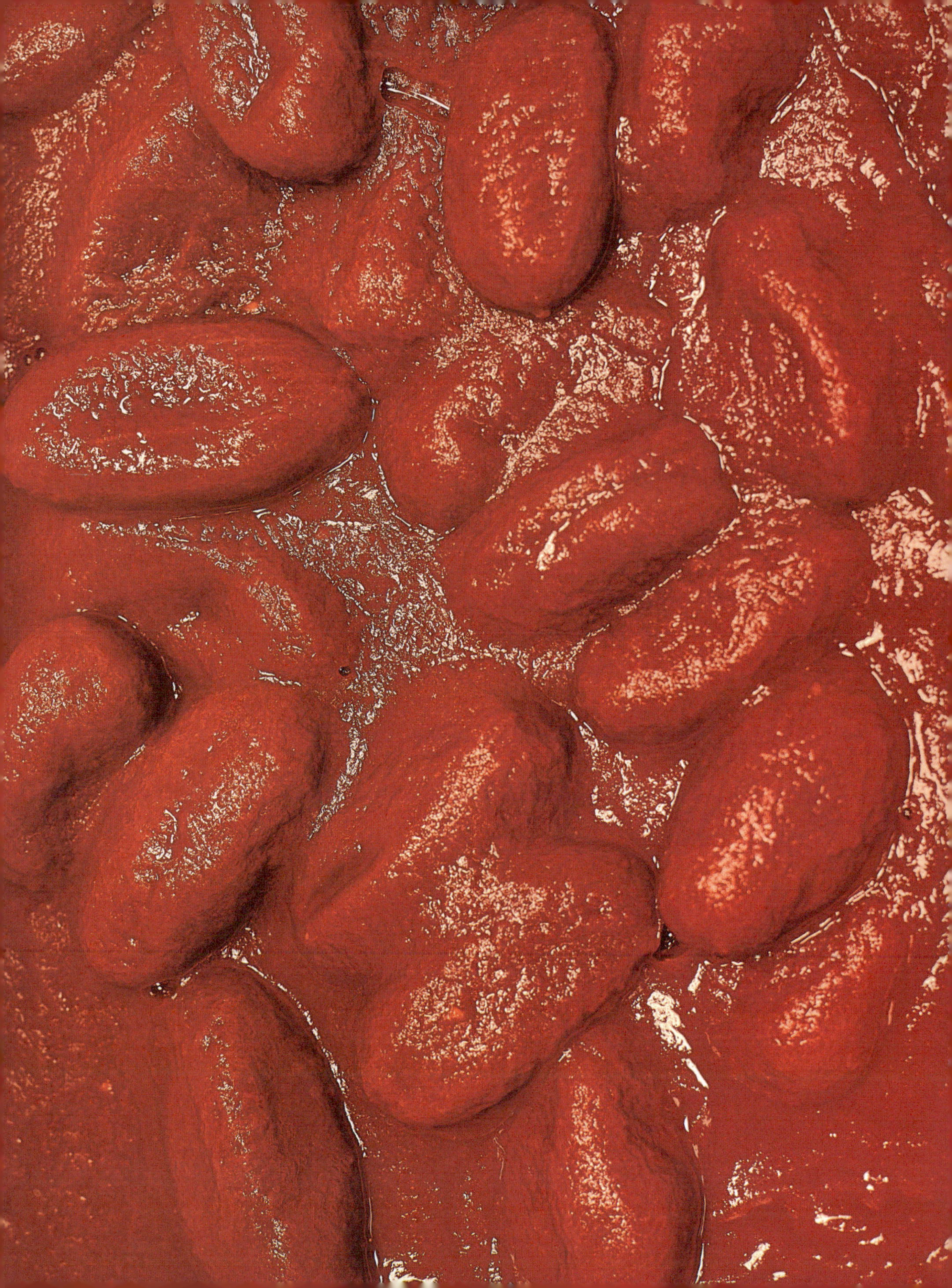

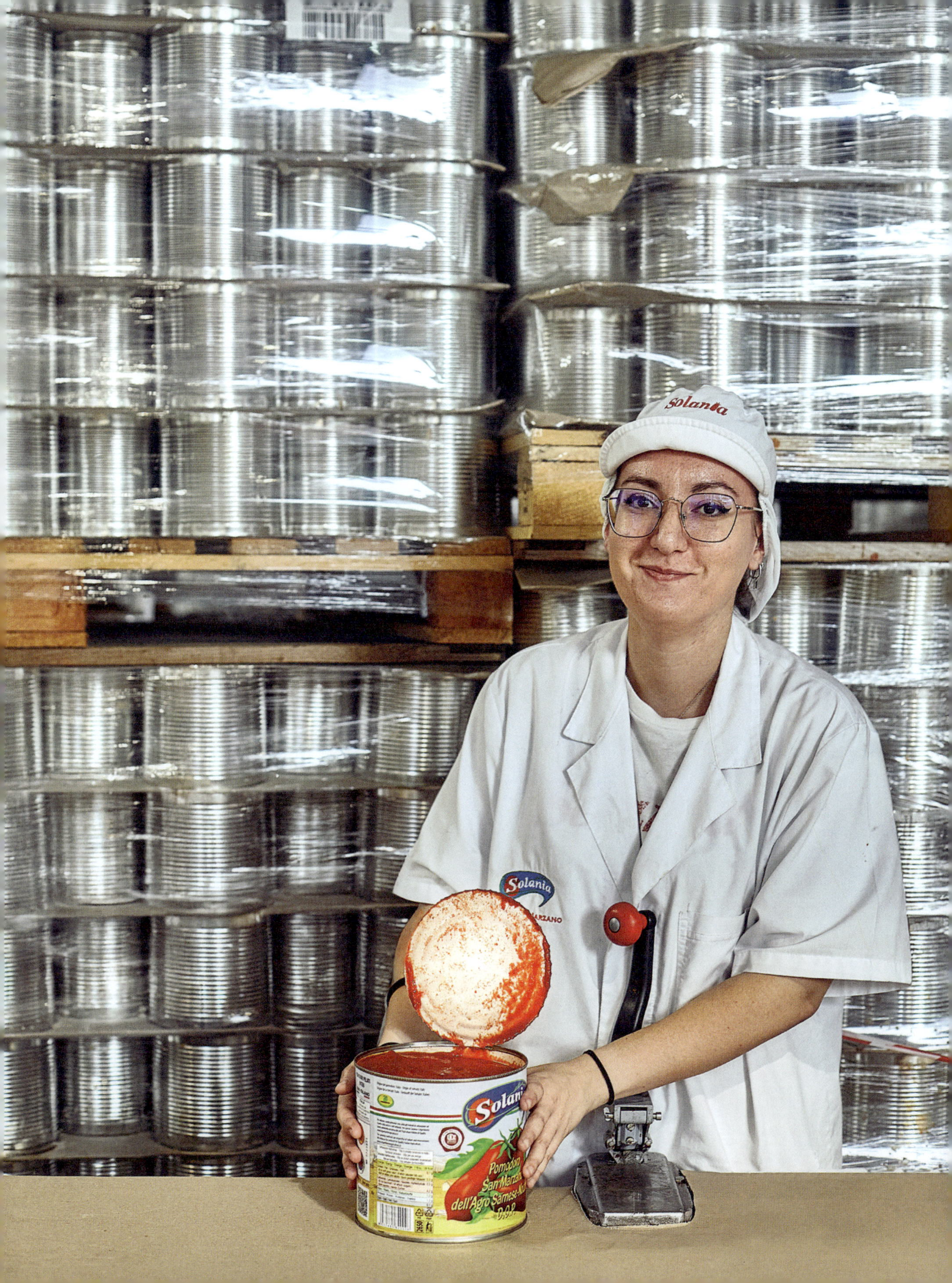
Solania
Solania
Solania

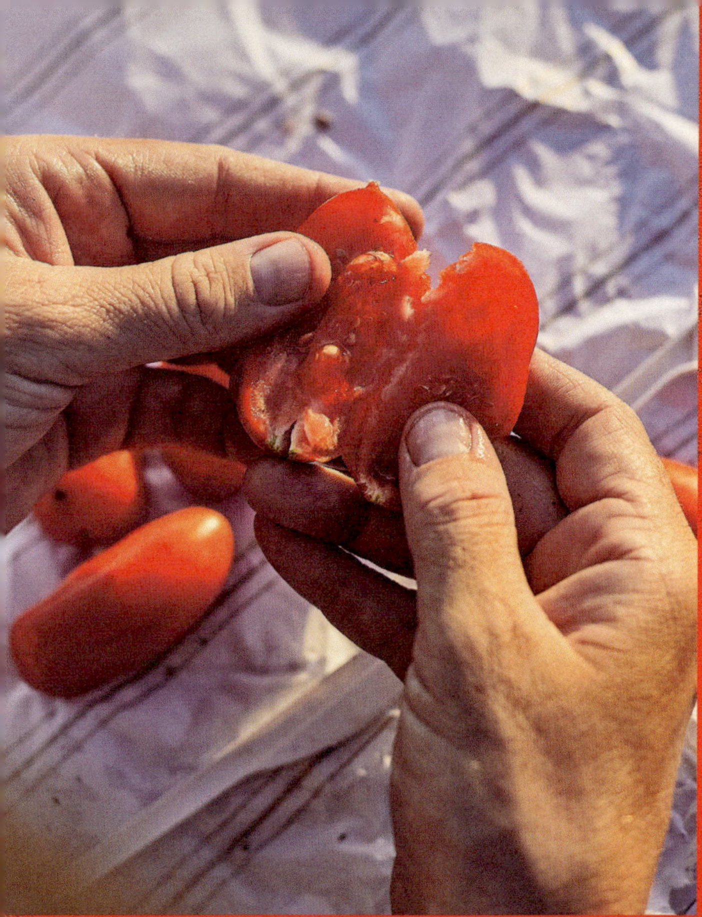
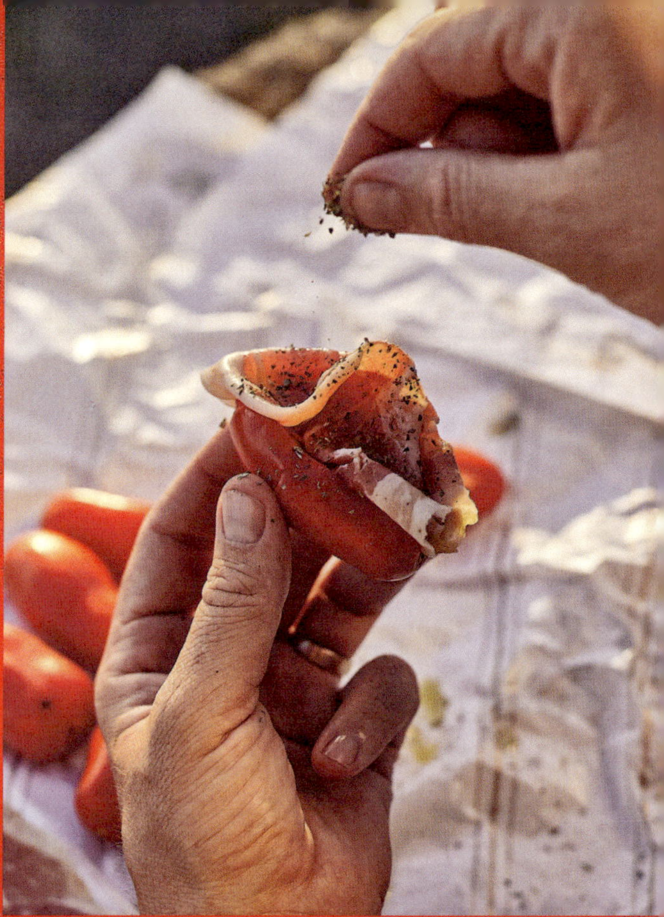
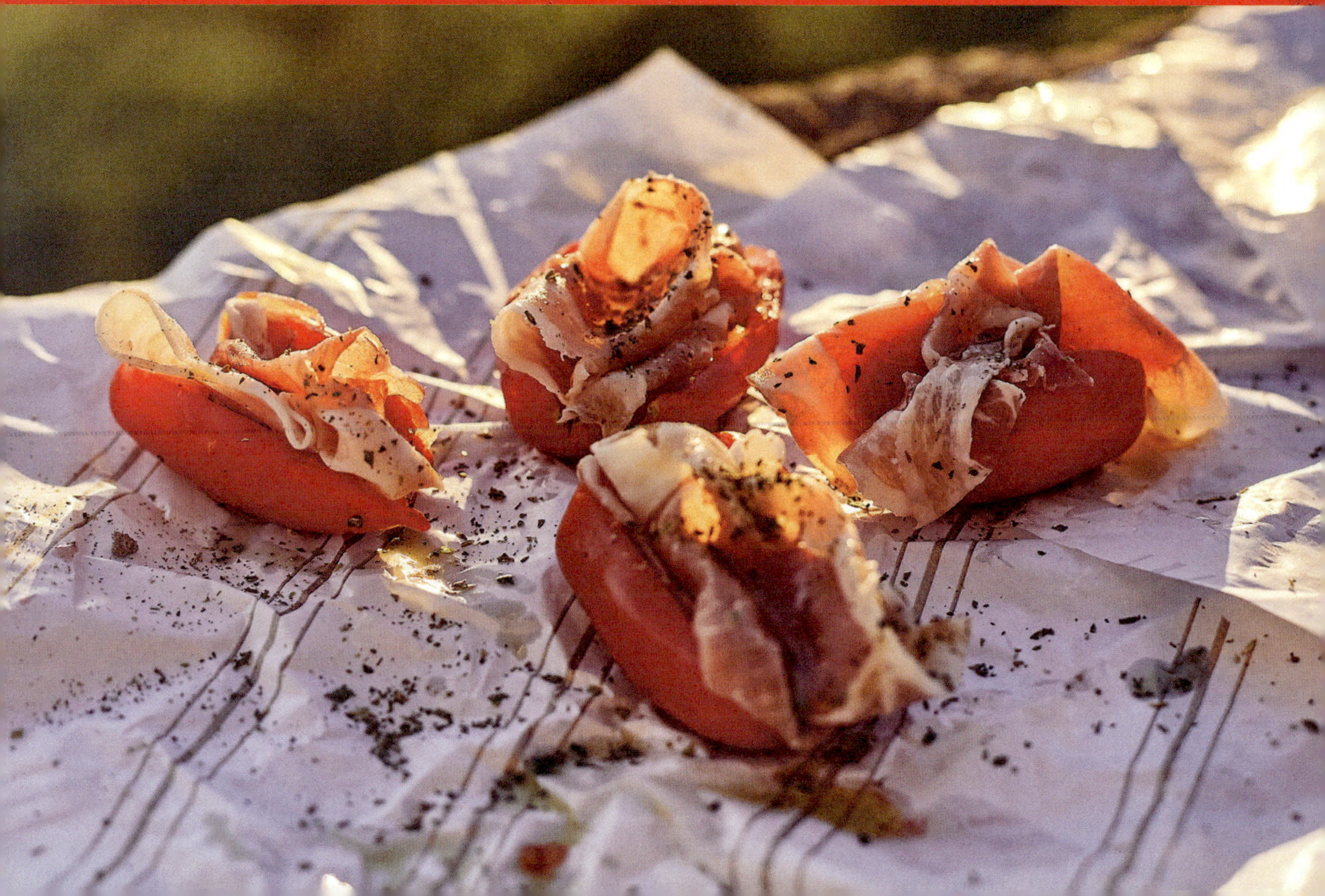

SAN MARZANO SANDWICHES

When we were in the field with Aniello, he told us about a little trick, and his favourite snack. You cut open a tomato, fill it with thinly sliced cured pancetta, oregano, a little salt and a drizzle of olive oil. 'Goes down well with a beer,' he said. We took that advice, nipped to the local *salumeria* (deli) and sat on the top of the old farmhouse stuffing our faces and feeling on top of the world as we watched the sun set behind Mount Vesuvius.

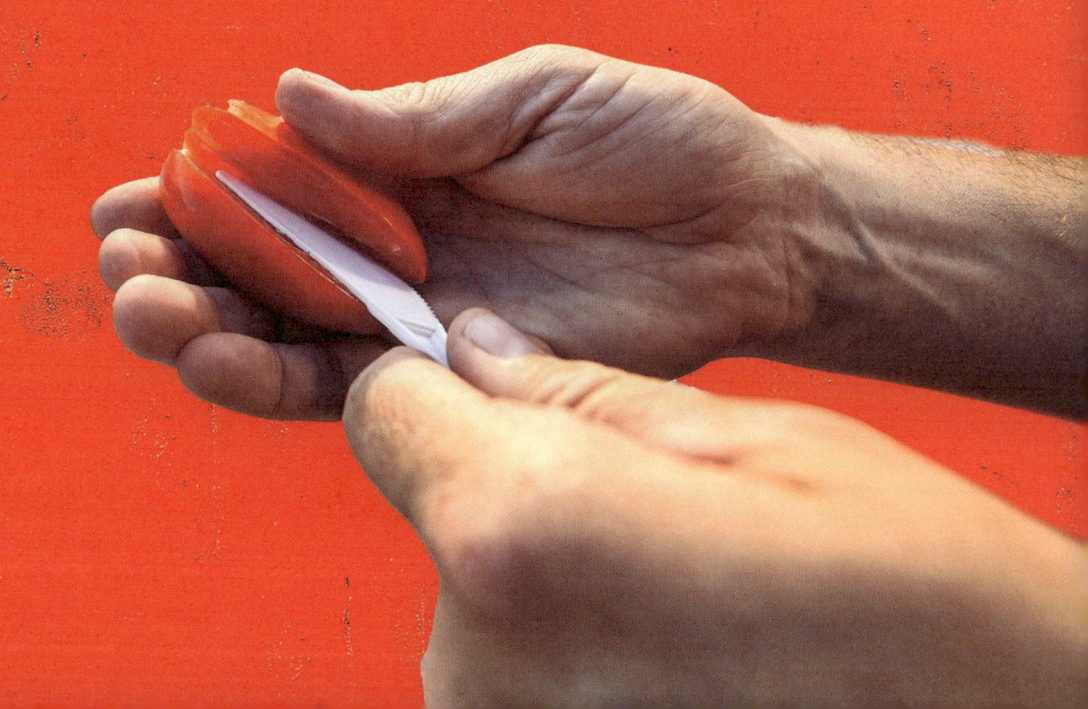

PIENNOLO

Pomodorino del Piennolo is a very unique variety of tomato. The plants love fertile soils and don't need much water, due to the fruit's thick skins, which makes the slopes of Mount Vesuvius – especially in the Somma Vesuviana region – a perfect place to grow them. They are then cut down in whole vines, tied into clusters and hung in a shady, well-ventilated area. The thick skins help to preserve the tomatoes and they can be stored for weeks, and even months, this way. They have a very intense, sweet and tangy flavour and are fantastic with just salt, oil and basil on bruschetta. Piennolos also preserve very well in jars. We use a lot in the pizzerias, especially on our Margherita Extra Extra, our swankiest Margherita with burrata, Piennolo tomatoes and fresh basil pesto. The pizza chefs also make a very simple pasta of Piennolo, basil, olive oil and salt for staff dinner: perfection.

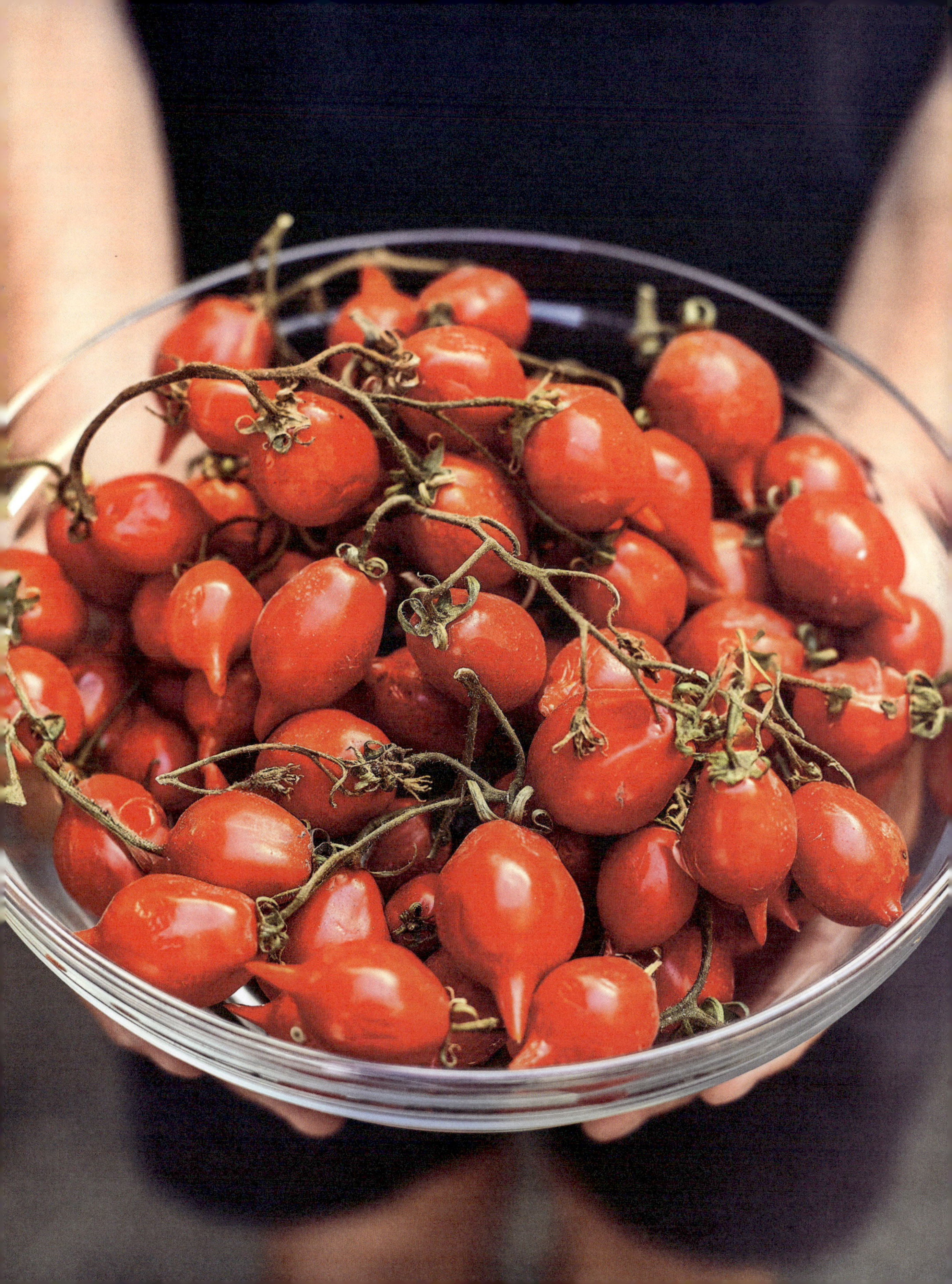

Latteria
SORRENTINA®
Arte Casearia dal 1880
CHEESE
MOZZARELLA DI BUFALA
CAMPANA
D.P.C.M. 10/05/1993
Reg. CE 1107/96
Aut. Consorzio Tutela
n. 014/10/1993
Certificato da Organismo
di Controllo Autorizzato
dal MIPAAF
Peso netto sgocciolato/ Drained net weight/
Nettogewicht/ Leeg nettogewicht/ Poids net égoutté/
Peso neto escurrido/ Peso líquido escorrido
250g℮

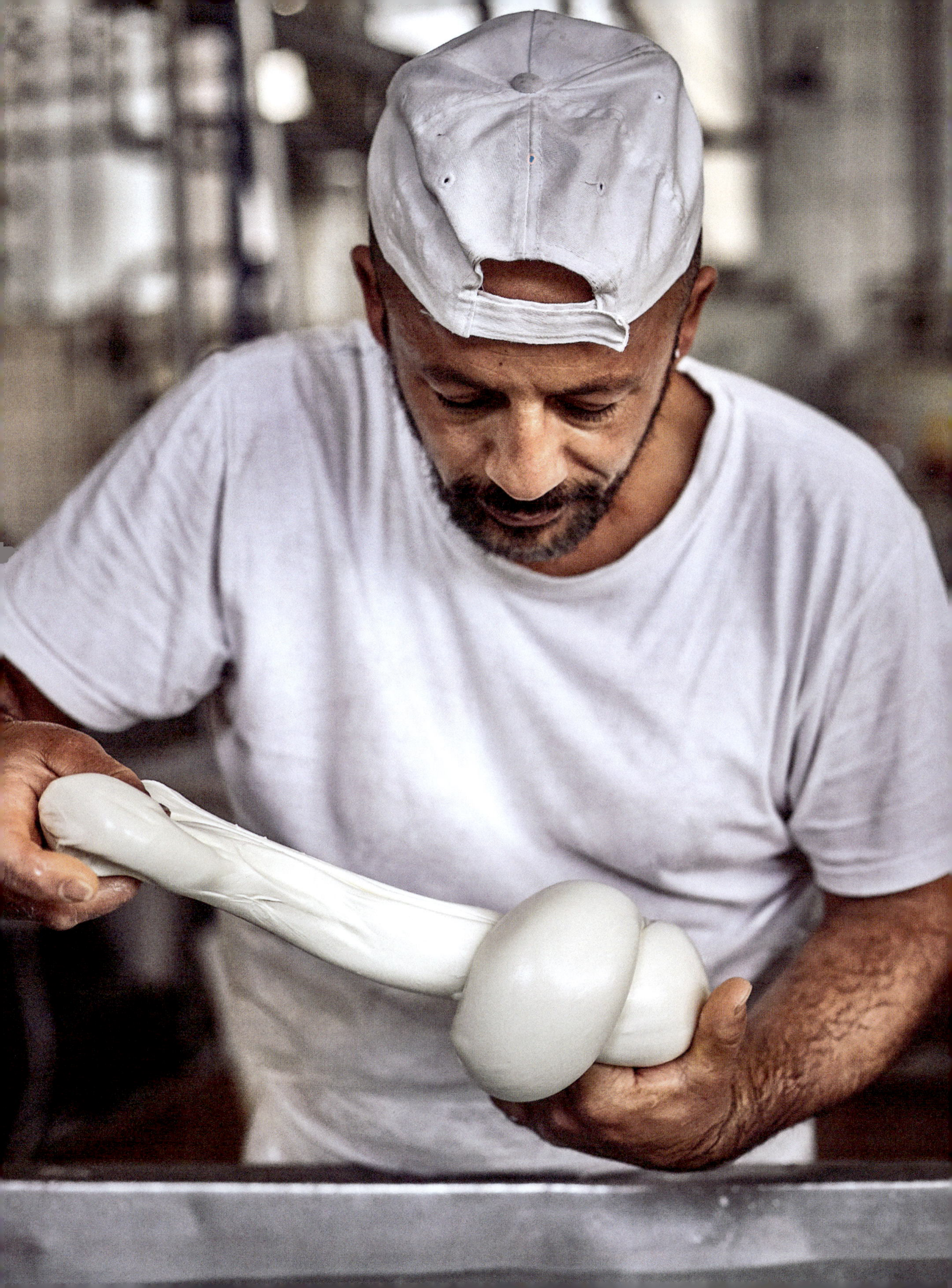

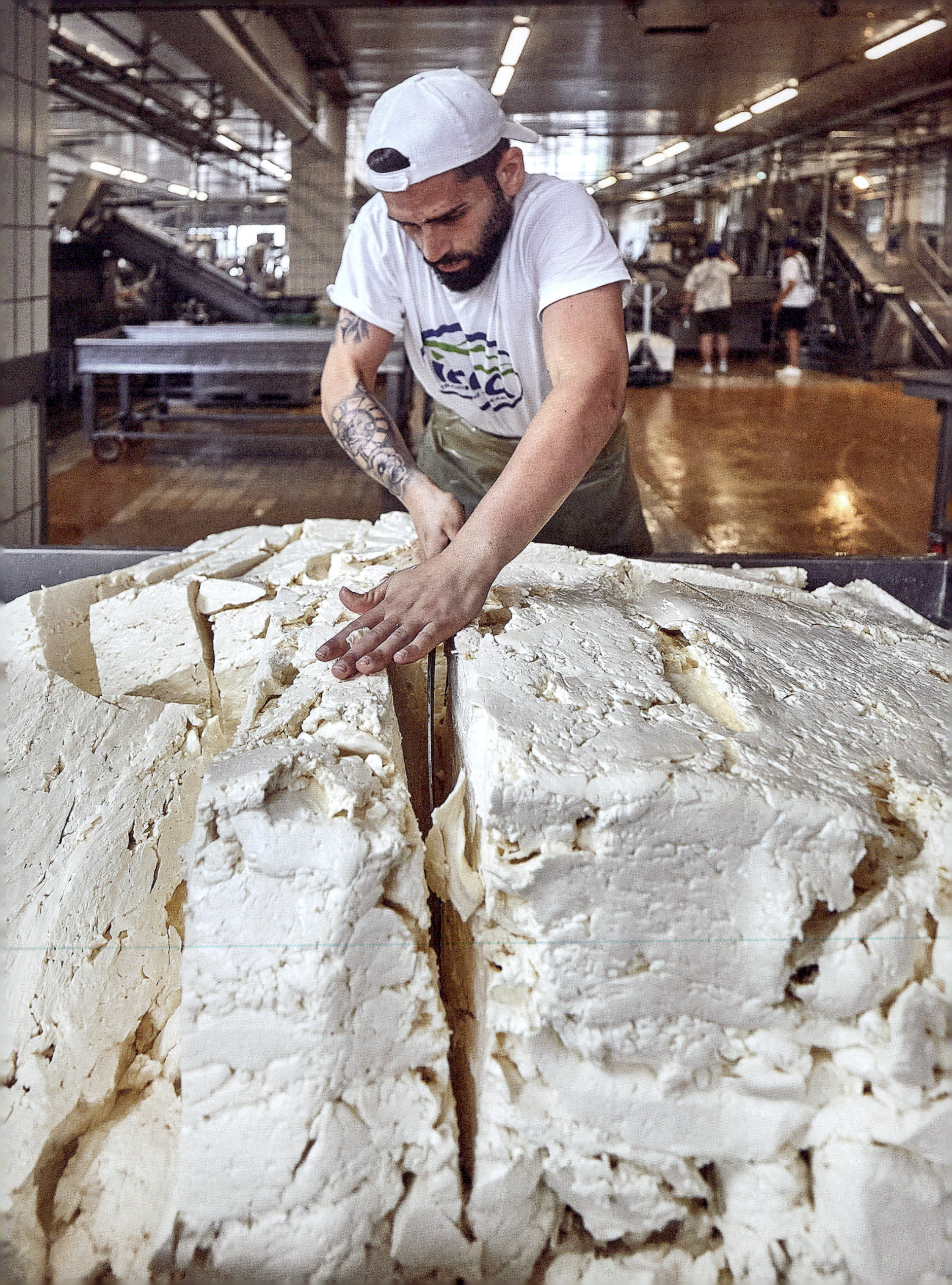

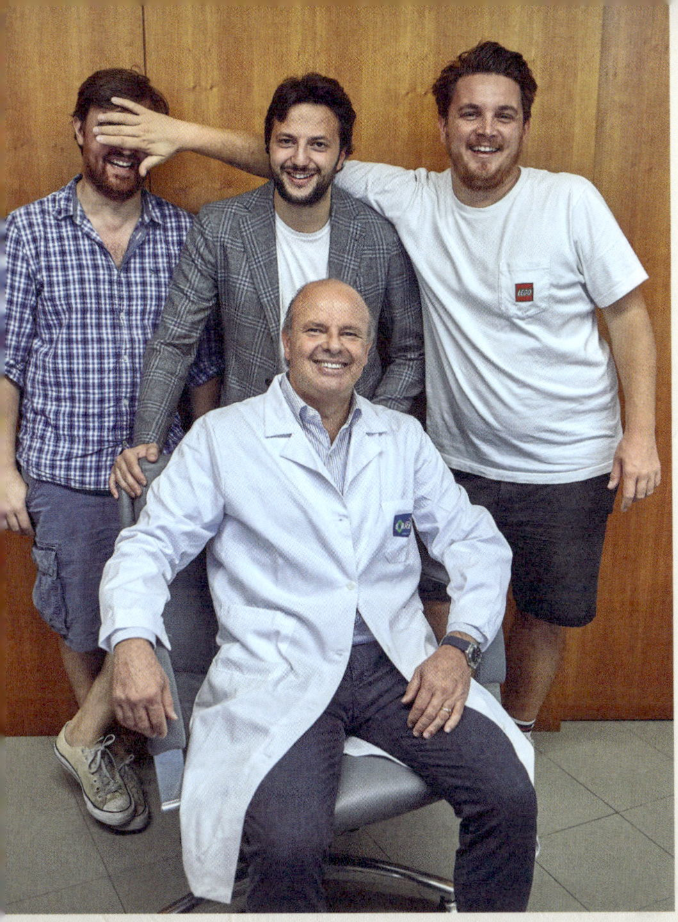

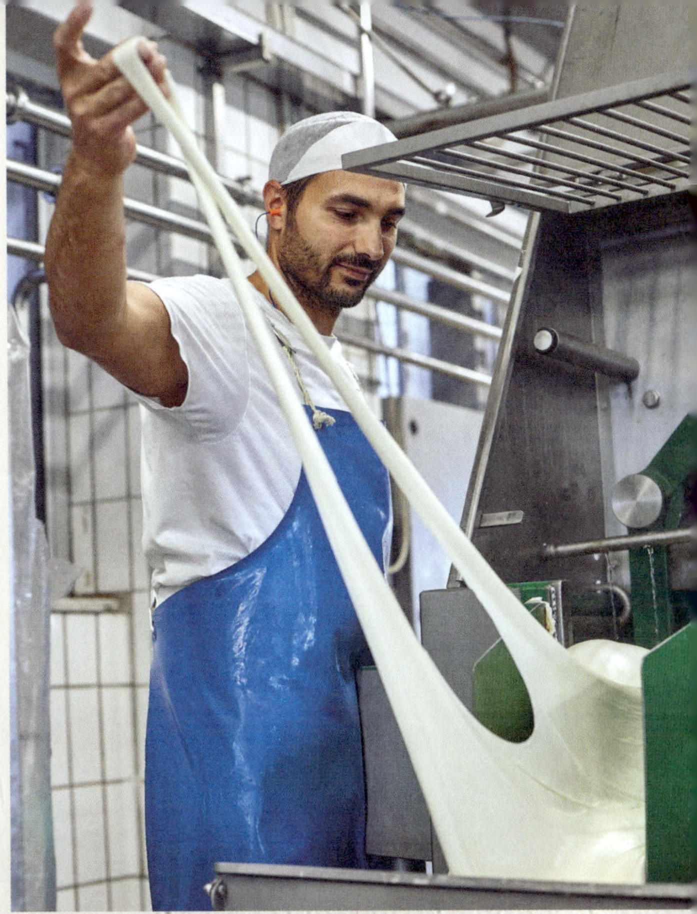

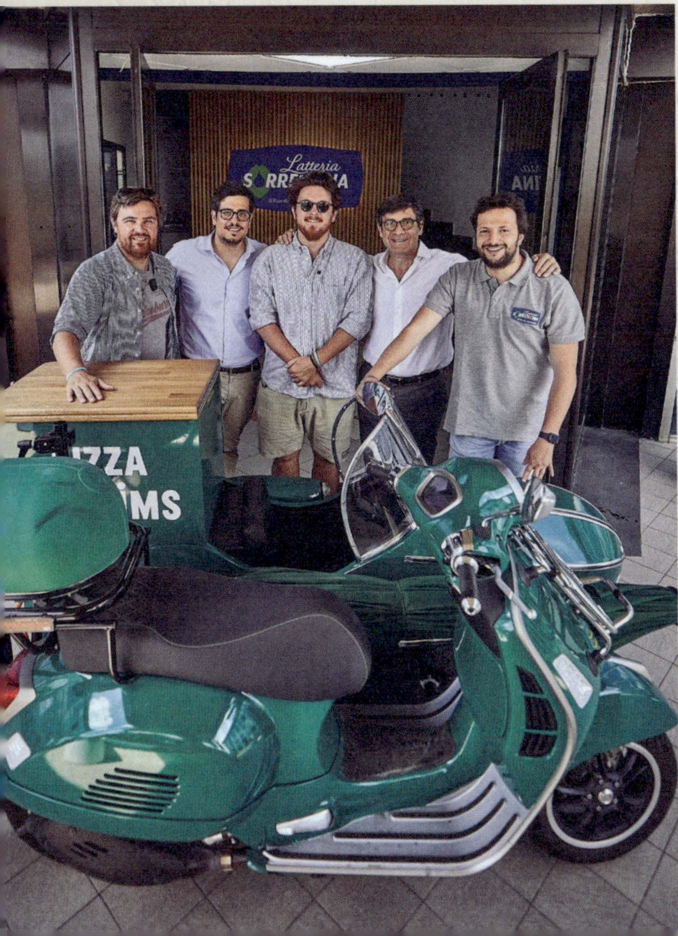
Latteria

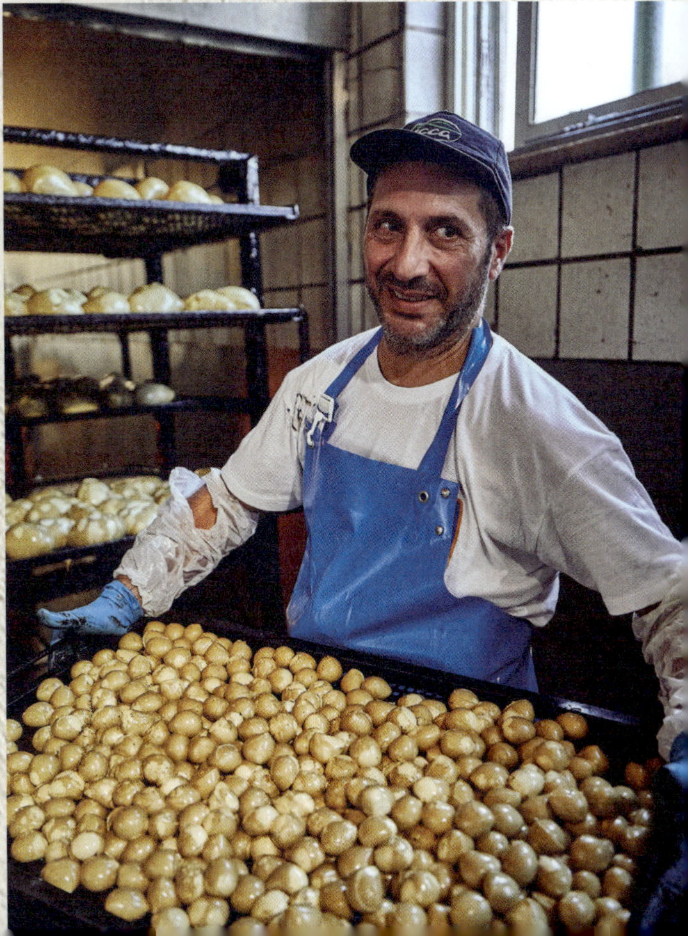

MOZZARELLA 101

Before we started Pizza Pilgrims, I (James!) worked for free at Pizzeria Di Matteo in Napoli to get some pointers. One morning, I was balling up the crocchè (page 247) when the mozzarella man arrived with a case of fresh bufala on his shoulder. 'Are you the English guy? Come here and taste this.' It was the best mozzarella I had ever tasted; a firm texture with good acidity and perfect flavour of milk. 'You will never get this in England!' And he turned and left. And it's true: mozzarella eaten the same day it's made is different. To transport it to England you have to chill it, which messes with the texture and flavour. Mozzarella is like a religion in Napoli, and they keep the best stuff for themselves.

You may already have a pretty good understanding of how mozzarella is made but, for the elimination of any doubt, let's run through the process from end to end. Who knows, maybe you'll be inspired to make some at home (we have and it was actually quite successful).

1. To begin, you need high-quality full fat (preferably raw) milk. The milk is heated to 34–38°C (93–100°F) while being stirred continuously to ensure even heating.

2. Then the rennet is added. This can be traditional animal rennet or a plant rennet (which will keep the mozzarella vegetarian). It is covered and left for 5 minutes; an enzyme called chymosin in the rennet curdles the casein in the milk to create curds.

3. Next, the curds are agitated and cut, using a special, fairly medieval, curd-cutting tool.

4. The curds are then allowed to ripen in the whey for 5 hours to develop acidity, before being separated from the whey. The whey can be cooked again to produce ricotta (more on that on page 84).

5. Water is heated to 76°C (169°F) and the curds are added.

6. Next comes a process called *pasta filata*, or 'spun curd', traditionally using a small bowl and a wooden stick to stretch the mozzarella curds as they begin to melt in the water. After about 5 minutes of stretching, you will see the structure of the curds start to change and take on a shiny consistency.

7. The mozzarella can then be formed into a number of different shapes. Most traditionally, balls are rolled and pinched using both hands. One way to tell hand-made mozzarella from industrial, is that hand-made will leave a 3-pointed seam on the mozzarella ball, whereas industrial mozzarella will have a small nipple where the machine has pushed the mozzarella from the mould. Other common shapes include plaiting the mozzarella into a *treccia*, knotting the mozzarella into *nodini* or forming tiny mozzarella pearls called *bocconcini*.

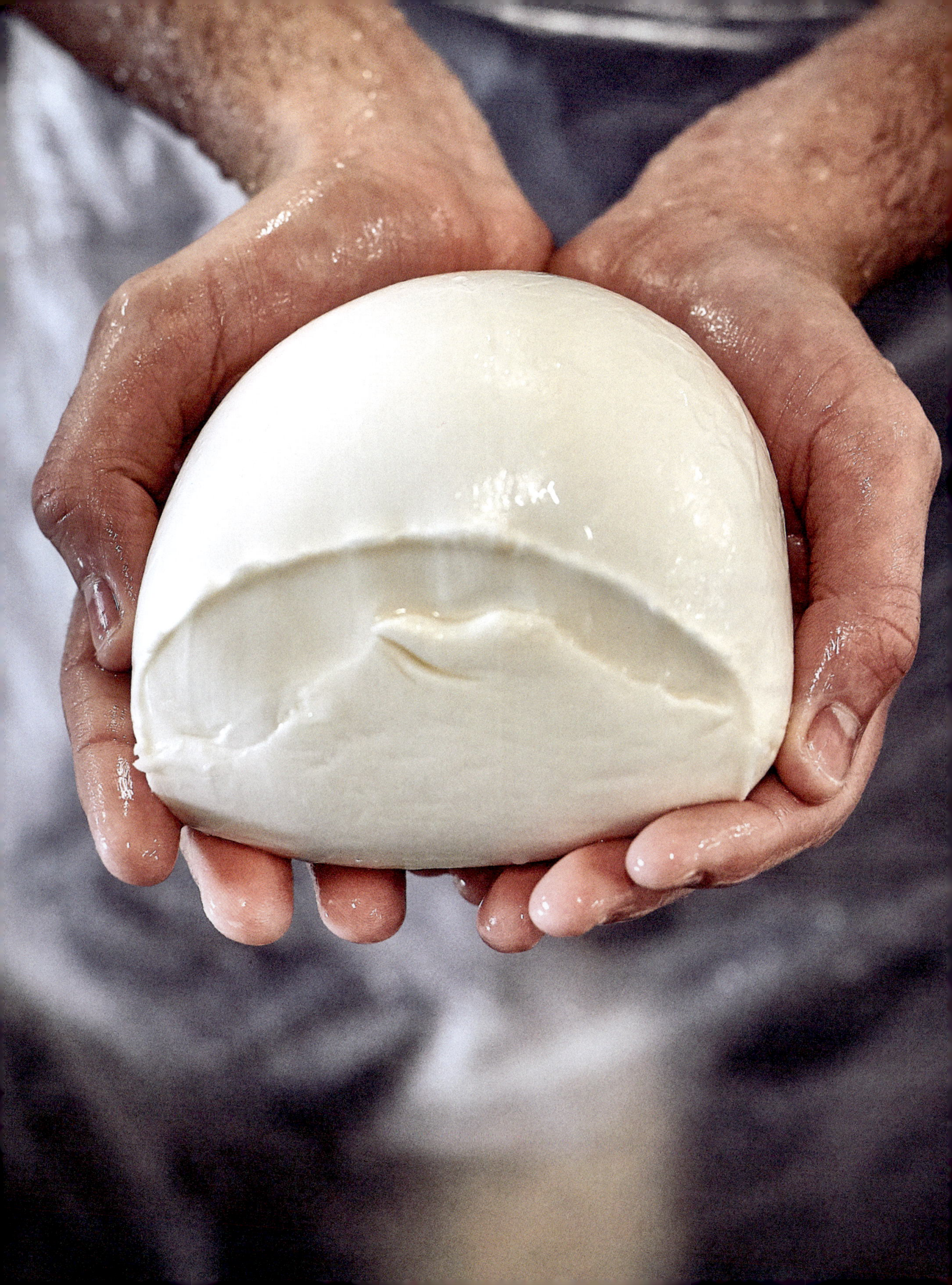

BUFALA

Buffalo mozzarella, or to give it its full name, Mozzarella di Bufala Campana DOC, really is the jewel in the crown of cheeses from Campania. As with so many products from Italy, its origins are a little murky, but the best story, and the one the Buffalo Mozzarella Consorzio is sticking to, is that water buffalo were introduced by the Arabs around AD 800 to the plains of Caserta and Salerno, as the buffalo were incredibly well suited to the watery marshes of the area. They were first used to pull ploughs and to clear flooded areas of vegetation. Then they began to be used for cheese made from their milk, and it was discovered that buffalo cheese was superior to cow's. Bufala really started to make a name for itself when the Bourbon royal family created an experimental cheese dairy in the 1700s to develop the standards and processes of bufala production. From then on, the cheese grew hugely in popularity, apart from a couple of tricky phases – during the Spanish occupation when 'buffalo hunts' came into vogue, then during World War II when the Nazis seized the entire buffalo stock of Campana. Mozzarella di Bufala Campana finally received its DOP status in 1993 and has continued to grow, being exported globally and featuring on almost every menu of every Italian restaurant around the world.

Molto bene

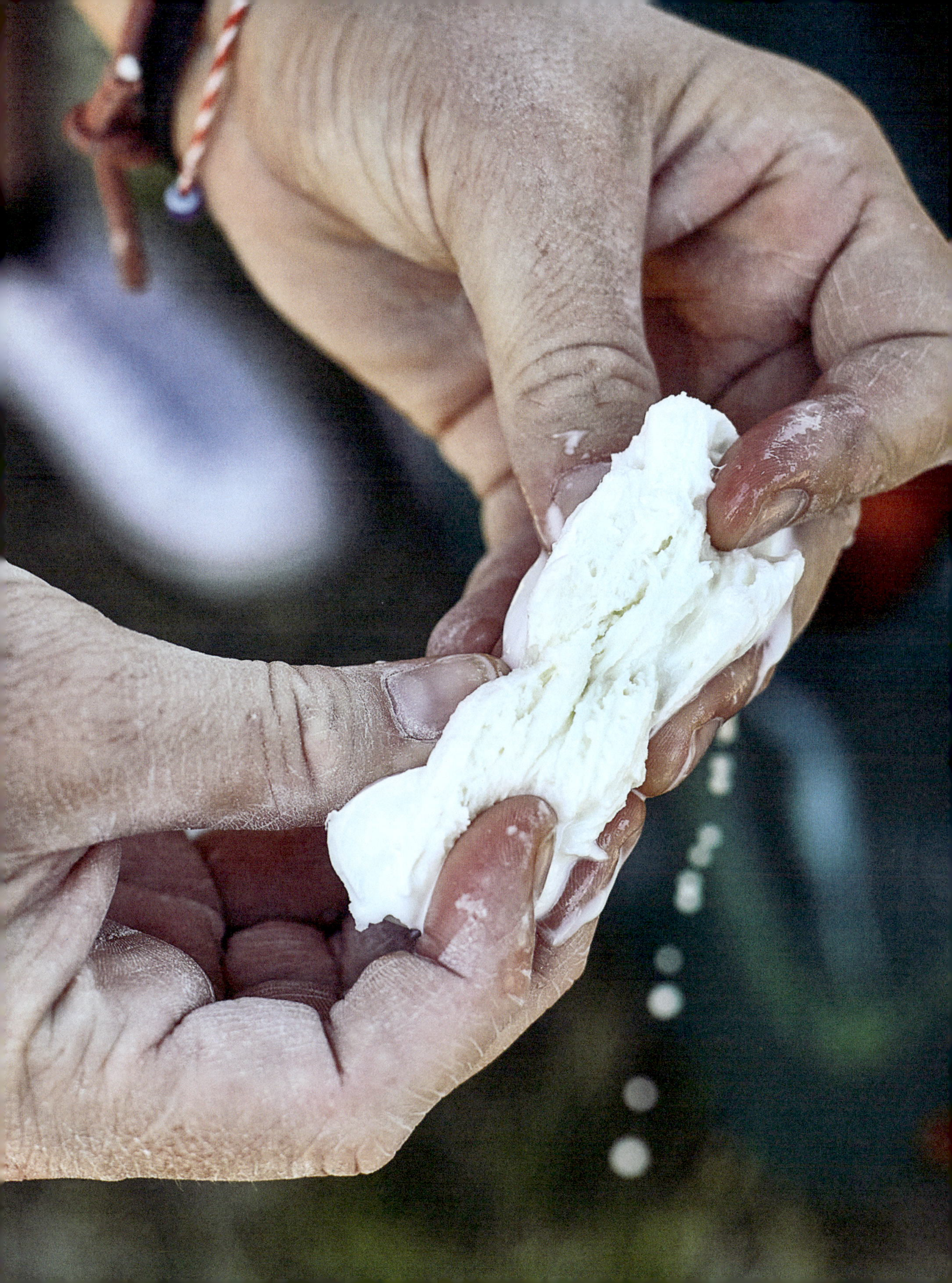

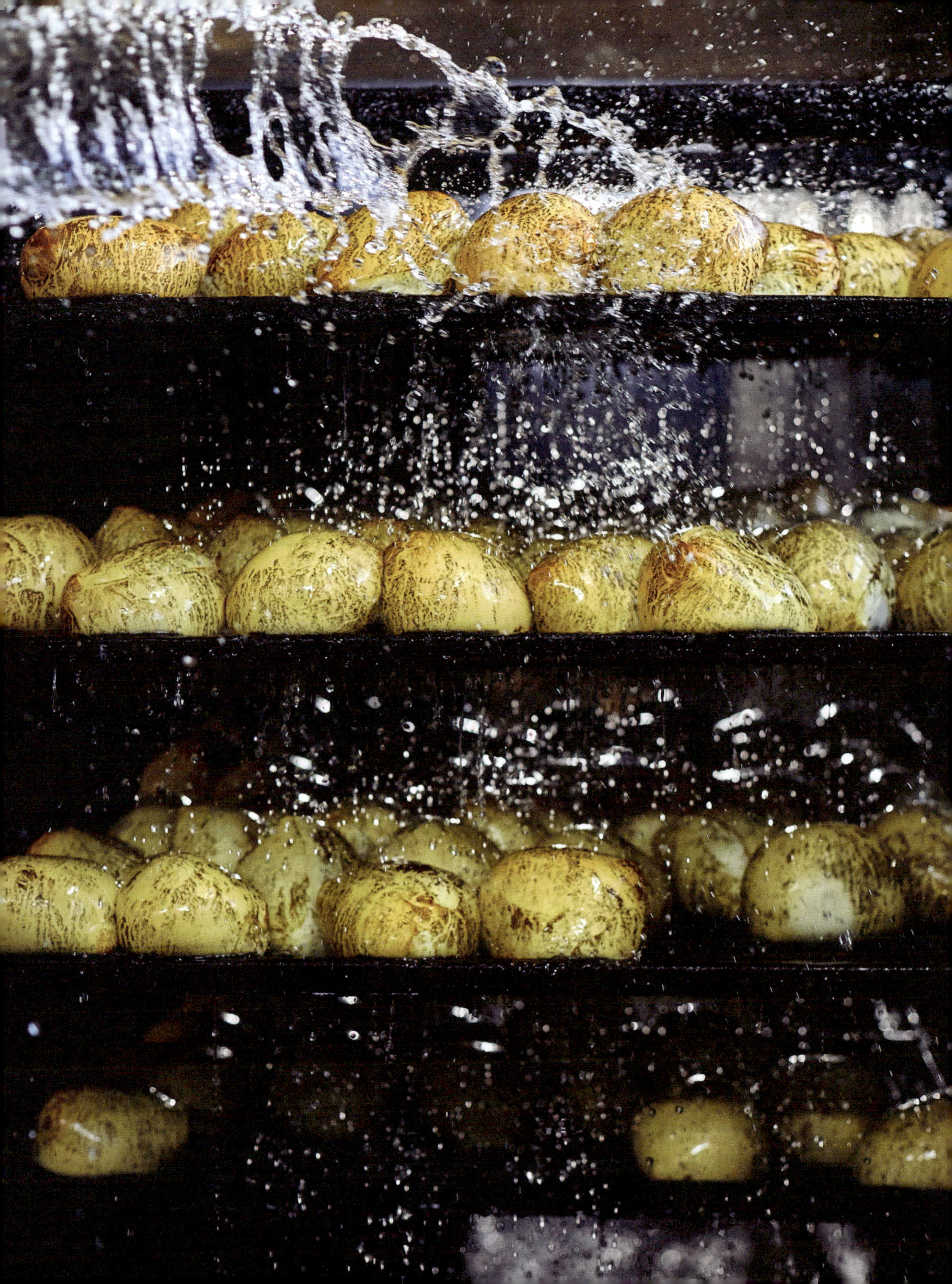

PROVOLA

Provola is the name for fresh smoked mozzarella, and you can get both cow's milk and buffalo milk varieties. Seeing provola being made is quite something. Huge metal racks on wheels, stained black with carbon from years of smoking, are loaded with hundreds of balls of fior di latte and buffalo mozzarella, straight off the production line. The racks are then wheeled through to the smoking room and loaded into the chamber where piles of hay are pitchforked in and set alight. The mozzarella stays in there for around 5 minutes and the smoky flavours immediately stick to the cheese. It's a remarkably simple process. The mozzarella is then wheeled out and tipped into a saltwater bath to take on more flavour and also to wash off any embers. The smoking process turns beautiful fresh mozzarella into a much more complex and savoury cheese. It pairs really well with strong meaty flavours as well as bringing some depth to fresh pizzas like the Provola e Pepe (page 108).

Provola is often confused with **provolone**, which is an aged cow's milk cheese. Napoli is also famous for provolone, and the Aurichio brand can be seen strung up in delis all over Italy. **Scamorza** is also often confused with provola – scamorza is a form of mozzarella that is dried for longer, characteristically tied up with string so that it droops as it ages. Scamorza is also a smoked cheese but the aging process gives the cheese a sweetness and nuttiness that you don't get in provola.

All these cheeses have their place on pizza but provola is the undisputed champion of smoked cheeses for the pizzaioli.

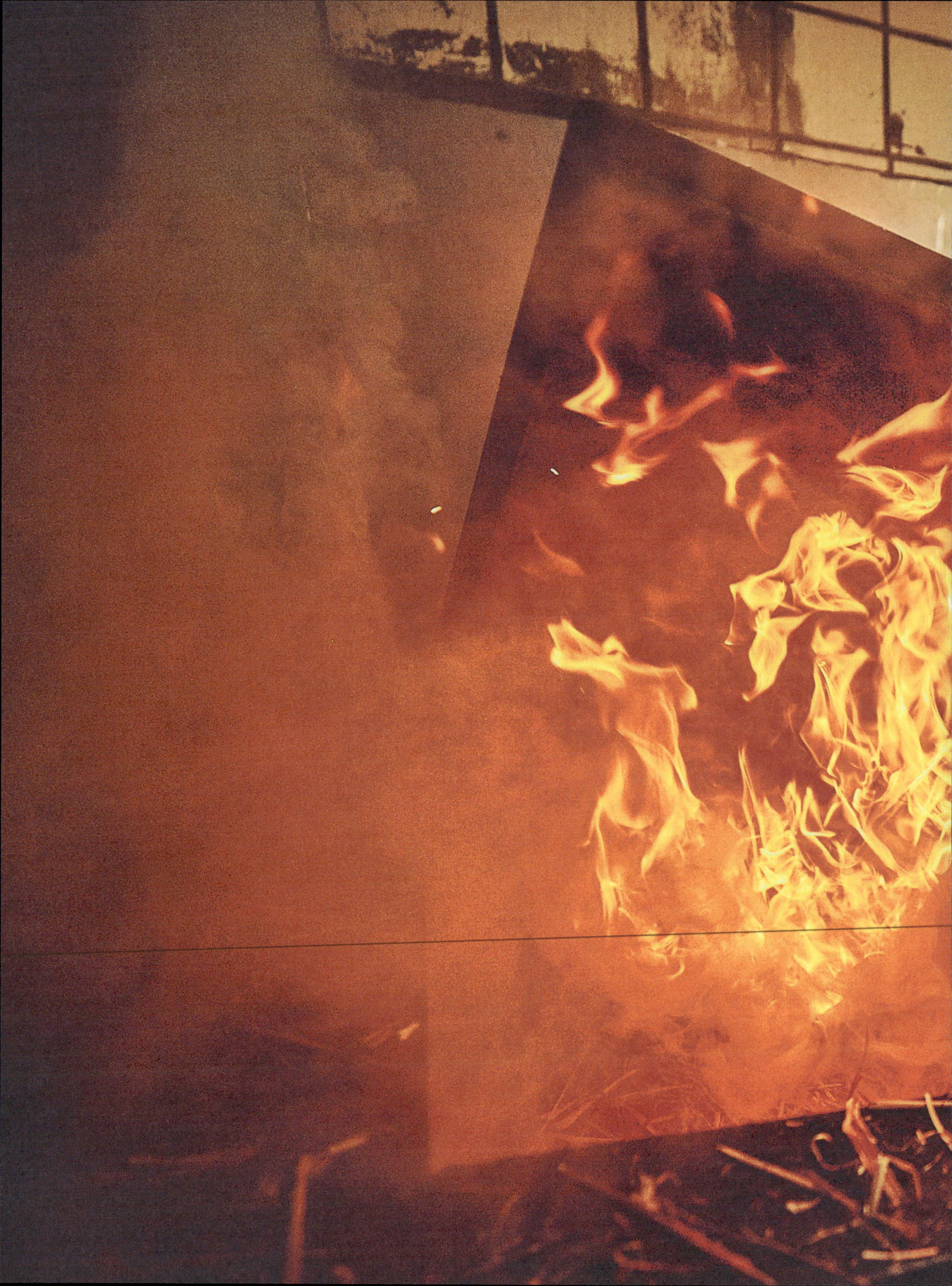

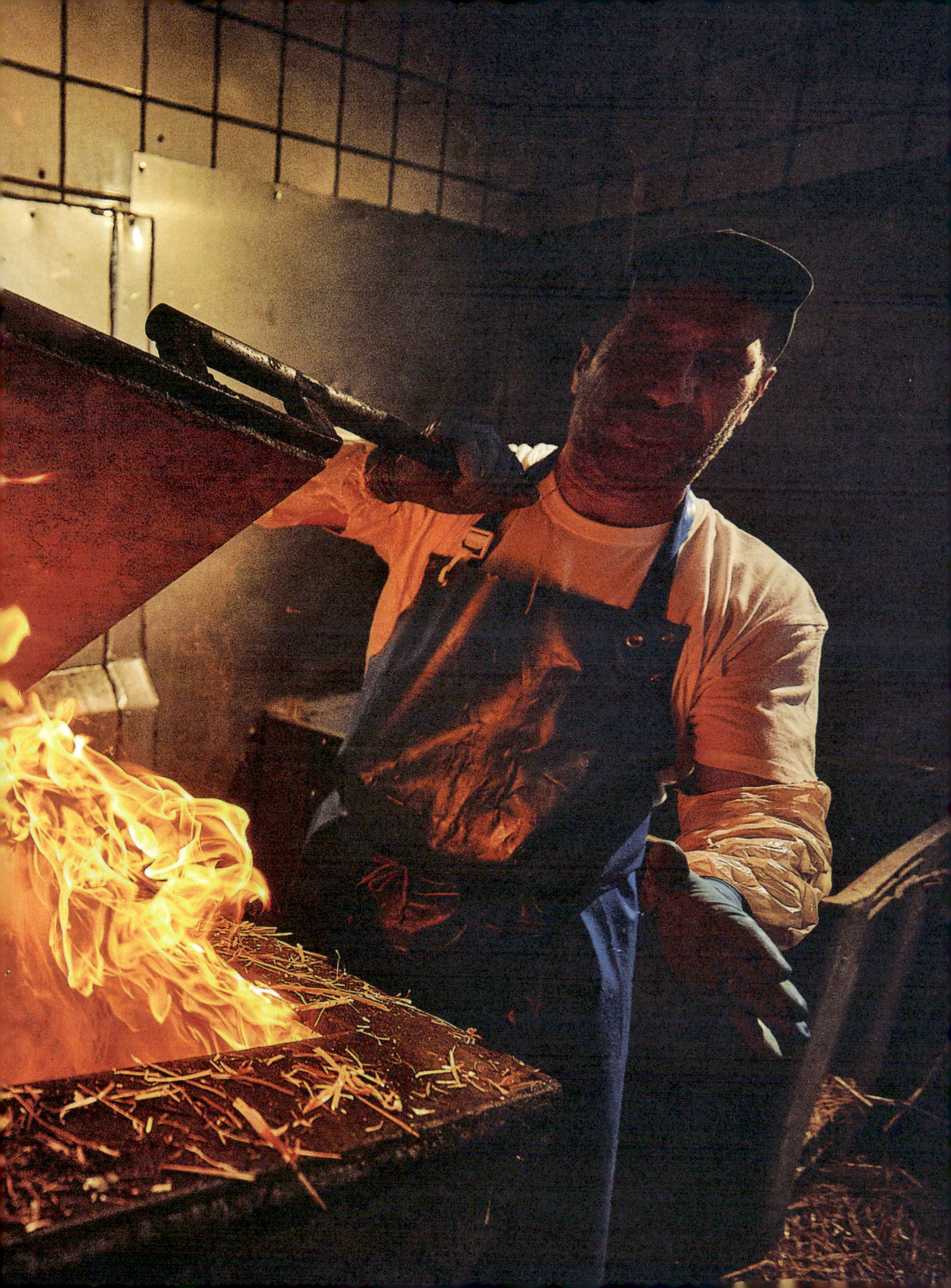

DEEP-FRIED MOZZARELLA BITES

We came up with this recipe, not so glamorously, round the back of our mozzarella supplier, in the car park, but perfectly positioned by a door next to the end of the provola production line. We think this must now be the most loved dish in our pizzerias – because it's got everything! Smoky, milky mozzarella with a crispy bread coating and some sweet chilli jam to balance out the richness. This recipe also has the benefit of being taste-tasted by the men who actually make the provola. Can't ask for a better seal of approval than that!

What you need

400g (14oz) provola (smoked) mozzarella

plain (all-purpose) flour

panko breadcrumbs

neutral frying oil

flaky sea salt

your favourite chilli jam (other dips work here too, such as truffle mayo or Marinara sauce), to serve

How to make it

Cut the provola into 4cm (1½ inch) cubes (small enough to melt all the way through but not small enough to over-melt and break through the breadcrumbs).

In a bowl, mix flour with cold water until it has the consistency of wet paint and season with salt. This is your pastella mix.

Tip your panko breadcrumbs onto a plate.

Throw the provola cubes into the pastella and, using a fork, fish them out straight into the panko. Roll them around until they are well covered. Repeat the process so they are double coated, to keep the melted mozzarella in.

Heat your frying oil to 180°C (356°F) in a deep-sided pan. Drop in your coated provola (ensuring not to overload the oil; fry in batches if necessary) and fry for 3–5 minutes until the crust is crispy and golden and the mozzarella inside has melted.

Drain on kitchen paper, season with flaky sea salt, then serve up with chilli jam and a cold beer.

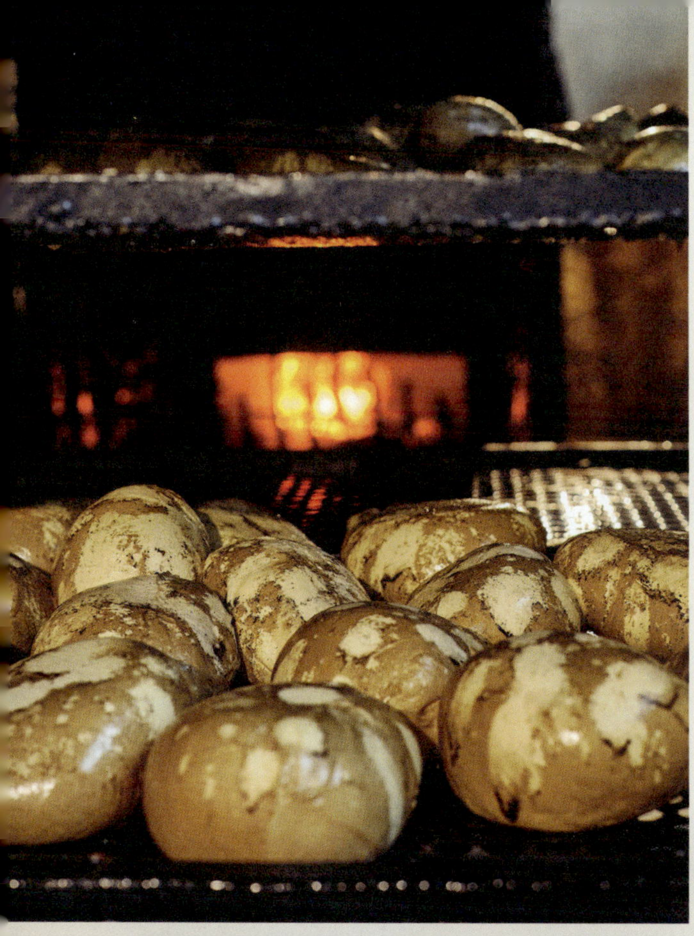

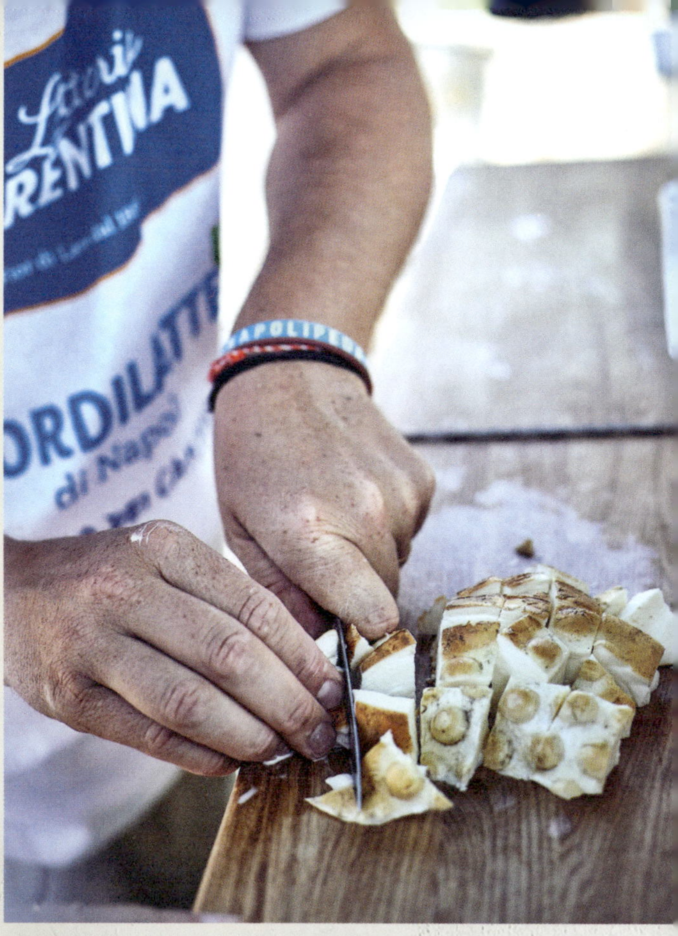
di Napoli

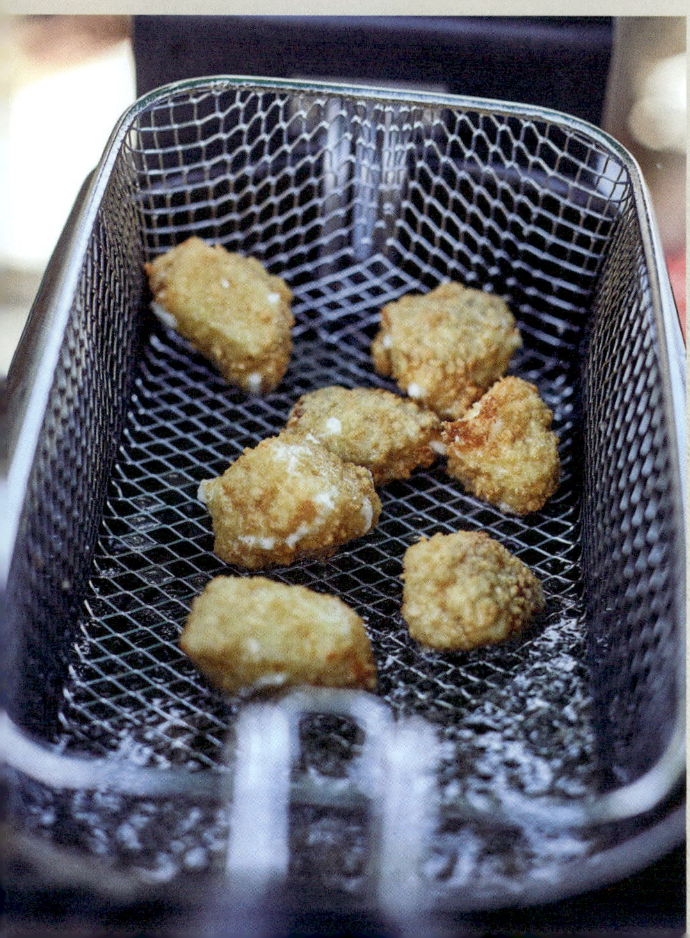

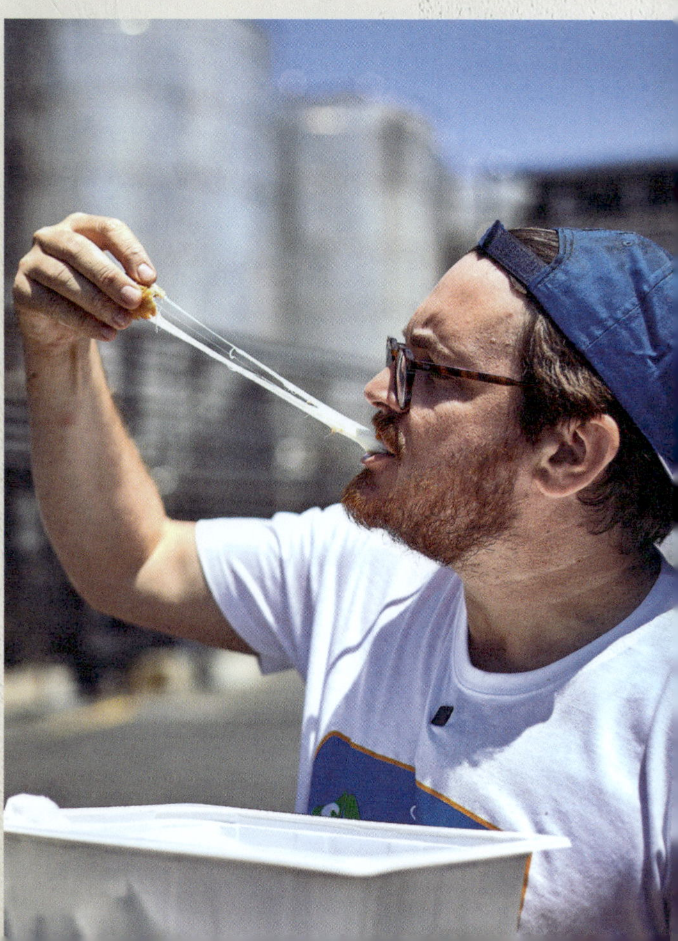

RICOTTA

We think ricotta is hugely underrated outside of Italy. It has a bit of a reputation in the UK as being like an Italian cottage cheese and very much mascarpone's cheaper cousin. However, in Italy it is a prized cheese and a staple of every kitchen. We think the problem might lie in access to 'the good stuff'. To eat ricotta straight off the production line in Campania is something quite special. It's thick, intensely milky and as smooth as clotted cream. We also know it mostly as an ingredient for pasta fillings, cannoli and cakes, but in Napoli they eat it straight, as an antipasti. We would love to see ricotta knock burrata off its top spot as *the* cheese to eat at the beginning of a meal with great tomatoes and olive oil, truffles or even warmed-through 'nduja and honey! It's also fantastic as a pizza ingredient, either as a replacement for tomato sauce on a pizza bianca, or piped on after cooking to bring a cool, fresh dimension to a rich pizza.

The process of making ricotta is also inventive, and has great sustainability credentials. It's made by almost every cheesemaker in Italy as it creates a whole new cheese from a waste product, and helps to bolster the finances. To get a little technical for a second, the protein strands that are used to make ricotta are mainly beta-lactoglobulin and alpha-lactalbumin, which is in the same family of molecules as egg white. When whey is heated to between 75°C and 85°C (167°F and 185°F), the strands of protein begin to form, much like egg white, and they can be sieved from the *scotta* (liquid that is left after production) and drained in moulds to make ricotta. The trick to making great ricotta is to allow the strands to form and not skim them until they have developed properly, but not so late that they become tough. It is a true art and there will often be a cheesemaker specific to ricotta making in every dairy, or *caseificio*.

BURRATA AND STRACCIATELLA

Burrata's rise to fame has been pretty astronomical in the past 10–15 years. It's creamy, salty, goes with everything, and has a party trick: the drama of cutting a burrata open table-side has been a hit with the social-media generation and caused the birth of Burratagram.

Burrata joins a long list of Italian ingredients that you imagine are hundreds of years old, but were actually created during the 20th century (ciabatta was invented in 1983?!). Originating during the 1920s in the region of Murgia in Puglia, it was said to be invented by a man called Lorenzo Bianchino Chieppa as a way of using up the leftovers of the cheese-making process – as Chieppa's son says, 'The cream came from the dense layer formed on top of the morning milking.' Any leftover mozzarella was then stripped by hand and added to the cream with salt to make the even more popular and hip stracciatella cheese.

When stracciatella is encased in a shell of mozzarella and crimped closed, you have burrata. The burrata casing had the extra benefit of protecting the cheese from the summer heat of Puglia, meaning it could be sold for longer at market.

PIZZA &

DOUGH

THE THREE CRUSTS OF NAPOLI (AND OURS TOO!)

When it comes to food, Neapolitans can be somewhat sceptical of innovation. One of the reasons Italian food culture is so strong is due to the deep respect of food history. Everyone's heard the seemingly arbitrary dining rules that are adhered to by everyone in the country: no cappuccino after 12pm; no cheese on seafood pasta; and, of course, no pineapple on pizza! The pizza scene was once guilty of moving at a fairly glacial rate in Napoli, with Neapolitan pizza not having vastly changed since its invention. However, there is one area in which the pizzaioli of Napoli are allowed to flex and develop their own personal style, and this is with the *cornicione,* or crust. The dough ingredients always stay the same but slight changes in the flour type, proving process, hydration, stretching and baking can, in the eyes of a Neapolitan, change everything in the pizza. We couldn't have written this crust-based bonanza without the help of our friend and 'Head of Pizza' at Pizza Pilgrims, Domenico (page 95). His passion for pizza runs deep and he is a constant source of information and inspiration. *Salute Dom!*

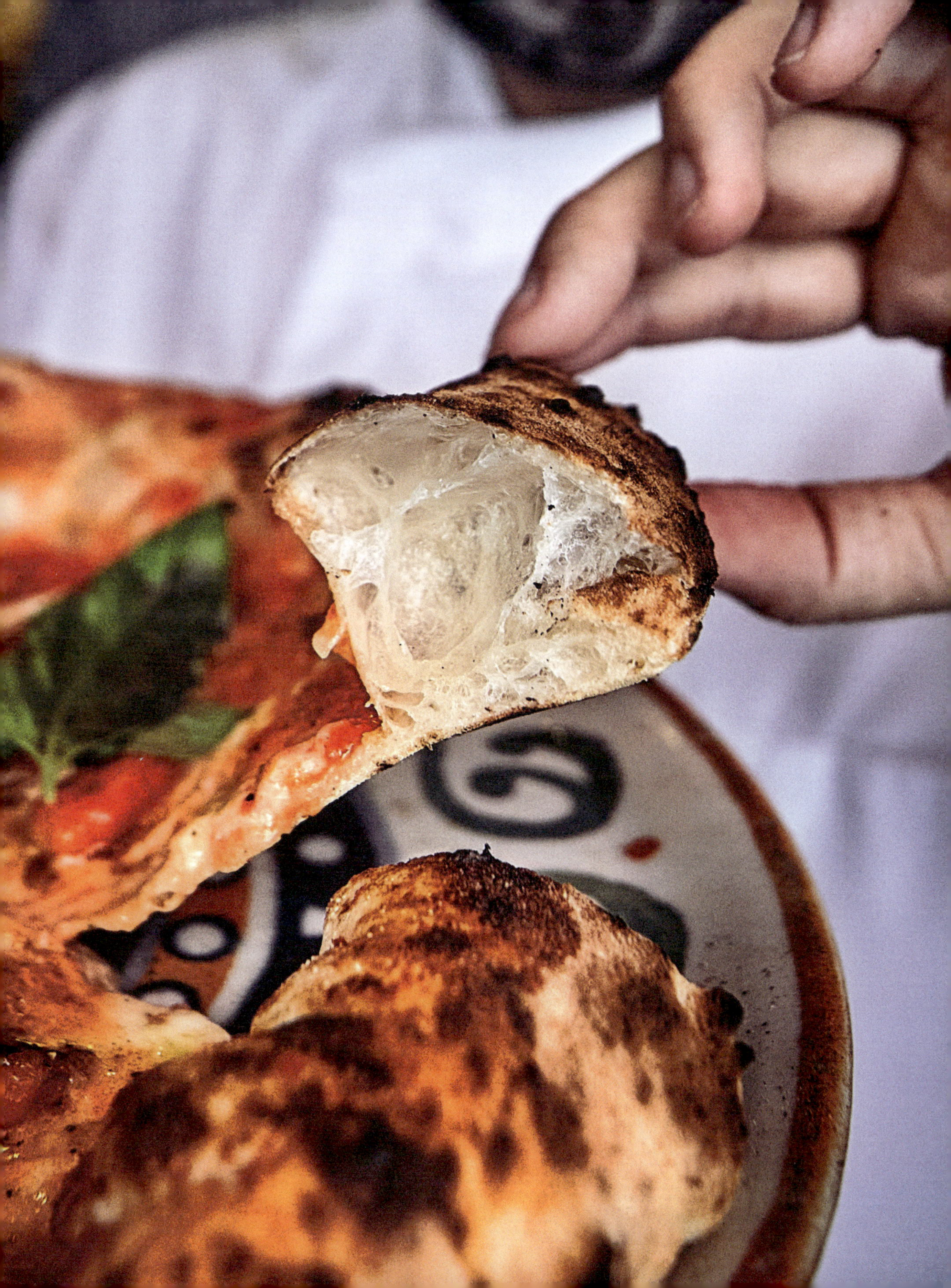

RUOTA DI CARRO

This is the most traditional style of pizza base in Napoli and is best exemplified in pizzerias like Da Michele (page 26) and Sorbillo (page 148). A couple of hundred years ago, pizza was placed in the middle of the table to serve a hungry family, so the pizza was huge and the crust was often thick and dense. Over the years, the Ruota di Carro style has become lighter, better to serve one, but has kept its size. The direct translation of the name in Italian is 'cartwheel' – the dough is stretched way over the edges of a large wooden peel when baked and it's served at the table with the crust of the pizza hanging off the sides of the plate. The crust has a low profile of 1cm (½ inch) and the middle of the pizza is wafer thin. The dough is a 'direct dough', meaning it's made in the pizzeria in the morning, balled and proved 'directly' for 6–8 hours for use that evening. As a result, the dough usually has a higher yeast percentage to help the dough prove quickly. Another characteristic of this dough is a lower hydration so that the dough ball is easier to stretch to a large size without tearing. Of the three classic styles, Ruota di Carro gives you the weightiest crust, with each individual dough ball weighing about 300g (10½oz), which lets you stretch the pizza to a massive 35cm (14 inches).

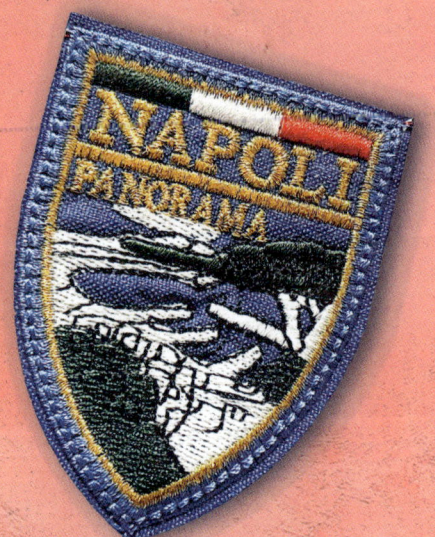

Makes 6 dough balls

What you need

600ml (20fl oz) cold water

2g (½ tsp) fresh yeast

1kg (2¼lb) 00 flour

30g (1oz) fine sea salt

How to make it

Add the water to a large mixing bowl (or the bowl of a stand mixer), then rub the yeast between your fingers under the water to dissolve it. Add half the flour and mix until smooth – the dough should have a consistency of a thick batter at this point. Add the salt and mix well to combine. Add the remaining flour in two batches, mixing until you have a scraggly dough.

Tip the dough out onto a clean work surface (if kneading by hand) and stretch and knead the dough for 10–15 minutes until elastic and smooth (if using a stand mixer, mix on slow for 10–12 minutes using the dough hook). Cover the dough with a cloth and leave to rest for 30 minutes.

Use a dough scraper to divide the dough into 300g (10½oz) portions, rolling each into a tight ball. Place the dough balls seam-side down in a large airtight container, then cover and leave to prove at room temperature for 6–8 hours until the dough has doubled in size, and you can smell a mild acidic fermentation.

The dough can now be used immediately or kept in the fridge for 1–2 days.

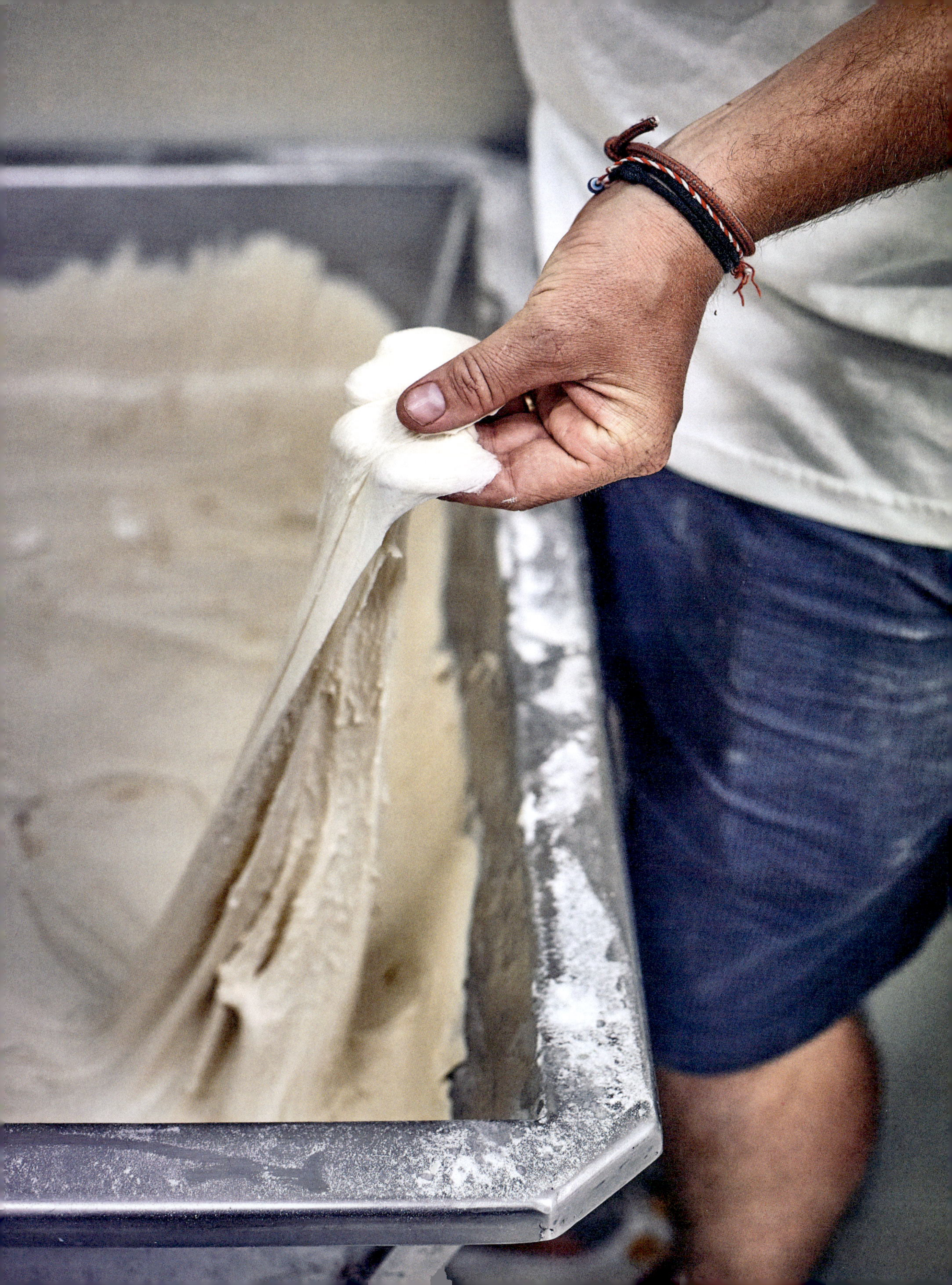

STG

In the mid '90s, the reputation of Neapolitan pizza was being dragged through the mud. Some pizza makers had lost their way and the word around Italy was that the pizza in Napoli was being made without passion and with cheap ingredients. Enter The Associazione Verace Pizza Napoletana (The Real Neapolitan Pizza Association, or AVPN). In a sort of Pizza Avengers moment, the great and the good of Napoli got together and decided to create a governing body to protect, celebrate and create a rulebook for true Neapolitan pizza (and they got really into it – the document outlining the rules for Margherita pizza is 27 pages long... front and back!). The result was Specialità Tradizionale Garantita (Traditional Speciality Guaranteed, or STG).

The principles of STG are as follows:

- The ingredients used should be local and of high quality.
- Tomatoes must be San Marzano.
- Cheese must be Parmigiano Reggiano and Mozzarella di Bufala Campana.
- You can use only extra virgin olive oil.
- The dough must be made using 00 flour and kneaded by hand or a slow spin mixer.
- The dough must be proved for at least 24 hours in a direct method.
- Each dough ball must be stretched by hand and cooked in a wood-fired oven at 485°C (900°F) for no longer than 60–90 seconds.
- The crust should not exceed 2cm (¾ inch) in height and the pizza should be 35cm (14 inches) wide.

Quite a lot of rules, huh? And that's just the beginning. However, the product of the AVPN and STG was a new pride and respect for traditional Neapolitan pizza, and is the reason why it is still considered the original and best to this day. Here's how to make the dough.

Makes 6 dough balls

What you need

650ml (22fl oz) cold water

1.5g (heaped ¼ tsp) fresh yeast

1kg (2¼lb) 00 flour

30g (1oz) fine sea salt

How to make it

Add the water to a large mixing bowl (or the bowl of a stand mixer), then rub the yeast between your fingers under the water to dissolve it. Add half the flour and mix until smooth – the dough should have a consistency of a thick batter at this point. Add the salt and mix well to combine. Add the remaining flour in two batches, mixing until you have a scraggly dough.

Tip the dough out onto a clean work surface (if kneading by hand) and stretch and knead the dough for 10–15 minutes until elastic and smooth (if using a stand mixer, mix on slow for 10–12 minutes using the dough hook). Cover the dough with a cloth and leave to rest for 30 minutes.

Use a dough scraper to divide the dough into 270g (9½oz) portions, rolling each into a tight ball. Place the dough balls seam-side down in a large airtight container, then cover and leave to prove at room temperature for 9–12 hours until the dough has doubled in size, and you can smell a mild acidic fermentation. Place the sealed container in the fridge and leave to prove for a further 12 hours.

Remove the dough from the fridge and allow come up to room temperature for 2–3 hours before using. The dough can now be used immediately or kept in the fridge for 2–3 days.

CONTEMPORANEA

This is the new hot dough on the scene... A younger generation of pizza chefs were looking for something to set themselves apart and the result was a dough that springs in the oven to create a high puffy crust often nicknamed *canotto* (directly translating as 'rubber dinghy'). This new style of dough made great social media content along with the often vibrant and interesting toppings used, like purple potatoes and raw red prawns. The dough style is also a flex of talent; to create a puffy dough like this you need a good understanding of dough management and the biga pre-ferment processes. It's also a high-hydration dough that is notoriously hard to stretch and work with on the bench. These two factors together made contemporanea a huge hit in Napoli and beyond. Will this cool wave of crust last? Let's see what the next generation brings to the table.

Makes 6 dough balls

What you need

For the pre-ferment

300g (10½oz) 00 flour

1g (¼ tsp) fresh yeast

150ml (5fl oz) water

For the dough

750ml (25¼fl oz) water

1g (¼ tsp) fresh yeast

450g (1lb) pre-ferment (see above)

700g (1½lb) 00 flour

20g (¾oz) fine sea salt

10g (⅓oz) extra virgin olive oil

How to make it

Begin by making your pre-ferment. Combine the flour, yeast and water in a bowl and mix until it becomes a rough dough. Cover and leave to ferment at 16°C (60°F) for 24 hours.

After the 24 hours, make your dough. Add the water to a large mixing bowl (or the bowl of a stand mixer), then rub the yeast between your fingers under the water to dissolve it.

Add the pre-ferment and massage it into the water using your hands. Add half the flour and mix until smooth, then add the salt and oil and mix well to combine. Add the remaining flour in two batches, mixing until you have a scraggly dough.

Tip the dough out onto a clean work surface (if kneading by hand) and stretch and knead the dough for 10–12 minutes until elastic and smooth (if using a stand mixer, mix on slow for 10 minutes using the dough hook). Cover the dough with a cloth and leave to rest for 30 minutes.

Use a dough scraper to divide the dough into 250g (9oz) portions, rolling each into a tight ball. Place the dough balls seam-side down in a large airtight container, then cover and leave to prove in the fridge for 10–12 hours until the dough has doubled in size, and you can smell a mild acidic fermentation.

Remove the dough from the fridge and allow it to come up to room temperature for 2–3 hours before using. The dough can now be used immediately or kept in the fridge for 1 day.

SPG

(aka Speciality Pilgrims Guaranteed!)
Our first dough recipe came from a pizza chef called Antonino Esposito who has a pizzeria in Sorrento called Ahum. James got some experience there before we first started out, to learn some tricks and tips and to get to grips with a good dough recipe. Eleven years have passed since then, and we estimate that over 500 pizza chefs have worked for Pizza Pilgrims in that period. Every chef has their own way of making dough that they learned from their mentors. We wanted to create a

dough that was unique and consistent to the brand, but we also wanted to learn and develop from new pizzaioli joining the business. So, we created the 'Pizza Pilgrims Summit'. It's an annual event where every head chef at the company comes together for a day to discuss nothing but dough: flour types, flour brands, hydration, proving methods, dough machine speeds and the changing seasons. We get it all out on the table, then finalize a recipe that all the chefs commit to using for the next 12 months. The recipe below is the culmination of 10 years of the Pizza Pilgrims Summit – we think of it as a greatest hits recipe and believe that our pizza style is a blend of all three classic styles. We want the pizza to hang off the edge of the plate; we need to use only the best ingredients; and we want a slow, double fermentation to create a more flavourful pizza and light puffy crust that looks amazing and melts in your mouth.

Makes 6 dough balls

What you need

630ml (21½fl oz) cold water

1.5g (heaped ¼ tsp) fresh yeast

1kg (2¼lb) 00 flour (we use Caputo Red)

30g (1oz) fine sea salt

How to make it

Add the water to a large mixing bowl (or the bowl of a stand mixer), then rub the yeast between your fingers under the water to dissolve it. Add half the flour and mix until smooth – the dough should have a consistency of a thick batter at this point. Add the salt and mix well to combine. Add the remaining flour in two batches, mixing until you have a scraggly dough.

Tip the dough out onto a clean work surface (if kneading by hand) and stretch and knead the dough for 10–15 minutes until elastic and smooth (if using a stand mixer, mix on slow for 10–12 minutes using the dough hook). Place the dough in an airtight container and leave to prove at room temperature for 2–3 hours, before transferring to the fridge to prove overnight.

The next morning, use a dough scraper to divide the dough into 280g (10oz) portions, rolling each into a tight ball. Place the dough balls seam-side down in a large airtight container, then cover and leave to prove at room temperature for 6 hours until the dough has doubled in size. Place the sealed container in the fridge and leave to prove for a further 12 hours.

Remove the dough from the fridge and allow it to come up to room temperature for 2–3 hours before using. The dough can now be used immediately or kept in the fridge for 2–3 days.

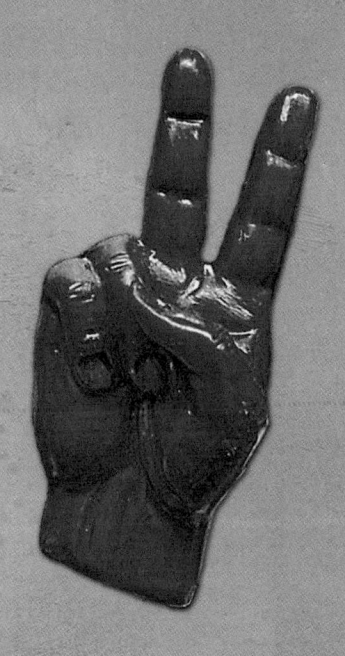

The man, the legend. Domenico, Head of Pizza at Pizza Pilgrims →

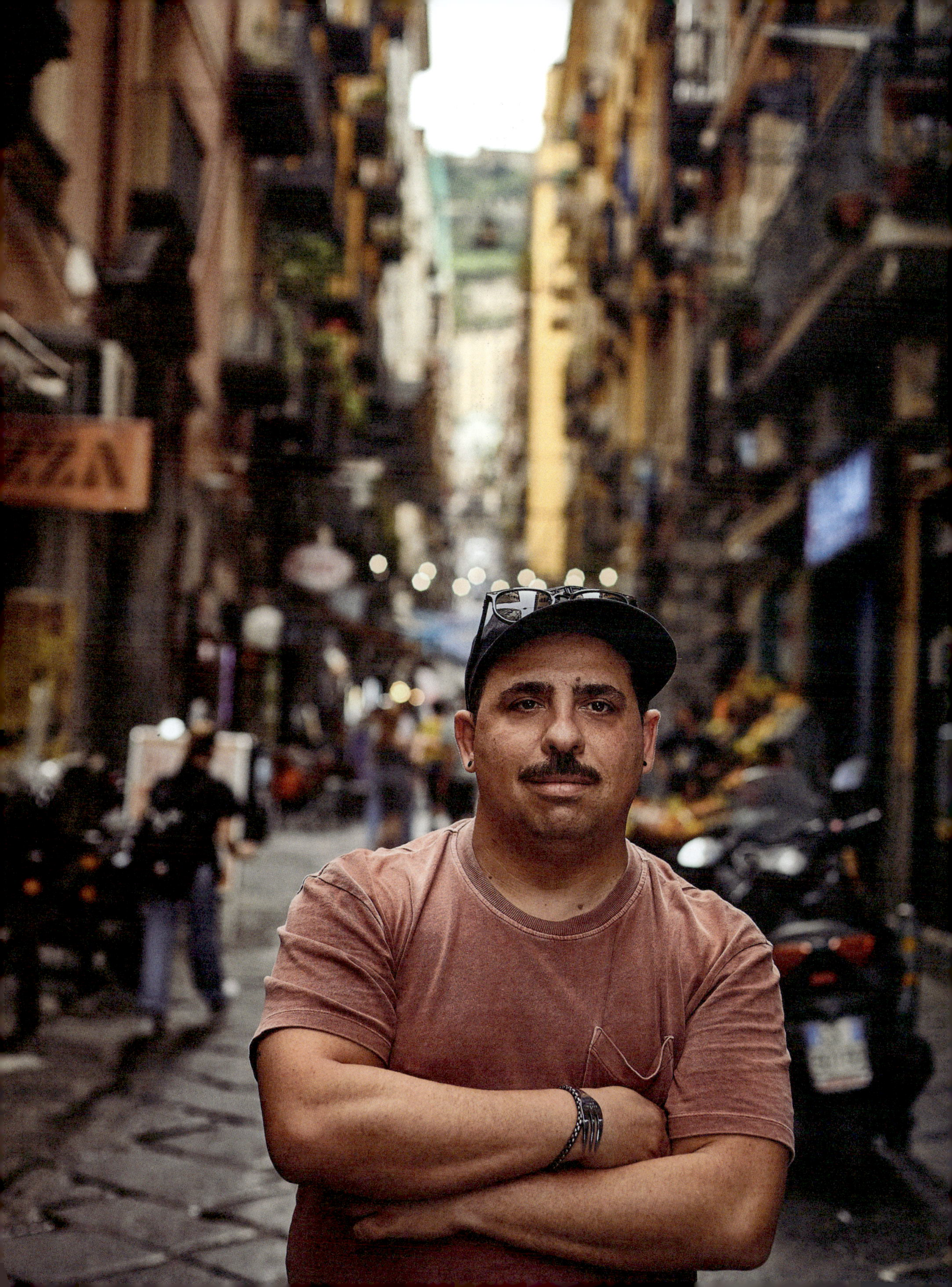
ZZA

OVENS

The most prized role in the pizza kitchen is undoubtedly that of the fornaio. The fornaio or 'oven man' oversees loading the pizzas, maintaining the fire intensity and cooking each pizza with equal care and attention. As a fornaio, you are given not one but two 1.5m (8ft) peels that must be wielded at speed, not to mention you must maintain a fire burning at pretty primal temperatures. Seriously cool stuff.

Wood-fired ovens have been used in Campania since the 1700s and are hugely important in Neapolitan cooking. You can walk into any number of letterbox-sized pizzerias in Napoli to see the huge imposing stone pizza ovens that take up almost half the room and realize how important they are to the pizza maker. The ovens become an extension of the pizza maker's personality. Giant double ovens sculpted into the shape of Mount Vesuvius; ovens adorned with the colours and logo of SSC Napoli; or even the pair of trilby hats that belong to one of our pizza legends, Salvatore Lioniello (page 204). The pizza-oven pride runs deep. Walk past a pizzeria late at night, just after service, and you will, without fail, see a fornaio on top of their oven, polishing the tiles with pride.

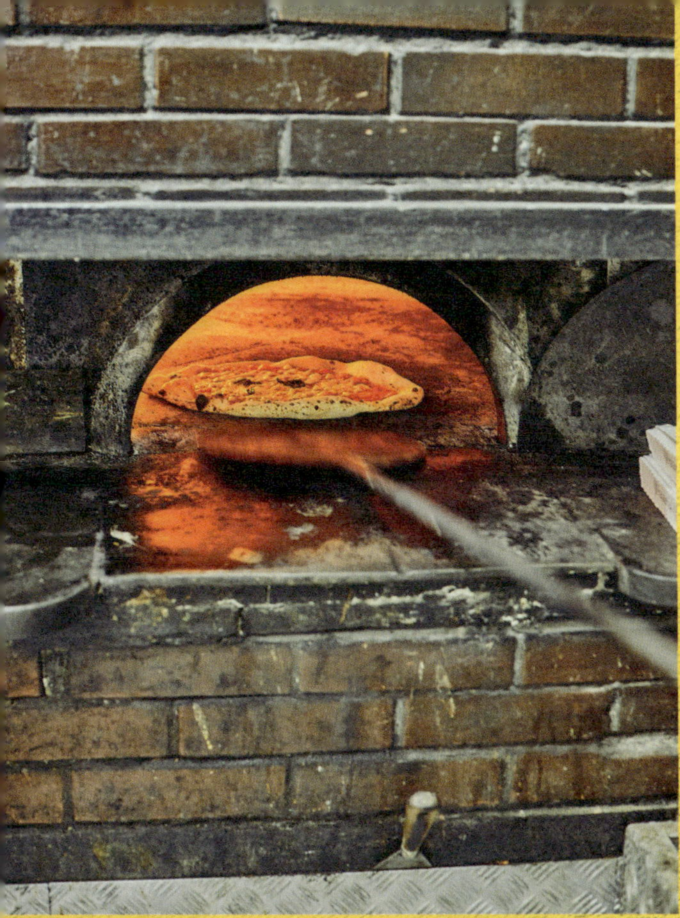

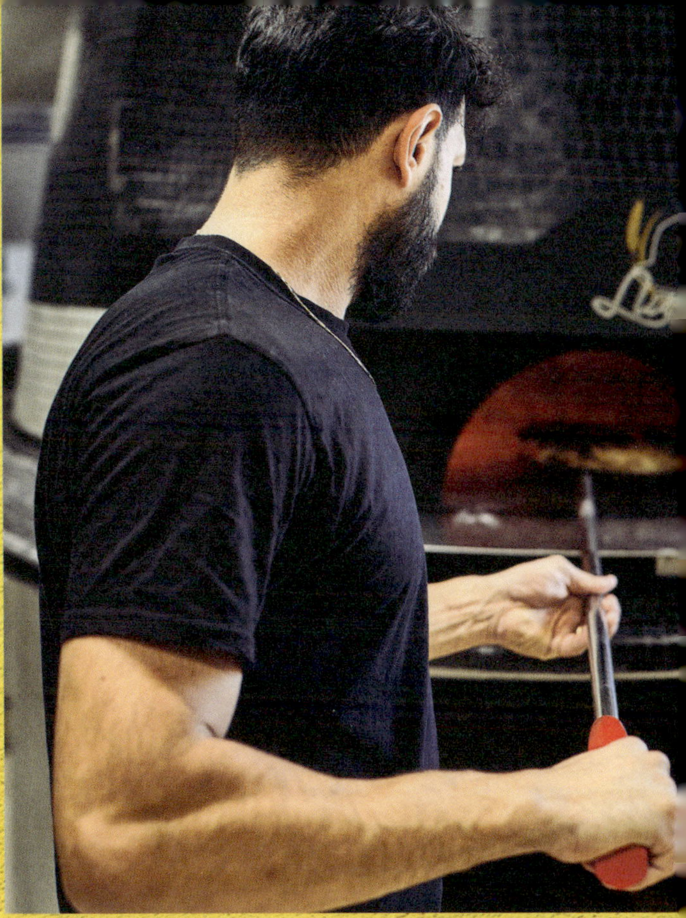

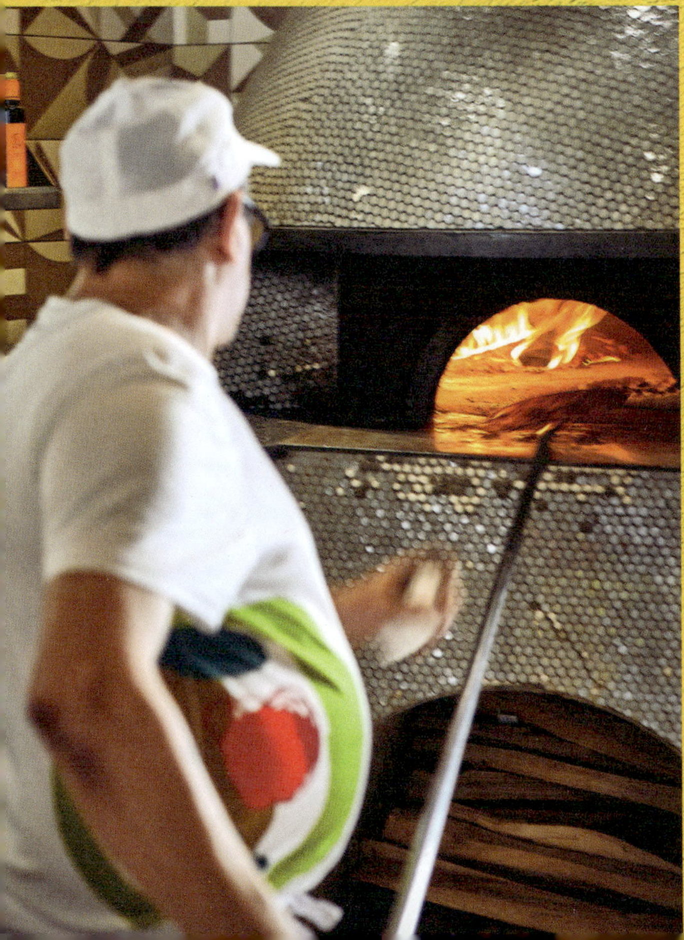

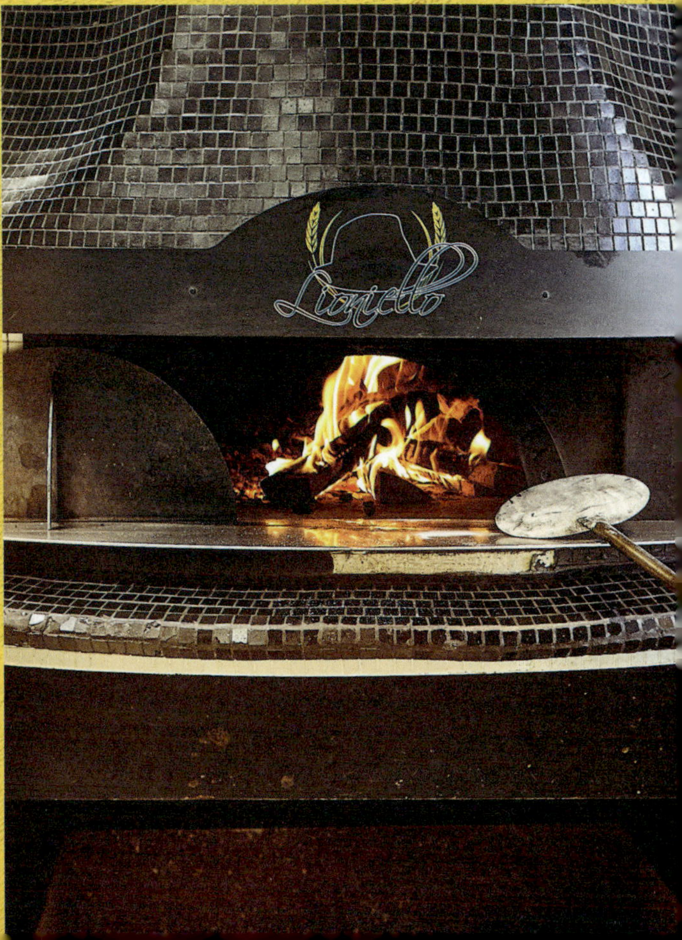
Lioniello

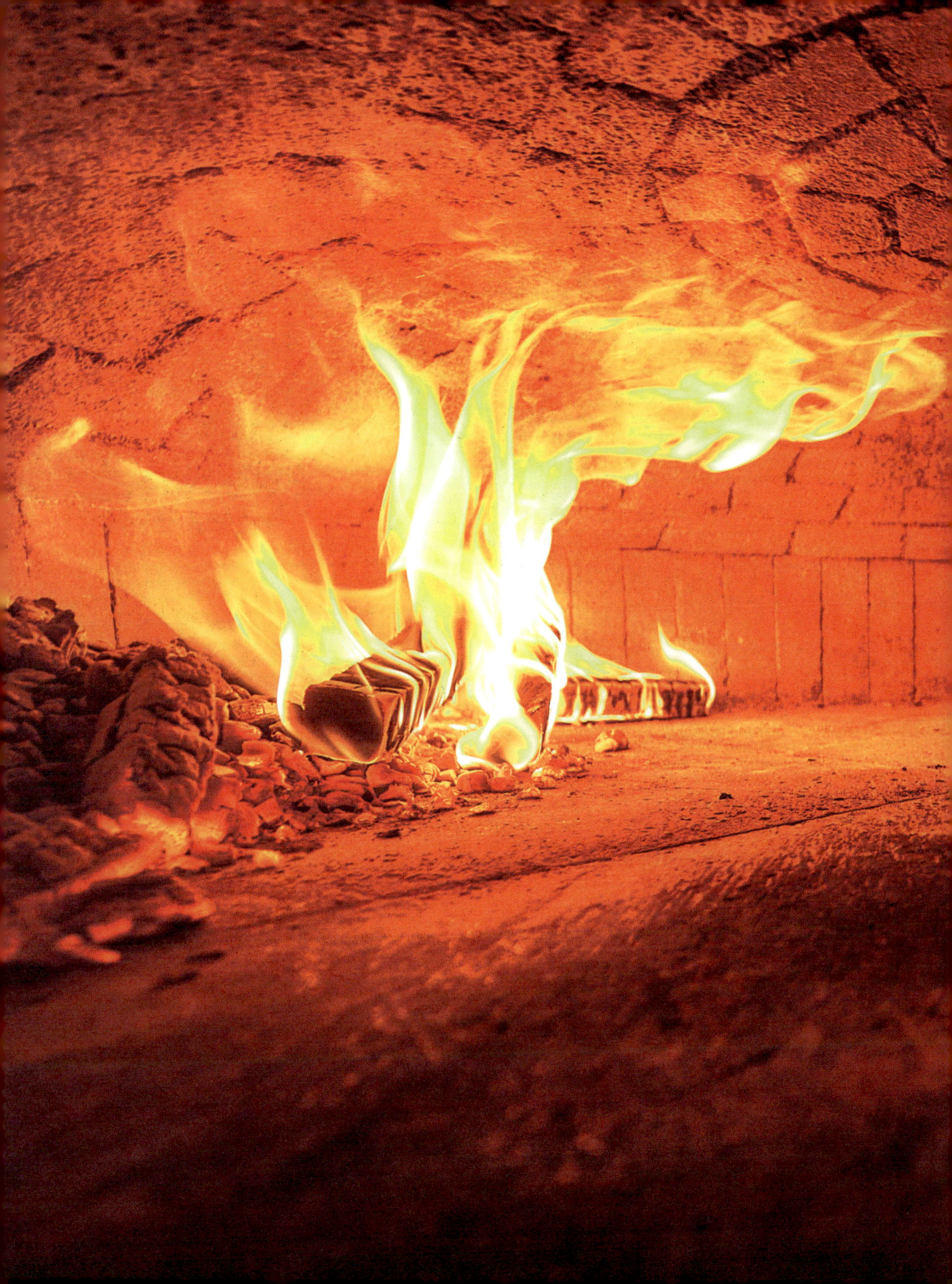

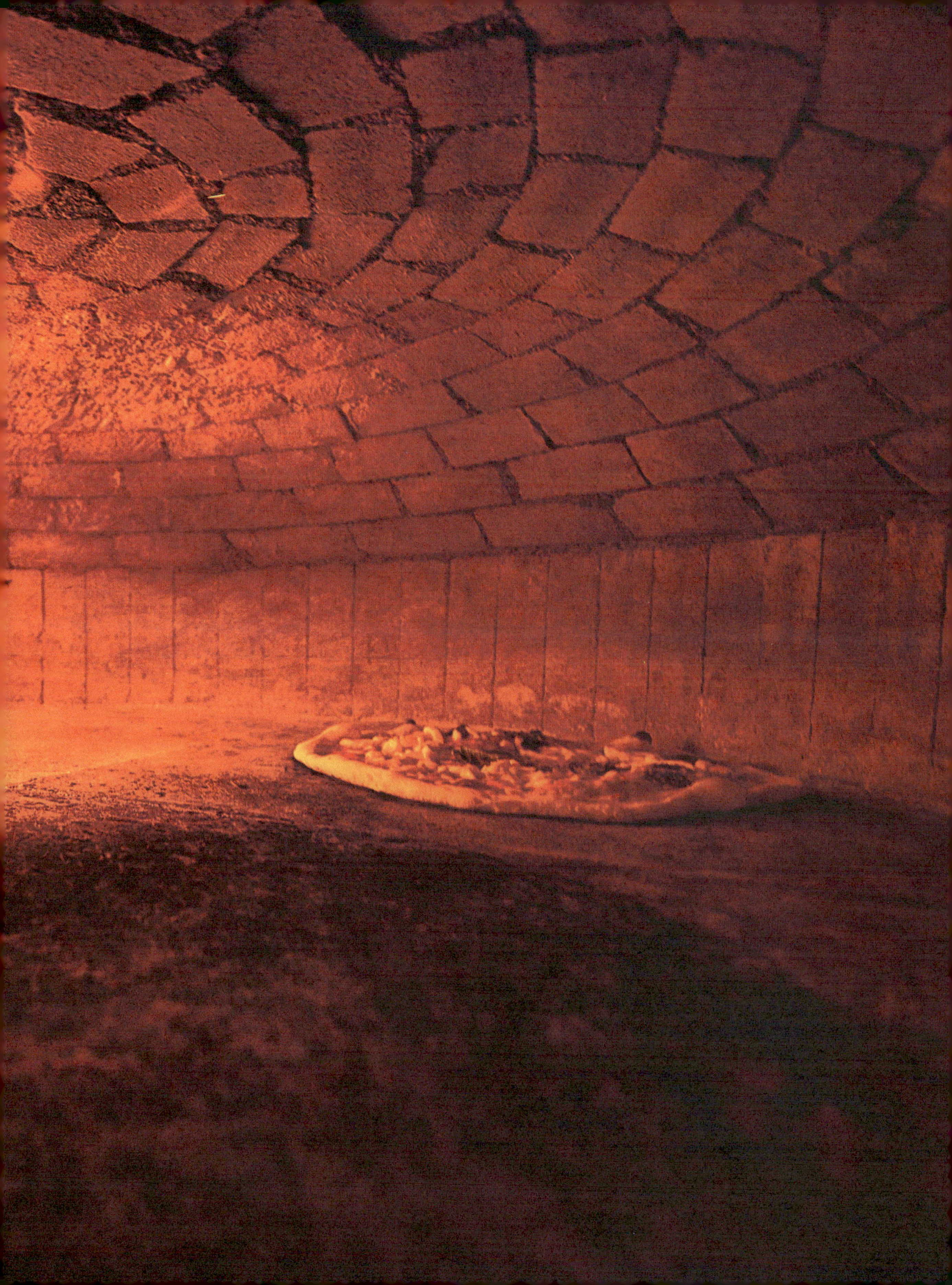

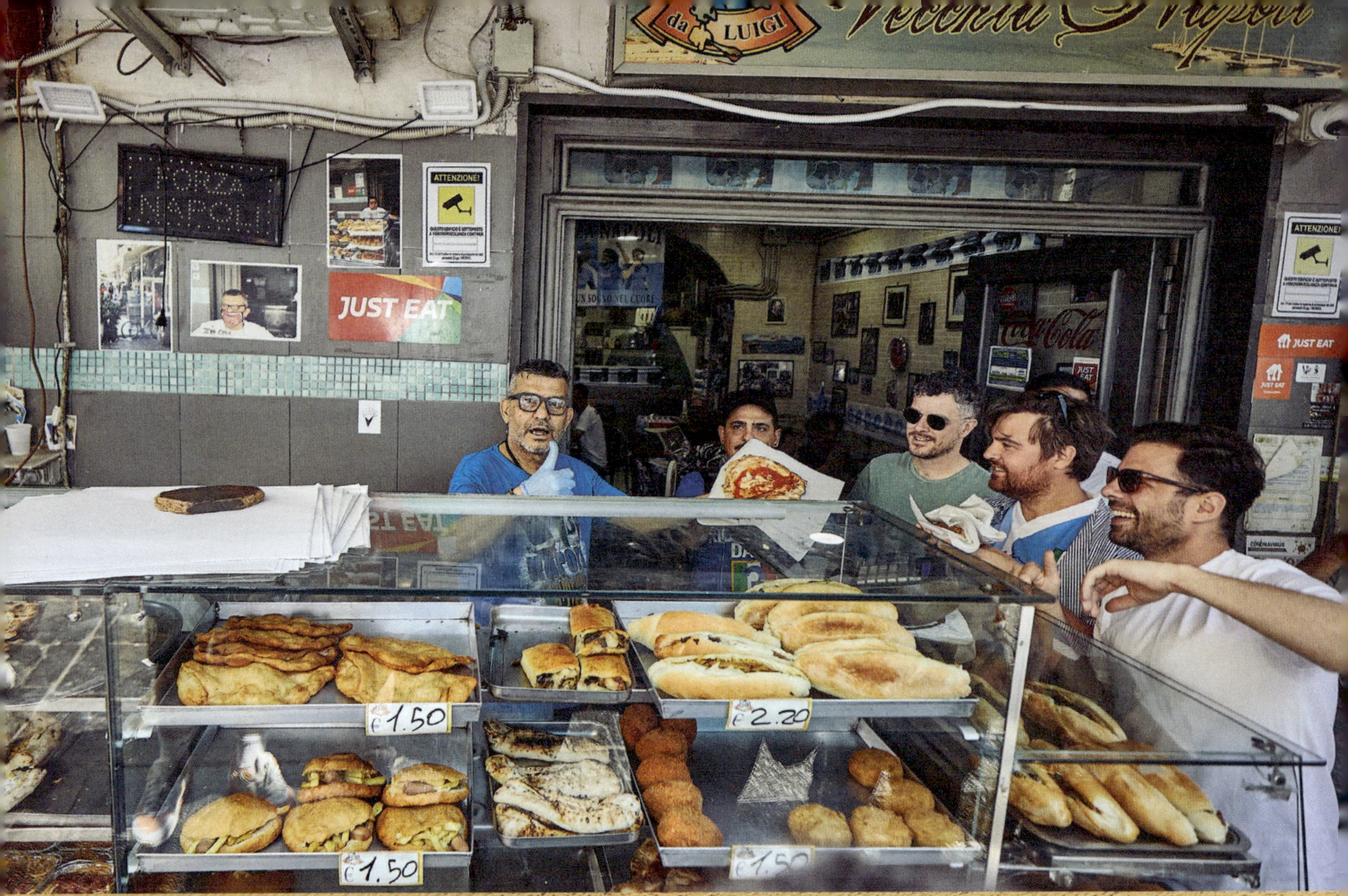
da LUIGI
ATTENZIONE!
JUST EAT
Coca-Cola
€1.50
€2.20
€1.50
€1.50

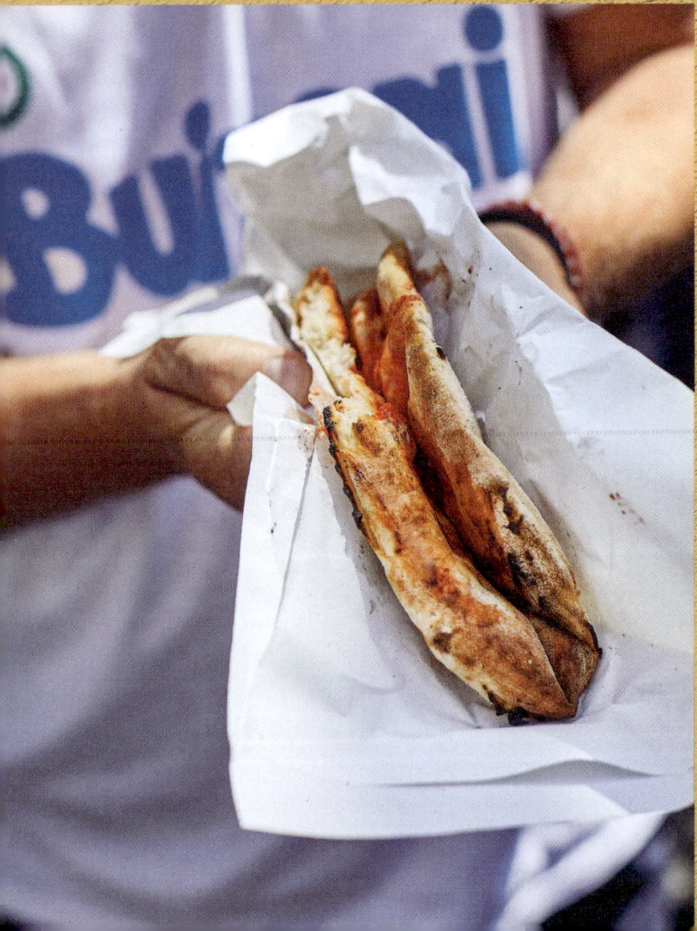

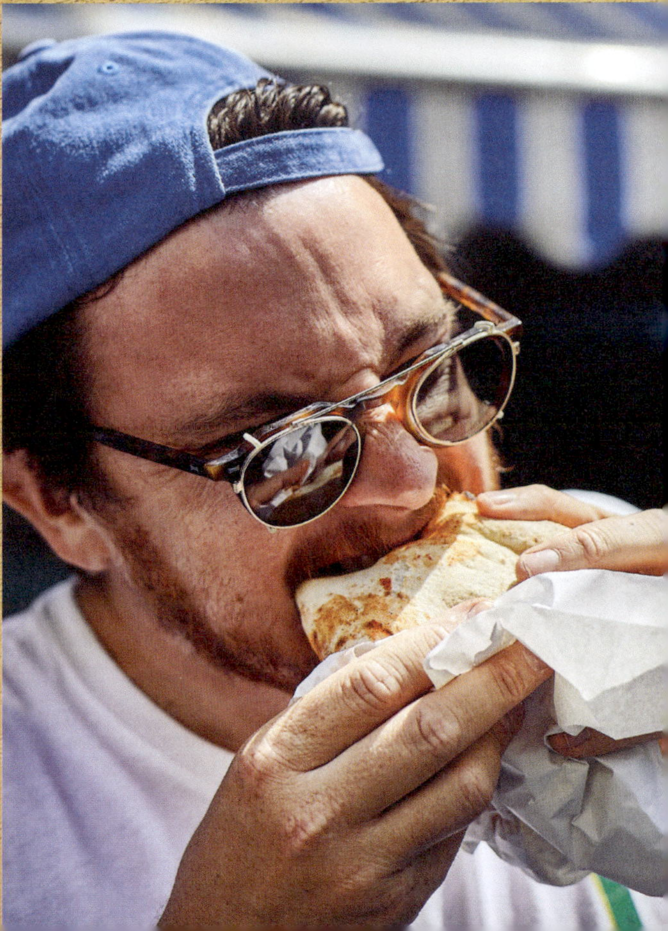

PIZZA PORTAFOGLIO

Trust the Neapolitans to come up with a way to eat a whole Neapolitan pizza on the move. Most pizzerias will have a little heated glass cabinet of joy that sits by the front door, loaded with goodies for the most time-poor of pizza fans. They bake off slightly smaller pizzas with a little handful of mozzarella in the middle and stack them up behind the glass. You hand over about €1.50 and they slide a pizza portafoglio onto a sheet of paper, fold it in half, then judo chop the halved pizza in half again with a little flick of the paper to create a folded pizza ready to go. You have two options for eating, but be warned: crusts first is for amateurs. Flip the pizza round so you eat the middle first and some of the tomato and mozzarella will slide down to adorn the crusts. Pro Napoli tip, that.

NAPOLI PIZZA CLASSICS

The Definitive 10 Pizzas of Napoli

There are certain things you can mess with when it comes to pizza in Napoli, and there are some things you know need to be left well alone. One major thing is celebrating the classic pizzas. A pizzeria is not always expected to have all of these but they need to have a good range to satisfy the most traditional of customers (for a lot of Neapolitans, ordering anything other than a Margherita is deemed unnecessary). Here is our top 10 list of pizzas you just need to be able to make to say you've mastered the Neapolitan classics.

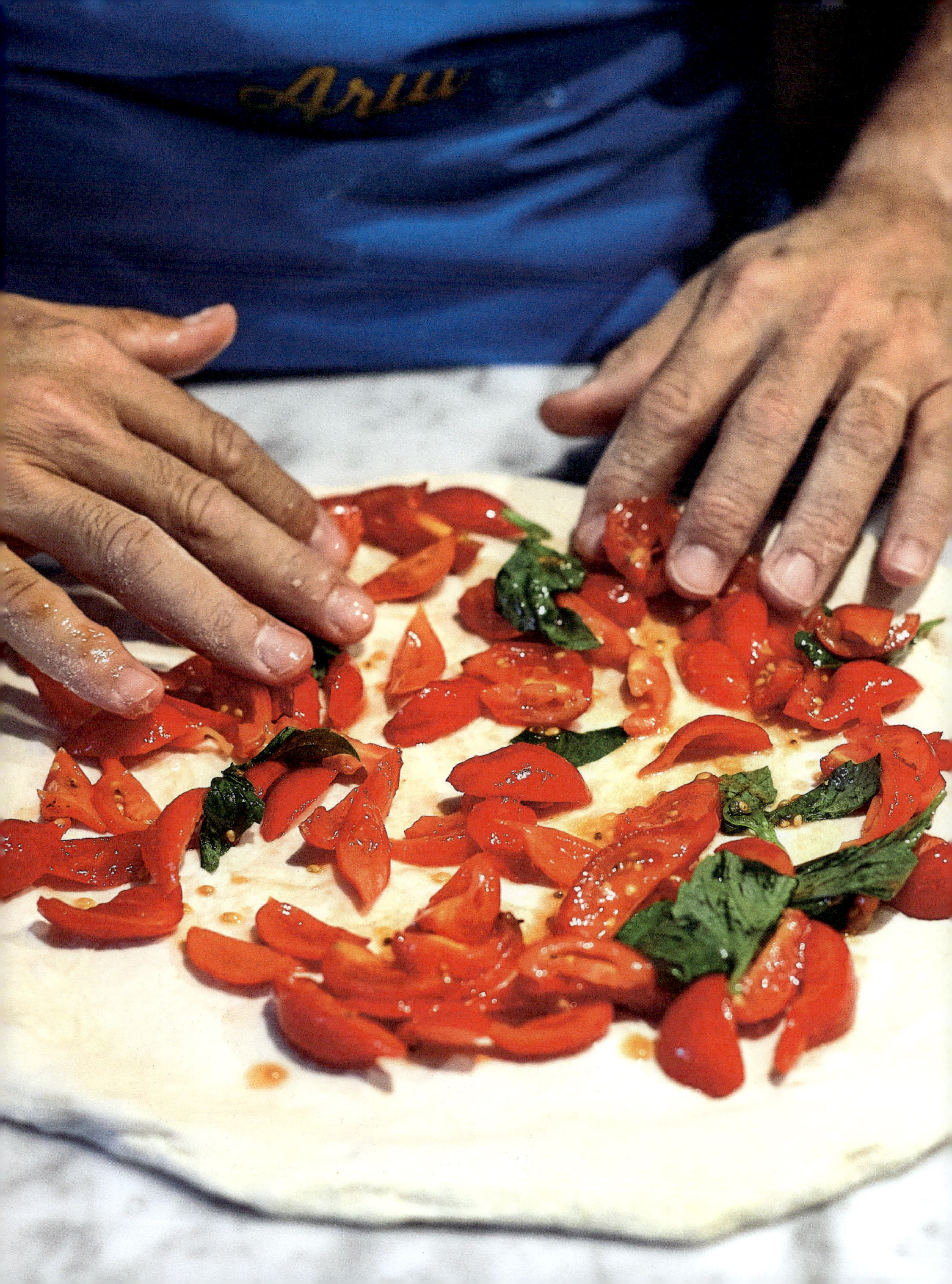
Ariu

MARGHERITA

The classic, the OG, the measuring stick that every god-fearing pizzaiolo will use to judge the quality of a pizzeria. The joy of the Margherita is its simplicity. There is nothing to hide behind and the quality of the ingredients and technical ability of the pizza chef is right there, plain to see. We think what sets apart a truly exceptional Margherita is the quality of the tomatoes and mozzarella, as well as not overloading your dough. It should be light, delicate and well balanced.

What you need

tomato sauce
fior di latte mozzarella
basil
Parmesan
extra virgin olive oil

BUFALA

An all-round more sloppy affair than the Margherita, buffalo mozzarella brings a deeper flavour with more tang and a higher moisture content, which makes the bufala probably the least eat-with-your-hands-friendly pizza on this list. People in the know order a Margherita at a pizzeria; people who order a bufala are true connoisseurs.

What you need

tomato sauce
buffalo mozzarella
basil
Parmesan
extra virgin olive oil

MARINARA

The Marinara is a hugely underrated pizza. We understand a pizza without mozzarella feels a bit lacking, but if you can get past that, the Marinara truly is one of the best pizzas in the game, and a true favourite with all our pizza chefs. A simple balance of tomatoes, herbs, garlic and oil, you are essentially cooking a tomato sauce on a pizza instead of in a pan. The most important thing is to only use the best San Marzano tomatoes and a really generous amount of olive oil.

What you need

tomato sauce

oregano

basil

extra virgin olive oil

sliced garlic

SALSICCIA E FRIARIELLI

Another truly classic Neapolitan flavour combo that isn't just limited to pizza but can be served as a primi, secondi, in a panini, in a pasta and even in a sfogliatella. Friarielli is a local kind of wild broccoli that is sautéed in a pan with olive oil, garlic, chilli and salt and served with grilled or roasted Italian sausages that are often flavoured with fennel seeds and have that beautiful coarse, meaty texture. On a pizza it is combined with provola mozzarella and fresh chilli to create the most popular pizza bianca of Napoli. It may seem like the salsiccia is the star of the show but it's really the quality of the friarielli that can bring a Neapolitan to their knees.

What you need

roasted Italian sausage

friarielli (sautéed fresh or from a jar)

provola (smoked) mozzarella

Parmesan

extra virgin olive oil

fresh chilli

CAPRICCIOSA

Capricciosa means someone who is unpredictable or impulsive in Italian, so it isn't a leap to guess how this pizza got its name. Capricciosas can vary from pizzeria to pizzeria but we think most people would agree that the definitive one includes prosciutto cotto, mushrooms, artichokes and olives. We serve ours on a Margherita base and finish with oregano. One way to elevate this pizza is to serve it bianca style on a mozzarella and olive oil base. We find it helps all the different flavours shine through a little more.

What you need

tomato sauce
fior di latte mozzarella
basil
extra virgin olive oil
prosciutto cotto
mushrooms
artichokes
black olives
oregano

DIAVOLA

Now, we might get ourselves into some hot water here, but we don't think Italians (excluding Calabrians!) handle spice all that well. We find peperoncino is used very sparingly with little pinches added to pastas and sauces to give a background heat rather that a knock-your-face-off vibe. The Diavola uses a spicy salami called spianata, and often that is it. Sometimes a pizzeria will add some extra fresh chilli or dried flakes, but all in all it's pretty PG when it comes to heat. The quality of the spianata is the most important thing here: it should always come from Calabria, the home of Italian chilli, and should always be cured to the right level so it crisps up and takes on a bacon-like flavour.

What you need

tomato sauce
fior di latte mozzarella
basil
Parmesan
extra virgin olive oil
spianata
chilli flakes (optional)

MIMOSA

Named after the mimosa flower that grows all over Italy, this is a pizza loved by every single one of our pizza chefs but isn't well known outside of Italy. Use the best cooked ham you can get hold of, but we find that canned sweetcorn works best on this pizza as it is already cooked and has a sweetness that balances the cream.

What you need

sweetcorn
prosciutto cotto
double (heavy) cream
fior di latte mozzarella
Parmesan
extra virgin olive oil
basil

ROMANA (AKA NAPOLETANA)

There's nothing more Neapolitan than doing things differently, so all over the world this pizza is commonly called a Napoletana or Napoli. However, in Napoli they call it a Romana and we rate them for it. An unlikely salty combo of anchovies, capers and olives, it's hard to say why so many salty ingredients work together so well but this is an absolute classic that needs to be on every menu.

What you need

tomato sauce
fior di latte mozzarella
Parmesan
basil
extra virgin olive oil
anchovy fillets
olives
capers

CALZONE RIPIENO

The direct translation here – 'stuffed trouser leg' – still makes me laugh. We feel it was the Americans who really made calzones popular (filling them with everything from buffalo chicken to meatballs). In Napoli there is only really one calzone: Napoli salami, ricotta, fior di latte mozzarella and tomatoes. It's all folded inside the dough, then a Margherita is built on top to create a sort of double-decker pizza. It is cooked more slowly in the mouth of the oven to ensure that the dough cooks all the way through.

What you need

ricotta
tomato sauce
fior di latte mozzarella
Parmesan
basil
Napoli salami
extra virgin olive oil

PROVOLA E PEPE

Now, this really is a pizza that doesn't seem to have made its way out of the city walls of Napoli. It's so simple but the flavour is completely different to a Margherita… even though it looks almost identical. The smokiness from the provola and the kick from the pepper transform this into a rich, complex pizza that you need to try.

What you need

tomato sauce
provola (smoked)
mozzarella
basil
extra virgin olive oil
Parmesan
black pepper

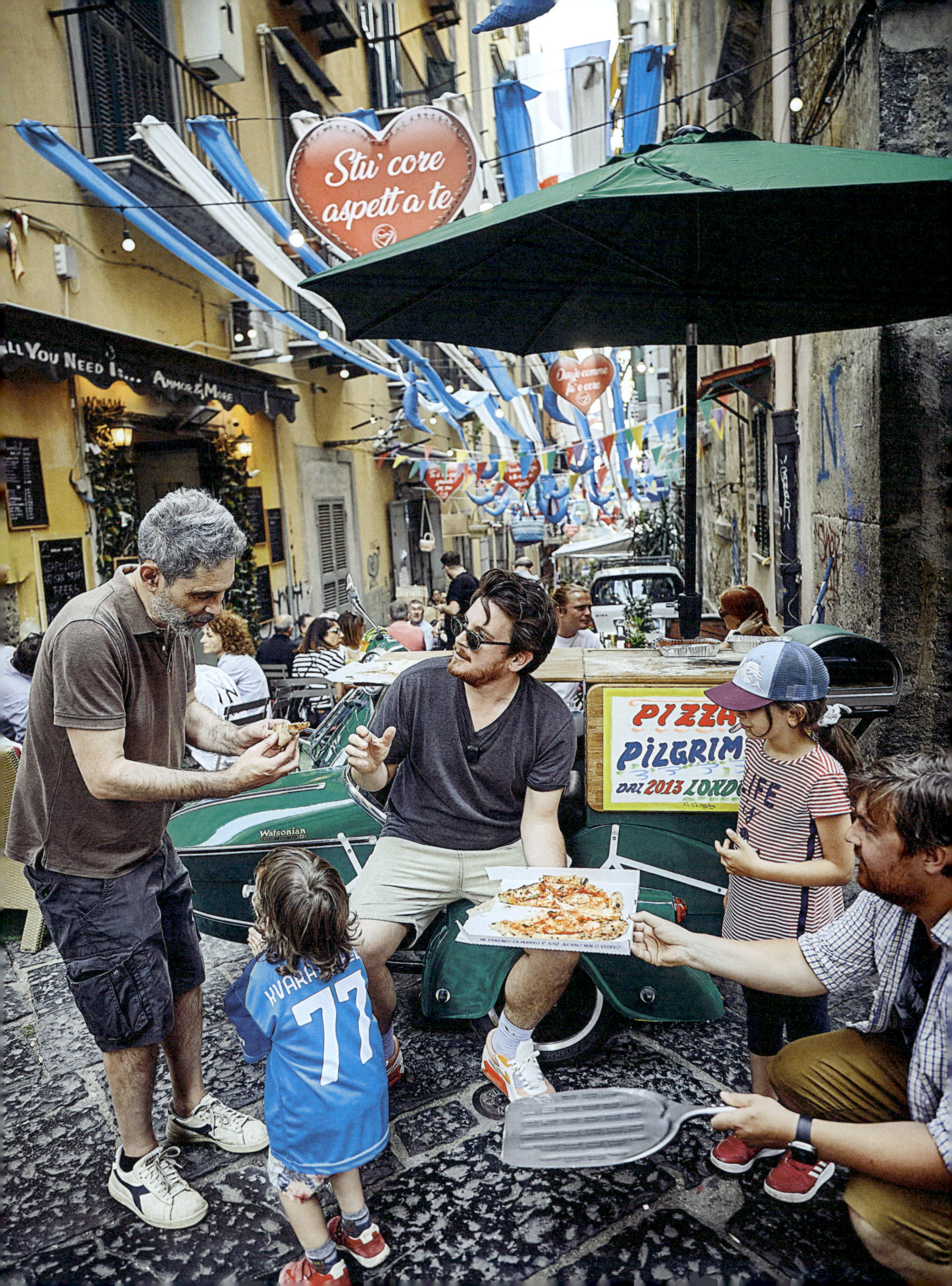
Stu' core aspett a te
PIZZA
PILGRIMS
Watsonian
77

PIZZA

LEGENDS

FRANCESCO MARTUCCI

Voted the best pizza chef in the world four times in a row by the 50 Top Pizza awards, Martucci is a mysterious figure and was a tough man to track down. We got wind that he was good friends with our flour supplier, but no luck. We briefly met him at a mozzarella party a few years ago and exchanged numbers, but when we messaged: no answer. Then Michele, a pizza chef from London, said he knew him and could organize a meeting. We were given a time to be at his pizzeria but heard nothing more. Martucci bases himself outside of Napoli on the outskirts of Caserta. The exterior of the pizzeria is very unassuming, but inside it is industrial and monochrome – more Brooklyn celeb haunt than rural Campania.

When the time finally came, it was hard not to be star-struck. Over 6ft tall, heavy set, with steely blue eyes, dressed head to toe in black and adorned with jewellery, he was quite the imposing figure. He suggested we 'eat first and talk later' (the whole thing feeling very Marlon Brando). The pizzas start coming out and were really something else. Yes, it was pizza, but the flavours and techniques were that of a fine dining restaurant – beautifully presented but not over the top. You could tell Martucci took his pizza very seriously.*

*Francesco keeps his complex recipes a very closely guarded secret so, instead of providing recipes on the following pages we've provided toppings and tasting notes so you can attempt to recreate them at home.

His triple-cooked technique is something we'd never come across before. First, the dough is steamed at 100ºC (210ºF) to make it puff, then fried at 180ºC (350ºF) to give crunch and finally baked at 400ºC (750ºF) for maximum flavour. When eating at his pizzeria there are 10 courses in total that take you on a journey through local and seasonal produce. It was impressive to say the least.

After lunch we headed back to the kitchen for a chat. As we talked, a much softer side to him came out. A big smile spread across his face when he spoke of starting out as a pizza chef aged just 10 years old – not out of passion but because he needed the money. He explained that I Masanielli is Italian for 'agitator' or 'revolutionary' and that's how he sees his pizza. Not Neapolitan in style but something of his own making. Because of this, he feels an immense duty to give his customers the best experience possible: 'they have given up their time and money, it's my job to repay that favour.' We asked if he is proud that his son is now a pizza chef, to which he says no... 'He has only been working for 2 years – we will see if he is a pizza chef.'

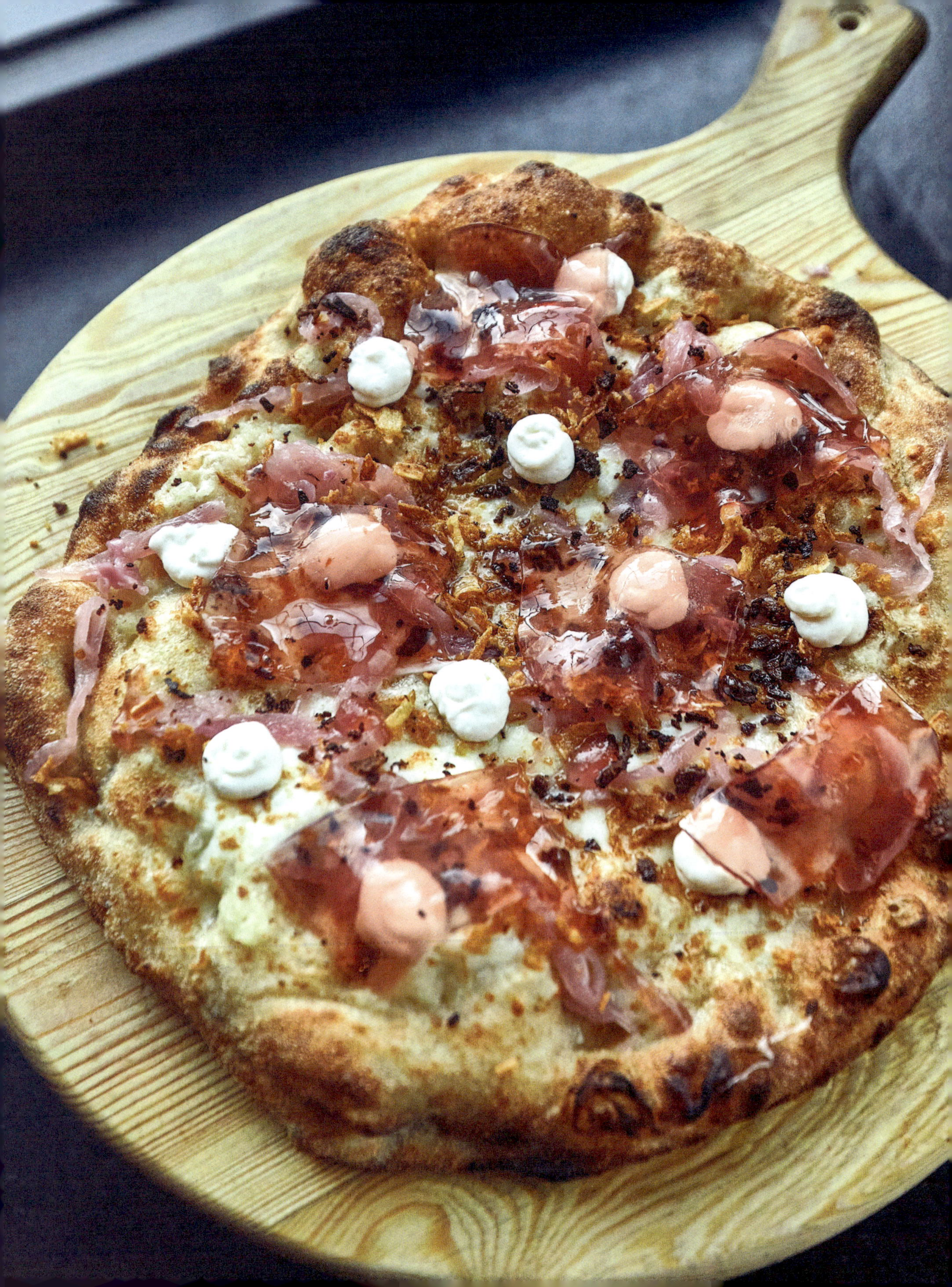

THE 7 CONSISTENCIES OF ONION

What you need

onion cream

pickled onions

crispy onions

burnt onion powder

onion mayonnaise

onion gel

onion jam

fior di latte mozzarella

What we think

This was one of Francesco's three-temperature doughs (page 113) and the result was a light and fluffy internal crust with a satisfying crunch on the outside. In terms of flavour, he really has managed to capture all the different notes of onion. The pickled onions give punch, the crispy onions give texture, and the burnt onion powder brings a bitter note that marries perfectly with the sweetness from the onion jam. For a pizza that has a lot going on, it was incredibly well balanced. Probably not a good one to order on a first date though…

ASSOLUTO DI CARCIOFO

What you need

fresh artichoke cream (crema di carciofi)

smoked provola cheese

sliced artichoke heart

gran riserva pecorino cheese

black pepper

parsley

smoked extra virgin olive oil

What we think

When we'd first arrived at Martucci's restaurant, we had noticed the team of chefs prepping the artichoke hearts; each one receiving a couple of minutes of careful attention – the tough outer layers removed to reveal the sweet, delicate centre. Artichoke is a tried-and-tested pizza topping, but this pizza took it to another level. The flavour was subtle but the artichokes were cooked until perfectly al dente, giving the pizza great texture. The smoky mozzarella and warming hit of black pepper gave the whole thing a complex and distinctly 'wintry' feel.

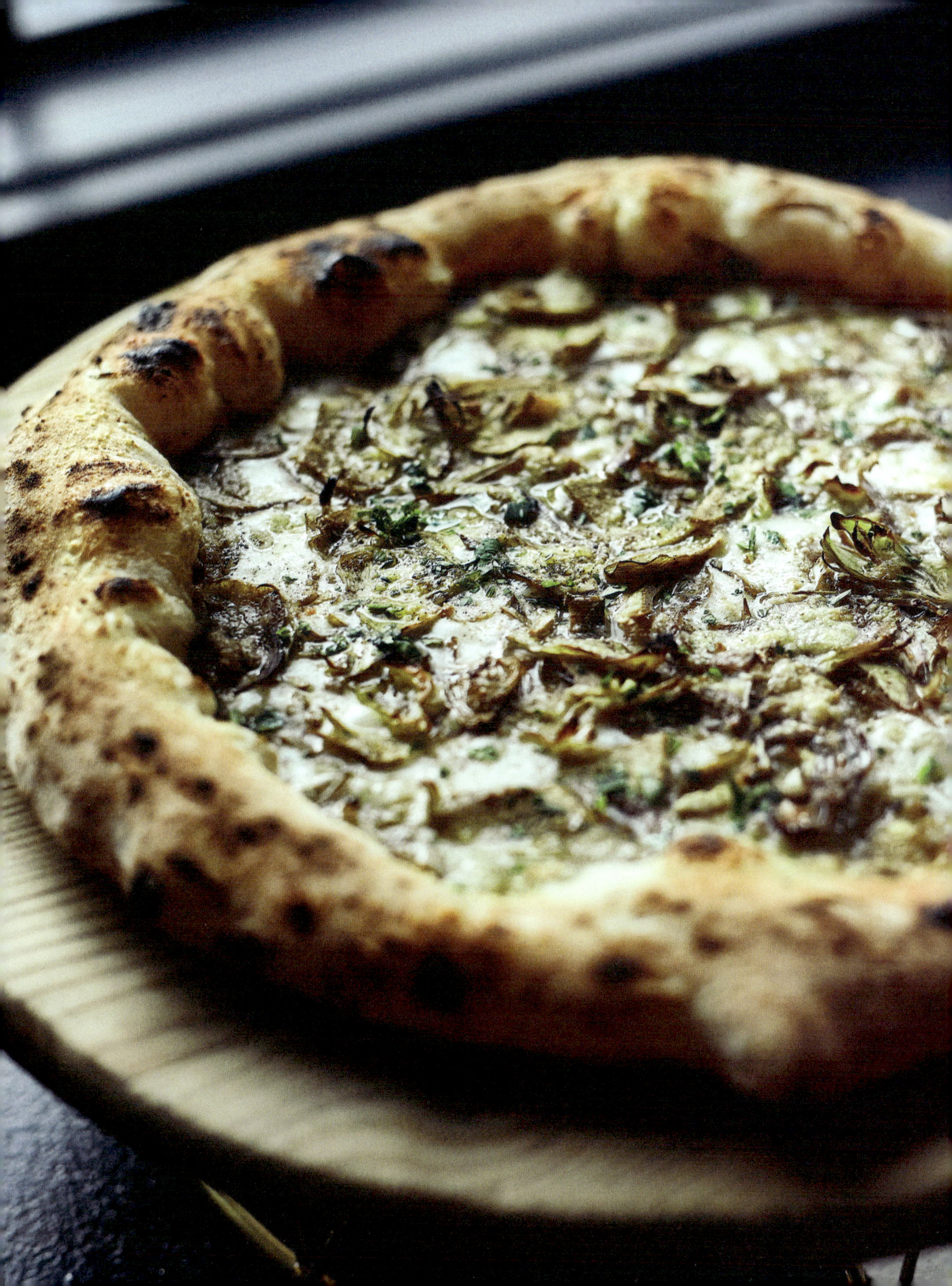

PIZZERIE
50 TOP PIZZA ITALIA 2021
I MASANIELLI - FRANCESCO MARTUCCI
50 TOP PIZZA ITALIA 2022
I Masanielli
Francesco Martucci
50 TOP PIZZA WORLD 2022
I Masanielli
Francesco Martucci

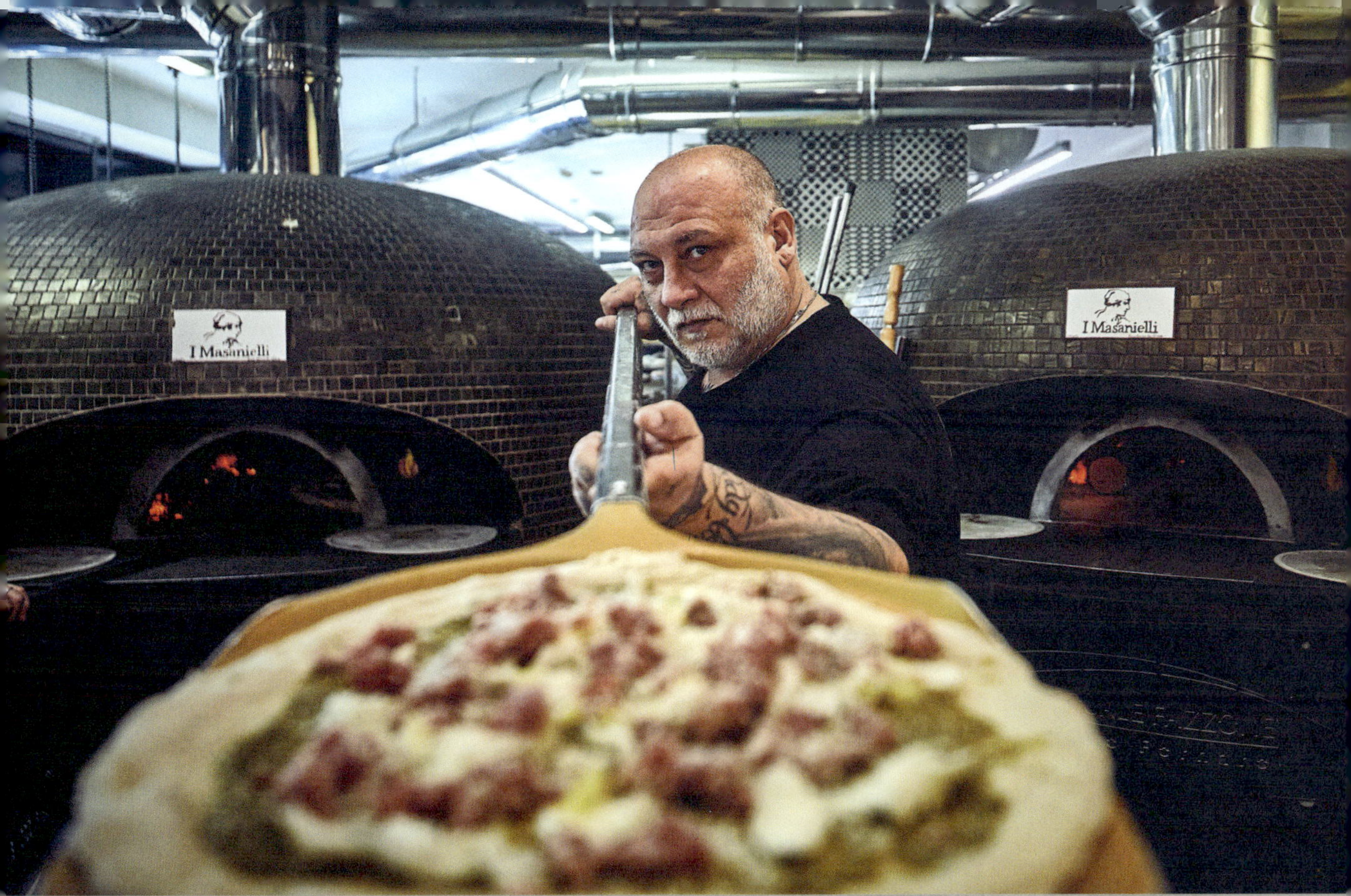
I Masanielli
I Masanielli

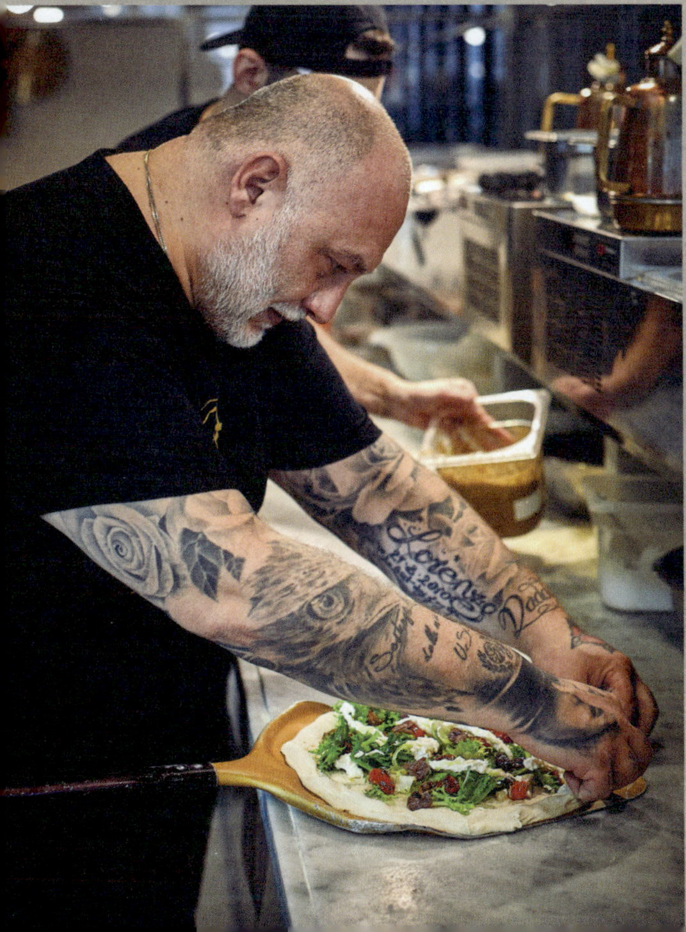

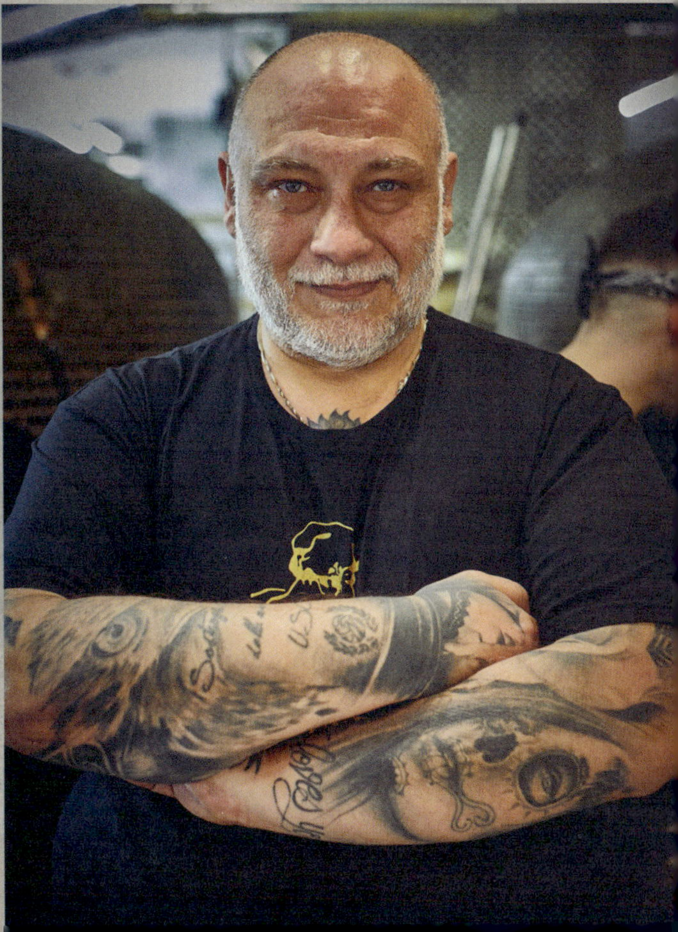

ASSOLUTO DI POMODORO

What you need

roasted cherry tomato cream

sautéed Piennolo tomatoes

San Marzano tomato mousse

sun-dried Piennolo tomatoes

red datterini chips

Piennolo tomato jam

extra virgin olive oil

basil

What we think

As you can imagine, this pizza was very… tomato forward! The skill and complexity that went into each topping element was a masterclass in technique and a far cry from what occurs in a standard pizza kitchen. The stand-out element on this pizza for us were the red datterini chips: crispy and acidic! Funnily enough, we didn't miss mozzarella at all on this pizza (the roasted cherry tomato cream provided just the right hit of creaminess).

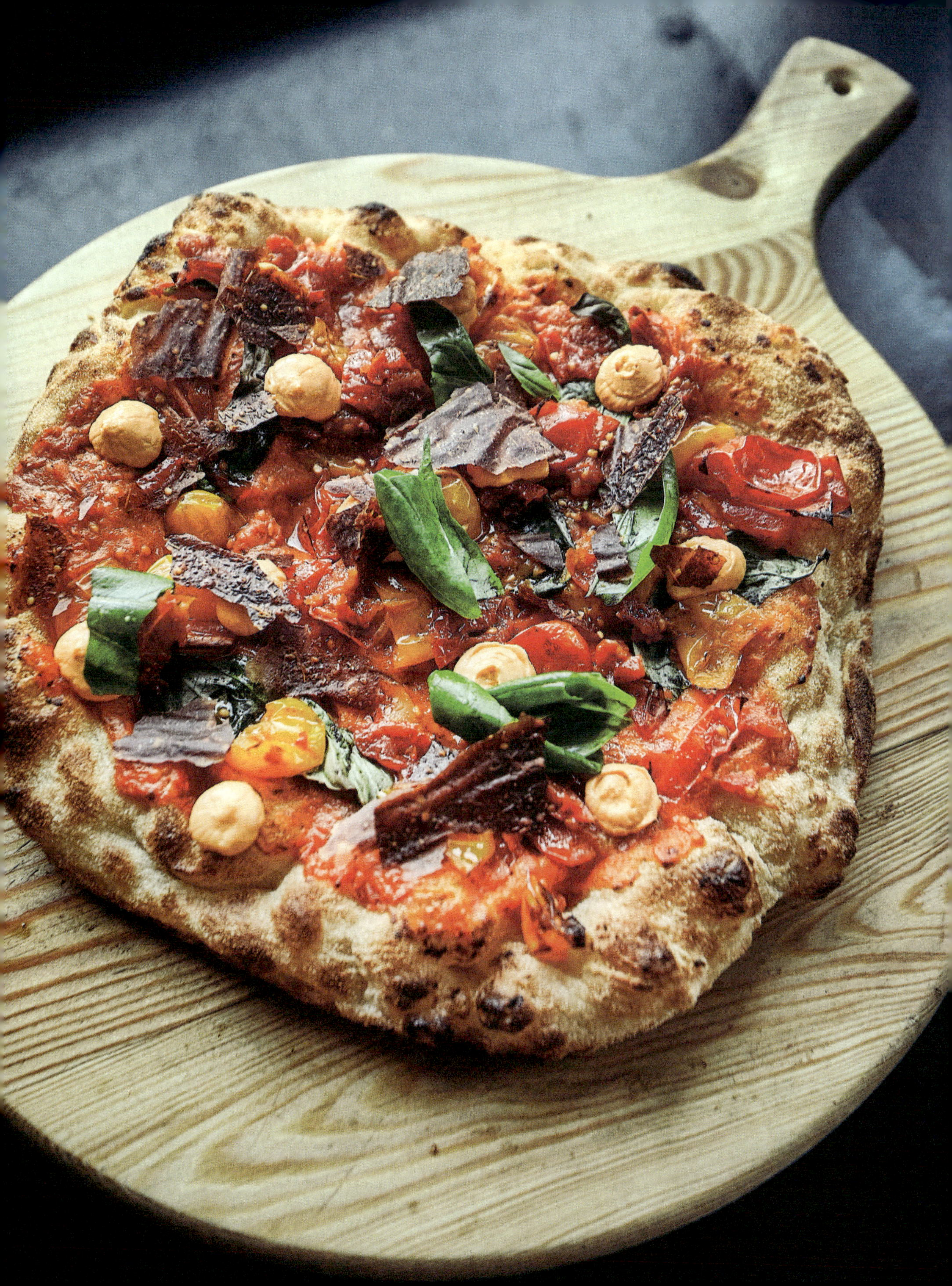

SATURNIA

What you need

roasted tomato cream

buffalo mozzarella

fermented black garlic and soy mousse

Caiazzo olive powder

Salina caper powder

crispy onions

bottarga

extra virgin olive oil

What we think

This pizza was all about mastering a perfect balance of flavour combinations. We get it, when you read the above list of toppings it sounds like a LOT, but somehow the combined saltiness of the soy, olive, caper and bottarga elements, matched with the mozzarella and tomato cream, worked brilliantly! The olive oil used to finish the pizza was also grassy and bitter, which was delicious.

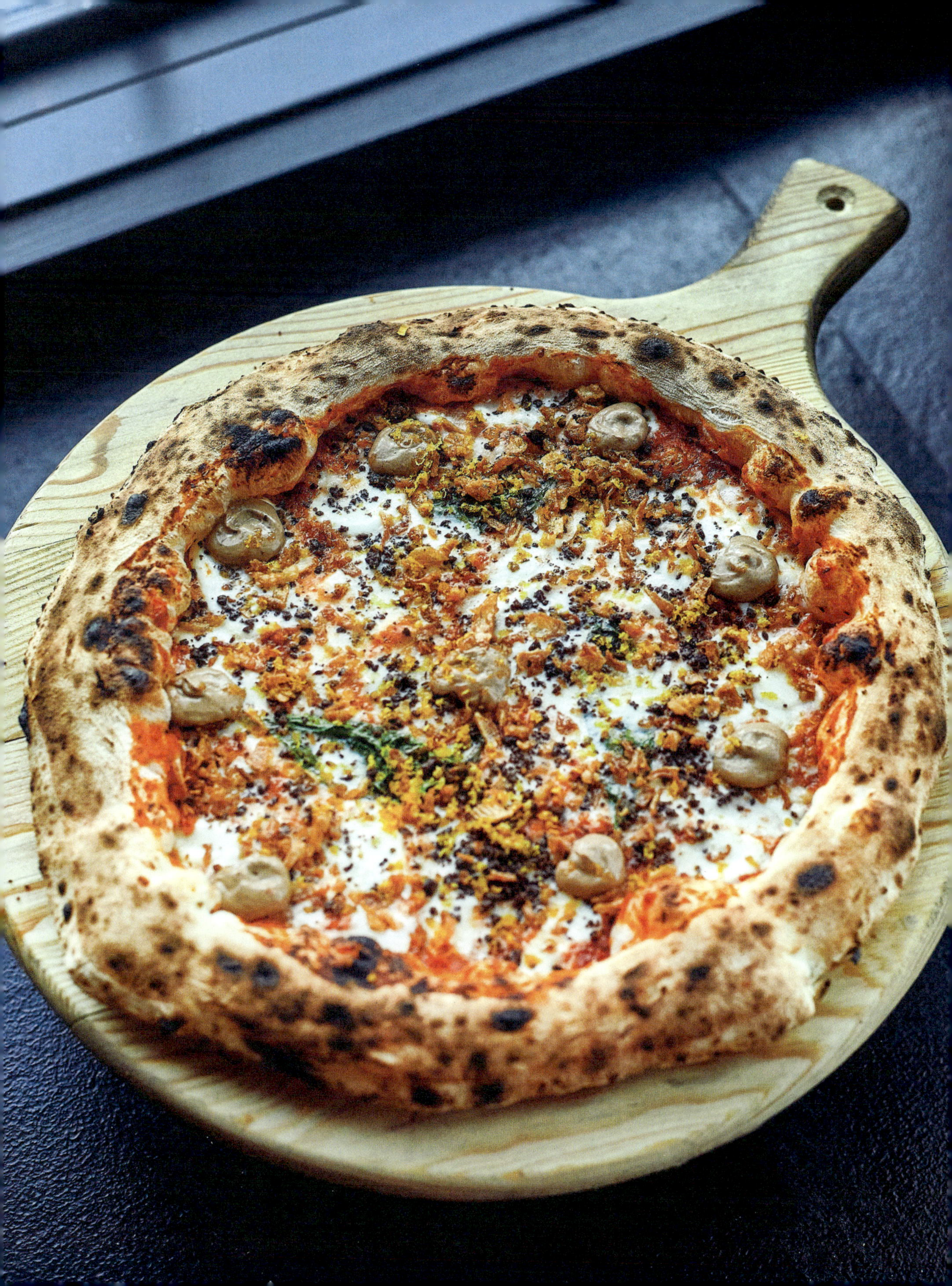

VINCENZO

Vincenzo Capuano

CAPUANO

'Yam ya!' is what Vincenzo shouts at the beginning of all his Instagram videos to his 737,000 followers. We don't think anyone encapsulates the new wave of pizza contemporanea more than this chef from Napoli. His puffy crusts and inventive toppings really grabbed attention and his pizzeria has become a celebrity hangout for footballers and pop stars.

As we pull up in the Vespa, Vincenzo and his grandfather, Vincenzo senior (page 254), literally stop traffic (impressive in Napoli!) to allow us to drive straight onto his terrace. They are a serious, three-generation pizza-making family and it's great seeing how closely Vincenzo and his grandfather work together. He rose to fame in 2022 when he won the Caputo Cup and since then he has grown his brand to 24 pizzerias across Italy, and is famed for his bespoke golden scissors that he uses to cut his light, puffy crusts.

We met up to discuss a very important subject, the surprising Neapolitan tradition of the Americana pizza – a pizza with hot dogs and fries on it. He says that, more than anything, pizza should be about enjoying yourself; the Americana started life as a pizza for kids but is secretly every Neapolitan grown-up's favourite pizza. It just shouldn't work, but one bite and you get the smoky notes from the wood-fired-oven frankfurters, the smoked mozzarella and the salty, sweet kick from the chips; it creates a combination so moreish you just… sorry, lost myself there for a second. Just trust me, it's a must try.

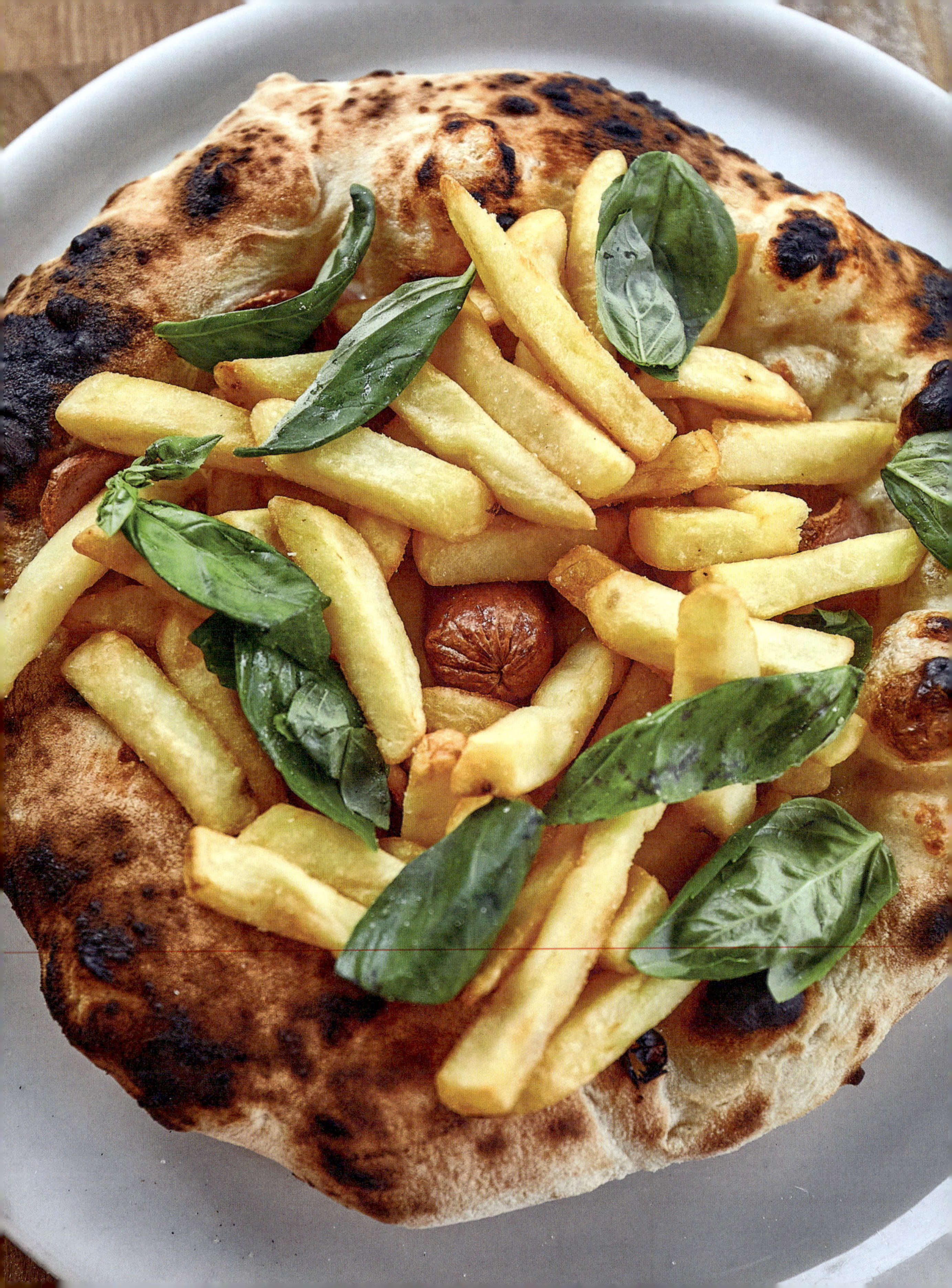

THE AMERICANA

What you need

- STG pizza dough (page 92)
- double (heavy) cream
- provola (smoked) mozzarella
- smoked frankfurters
- Parmesan
- chips/fries
- basil

How to make it

Stretch a ball of dough out and start with a base of cream. Top with provola, thinly sliced frankfurters, more cream and grated Parmesan.

Bake in the oven, then top with a generous portion of baked or deep-fried chips or fries and finish with fresh basil leaves.

PRAWN TARTARE AND STRACCIATELLA

What you need

contemporanea pizza dough (page 93)

extra virgin olive oil

Parmesan

stracciatella cheese

prawn (shrimp) tartare (see below)

lemon zest

basil

How to make it

Stretch a ball of dough out, brush with olive oil and sprinkle over a generous amount of grated Parmesan. Bake in the oven.

Top the pizza with a good amount of stracciatella so it covers the base.

Scatter over the prawns and finish the pizza with lemon zest, basil leaves and a drizzle of olive oil.

For the prawn tartare (makes enough for 4 pizzas)

250g (9oz) raw, shell-on red prawns (shrimp)

squeeze of lemon juice

pinch of sea salt

Peel and chop your prawns and toss them in the lemon juice and salt.

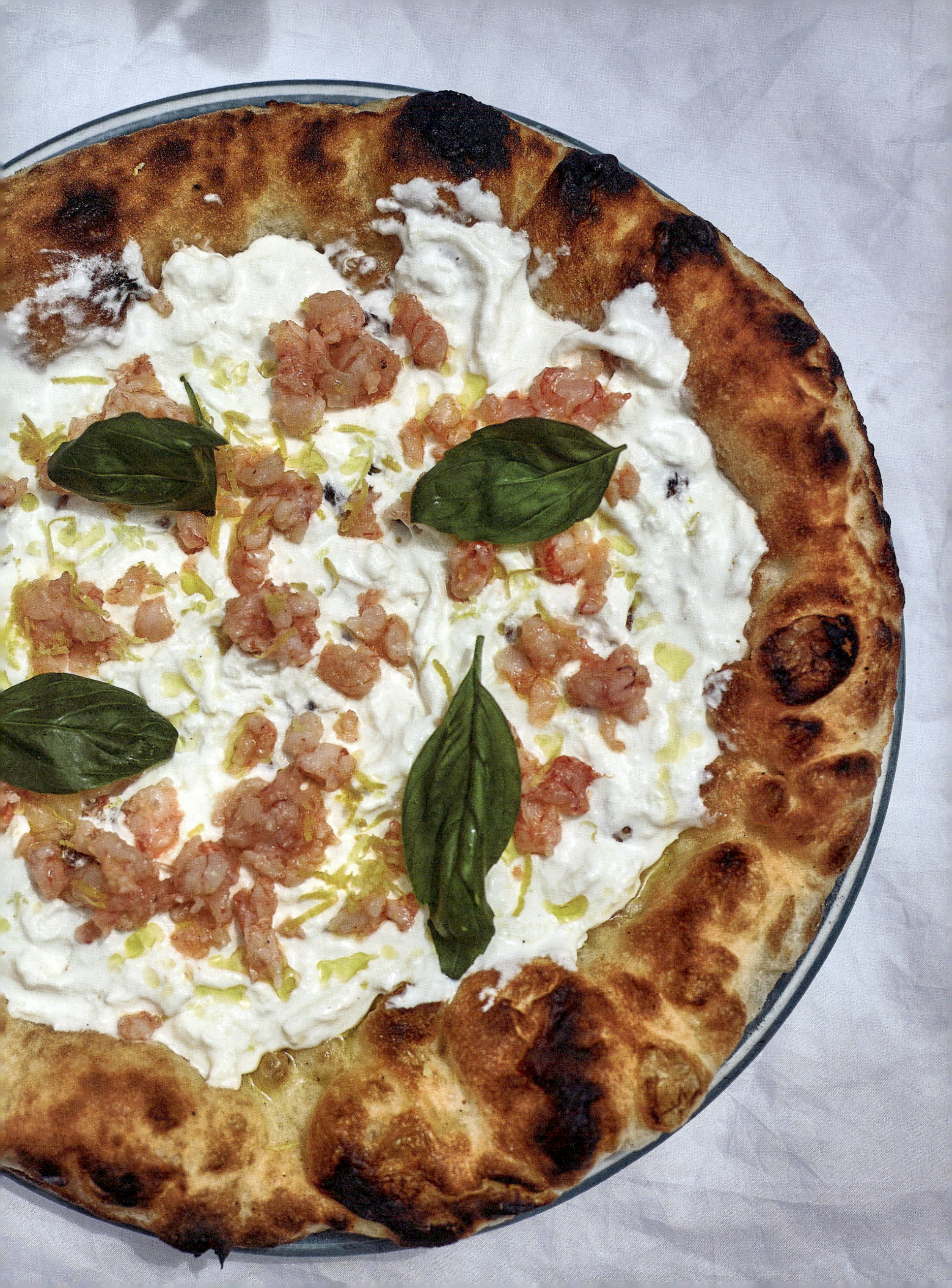

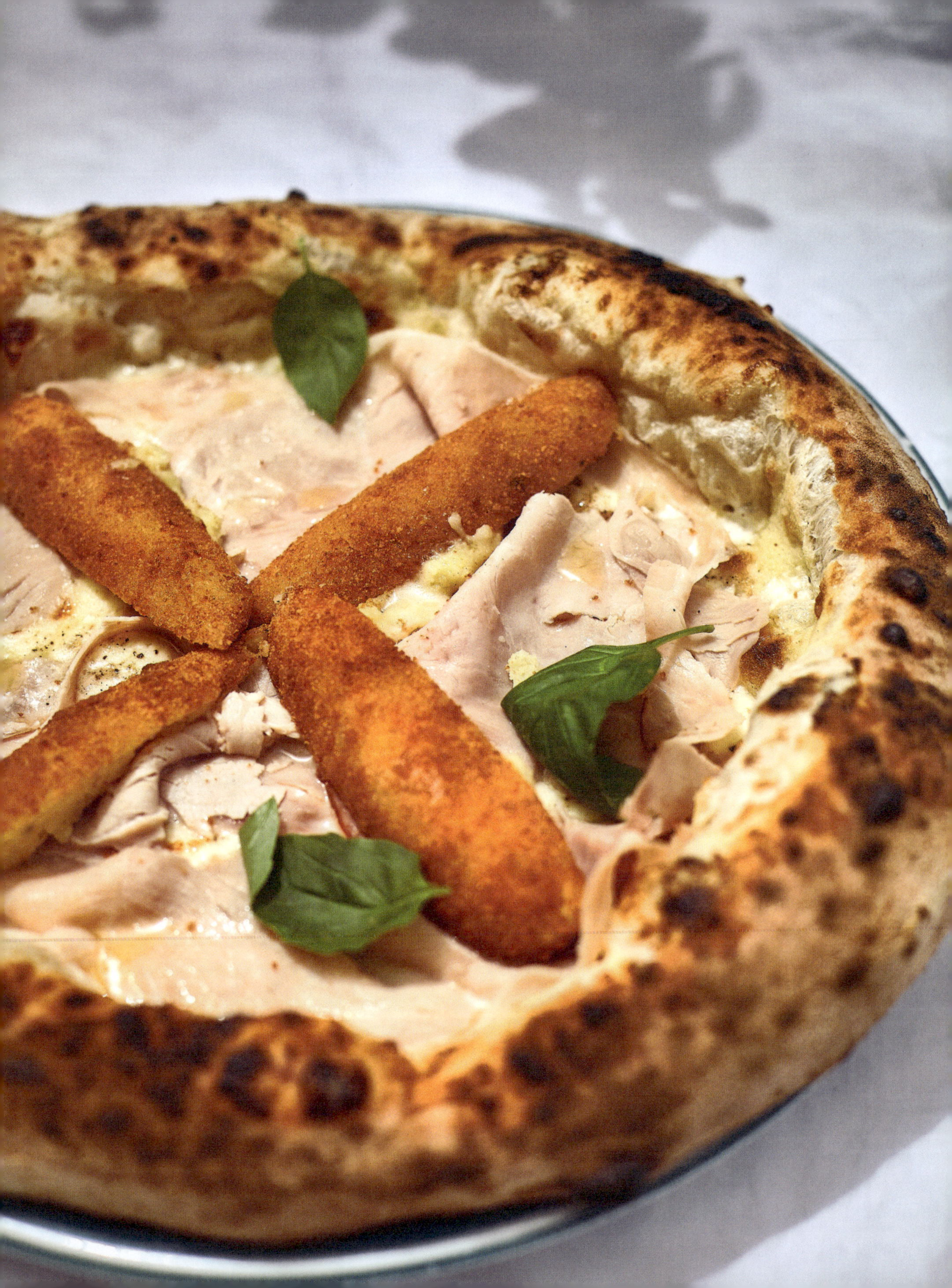

What you need

contemporanea pizza dough (page 93)

ricotta

fior di latte mozzarella

Parmesan

prosciutto cotto

potato crocchè (page 247)

extra virgin olive oil

basil

How to make it

Stretch a ball of dough out, spread with ricotta and top with mozzarella and grated Parmesan.

Bake in the oven, then drape over thin slices of prosciutto cotto.

Meanwhile, deep-fry your crocchè and slice lengthways. Lay on the pizza in star formation.

Finish with olive oil and basil leaves.

CROCCHÈ E PROSCIUTTO COTTO

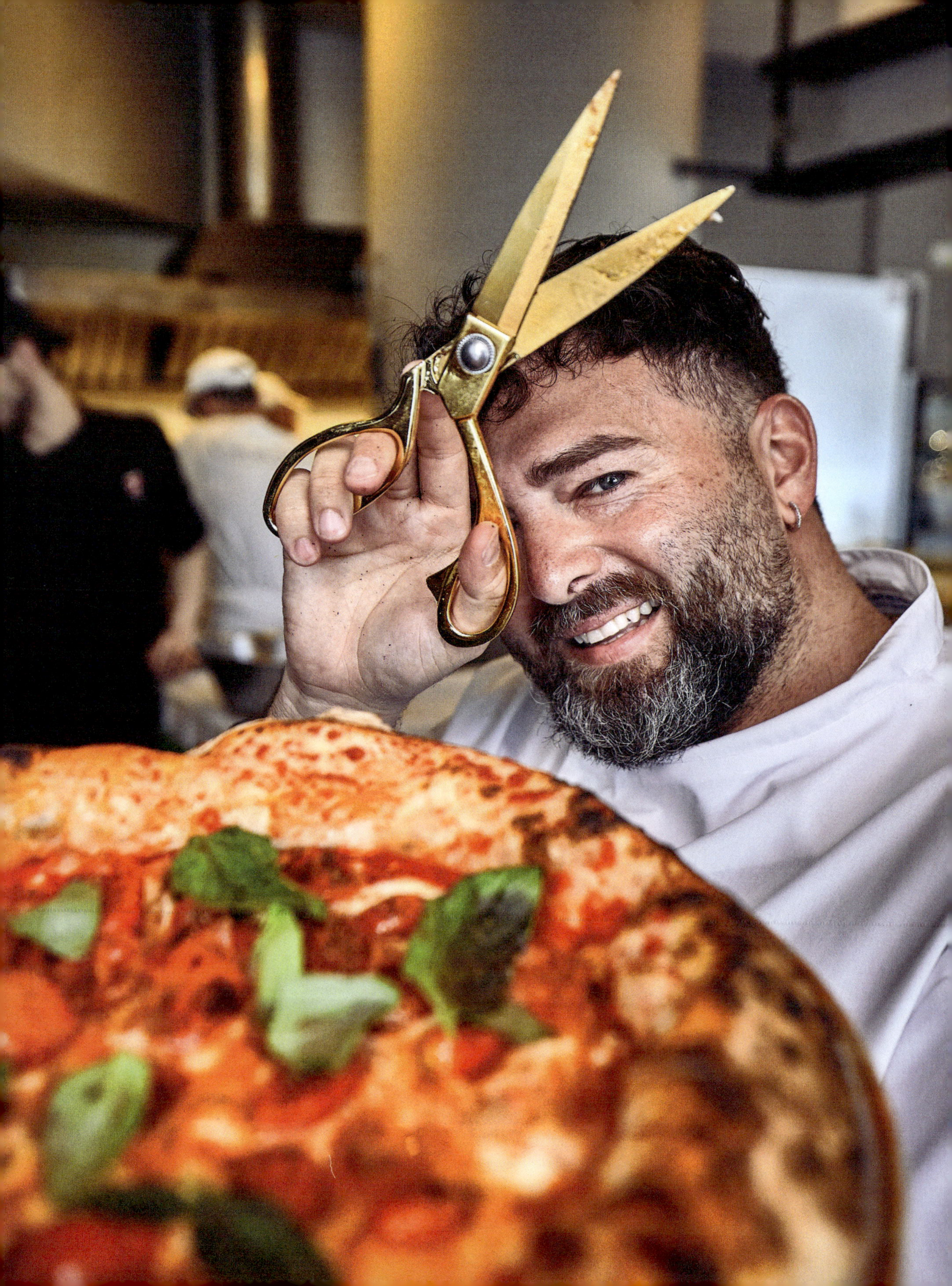

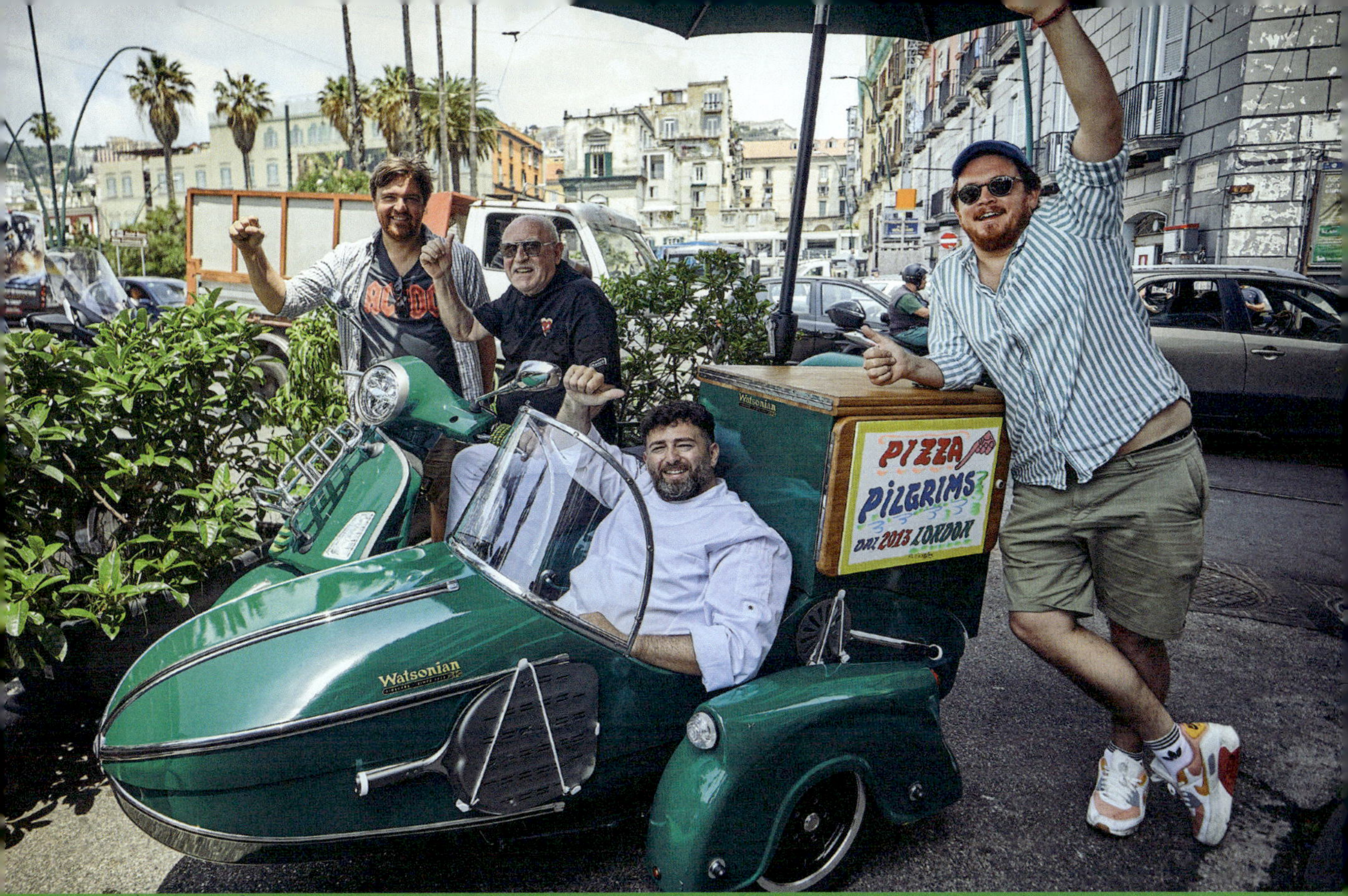
PIZZA
PILGRIMS
DAL 2013 LONDON
Watsonian

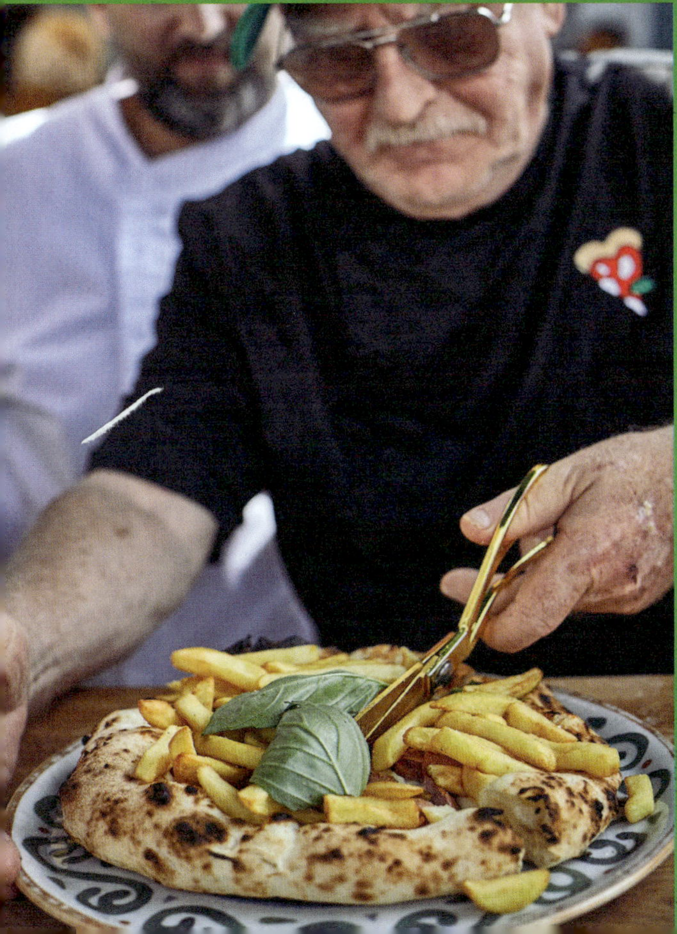

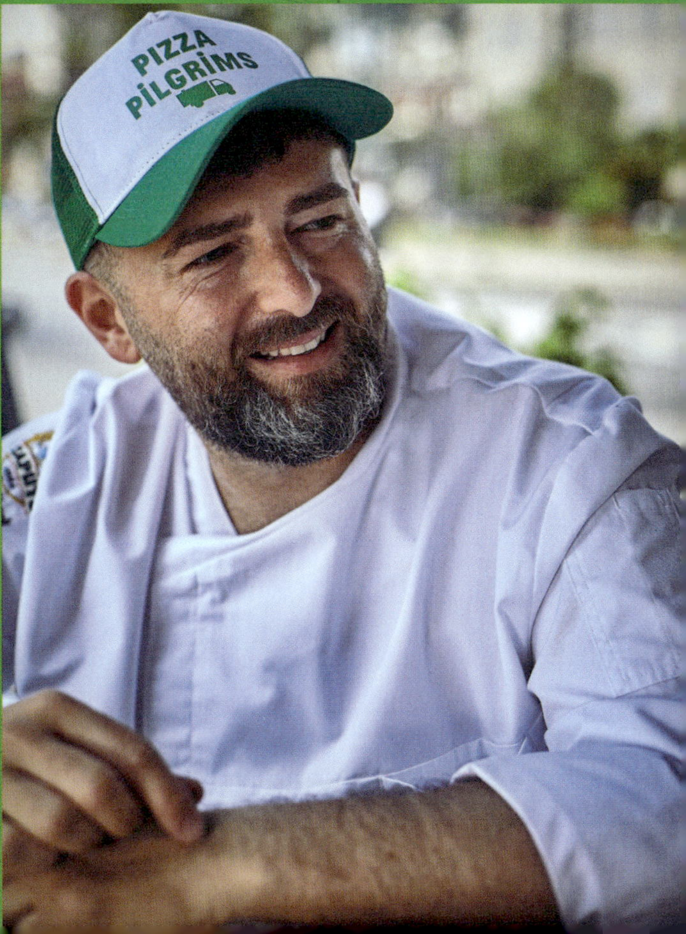
PIZZA
PILGRIMS

CENTRO CALABRIA

What you need

contemporanea pizza dough (page 93)

tomato sauce (page 190 or 209)

provola (smoked) mozzarella

Neapolitan cooked sausage

Calabrian 'nduja

extra virgin olive oil

basil

How to make it

Stretch a ball of dough out and spread tomato sauce over it. Top with provola, sausage and 'nduja.

Bake in the oven, then finish with olive oil and basil leaves.

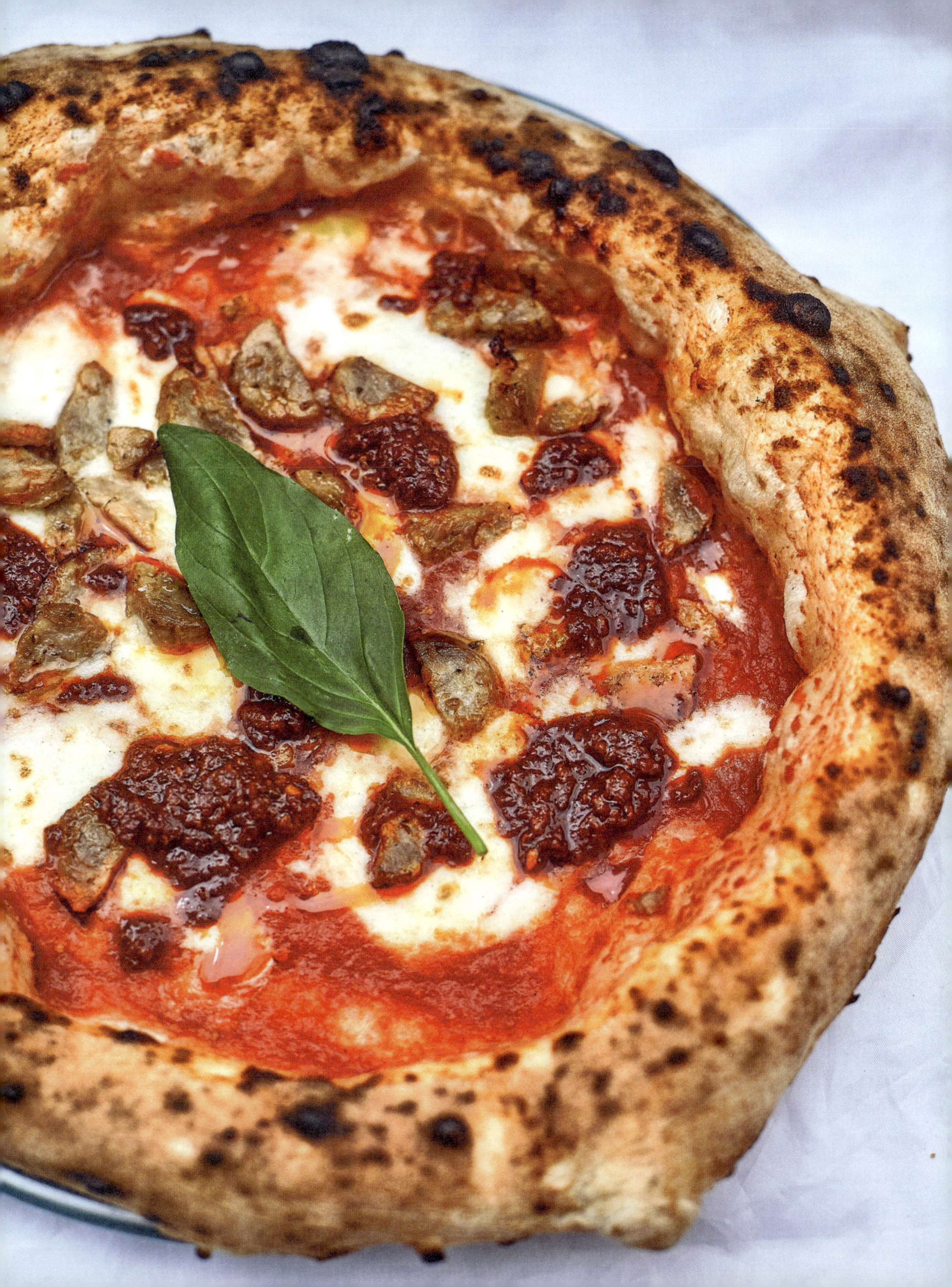

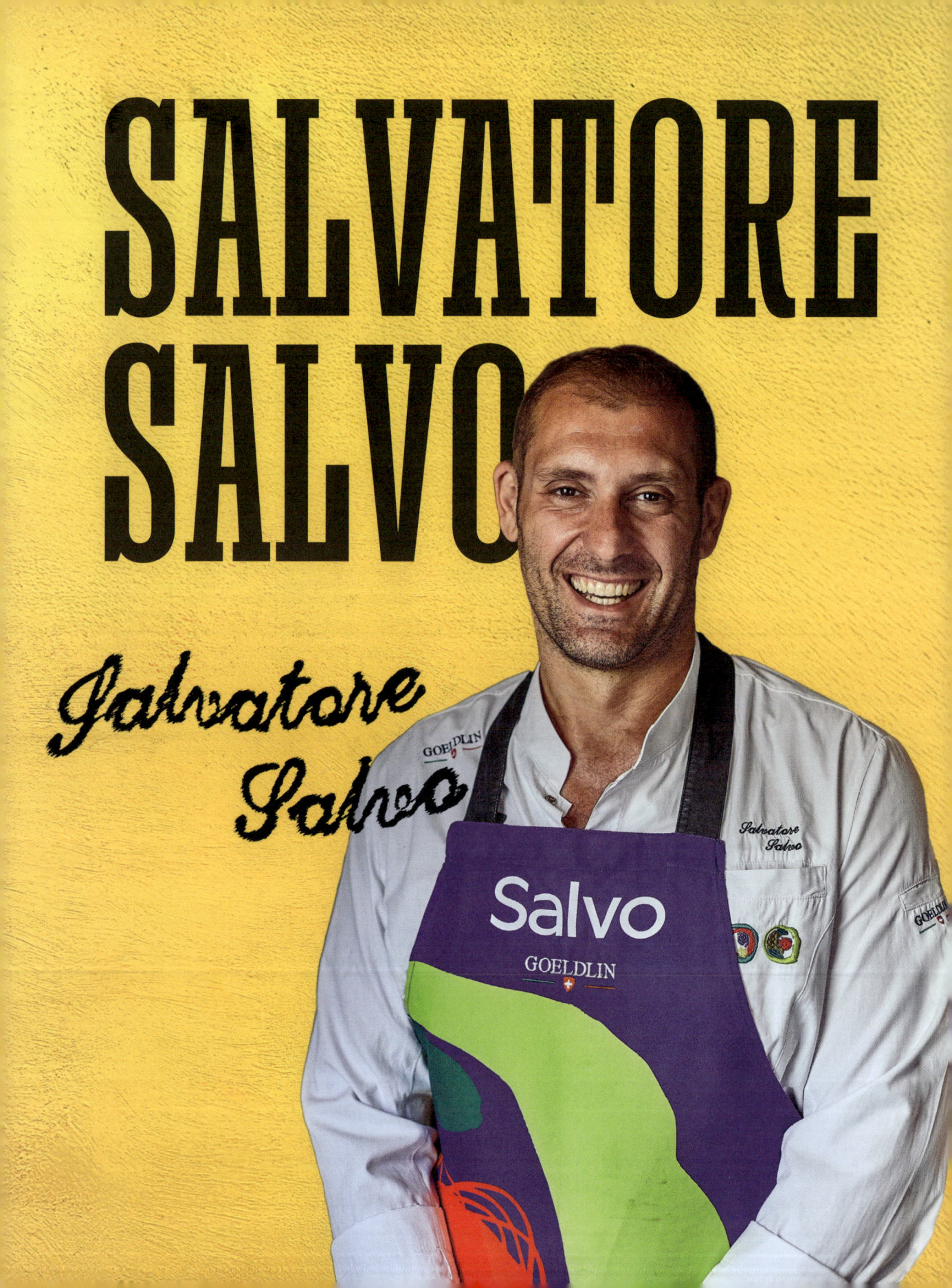

SALVATORE SALVO

Salvatore Salvo

Salvatore and his brother Francesco are something of a legend on the Napoli pizza scene. They are the third generation of a famous pizza family who have had pizzerias in Napoli and neighbouring Portici for decades. At 6ft 5 inches, he comes across more like a rival to Rocky Balboa than a pizza chef, but as we walk in he cracks a huge smile and it becomes instantly clear that he is a gentle giant with a huge passion for pizza and his city.

'Ten years ago the reputation of Neapolitan pizza was on rocky ground. Roman pizza ruled supreme and Gabriele Bonci famously said that pizza from Napoli was "the bottom of pizza, cheap ingredients made badly".' Salvatore says it was at that time that he and his brother decided to try and turn around the pizza scene in Napoli. He agrees that people were buying cheap ingredients from huge suppliers and that the quality was poor. They began encouraging small local suppliers to start producing low-volume, high-quality produce like tomatoes, courgettes (zucchini), mozzarella and salami, and he also began to collaborate with 2-Michelin-starred chefs like Gennaro Esposito and Antonino Cannavacciuolo, challenging them to create pizzas worthy of their restaurants. At first the people of Napoli worried that this approach would ruin 'real pizza', but as time went by they got busier and busier and he gained the trust of the city. He is famous for championing a locally loved but not widely known pizza, the Cossaca. Invented in 1935 when Tsar Nicholas II was visiting Napoli from Russia, this tomato and Parmesan pizza is the picture of simplicity but relies on perfect ingredients. The Tsar wanted a pizza that paid tribute to the Ural mountains of Russia, so the tomato pizza was topped with Parmesan 'snow'.

Salvatore runs his kitchen much like a Michelin-starred chef and nods to his obsession with produce, such as in a pizza featuring six different preparations of tomato. The olive oil shelf next to the pass also features 18 different oils to finish every different pizza. He believes that Napoli is now back to form and is the best city in the world again for pizza. The ingredients are unrivalled and people travel from all over the world to try the best.

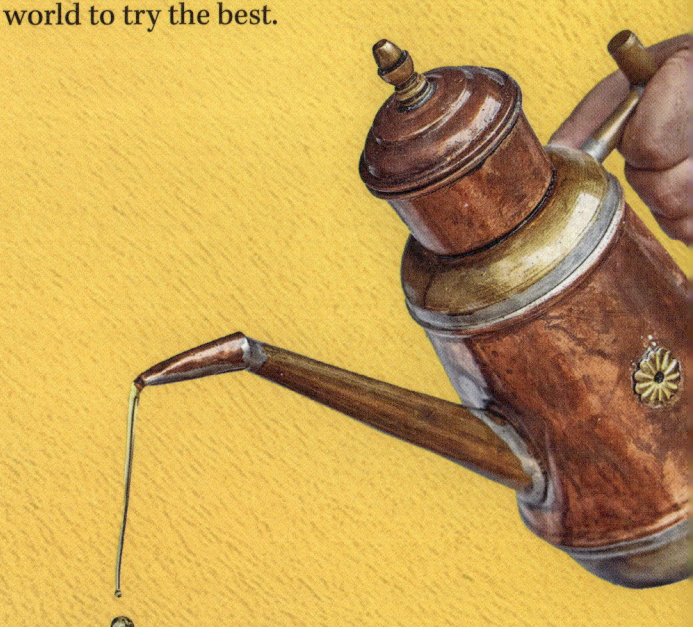

COSSACA

What you need

STG pizza dough (page 92)

tomatoes from Corbara

olive oil from Fratelli Pinna

basil

pecorino from Bagnoli

sea salt

How to make it

Stretch a ball of dough out. Crush peeled tomatoes by hand and add salt to taste.

Start with a generous amount of the tomatoes over the base, then add a good drizzle of olive oil and basil leaves.

Bake in the oven, then finish with freshly grated pecorino and another drizzle of olive oil.

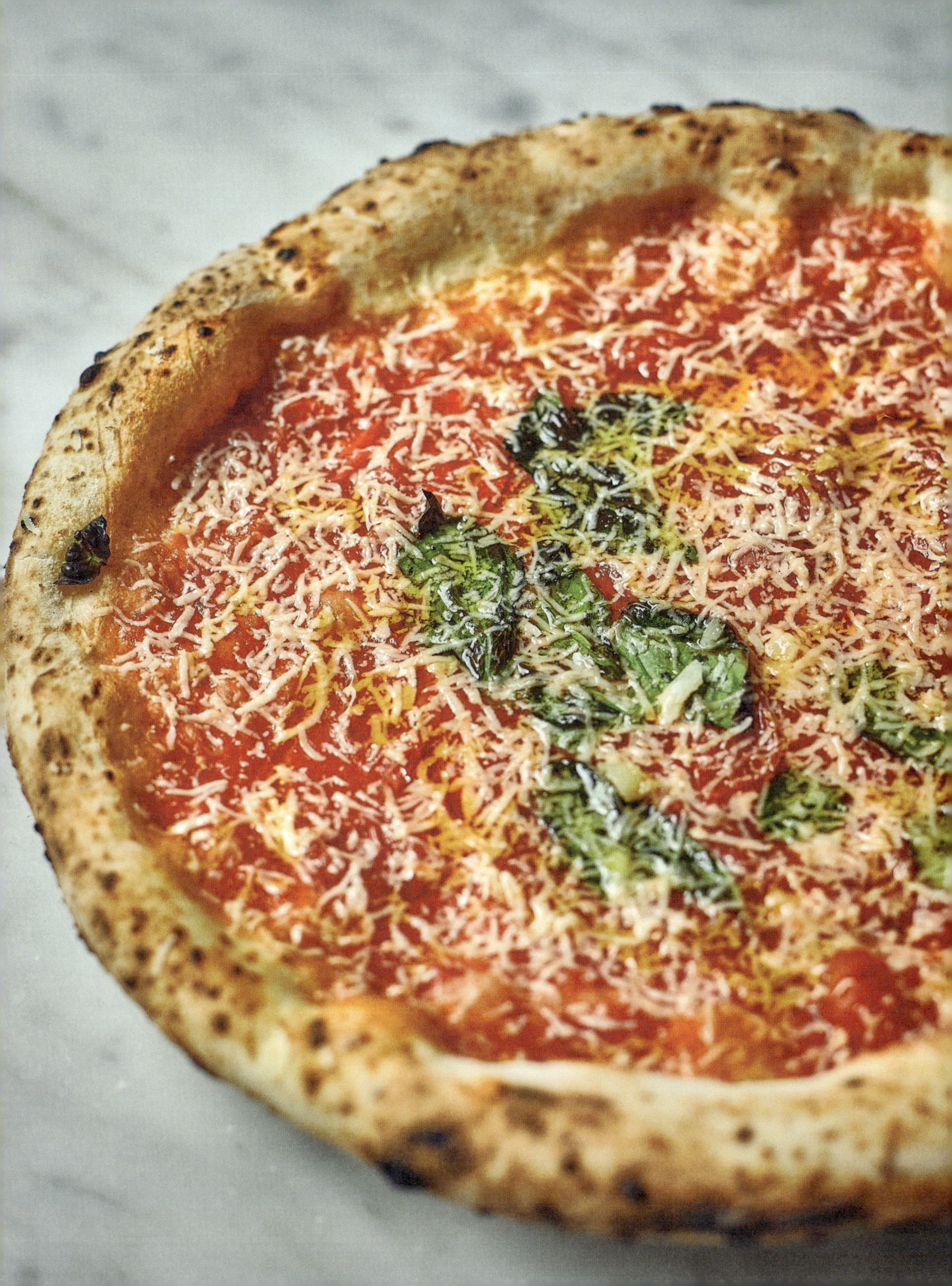

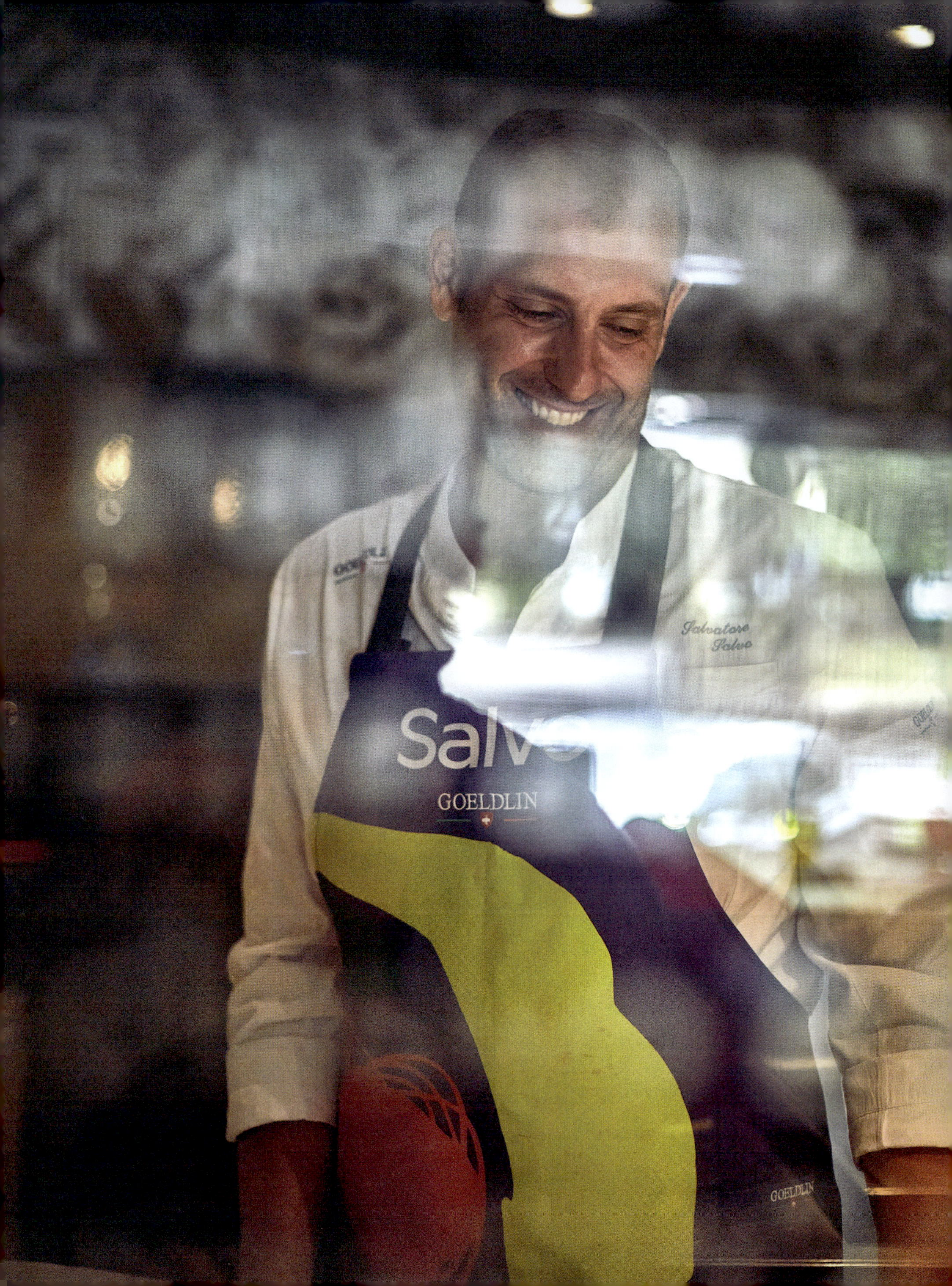
Salvatore
Salvo
Salv
GOELDLIN
GOELDLIN

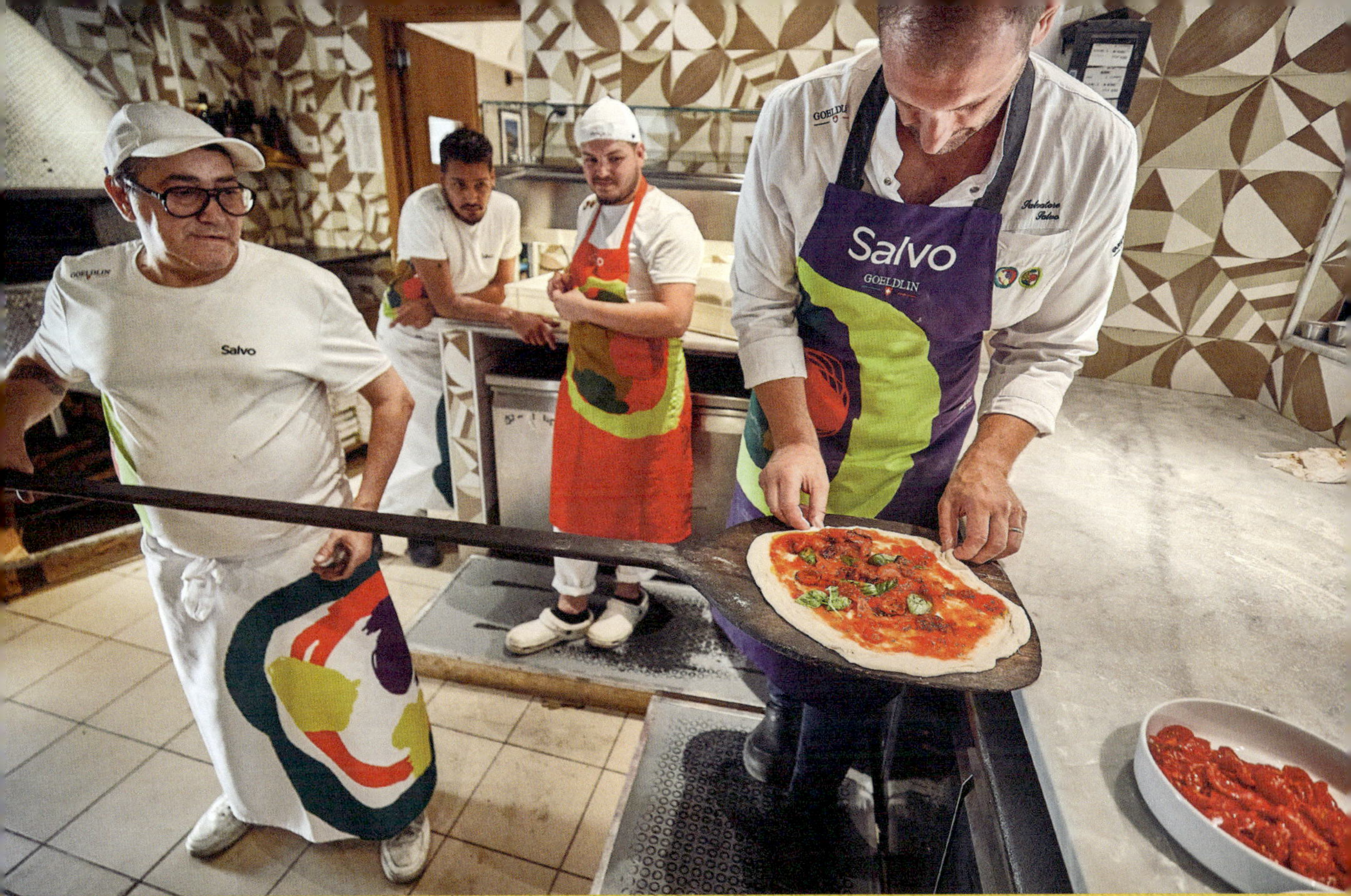
Salvo
GOELDLIN
Salvo

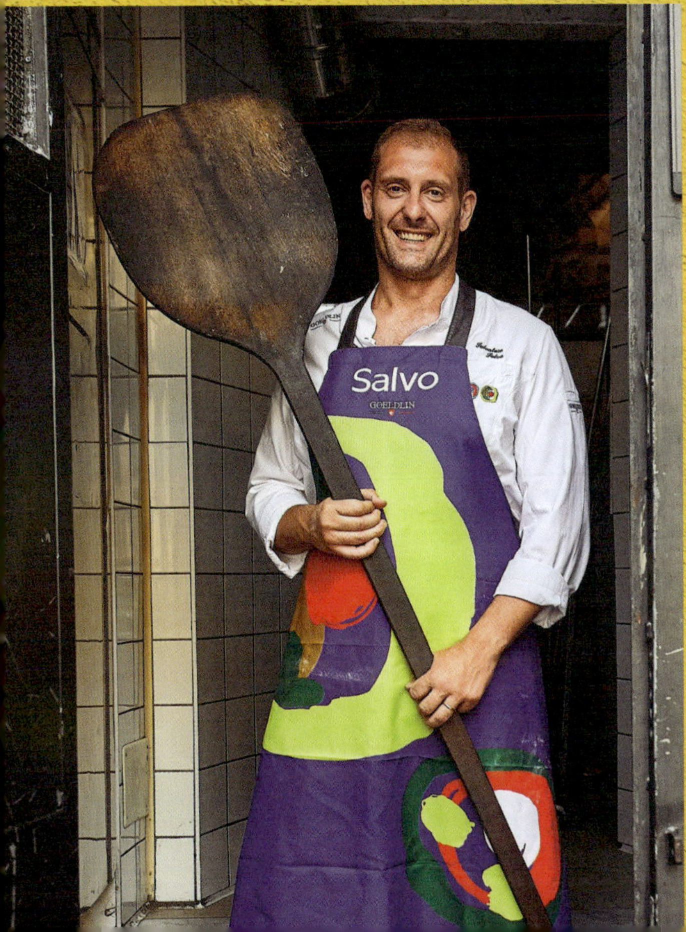
Salvo
GOELDLIN

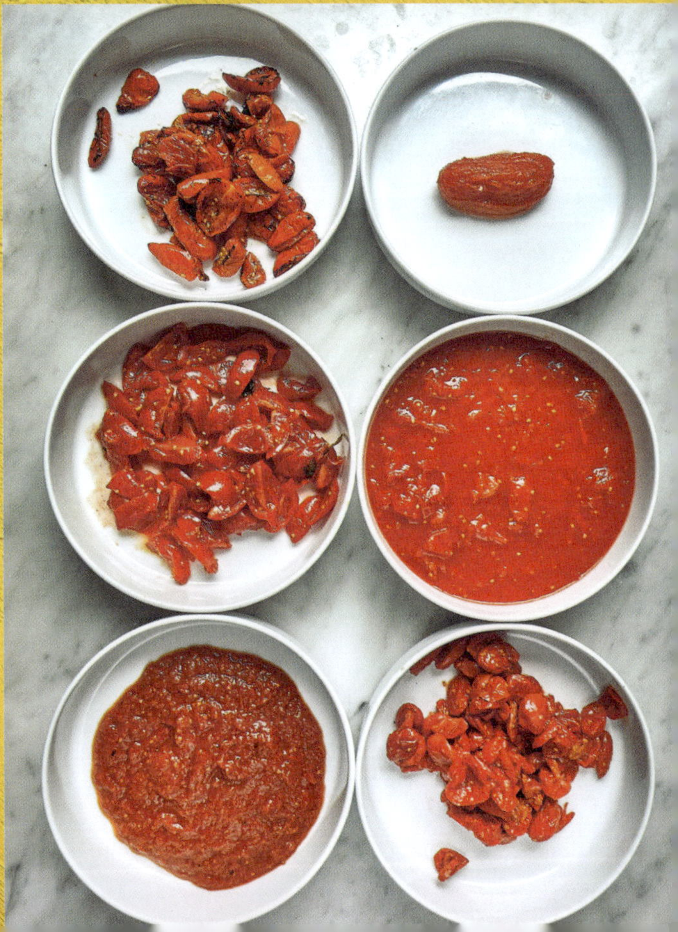

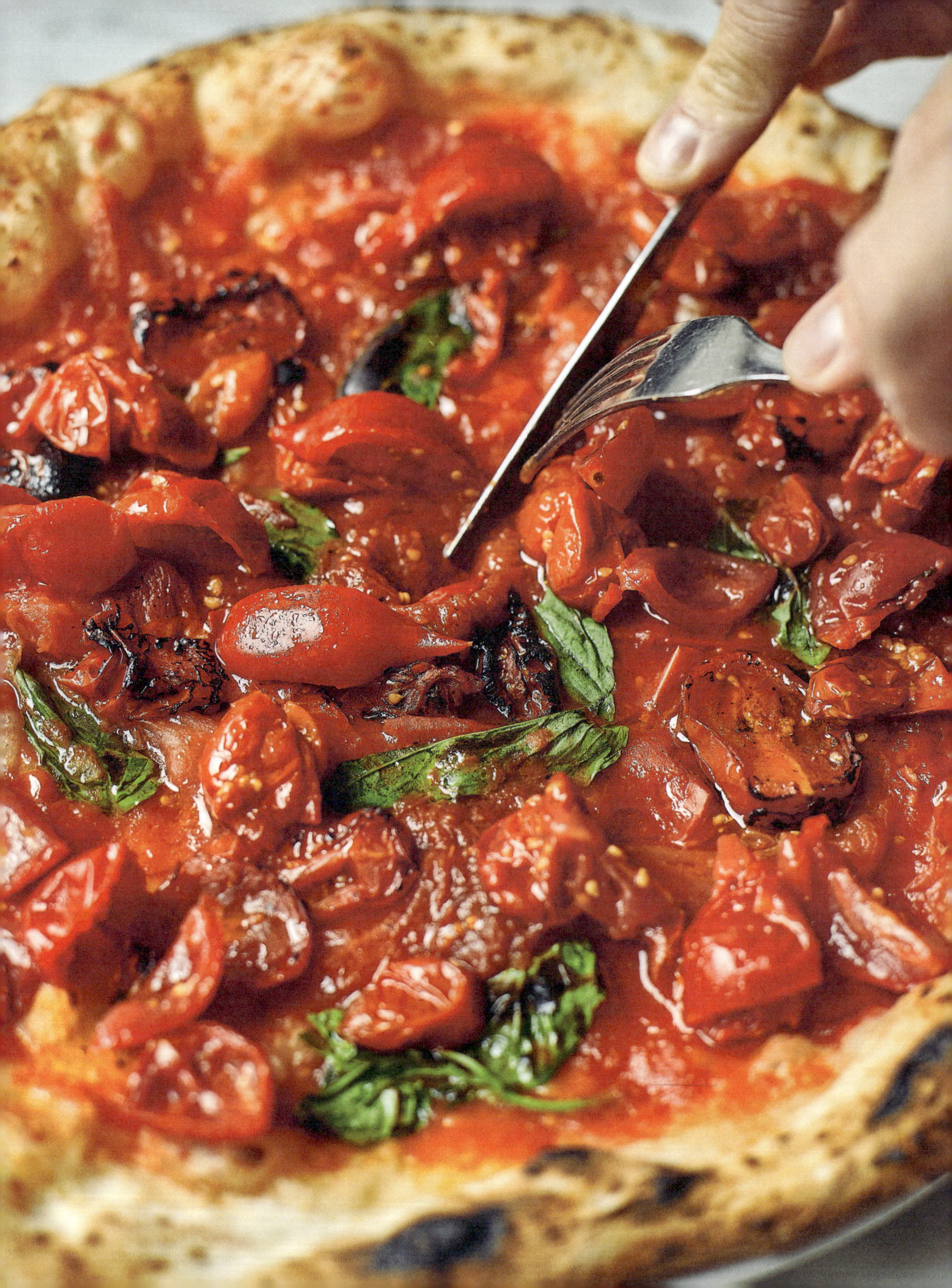

PIZZA POMODORO

What you need

STG pizza dough (page 92)

canned Corbarino tomatoes (see below)

San Marzano tomato

smoked sun-dried tomatoes (see below)

datterini tomatoes (see below)

basil

extra virgin olive oil

marinated Piennolo tomatoes (from a jar)

How to make it

Stretch a ball of dough out and start with a base of Corbarino. Next take a single San Marzano tomato and break it up onto the pizza. Drop little spoonfuls of the smoked sun-dried tomatoes around the pizza. Add a few of the grilled datterinis, some basil leaves and olive oil.

Bake in the oven, then finish with a few oven-dried datterinis, 120g (4oz) marinated Piennolo tomatoes and a good glug of olive oil.

For the Corbarino tomatoes (makes enough for 4 pizzas)

400g (14oz) can of Corbarino tomatoes (an ancient variety available online)

sea salt

Crush the tomatoes by hand and add salt to taste.

For the datterini tomatoes (makes enough for 4 pizzas)

500g (1lb 2oz) datterini tomatoes, halved

good drizzle of extra virgin olive oil

pinch of dried oregano

Season half the datterini with olive oil, salt and oregano and place in a single layer on a baking sheet. Place in a 90°C (195°F) oven for 2 hours until they have dried out and intensified.

Season the remaining halved datterini with oil and salt and grill (broil) in the pizza oven or under an oven grill until they are charred and juicy.

For the smoked sun-dried tomatoes (makes enough for 4 pizzas)

100g (3½oz) drained, smoked sun-dried tomatoes

Blend with a stick blender to a smooth chutney.

OSHIRASE

What you need

STG pizza dough (page 92)

fior di latte mozzarella

Sicilian extra virgin olive oil

marinated beef fillet (see below)

friarielli cream (see below)

How to make it

Stretch a ball of dough out and top with mozzarella and olive oil. Bake in the oven, then top with the marinated beef and drops of the friarielli cream.

Finish with a good drizzle of olive oil.

For the marinated beef fillet (makes enough for 4 pizzas)

240g (8½oz) beef fillet

50ml (1¾fl oz) soy sauce

1 tbsp honey

Thinly slice your beef fillet into pieces the same size as a large anchovy. Marinate in the soy and honey for 1 hour.

For the friarielli cream (makes enough for 4 pizzas)

100g (3½oz) jarred sautéed friarielli

Using a stick blender, blend the friarielli with the oil from the jar to make a smooth sauce.

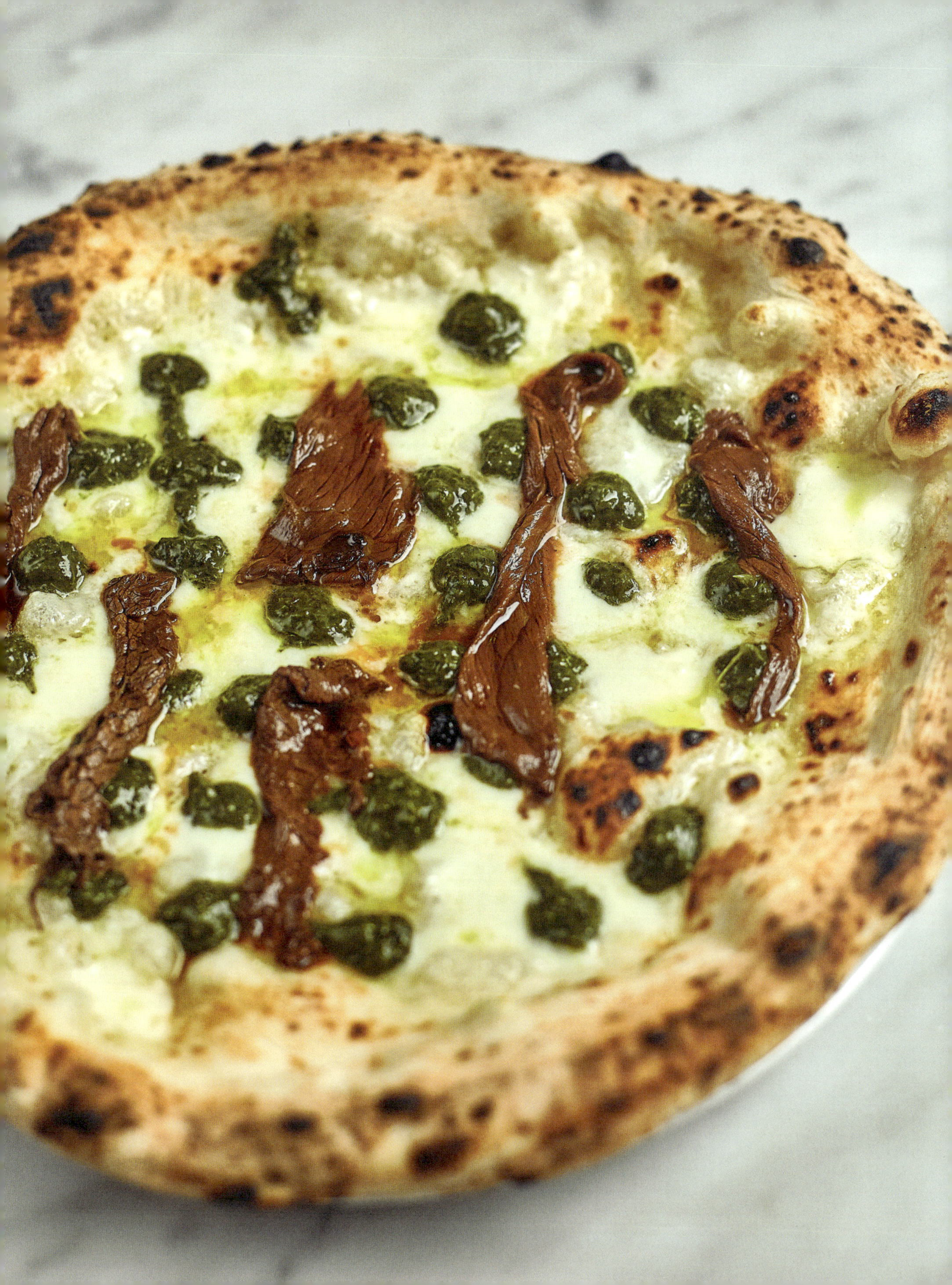

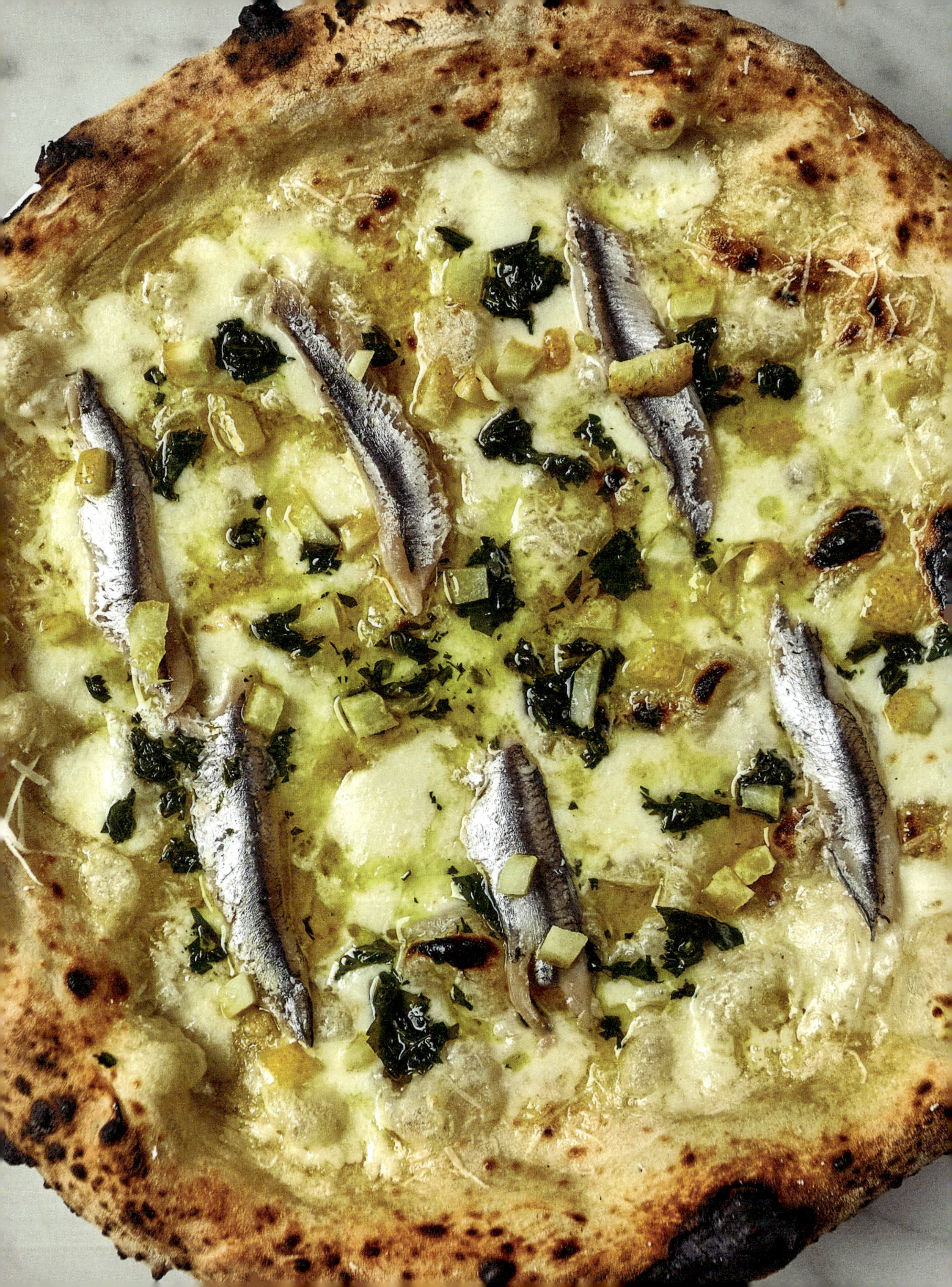

PROFUMO DI COSTIERA

What you need

STG pizza dough (page 92)

fior di latte mozzarella

pecorino

extra virgin olive oil

marinated anchovies (see below)

lemon and parsley salad (see below)

How to make it

Stretch a ball of dough out and add a base of mozzarella, grated pecorino and olive oil.

Bake in the oven, then arrange the anchovies on the pizza in lines. Finish by spooning over the lemon and parsley salad.

For the anchovies (makes enough for 4 pizzas)

80g (3oz) white anchovies in oil from Cetara

1 tbsp white vermouth

On a plate, lay out the white anchovies, drizzle with white vermouth and leave to marinate for 1 hour.

For the lemon and parsley salad (makes enough for 4 pizzas)

1 lemon

50ml (1¾fl oz) extra virgin olive oil

small handful of parsley, chopped

pinch of sea salt

drizzle of colatura di alici (anchovy essence) from Cetara

Peel the lemon and dice the skin into small cubes. In a bowl, mix the cubes with the juice squeezed from the lemon, the olive oil, parsley, salt and anchovy essence.

GINO AND

TOTO SORBILLO

Brothers? In pizza? That'll never work… Toto and his brother Gino have been such a huge part of the Neapolitan pizza scene for over 20 years. Their flagship pizzeria in the heart of the Centro Storico of Napoli on Via Tribunale is a genuine pilgrimage for any pizza lover coming to the city. The queues famously snake around the block and for good reason. The brothers celebrate the most traditional style of pizza in Napoli. The dough is Ruota di Carro (page 90) and when the pizza arrives at the table it is giant, spilling over the edge of the plate. The brothers obsess about the quality of the ingredients and all are locally sourced from the area. The pizzeria is run by what they call their 'army' of pizza chefs, and it is a well-oiled machine. A team of 10+ pizza chefs dance around each other in what is a tiny kitchen. Heads duck as pizzas are swung around on peels and loaded into the oven. When they hit the plates the waiters in red t-shirts and sweatbands run them to the tables. It's only men in the Sorbillo team and it feels like a football squad in training.

Their mother sits outside the pizzeria with a PA system calling the names of people who have sometimes queued up to 3 hours for a chance to try the pizza. Sorbillo is a big brand now and you can find their little pizza fritta shops all around Napoli, along with pizzerias in Rome, Milan and Turin. But Gino tells us that back when they first started, the goal was to open a pizzeria to help a community that was suffering under the control of the Camorra. Gino describes the area as a war zone when they first opened. Customers would come for pizza and have their Rolex watches stolen off their arms as they left the pizzeria. Twenty years on and this has all changed – the place is an institution and we would say still most people's favourite pizzeria in the city (and the best known). When we last turned up on the Vespa we thought it would be a good idea to feed the queues a little slice of pizza while they waited. Toto came out to meet us a little bemused, but then quickly got into the swing of things and started making pizza with us. Napoli in a nutshell.

ANANAS

What you need

butter

fresh pineapple rings

Ruota di Carro dough (page 90)

provola (smoked) mozzarella

buffalo mozzarella

basil

extra virgin olive oil

salted goat's ricotta

How to make it

In a large frying pan heat some butter until it has melted and is foaming. Add about 4 pineapple rings and fry on both sides until the fruit has softened and caramelized. Set to one side to cool.

Stretch a ball of dough out and distribute the provola and buffalo mozzarella evenly, then top with the pineapple.

Finish with a couple of basil leaves and bake in the oven.

Once out of the oven, drizzle with some extra virgin olive oil and grate the goat's ricotta over the crust.

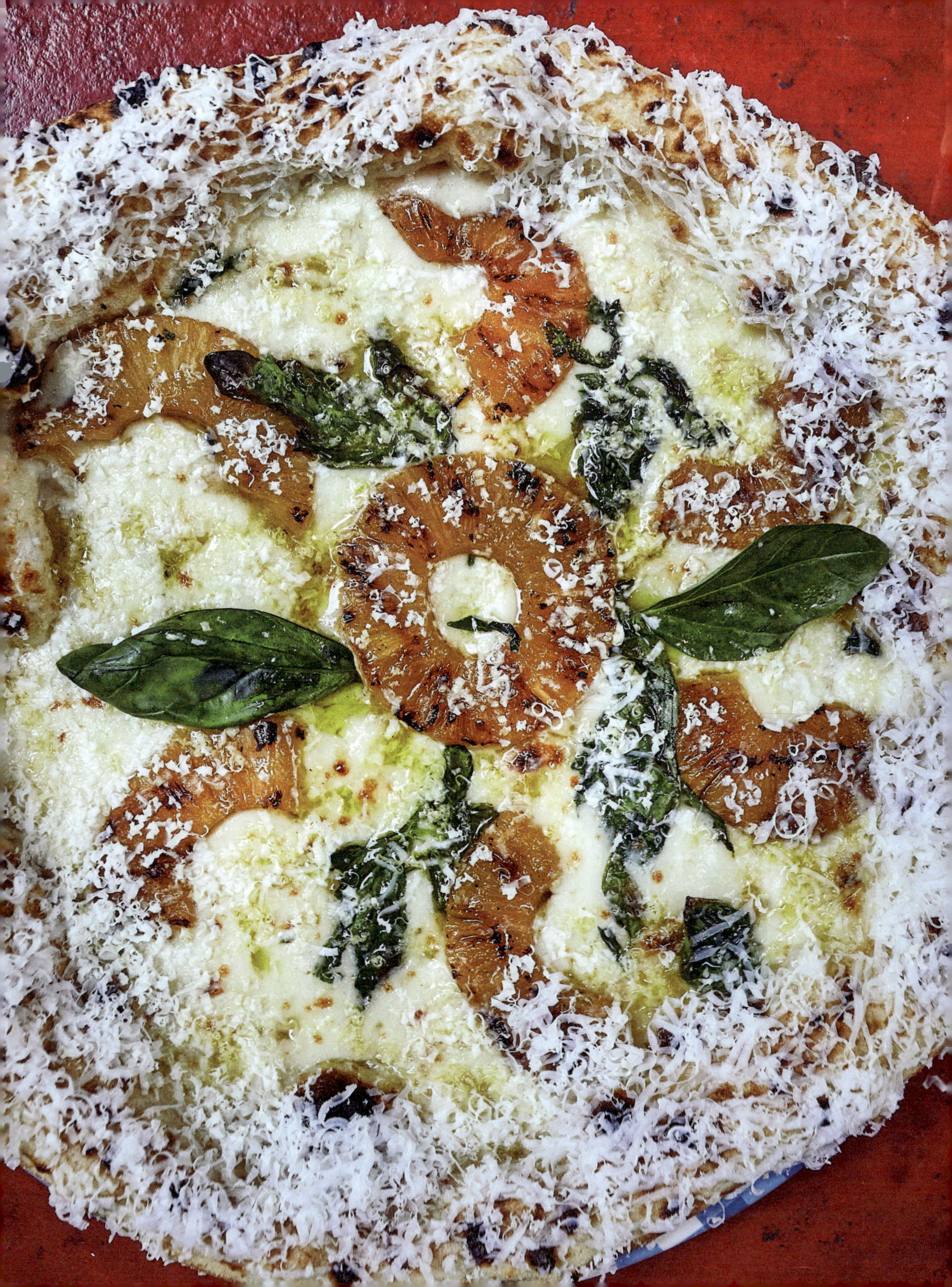

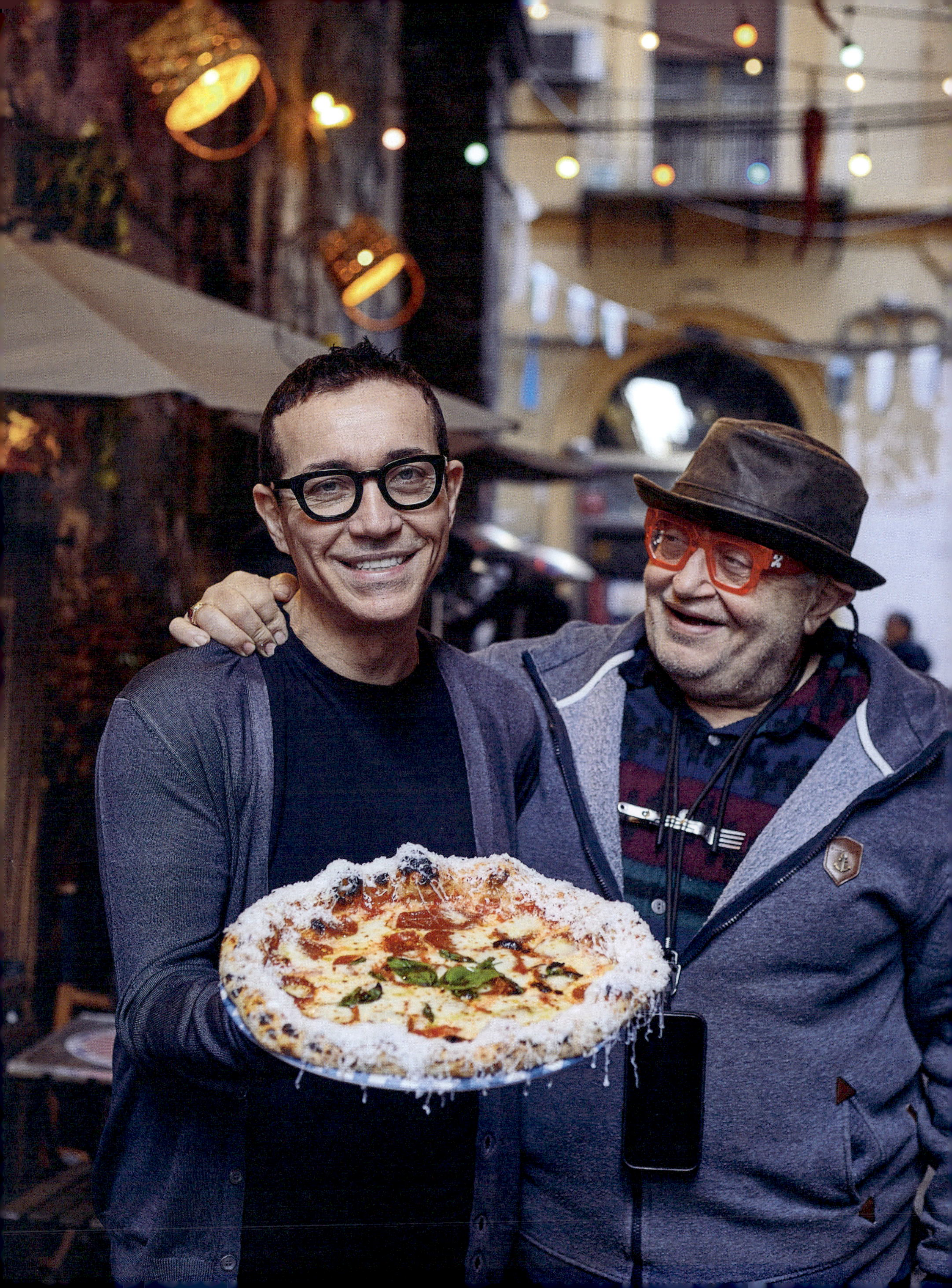

Birra
Limoncello Spritz
Gino e Toto
Sorbillo
Pizza dal 1935

APEROL SPRITZ 2,50
Limoncello Spritz
Sorbillo

Gino e Toto
Sorbillo
International Pizza since 1935
ORIGINAL

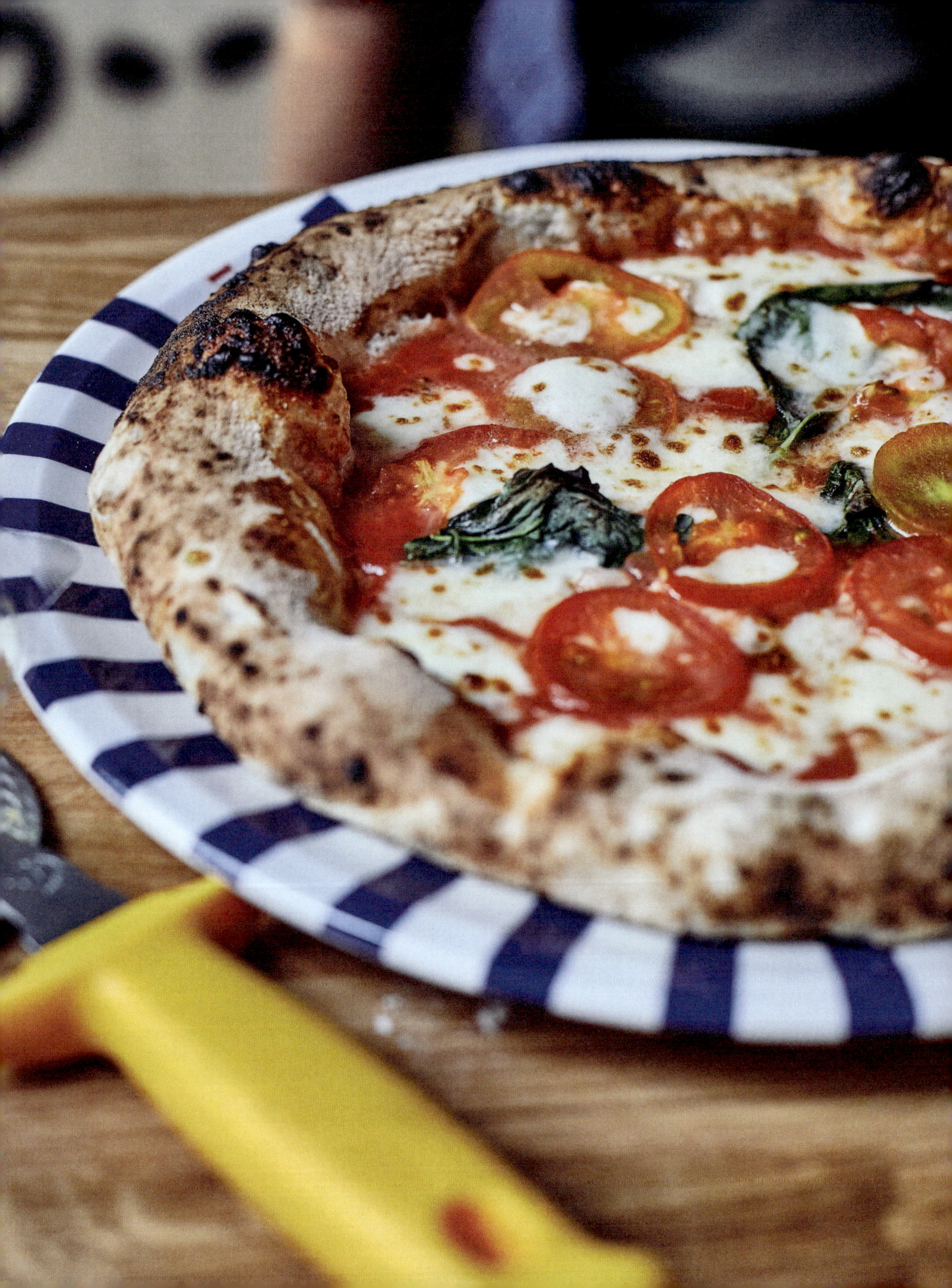

What you need

Ruota di Carro dough (page 90)

tomato sauce, preferably made with San Marzanos (page 190 or 209)

buffalo mozzarella

fresh San Marzano tomatoes, thinly sliced

extra virgin olive oil

basil

How to make it

Stretch a ball of dough out and add a base of tomato sauce, then top with some buffalo mozzarella.

Season the freshly sliced San Marzano tomatoes with a little salt then place some on the pizza. Bake in the pizza oven.

Finish with extra virgin olive oil and basil leaves.

MARGHERITA EXTRA EXTRA

SALAMI NAPOLI PICCANTE

What you need

cacioricotta cheese, grated

double (heavy) cream

Ruota di Carro dough (page 90)

tomato sauce, preferably made with San Marzanos (page 190 or 209)

buffalo mozzarella

basil

spicy salami (salame Napoli piccante), sliced

extra virgin olive oil

aged Parmesan

How to make it

Combine equal parts of cacioricotta and double cream in a small saucepan and set over a low heat. Stir continuously until it is melted and smooth, then set aside to cool.

Stretch a ball of dough out and add a base of tomato sauce, then top with some buffalo mozzarella and a few spoonfuls of the cooled cacioricotta cream.

Add basil leaves and spicy salami, then bake in the oven.

Finish with more basil leaves and a drizzle of extra virgin olive oil, then grate aged Parmesan onto the crust.

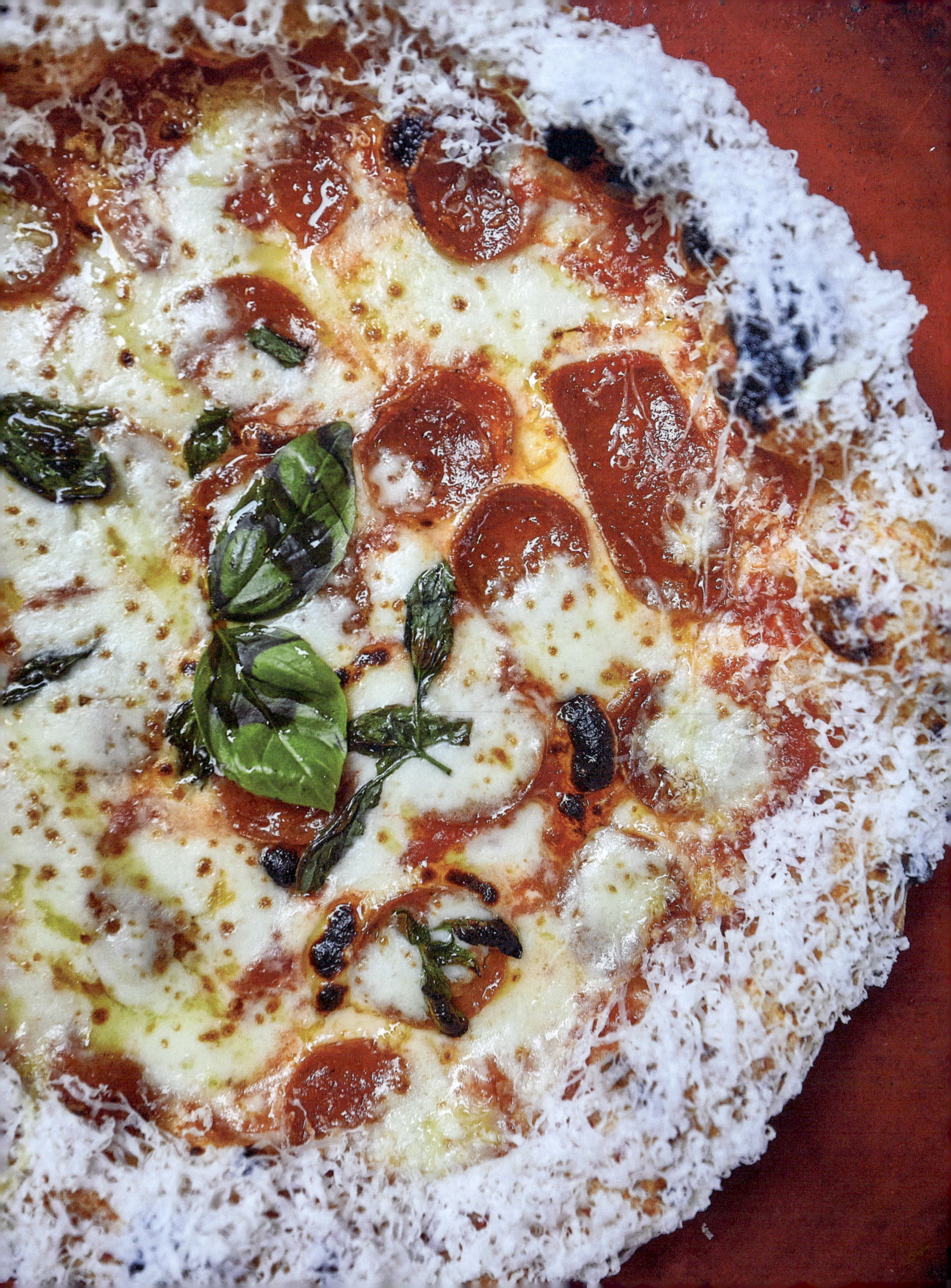

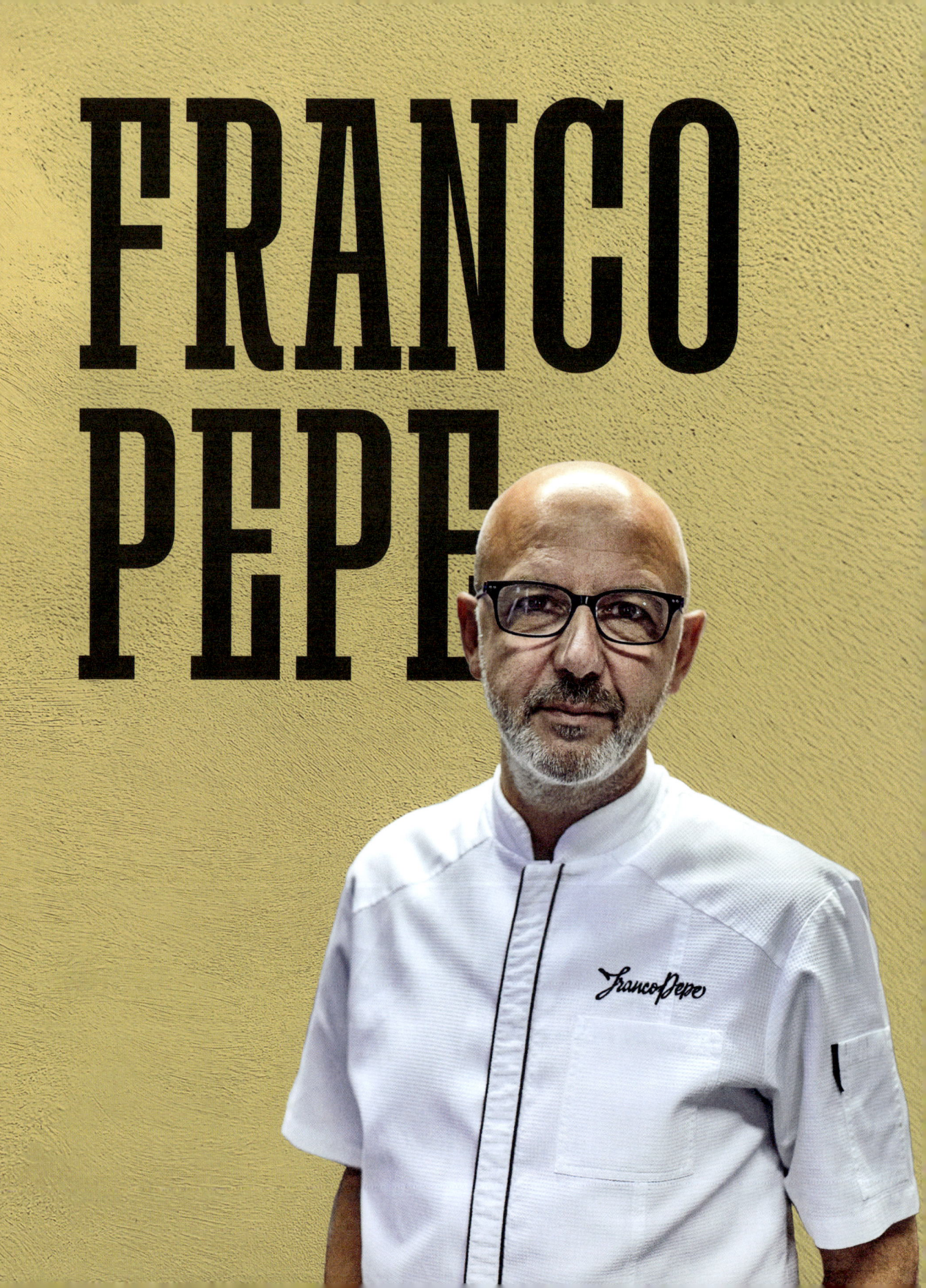

FRANCO PEPE

Franco Pepe

If there was one stop we had to make on our second pilgrimage, it was to Franco Pepe. It's a form of pilgrimage in itself, as he is based up in a sleepy little town of just 6,000 inhabitants, about an hour north of Napoli, called Caiazzo.

If pizzaioli were actors, then Franco would be a kind of Daniel Day-Lewis character: extremely talented, mysterious and aloof, with an all-consuming passion for his craft. His grandfather was a baker, his parents restaurateurs, and he took on the family business with his brother back in 1996. Pepe's obsession with pizza developed there and in 2012 he parted ways with the family business to open his temple to pizza, Pepe in Grani. His philosophy was to only use the best of the best from producers as local as he could find. He also obsesses over the methods by which he makes his dough, and to this day the dough is made by hand (no dough machine!) in the huge wooden troughs of his dough lab, by his squad of young pizza chefs, to a very specific recipe that blends three flours all milled on site. Yup, he's obsessed.

Pepe also brings a fine-dining approach to pizza that is rare, and encourages a tasting menu of pizza creations that play with the very strict rules of Neapolitan pizza. Expect gels, dehydrated powders and foams a-plenty. This approach has garnered him some criticism from the trad pizza world and people thought that such an experimental pizzeria, so far from town, would fail. Twelve years on and he has won every accolade possible, and the queue is out the door.

The cool thing about Pepe in Grani is that you can go for the all-out Willy Wonka experience but you can also go for a simple, beautifully made Margherita for less than ten euros. We also hugely respect the fact that he hasn't fallen to the temptation of rolling his pizzerias out around the world, instead driving all his energy into his restaurant in Caiazzo. We have visited three times now and every time he is in the kitchen, walking the tables and ensuring everyone is having a good time. We've only been allowed to witness the process of making his Margherita sbagliata, so while the method is included for that recipe, for the other pizzas you'll have to use your imagination to recreate them!

MARGHERITA SBAGLIATA

Franco Pepe's most famous pizza plays with the form of the most traditional pizza. This is a must on every visit!

What you need

STG pizza dough (page 92)

fior di latte mozzarella

extra virgin olive oil

tomato sauce (page 190 or 209)

basil oil (see below)

How to make it

Stretch a ball of dough out and start with a base of fior di latte mozzarella and a little olive oil.

Bake in the oven, then top with lines of tomato sauce, then dot with basil oil to finish.

For the basil oil (makes enough for 10–15 pizzas and keeps for 2 weeks)

large handful of basil leaves

100ml (3½fl oz) extra virgin olive oil

Drop the basil leaves into boiling water for 2–3 seconds and then transfer them to a bowl of ice-cold water (this process locks in the colour of the basil). Drain, then blend with the olive oil to make a smooth basil sauce.

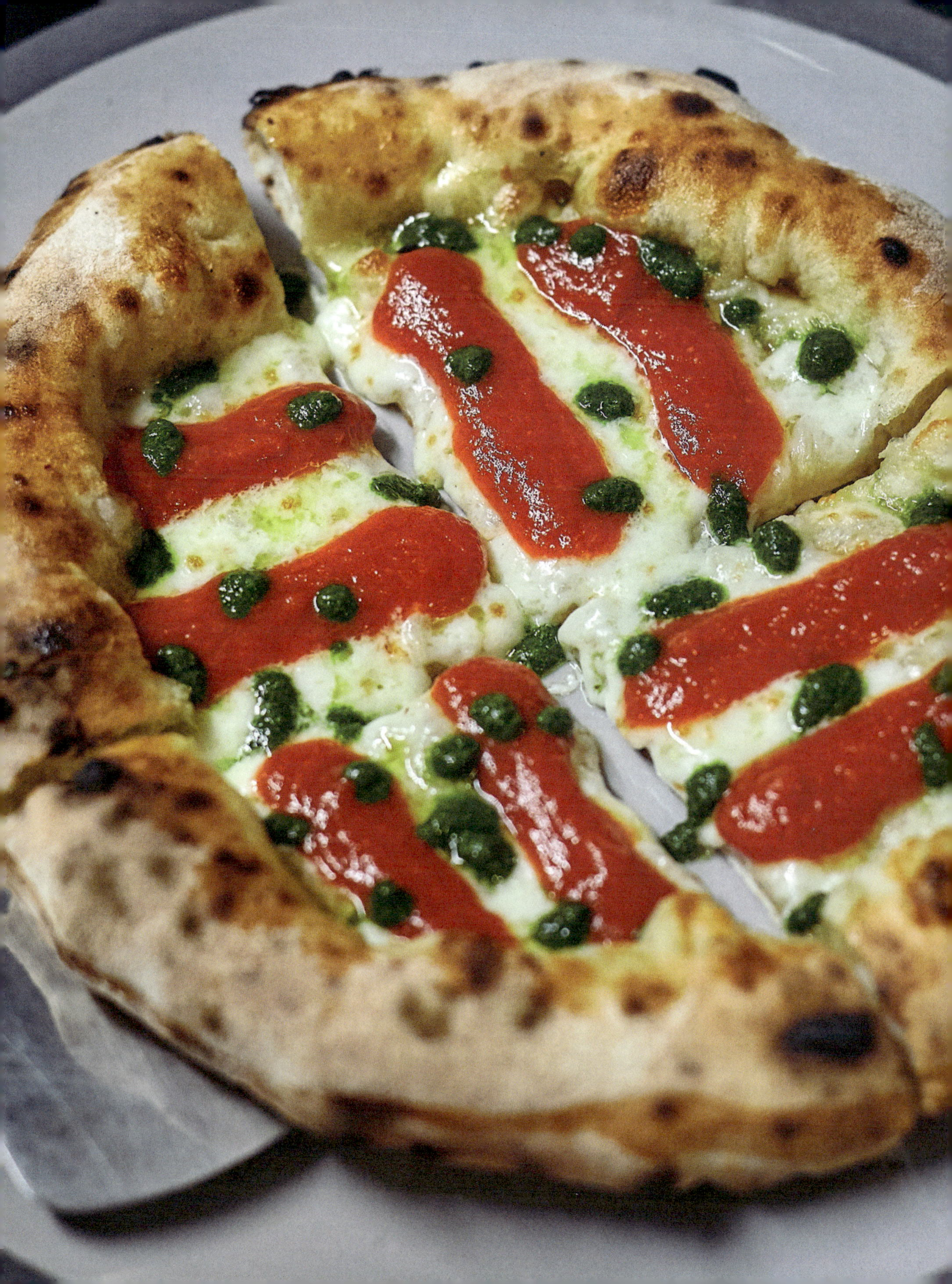

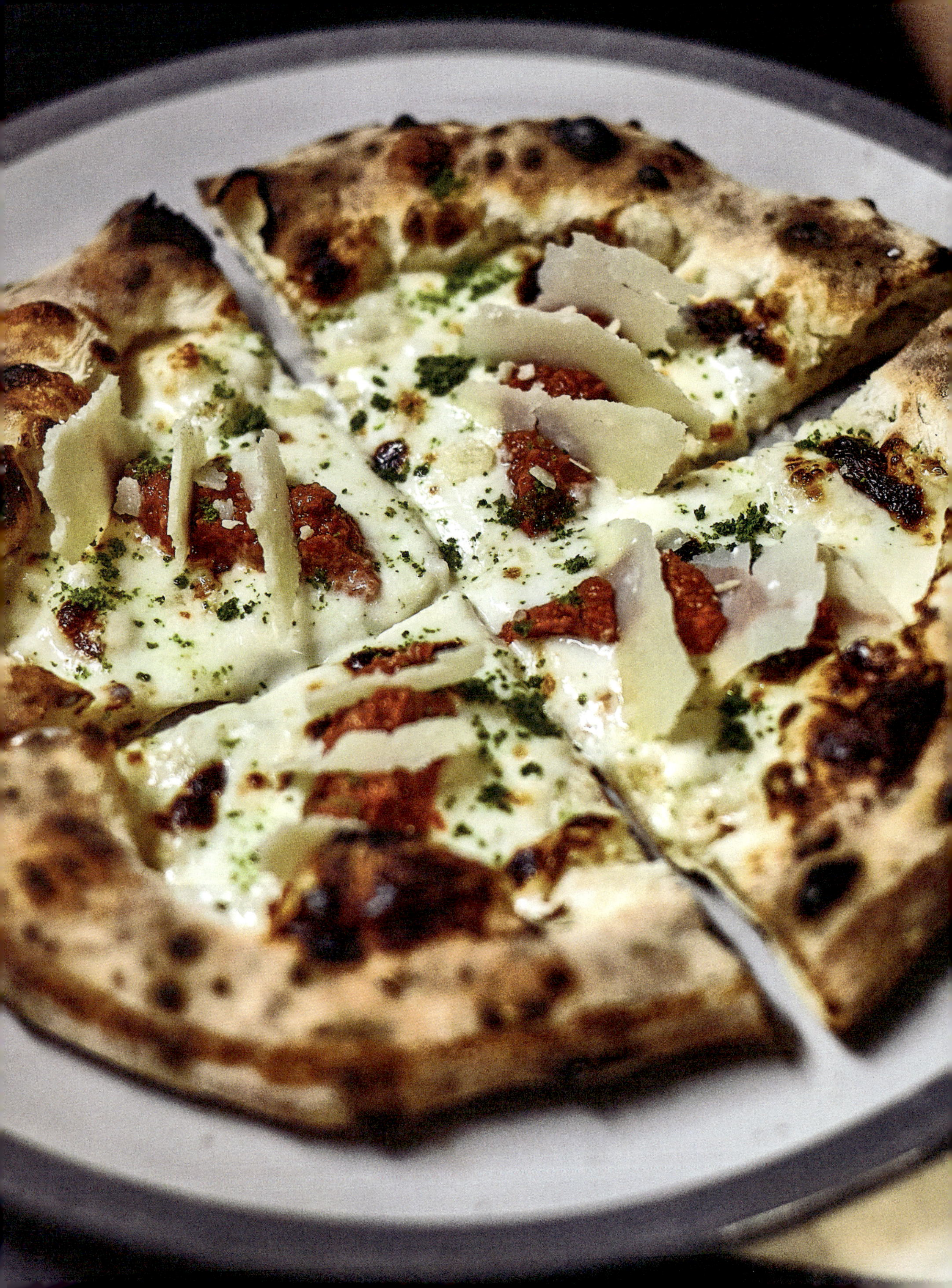

SCARPETTA

What you need

STG pizza dough (page 190 or 209)

fior di latte mozzarella

raw tomato compote

basil leaf powder

Parmesan

extra virgin olive oil

What we think

This is Pepe's pizza tribute to that moment at the end of eating a bowl of pasta, when you use bread to mop up the leftover sauce and cheese.

Have a go at making this one and see if you can match it to the photo opposite (we want to see those upright Parmesan shards!).

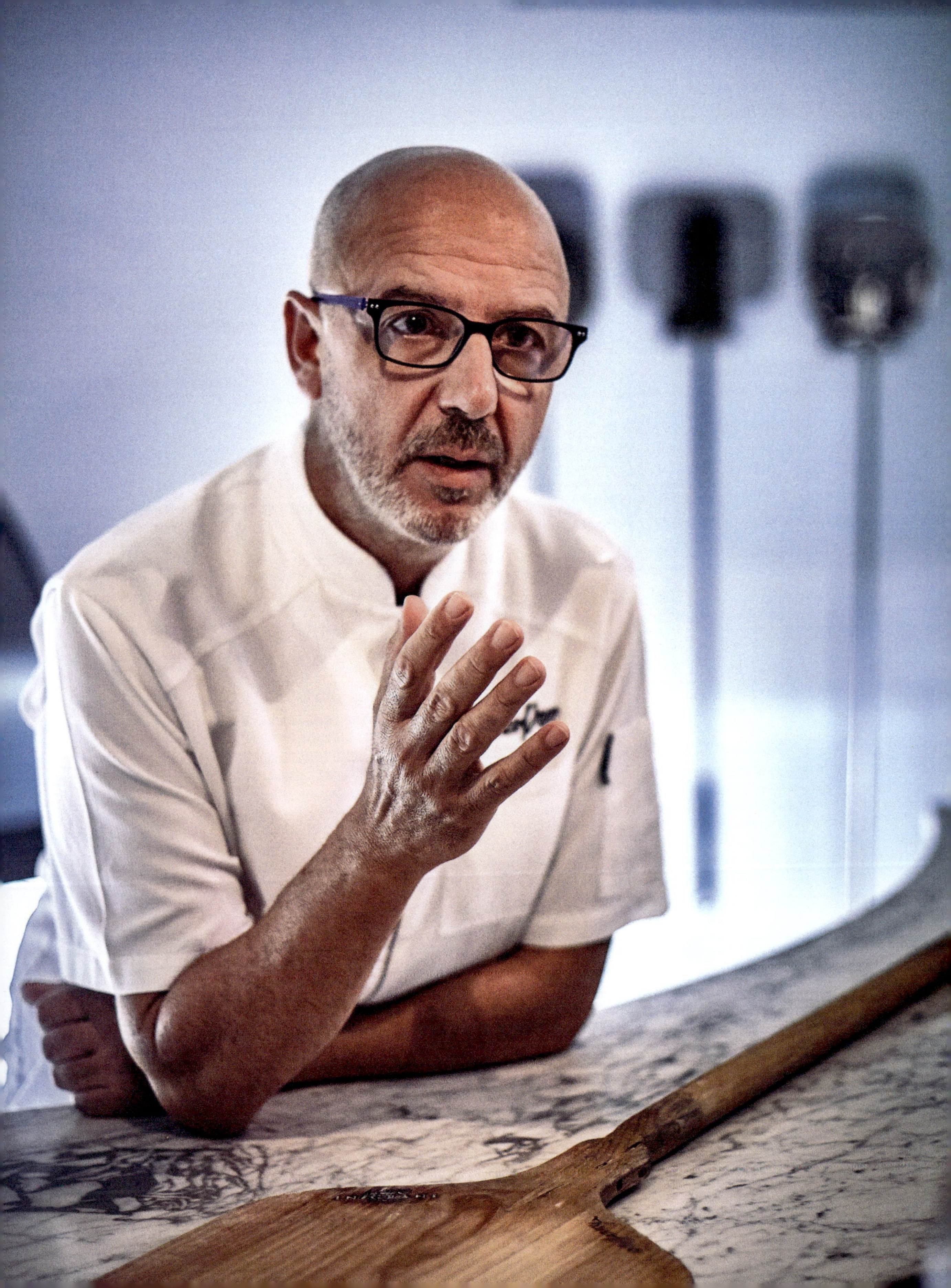

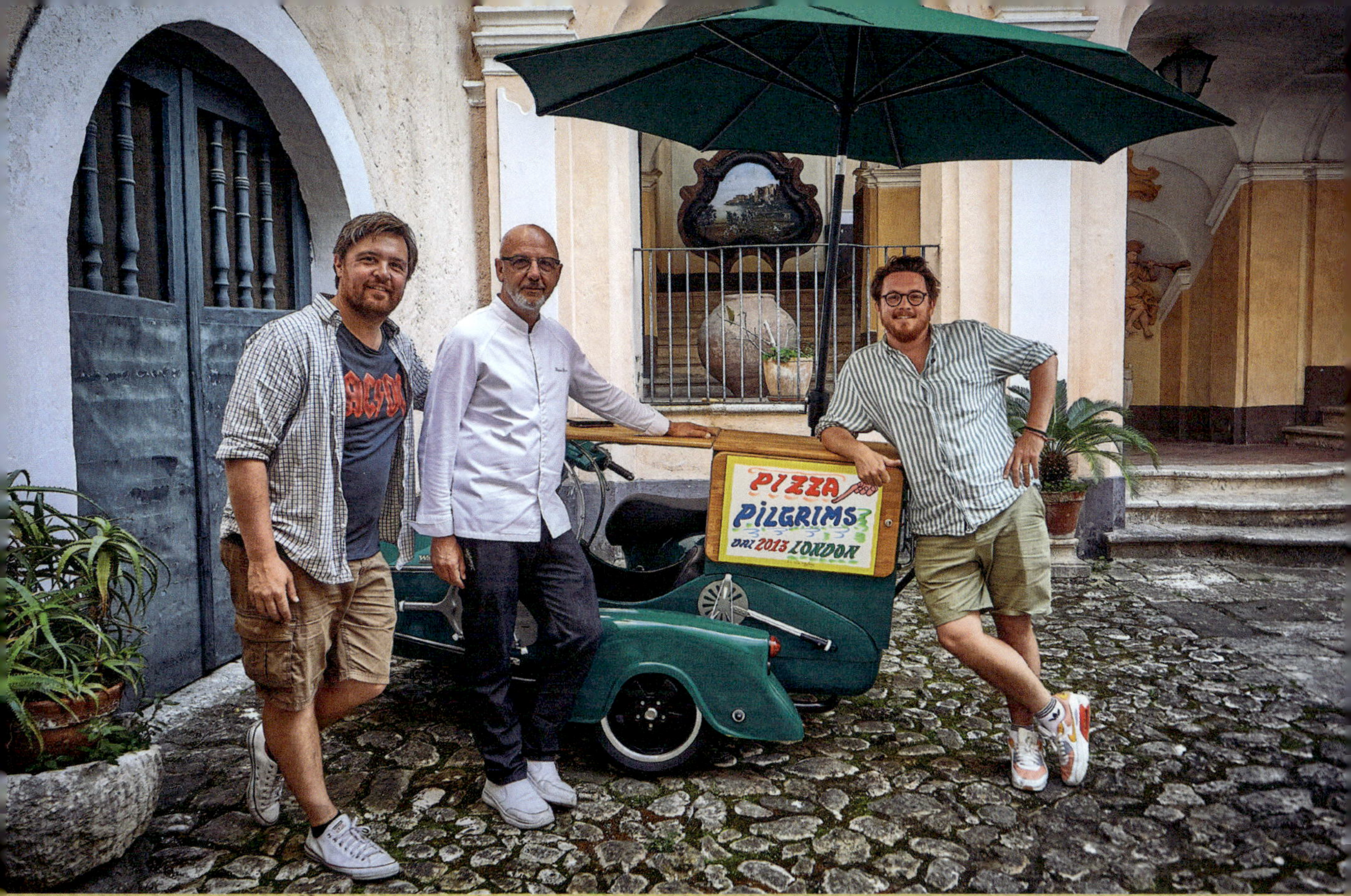
PIZZA
PILGRIMS
dal 2013 LONDON

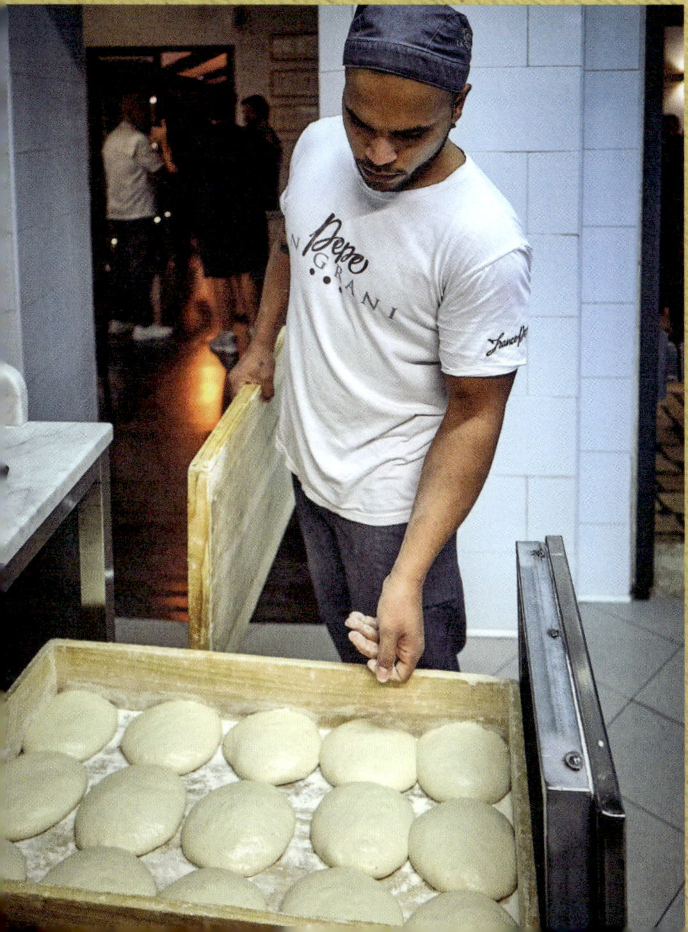
Pepe
IN GRANI

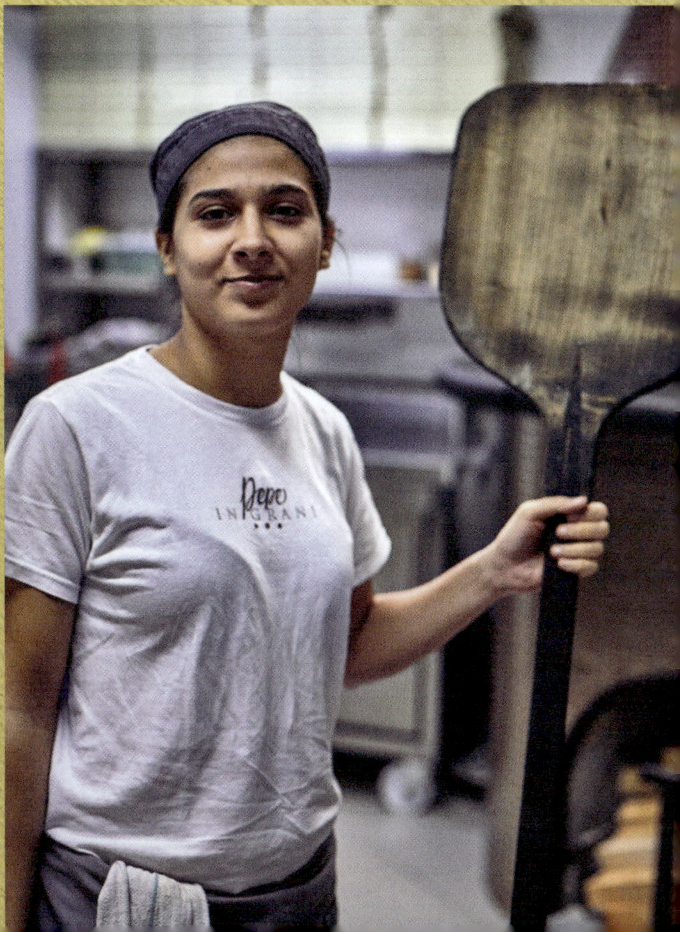
Pepe
IN GRANI

ANANASCOSTA

What you need

deep-fried pizza dough horn (page 231)

fresh pineapple

San Daniele prosciutto

12-month Grana Padano fondue

liquorice powder

What we think

This is Pepe's answer to the Hawaiian. He says that the issue with pineapple on pizza is because it is combined with tomato, giving an unpleasant double acidity. By switching tomato for a cheese sauce, the balance works much better.

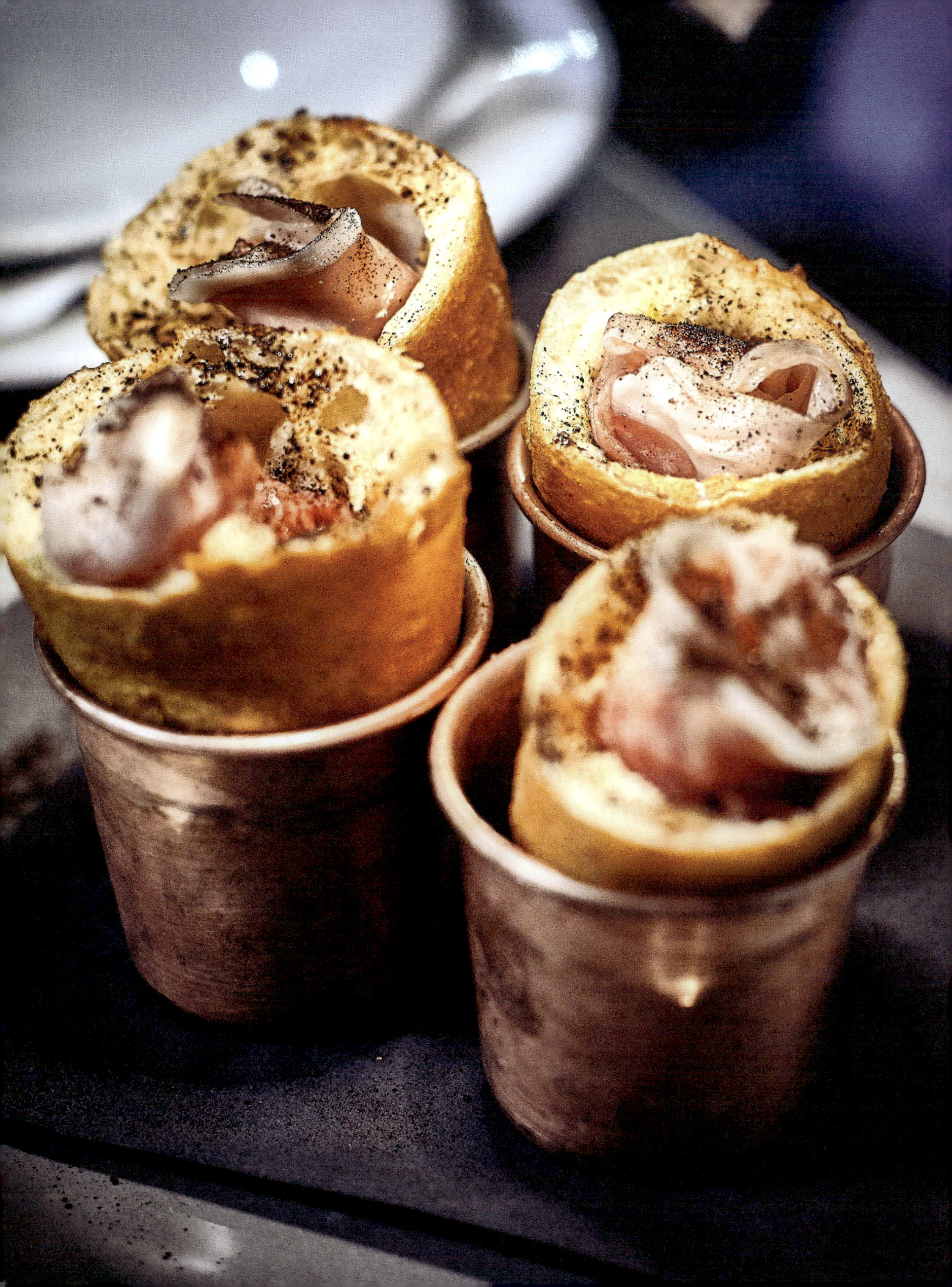

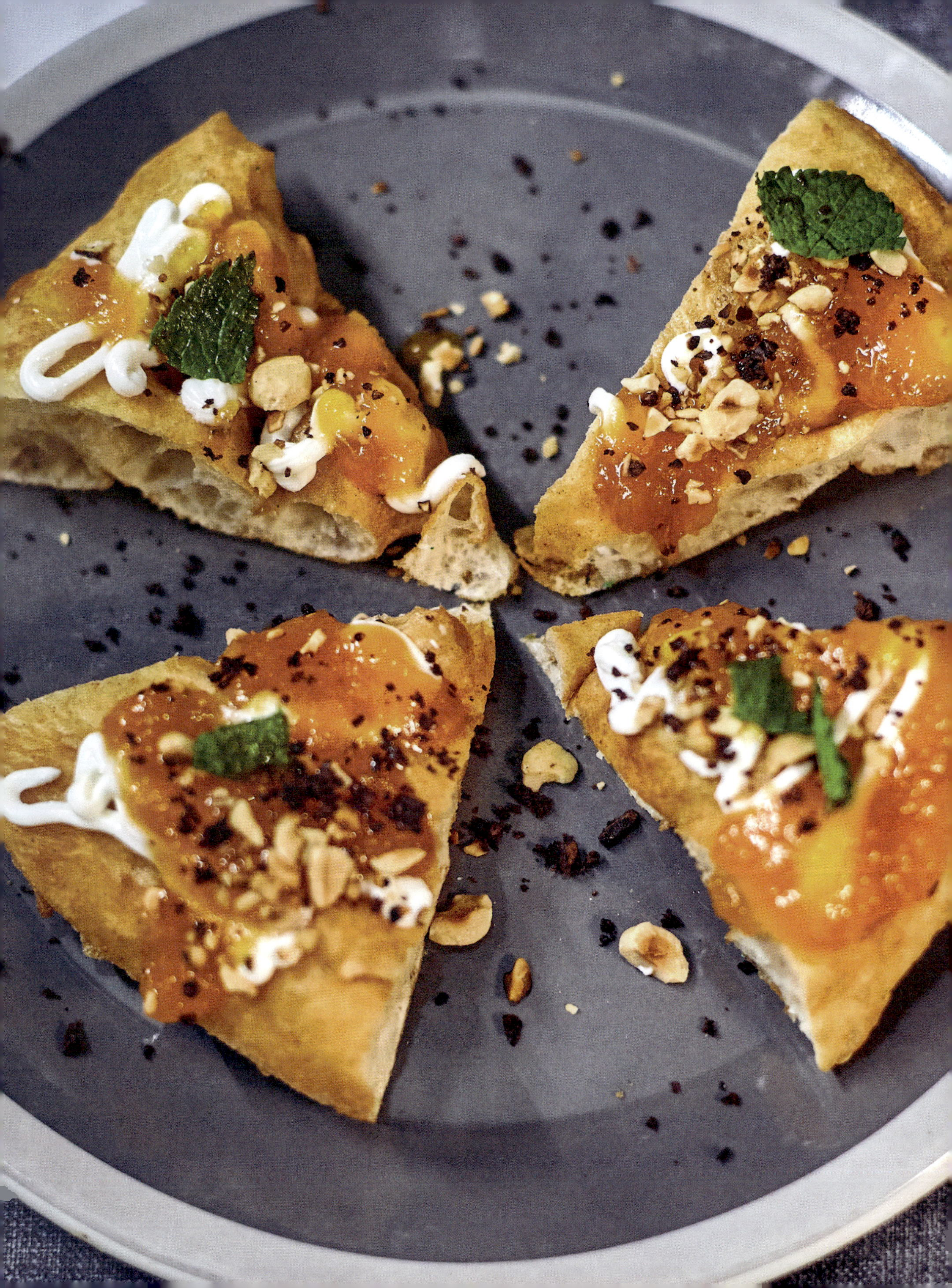

LA CRISOMMOLA

What you need

deep-fried pizza base (try using the base from page 232)

buffalo ricotta mixed with a little orange zest

apricot jam

toasted hazelnuts

black olive powder

mint

What we think

Having this pizza as the dessert at the end of a 10-course pizza-tasting menu is something we didn't know we needed until we tried it!

This creation is a celebration of the local produce that Pepe is so passionate about.

ERRICO PORZIO

PIZZERIA Errico Porzio
s'adda sape fà

Errico Porzio seems to be the new big name in Napoli for pizza. He is famed for his entertaining social media content and being a stickler for the rules. You will NOT see him put pineapple on pizza. Online he has a funny, almost Charlie Chaplin-like, slapstick persona. In real life he is quite serious about his pizza, and clearly a businessman. His empire is growing and he has just expanded out of Napoli, into Rome. One of his pizza creations got a lot of media attention recently; it is a kind of tasting menu of pizza, all on one plate. Move aside four seasons, Errico's in town...

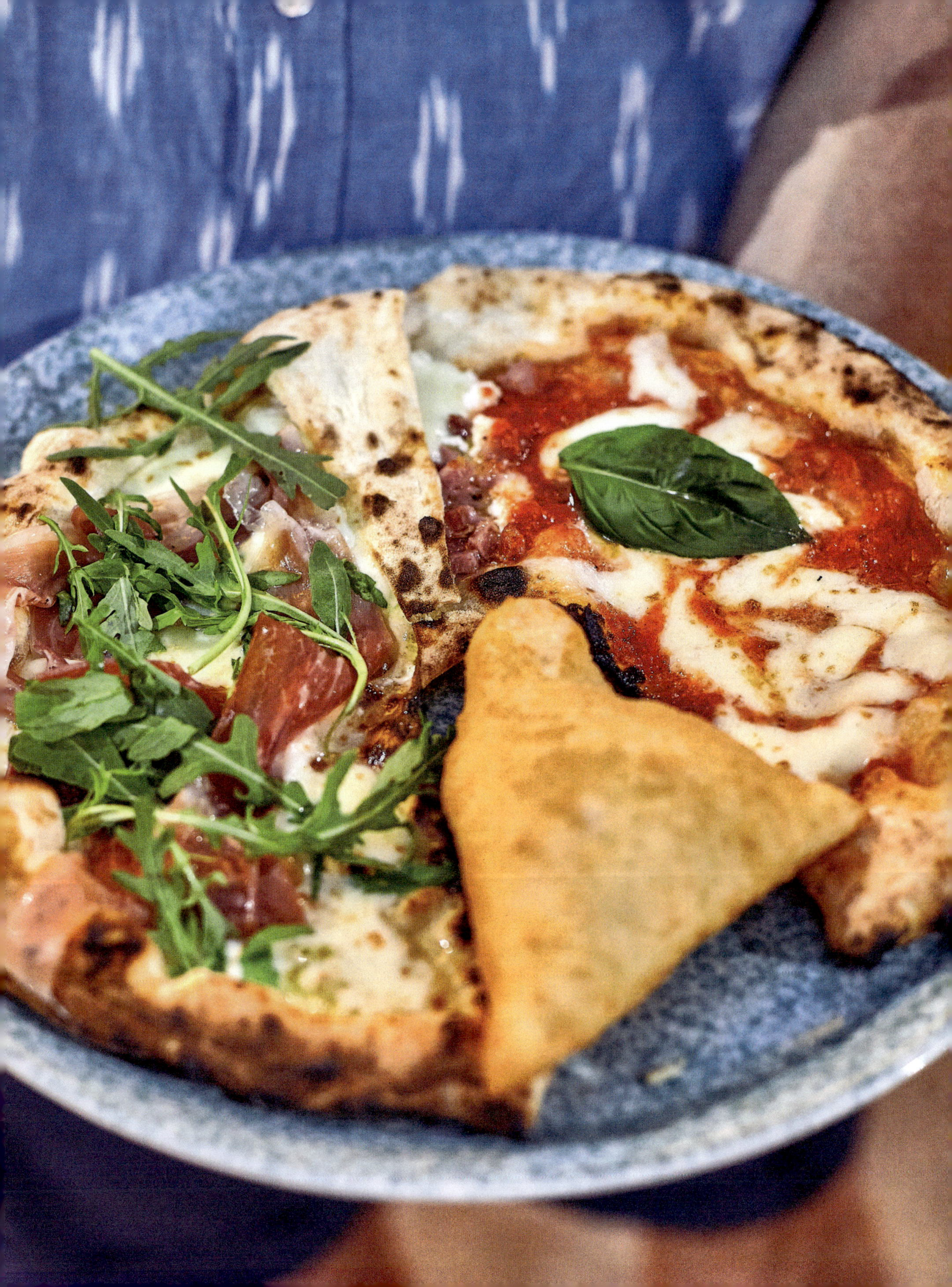

POKER

What you need

contemporanea pizza dough (page 93)

tomato sauce (page 190 or 209)

fior di latte mozzarella

basil

extra virgin olive oil

Napoli salami

ricotta

provola (smoked) mozzarella

mushrooms (sliced chestnut/cremini, either from a jar, or sautéed in olive oil)

neutral frying oil

prosciutto di Parma

rocket (arugula) leaves

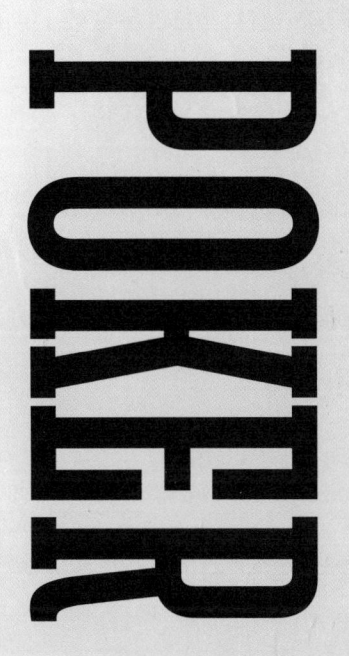

How to make it

Stretch a ball of dough out and, using a pizza wheel, cut a V shape into one quarter like a slice, leaving it connected in the middle.

Top one quarter with tomato sauce, fior di latte, basil and olive oil.

Top another quarter with sliced Napoli salami, ricotta and olive oil and fold the slice-shaped piece of dough over to create a calzone.

Top another quarter with provola and olive oil.

Stretch it onto the peel, ensuring that you leave a one-quarter-sized hole.

Bake in the oven for 2–3 minutes, until the crust is baked and the mozzarella has melted.

In the meantime, stretch another pizza ball out and cut out one quarter of it. Fill this quarter with mushrooms and mozzarella, then fold and seal it into a triangle roughly the same size as the hole left in the first pizza.

Heat your neutral frying oil to 180°C (356°F) in a deep-sided pan, deep enough to cover your stuffed pizza pocket, then fry the pizza pocket for 4–5 minutes until golden brown.

Once everything is cooked, assemble the pizza by adding in the pizza fritta to the baked pizza, then top the provola section of the pizza with prosciutto di Parma and rocket.

Pizza Legends

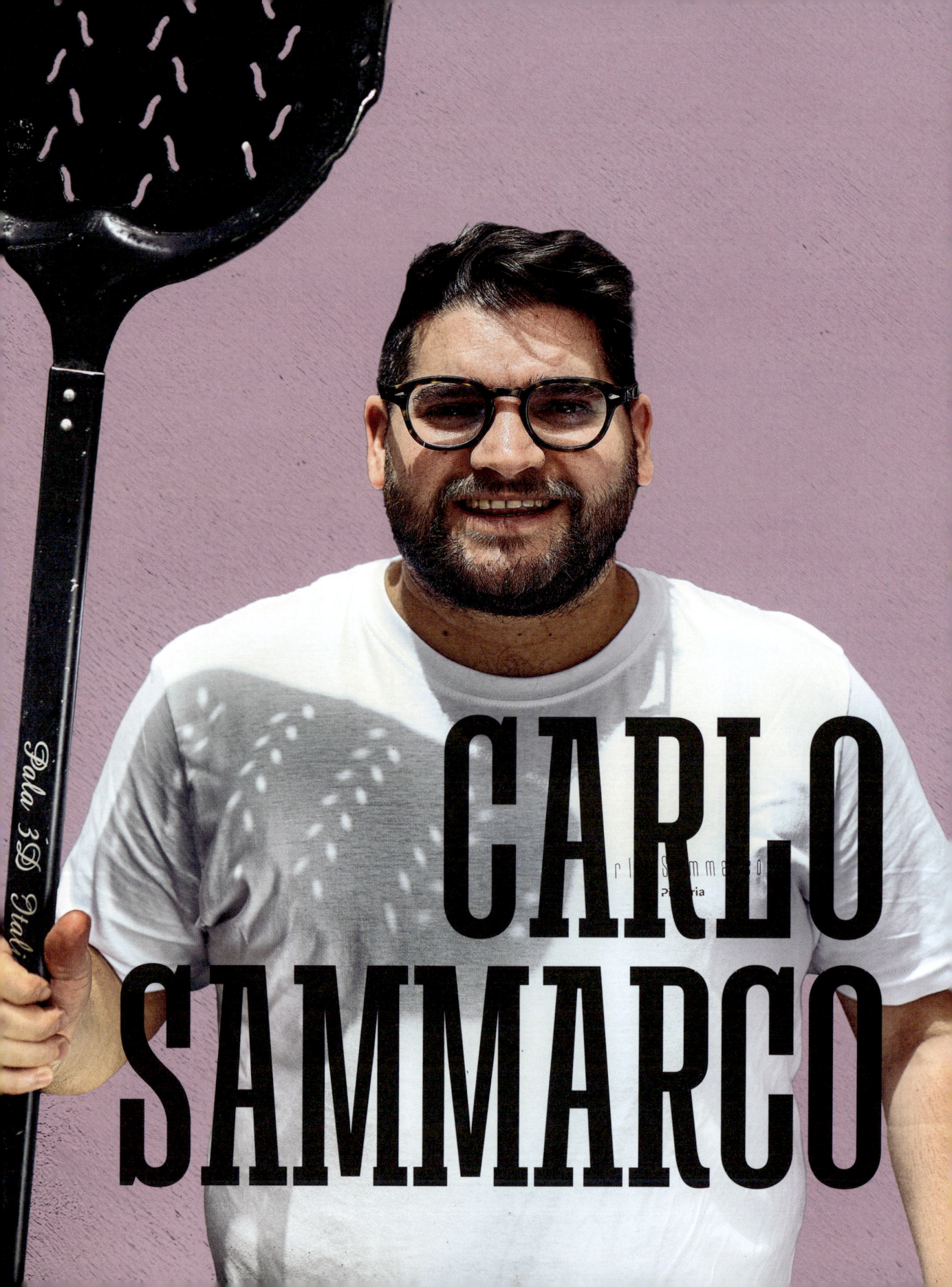

CARLO SAMMARCO

Carlo Sammarco
Pizzeria

Carlo picks up a purple potato that he imports from France ('it looks like a dog shit!') and breaks into a full belly laugh. That pretty much sums up Carlo Sammarco. He is obsessed with seasonal produce and colour but doesn't take himself too seriously. Carlo is part of a growing group of young, marketing-savvy pizza personalities who are developing brands that aren't just about the pizza. He's based on the outskirts of Caserta and we walk from sweltering 40°C (100°F) June heat into his giant, sleek pizzeria with ice-cold air con and a living moss wall on one side. There are about 200 seats inside, and still queues out the door. Any pizzeria on the outskirts of town that can pull numbers like that must be very special. As we step into the kitchen, Carlo's energy is clear. He bounces round the kitchen, picking up ingredients and jamming them in our hands to try. The kitchen is a hive of activity and you can tell that his team love him.

Carlo grew up in a restaurant on Piazza Garibaldi in Napoli, a tough area near the station. He says by aged 13 he was smitten with pizza and has never looked back. He loves the city and says that Napoli is best pizza city in the world because the ingredients are unrivalled. He picks up a basil leaf the size of a Porterhouse steak: 'See this? This only grows like this outside Caserta in the month of June. You can't beat that!'

Carlo changes his menu four times a year because seasonality is the most important thing to him. He also says that colour has to be one of the first things you think about when it comes to making pizza because 'your eyes have taste buds'.

These three pizzas are the ones that represent him and his team the best: fun, delicious and colourful!

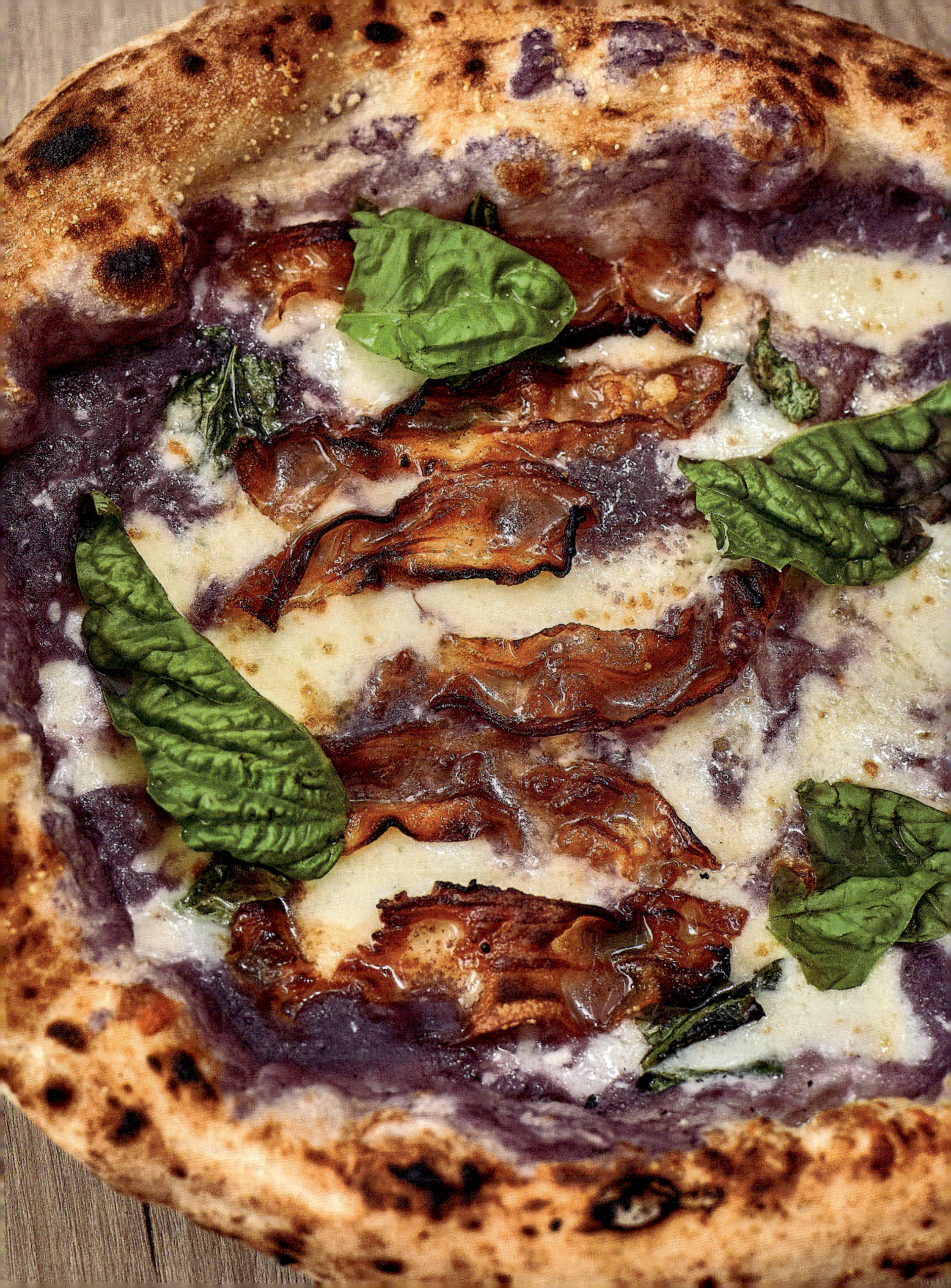

VELOUTÉ

What you need

STG pizza dough (page 92)

purple French potatoes (see below)

basil

Parmesan

fior di latte mozzarella

pancetta from the black pigs of Caserta

How to make it

Stretch a ball of dough out and spread with a base of potatoes. Top with basil, grated Parmesan and mozzarella before finishing with pancetta slices.

Bake in the oven, then finish with some extra basil leaves.

For the purple potatoes (makes enough for 4 pizzas)

200g (7oz) purple potatoes from France

extra virgin olive oil

sea salt

Boil the potatoes until soft, then push through a potato ricer (mashing is also fine, but make sure you get it really smooth). Add olive oil and salt to taste and allow to cool.

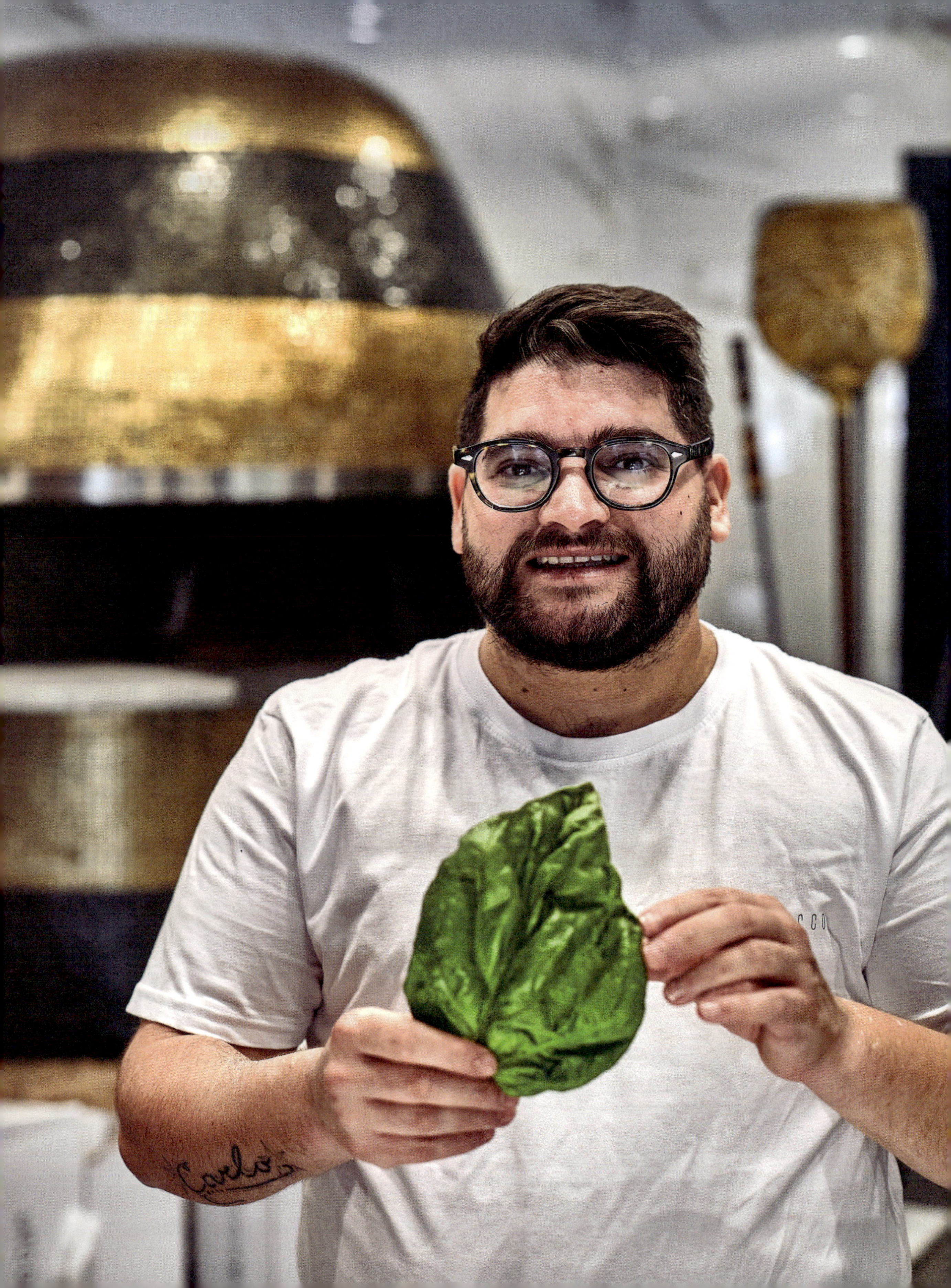
Carlo

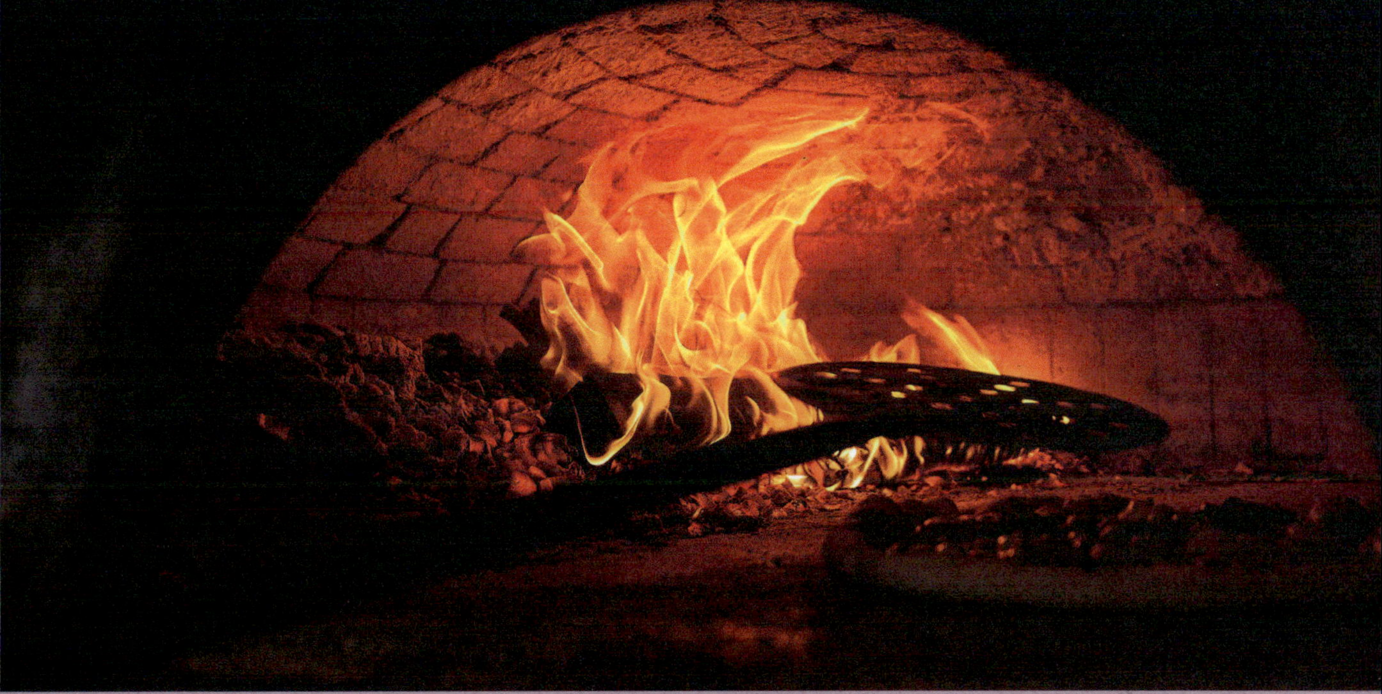

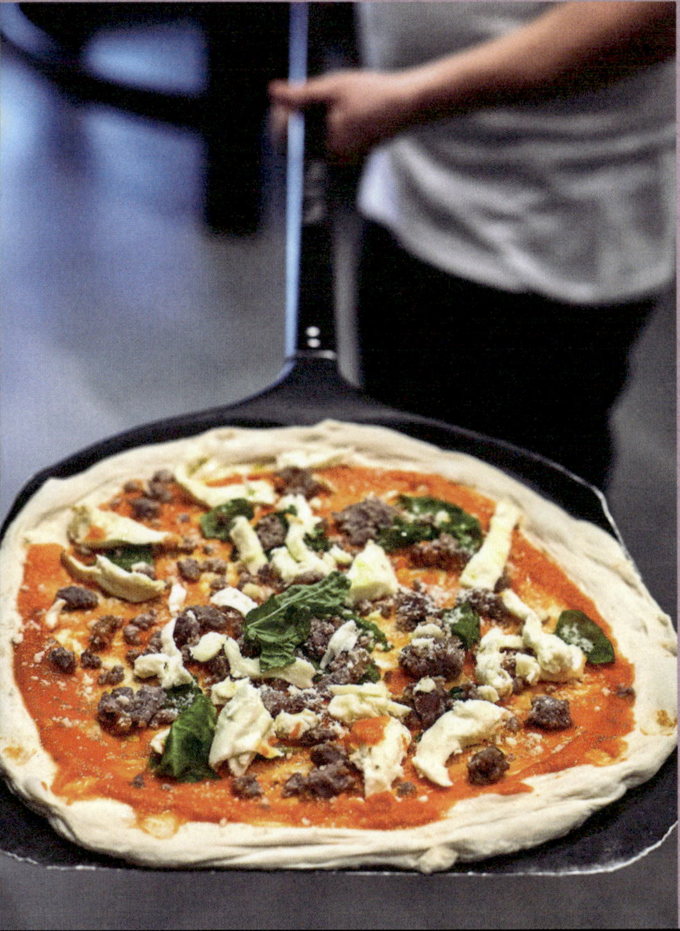

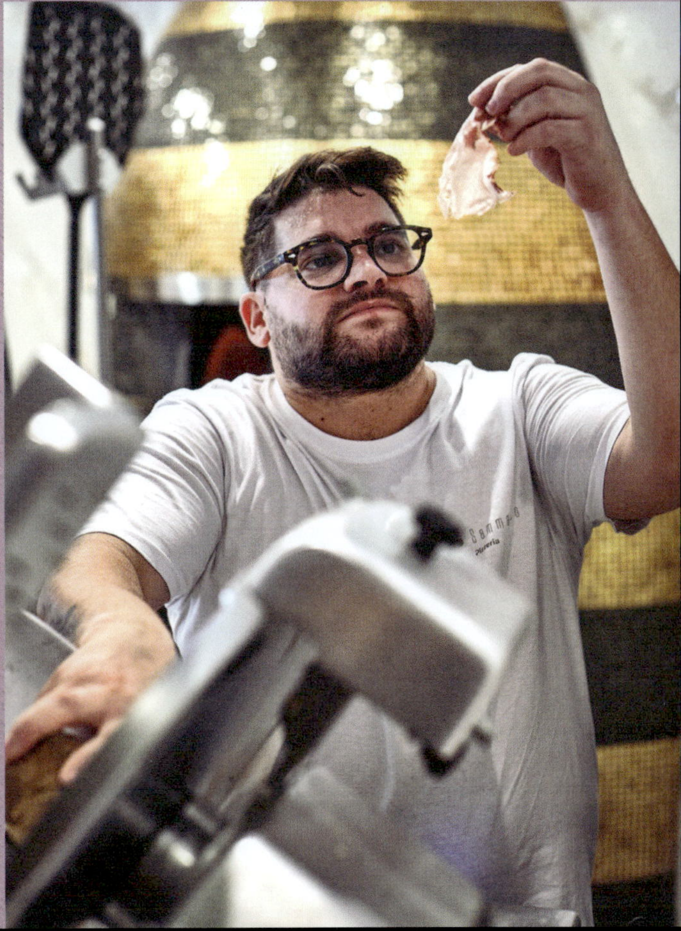

AUTUNNO

What you need

STG pizza dough (page 92)

provola (smoked) mozzarella

chiodini mushrooms (see below, or use jarred)

extra virgin olive oil

Capocollo di Martina Franca (a cured pork salami that comes from the neck of the pig), sliced wafer thin

basil

How to make it

Stretch a ball of dough out and arrange some provola and mushrooms on the base. Drizzle with some olive oil.

Bake in the oven, then drape over 6–8 slices of capocollo. The heat from the pizza will soften the fat and bring out the flavour.

Finish with basil leaves and a drizzle of olive oil.

For the chiodini mushrooms (makes enough for 4 pizzas)

250g (9oz) chiodini mushrooms (or any mushrooms will work here),

extra virgin olive oil

sea salt and freshly ground black pepper

Sauté the mushrooms in olive oil over a medium heat, adding salt and pepper to taste. Leave to cool.

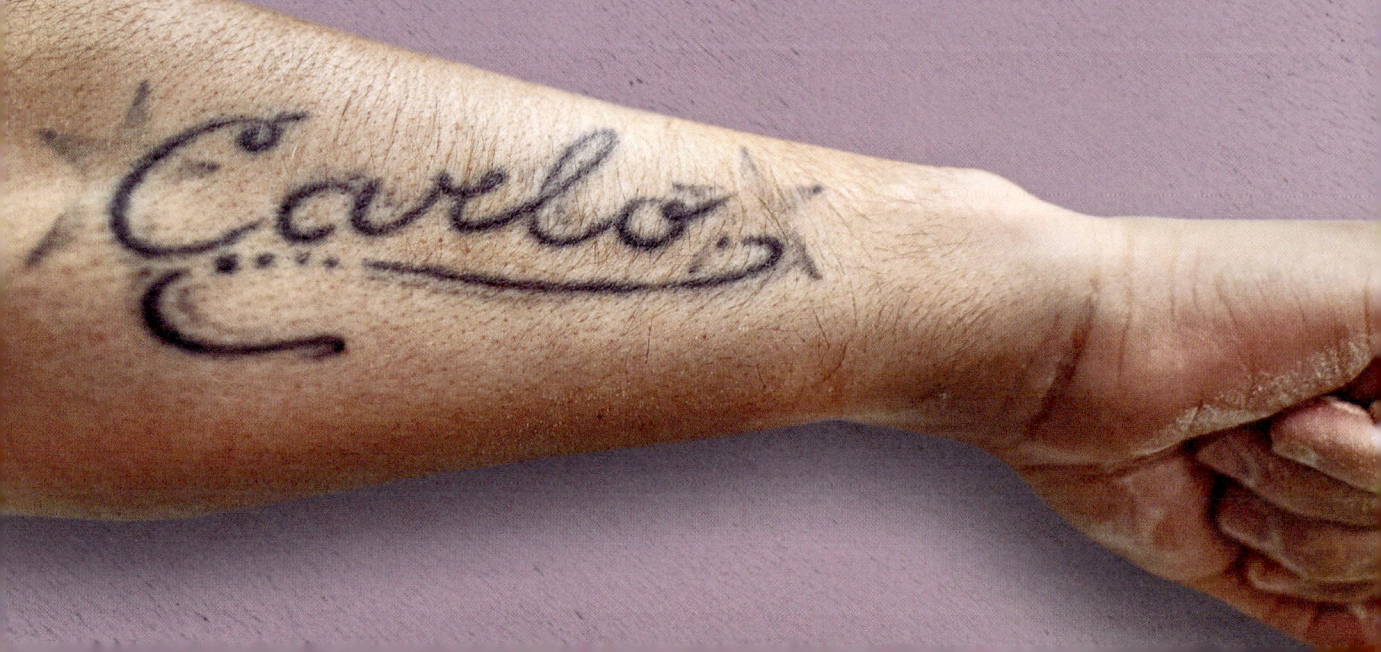

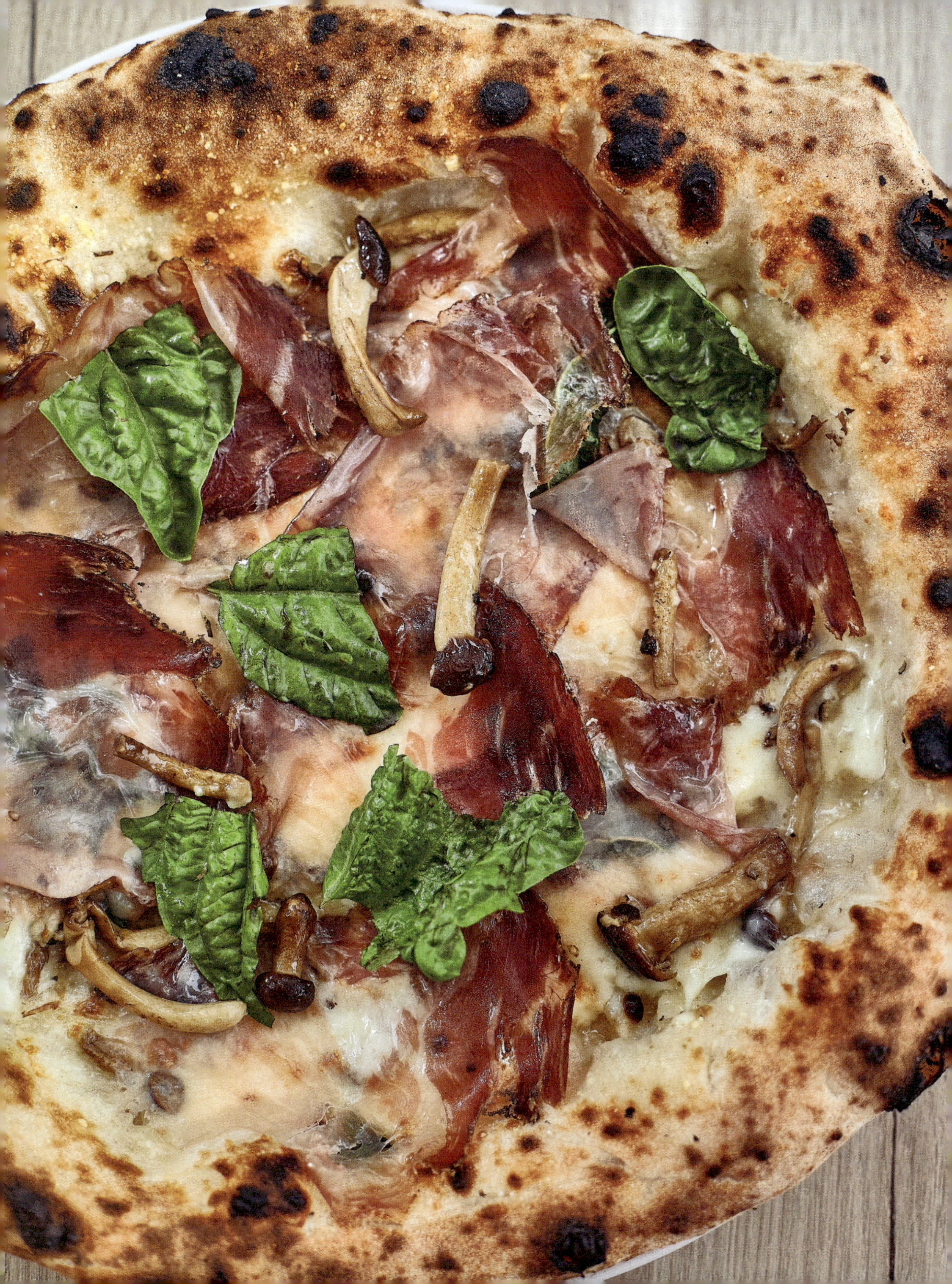

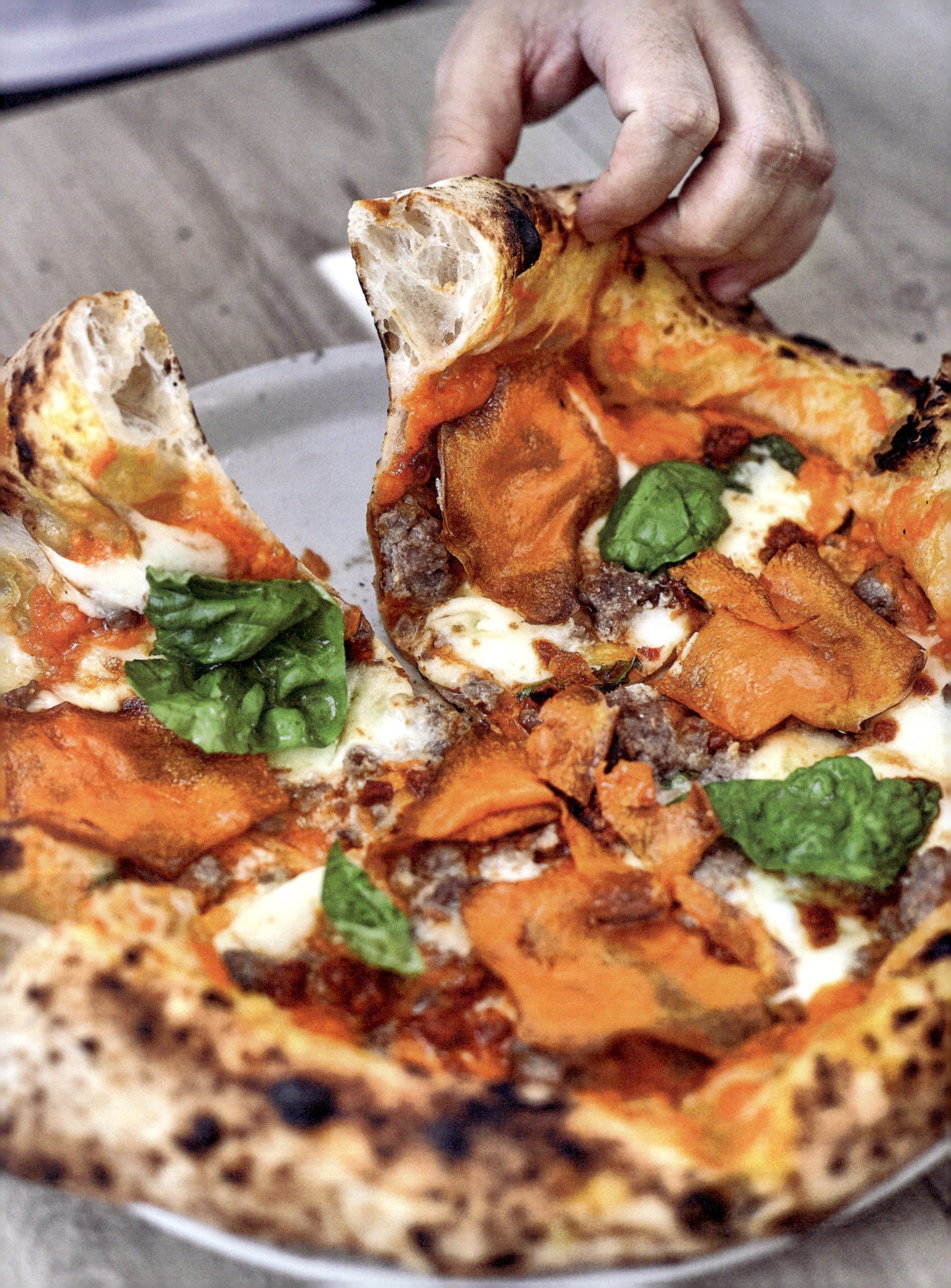

ZUCCA E 'NDUJA

What you need

STG pizza dough (page 92)

pumpkin purée (see below)

basil

cooked salsiccia

'nduja di Spilinga

provola (smoked) mozzarella

fried pumpkin slices (see below)

How to make it

Stretch a ball of dough out and spread the base with some pumpkin purée. Top with basil, salsiccia, 'nduja and provola.

Bake in the oven, then finish with the slices of fried pumpkin.

For the pumpkin purée and fried slices (makes enough for 4 pizzas)

240g (8oz) peeled pumpkin

extra virgin olive oil

2 garlic cloves, chopped

sea salt

Take three-quarters of your peeled pumpkin and cut it into 2cm (¾ inch) dice. Fry slowly in olive oil over a low heat, with the garlic and some salt, until tender. Once cooked, remove from the heat and blend with a stick blender, adding a splash of water if needed, to produce the consistency of tomato sauce.

Very thinly slice the remaining pumpkin. Heat a moderate layer of oil to 180°C (356°F) in a deep-sided pan, add the sliced pumpkin and fry until crisp and tender. Remove with a slotted spoon and leave to drain on kitchen paper.

CIRO CASCELLA

3.0
Ciro Cascella
Maestro Pizzaiolo

Ciro is a self-proclaimed *scugnizzo*, which roughly translates from Italian as 'street urchin'. The term has been romantically adopted by Neapolitans to refer to someone who grew up on the streets of Napoli, going to school only when they had to and generally hustling their way through life doing odd jobs and dabbling in petty crime. Imagine a kind of Neapolitan Artful Dodger character.

For Ciro, this is a badge he wears with pride. He got out of petty crime and became a pizza chef when he was 17 and 'stole' his pizza knowledge from the best. He says that his upbringing deeply connects him to the city and his pizza is a reflection of that. He called his pizzeria Ciro Cascella 3.0 to signify his pizza philosophy of respecting the traditions of the ancient pizza makers while embracing the innovations of the pizza contemporanea scene. And this is reflected in his pizza. He uses very traditional recipes like Genovese sauce, scarola (a bitter salad leaf) and cigoli (a pressed pork belly from Napoli) but adds puffy crusts, Instagram-friendly garnishes and slick, modern pizzeria interiors. These are his three signature pizzas that he says reflect his pizza philosophy best.

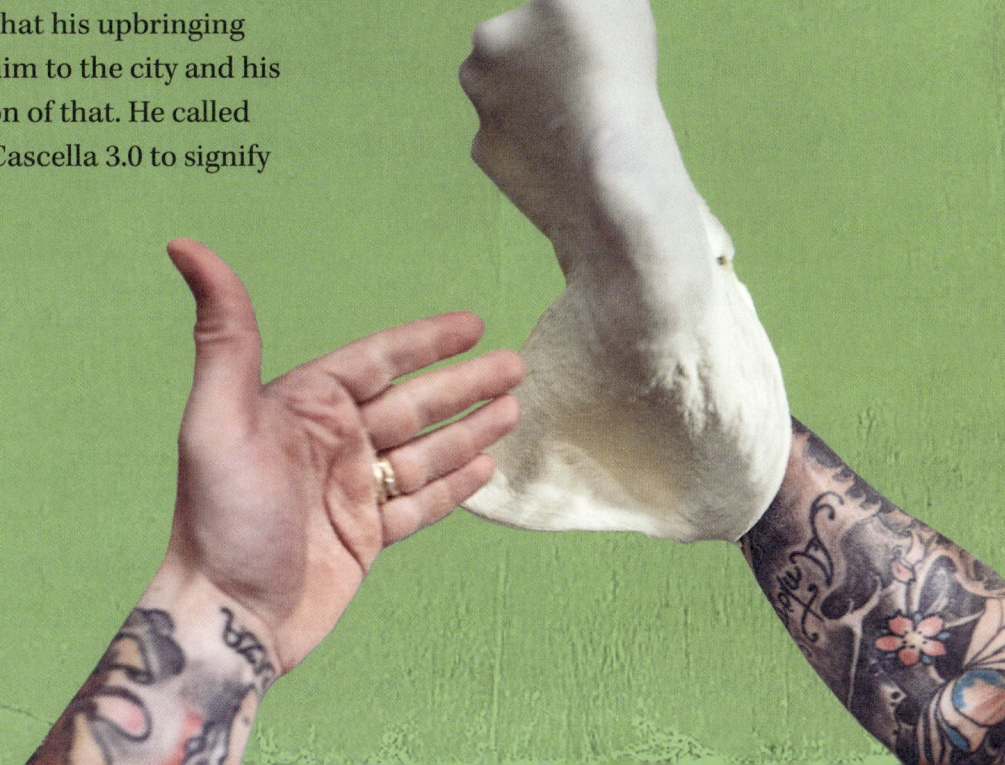

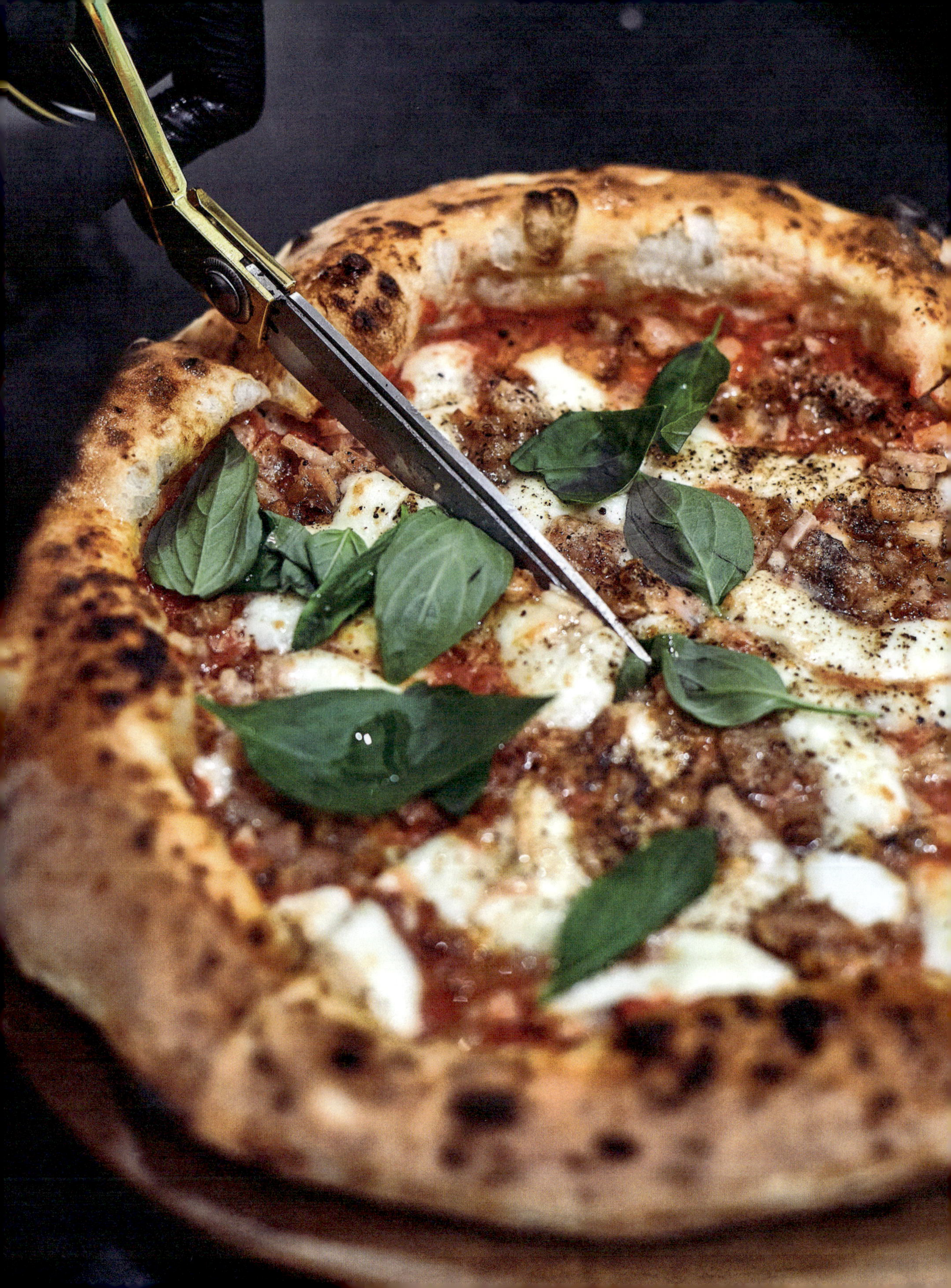

SCUGNIZZO PER SEMPRE

What you need

contemporanea pizza dough (page 93)

tomato sauce (page 190)

cubed cigoli (pressed pork belly from Napoli) or pancetta

provola (smoked) mozzarella

cracked black pepper

basil

extra virgin olive oil

How to make it

Stretch a ball of dough out, then spread the base with some tomato sauce. Top with cigoli, provola and some cracked black pepper.

Bake in the oven, then finish with basil leaves and a drizzle of extra virgin olive oil on the crust.

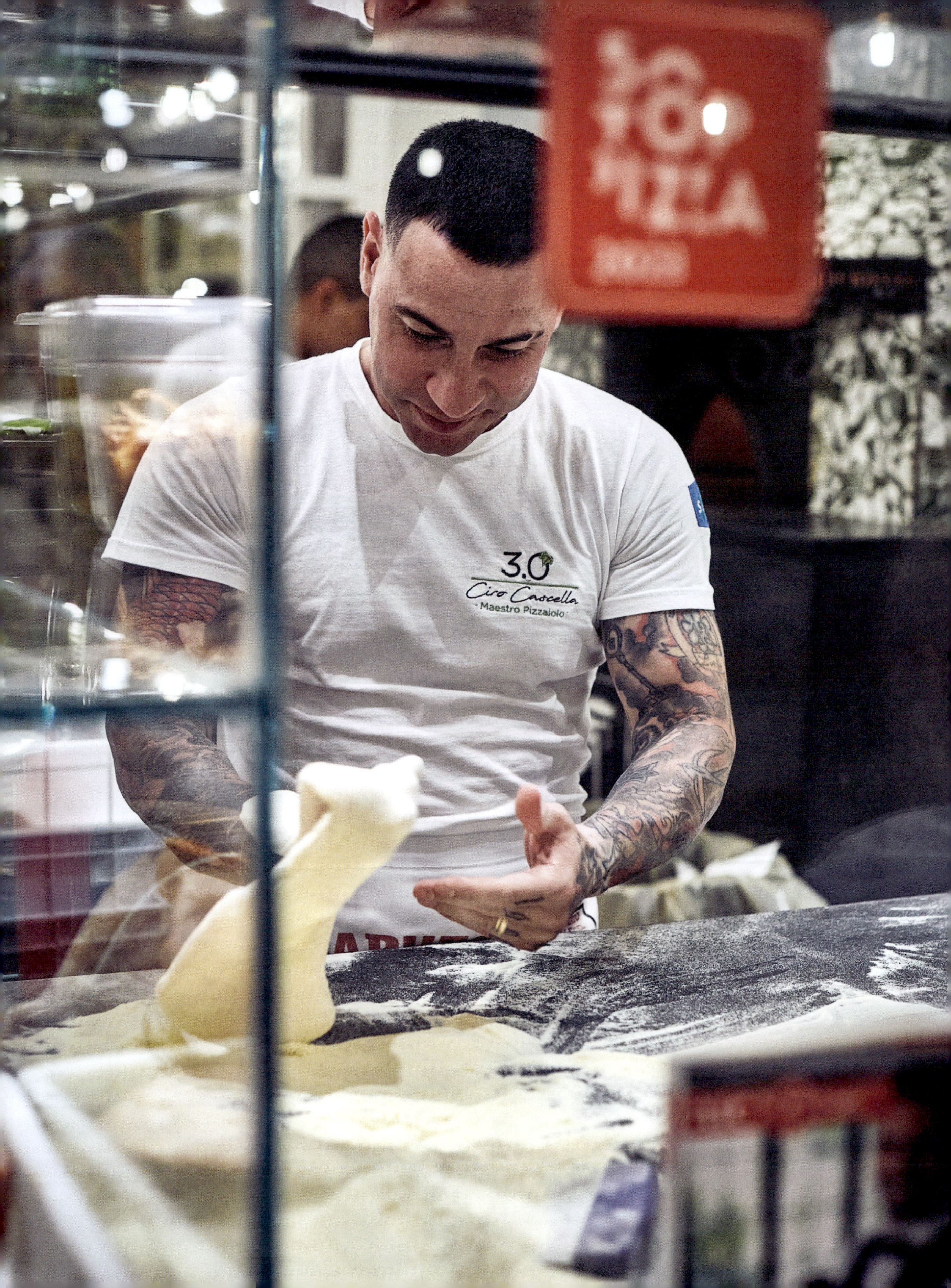
3.0
Ciro Cascella
- Maestro Pizzaiolo -

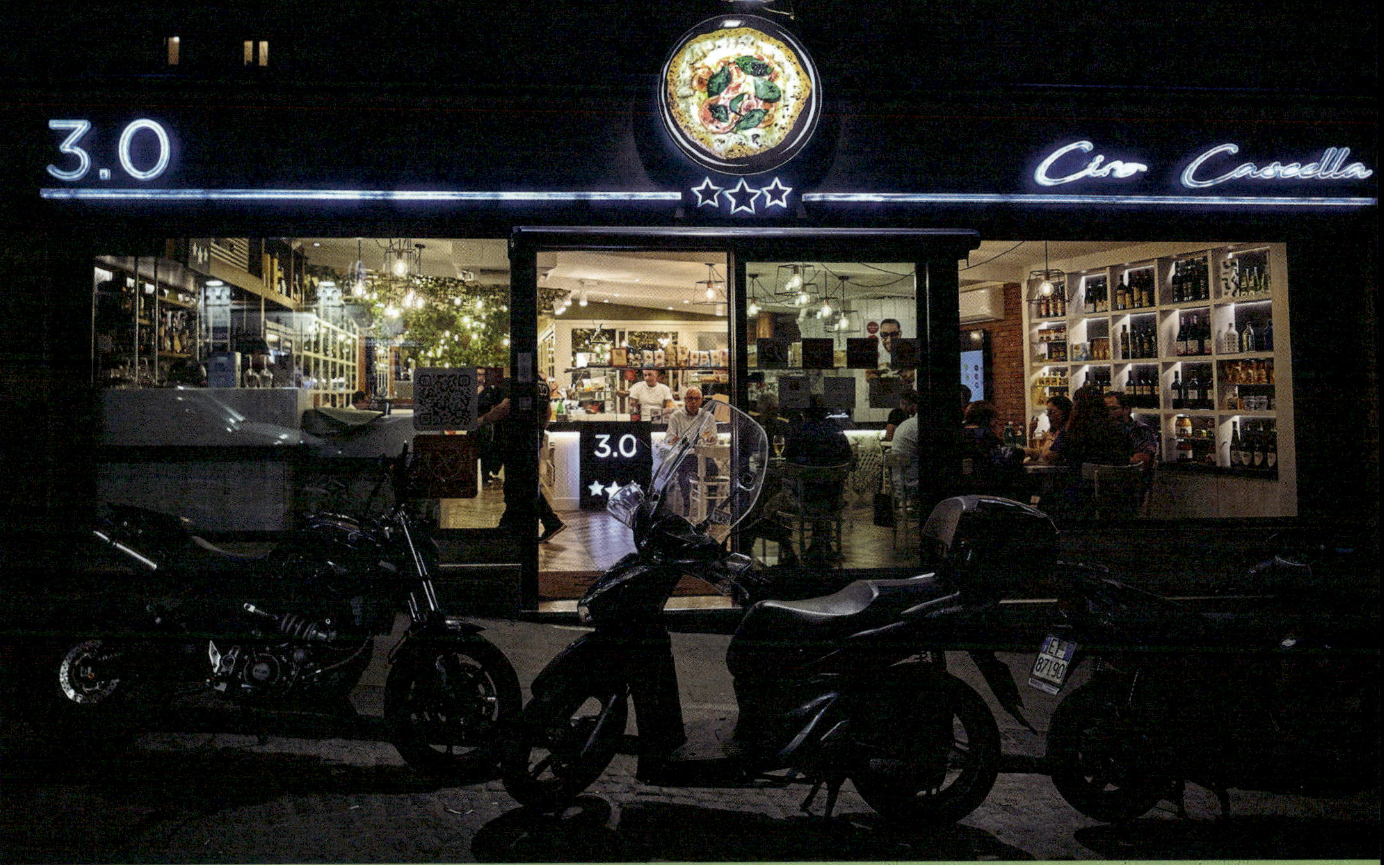
3.0
Ciro Cascella
3.0

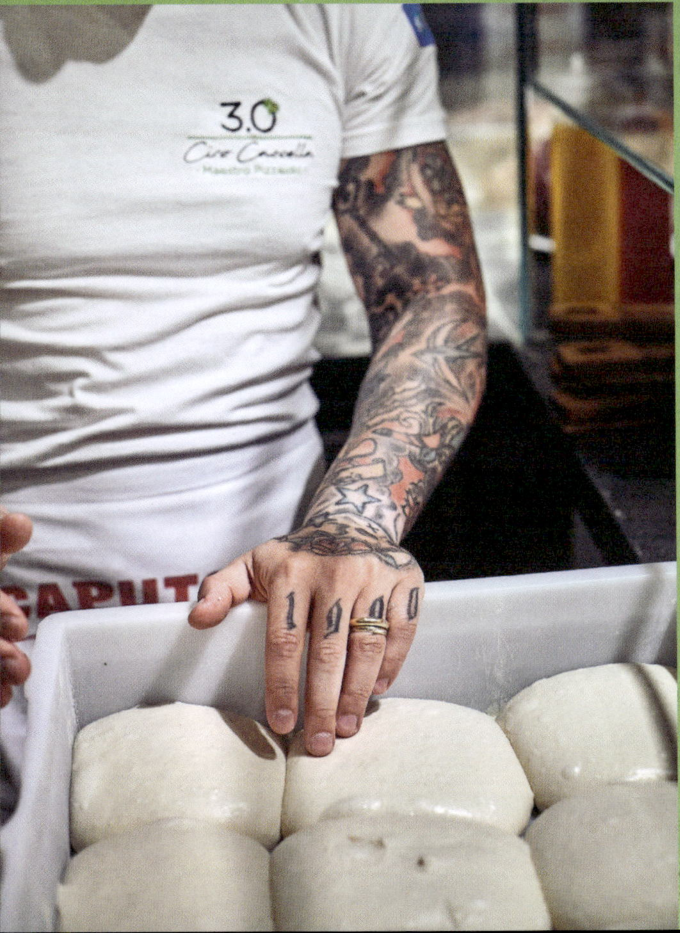
3.0
Ciro Cascella

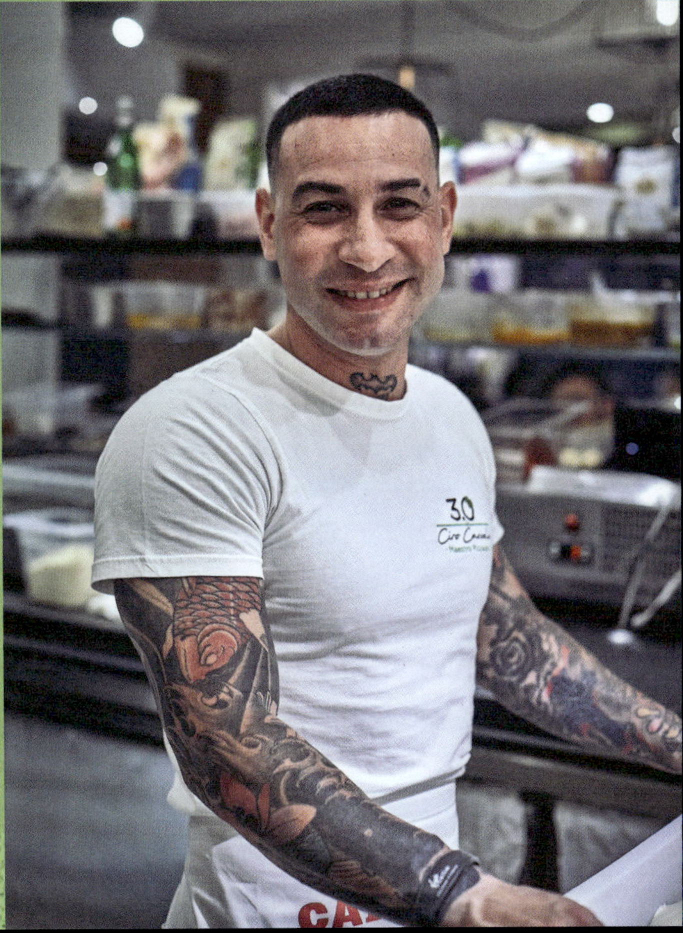
3.0
Ciro Cascella

ECCELLENZA CAMPANA

What you need

contemporanea pizza dough (page 93)

tomato sauce (see below)

buffalo mozzarella

Grana Padano

basil

extra virgin olive oil

How to make it

Stretch a ball of dough out and spoon on some tomato sauce. Top with the buffalo mozzarella and a generous sprinkle of grated Grana Padano.

Bake in the oven and finish with basil and olive oil.

For the tomato sauce (makes enough for 4 pizzas)

50ml (1¾fl oz) extra virgin olive oil

2 garlic cloves, chopped

400g (14oz) Piennolo tomatoes, halved

Heat the olive oil in a pan with the garlic until the garlic starts to take on some colour.

Add the tomatoes and season with salt to taste. Cook for 5–7 minutes until the tomatoes soften and the sauce reduces slightly. Leave to cool completely.

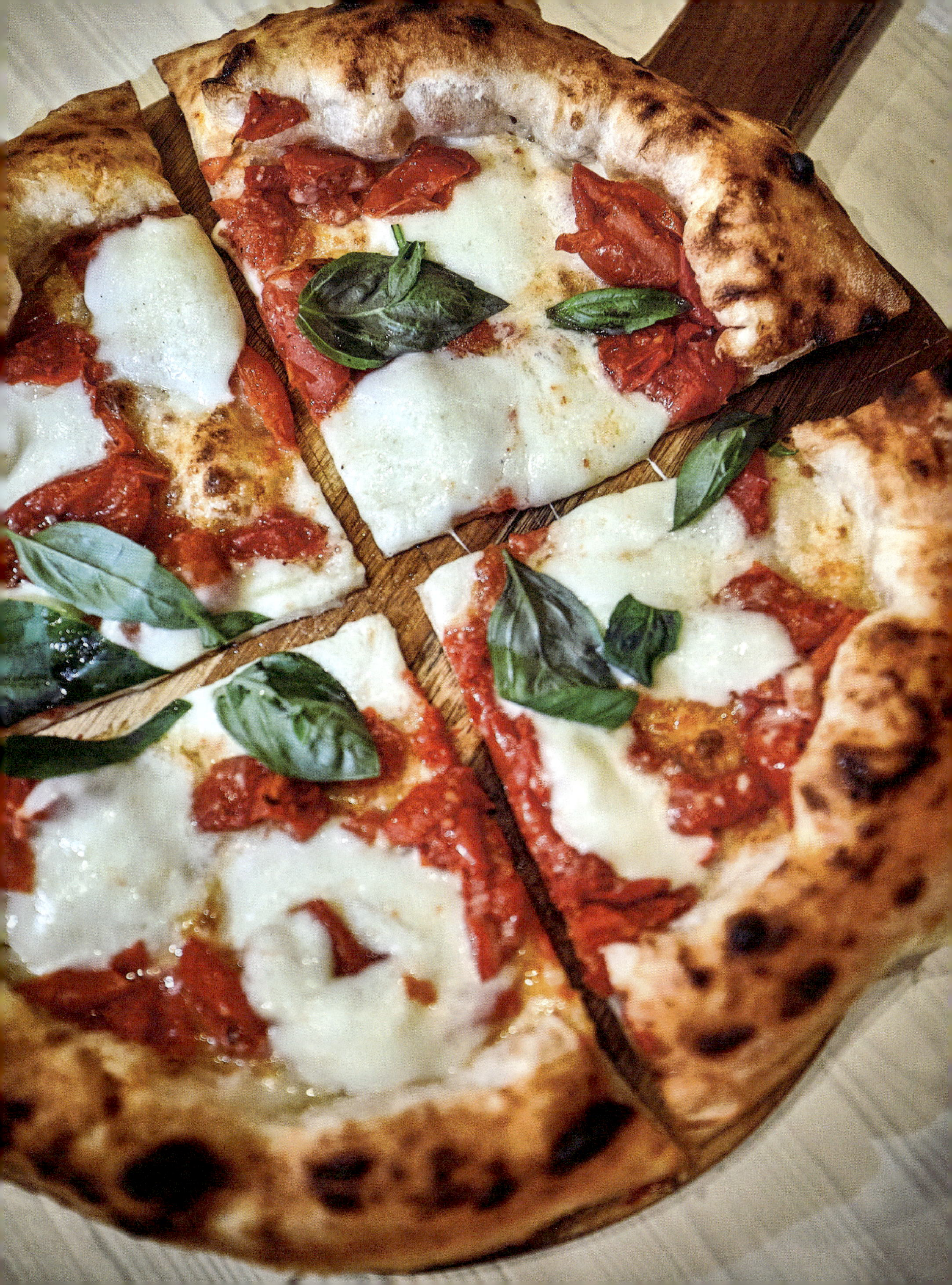

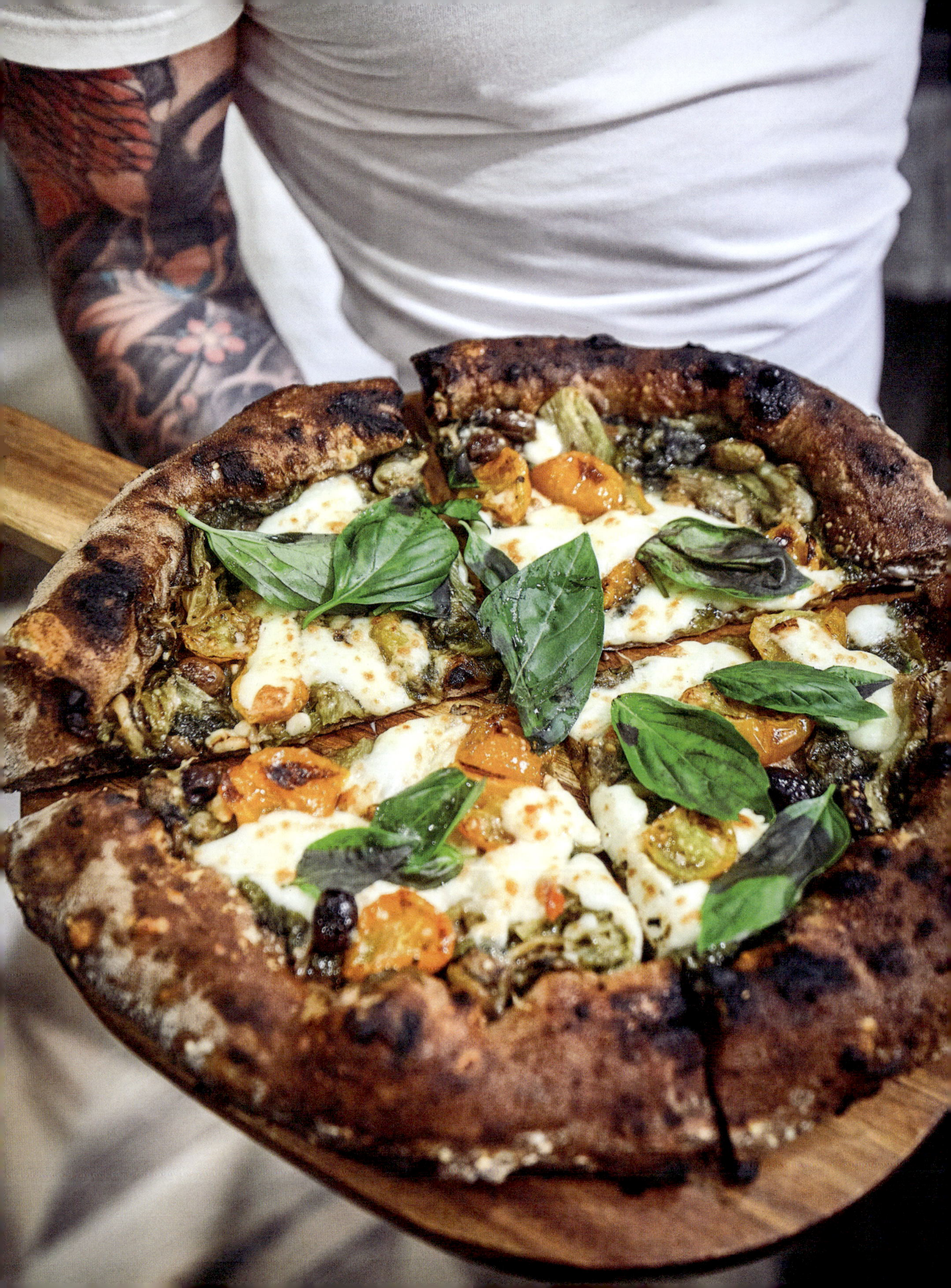

SOGNI

What you need

contemporanea pizza dough (page 93)

scarola (see below)

yellow cherry tomatoes

provola (smoked) mozzarella

Grana Padano

basil

extra virgin olive oil

How to make it

Stretch a ball of dough out and spread the base generously with your cooled scarola mix. Top with sliced yellow tomatoes, provola and grated Grana Padano.

Bake in the oven and finish with basil leaves and olive oil.

For the scarola (makes enough for 4 pizzas)

extra virgin olive oil

200g (7oz) scarola leaves (a bitter salad leaf from Napoli; endive/chicory will also work well)

sea salt

Heat some olive oil in a pan and drop in the scarola leaves with a pinch of salt. Gently cook for 3–5 minutes until the leaves have softened. Allow to cool.

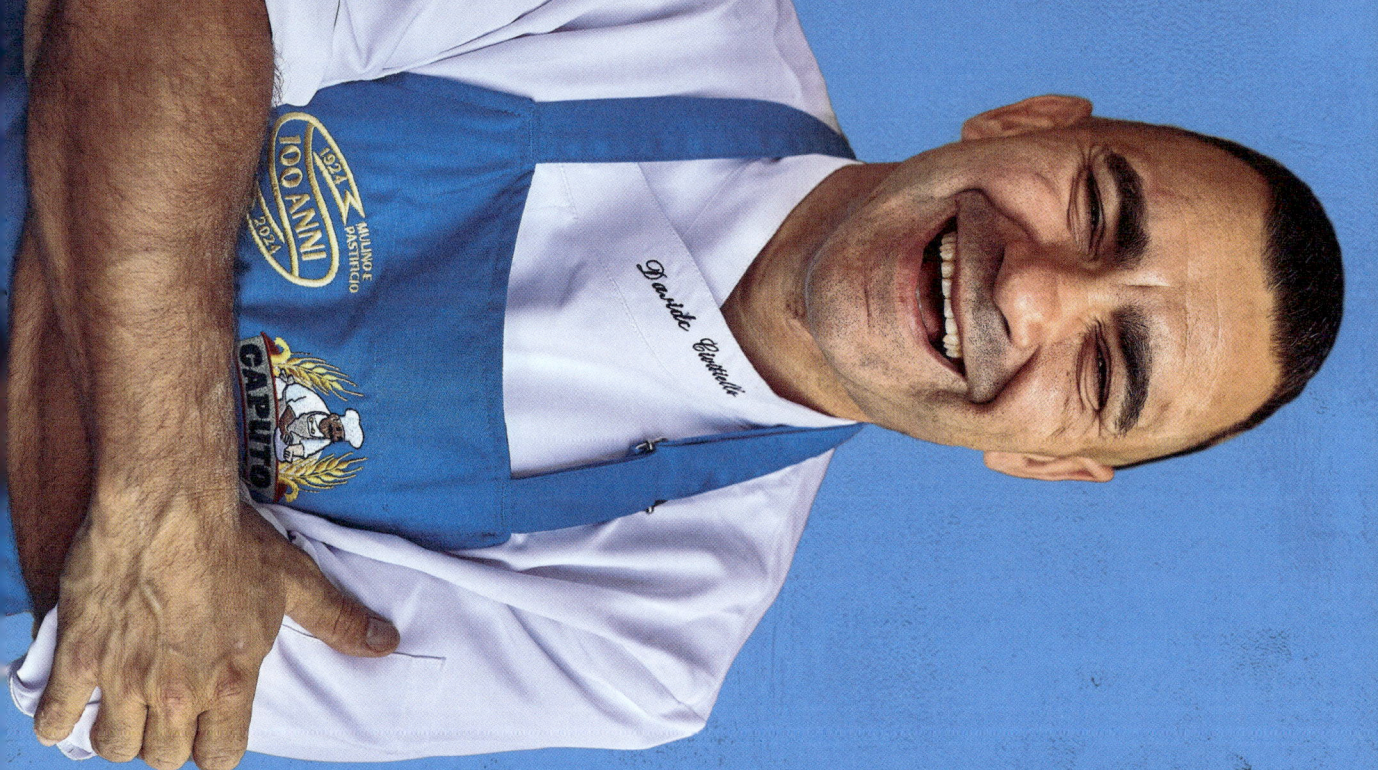

DAVIDE CIVITIELLO

Davide Civitiello

Davide has become a good friend over the years. We first met him through Antimo and the team at Mulino Caputo (page 48) back in 2013, when he had just become the Pizza World Champion. We had just started our first pizzeria and still had no idea what we were doing. He was so generous with his time and gave us lots of advice on everything from dough tips to how to look after pizza chefs from Napoli and how they like to work. Davide now travels the world spreading the good word of pizza in an official capacity for Caputo. When a new Neapolitan pizza scene kicks off, Davide is first boots on the ground, showing people how to maintain their wood-fired ovens and what the best proving technique is for the specific humidity of the country.

Davide is also the star judge every year at our annual head chef 'Doughdown' – a boxing-themed pizza competition we run at Pizza Pilgrims. He always gives incredibly eloquent feedback to our chefs, while also being a good sport and wearing giant blow-up boxing gloves. That is how much of a pizza legend Davide is.

We met up with him in Caputo's test kitchen and asked him to make three pizzas that reflected his style. Cool as a 'cetriolo', Davide nipped to the shops and came back with two bags of shopping. He knocked up these three pizzas on the fly and they may have been our favourite pizzas of the trip!

FILETTI DEL VESUVIO

This is a really simple pizza and is essentially a riff on a Marinara but using fresh tomatoes. All the ingredients that Davide uses are sourced from the foothills of Mount Vesuvius, which we understand might be difficult if you don't live in the foothills of Mount Vesuvius as Davide does. The best the supermarket has to offer will do fine, but this is a good pizza to make in summer when tomatoes are at their best.

What you need

Ruota di Carro pizza dough (page 90)

Piennolo tomatoes with basil and garlic (see below)

dried oregano

basil

extra virgin olive oil

How to make it

Stretch a ball of dough and scatter some of the tomato mix over the base. Bake in the oven.

To finish, sprinkle with a generous amount of dried oregano, top with basil leaves and drizzle with olive oil.

For the tomatoes (makes enough for 4 pizzas)

400g (14oz) Piennolo tomatoes

small handful of basil, torn

1 garlic clove, crushed

extra virgin olive oil

sea salt

Quarter the tomatoes and add to a bowl with the basil and garlic, then season with olive oil and salt to taste. Mix well.

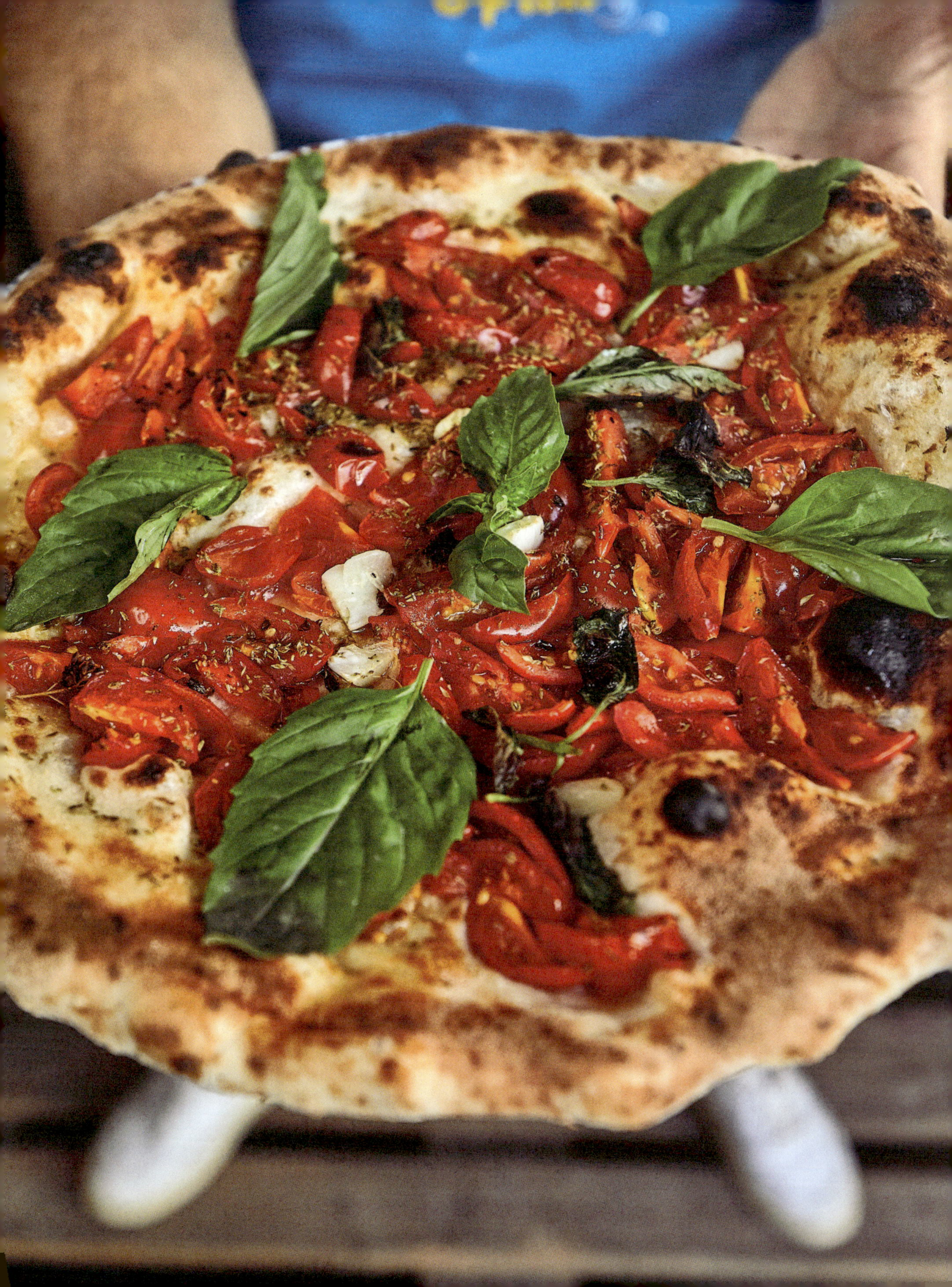

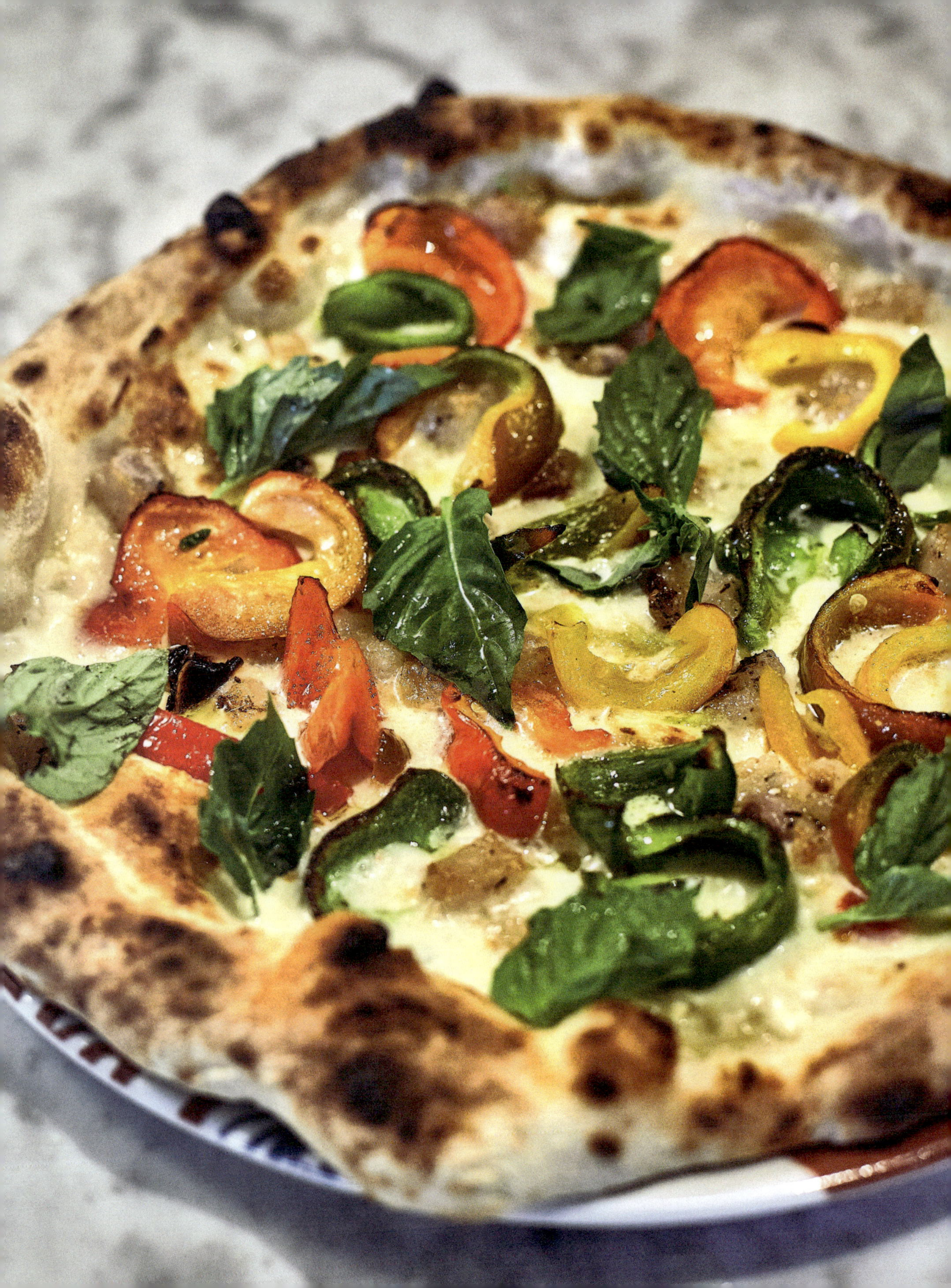

Papacella peppers are a specific type of bell pepper from Campania that are amazing when in season and have a perfumed, sweet flavour that is hard to beat. Davide pairs the peppers with big cubes of lardo to balance out their sweetness, and the combination is a winner.

What you need

Ruota di Carro pizza dough (page 90)

provola (smoked) mozzarella

Papacella peppers (see below)

lardo, cubed

Parmesan

basil

How to make it

Stretch a ball of dough out and spread the base with provola mozzarella.

Scatter over some of your cooled peppers and some lardo, then finish with a sprinkling of grated Parmesan.

Bake in the oven, then finish with basil leaves.

For the peppers (makes enough for 4 pizzas)

250g (9oz) Papacella peppers (regular bell peppers will work too)

extra virgin olive oil

sea salt

Remove and discard the pepper stalks and seeds, then cut the flesh into 1cm (½ inch) slices. Place in a roasting tin with oil and salt and roast in a hot pizza oven for 10 minutes until they have softened and charred at the edges. Set aside to cool.

LARDO E PAPACELLA

1924
MULINO E PASTIFICIO
100 ANNI
S. GIOVANNI A TEDUCCIO
2024
CAPUTO
Il mulino di Napoli - 1924

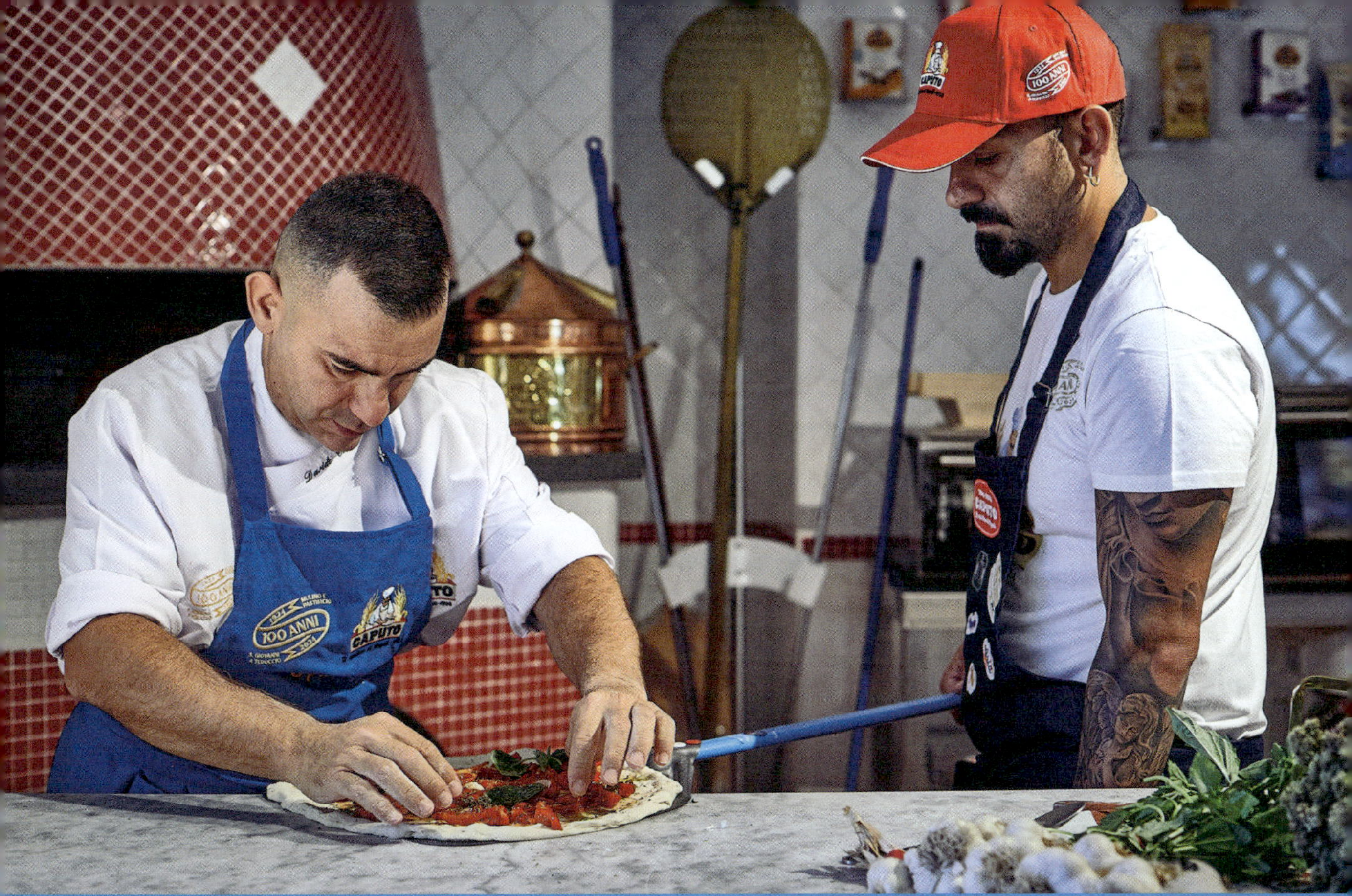
100 ANNI
CAPUTO

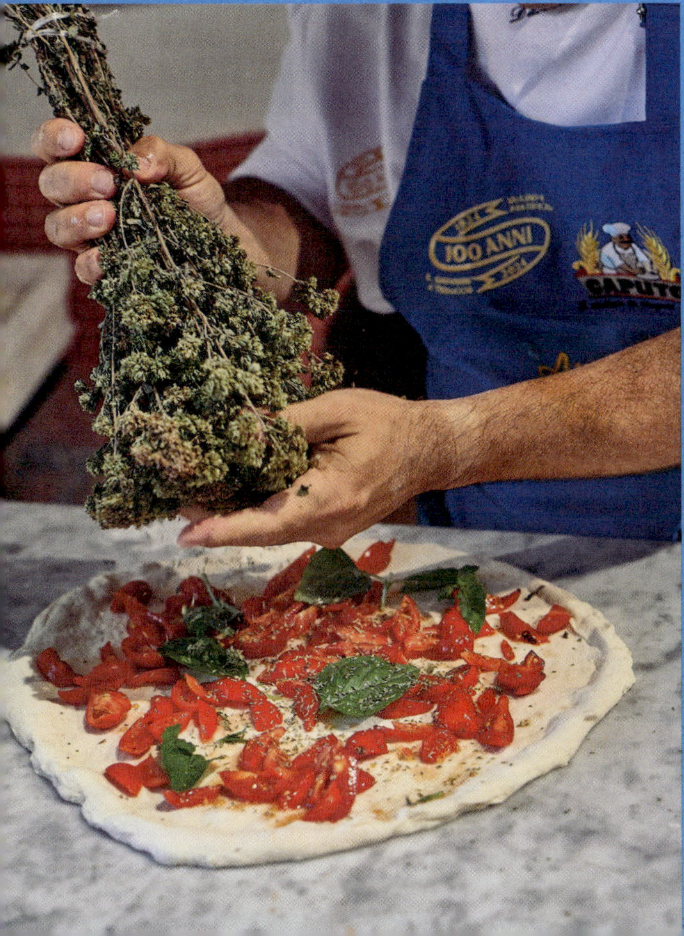
100 ANNI
CAPUTO

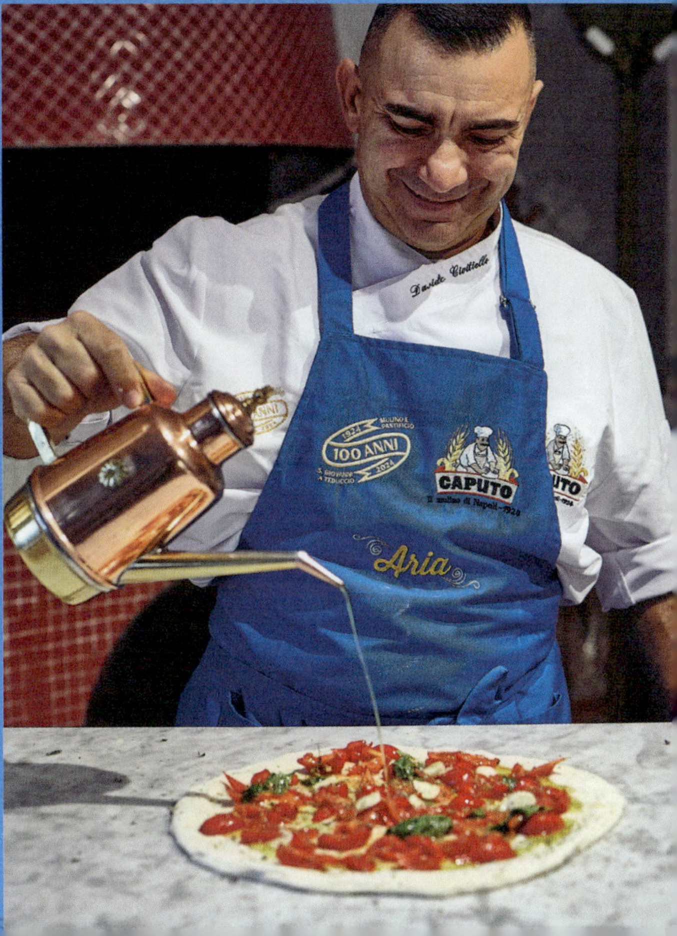
100 ANNI
CAPUTO
Aria

SALSICCIA E ZUCCHINI

What you need

Ruota di Carro pizza dough (page 90)

courgettes (zucchini), see below

provola (smoked) mozzarella

fresh Italian sausage

basil

extra virgin olive oil

cracked black pepper

How to make it

Stretch a ball of dough out and spread the base with the courgette mixture. Top with provola mozzarella.

Squeeze the sausage so that the sausage meat comes out of the casing, and drop bite-sized pieces of sausage meat over the pizza. Ensure the pieces are small enough to cook in the same time as the pizza dough.

Bake in the oven, then finish with basil leaves, a drizzle of olive oil and some freshly cracked black pepper.

For the courgettes (makes enough for 4 pizzas)

2 medium courgettes (zucchini)

extra virgin olive oil

sea salt

Using the wide-holed grater, grate the courgettes into a bowl, then season with olive oil and salt and stir well.

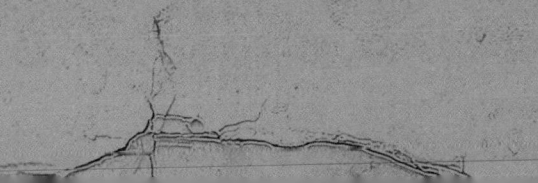

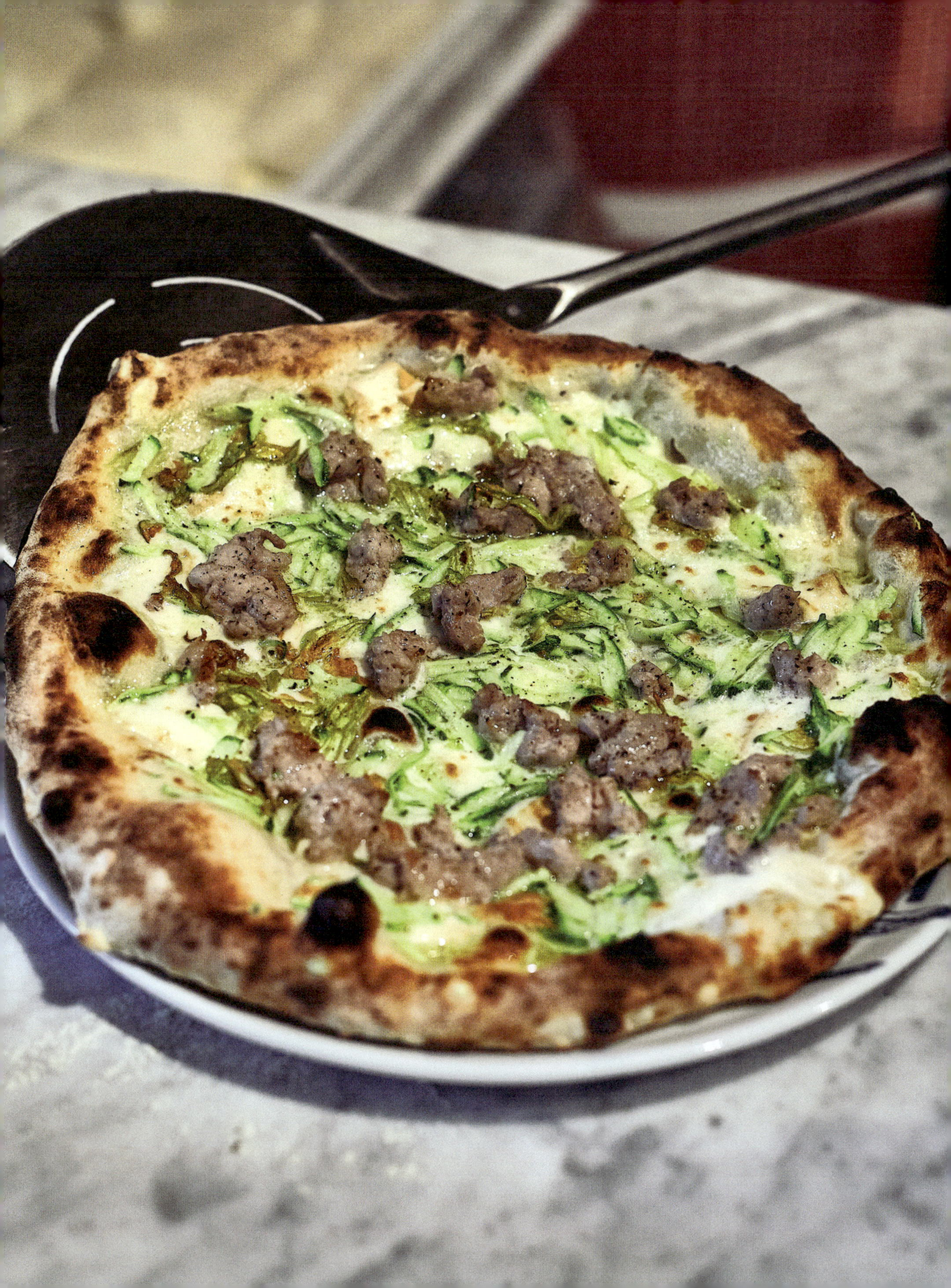

SALVATORE LIONIELLO

Lioniello

Salvatore Lioniello

When we arrived at the pizzeria just outside Caserta, we walked into the kitchen and were met with a giant pair of ovens in the shape of trilby hats. Salvatore, AKA The Pizza Chef with the Hat, arrived at the pizzeria two hours late with what can only be described as serious swag... A double espresso and a quick change into chef whites and the inimitable hat, and he was ready for business. Lioniello became famous for his disruptive style when pizza in Napoli was staunchly traditional. He was one of the first chefs to work with biga dough fermentation and high-hydration percentages (north of 75%) as well as collaborations with glamorous Michelin-starred chefs.

Lioniello and his brother Michele grew up in a pizzeria run by their father. He remembers 'electric oven, cheap ingredients; just a local place'. At first, he took no interest and became a builder, but before long he and his brother began to discuss how they could do things differently. They opened their first place in 2015 and began to work on their style. They started to create a menu of pizzas that pushed the boundaries of traditional Neapolitan pizza, leaning on techniques from high-end kitchens. Salvatore's kitchen is not like a normal pizzeria – there is a huge back cook line filled with fryers, grills, steam ovens and gadgets to prepare pizza toppings in inventive ways.

He says he was criticized at first and that the old-school pizza scene didn't like the way he was messing with tradition. They also said his pizzeria was too far from Napoli to visit. But slowly the pizzeria began to grow its reputation and today it sits firmly on the map as a sophisticated pizzeria serving incredibly inventive contemporary pizzas in a chic setting... they even have a mineral water menu.

It's a far cry from the pizza portafoglio (page 101) of the Spanish Quarter, but there is no doubt that his style helped inspire a new generation of pizza makers.

NERANO MONTENARA

What you need

pizza fritta dough (page 229)

neutral frying oil

courgette (zucchini) cream (see below)

stracciatella cheese

courgette flowers

lemon oil (page 215)

courgette chips (see below)

provolone

How to make it

Stretch the pizza dough evenly like a focaccia, ensuring no crust or thin middle. Heat the neutral frying oil in a deep-sided pan to 190°C (374°F). Add the dough and fry for 3–4 minutes until light golden brown.

Top the fried dough with courgette cream and bake for 2 minutes in the oven, then top the cooked pizza with stracciatella. Toss the courgette flowers with a little lemon oil, then drape these over the pizza. Finish with the courgette chips and some grated provolone.

For the courgette cream and chips (makes enough for 4 pizzas)

1 medium courgette (zucchini)

50g (1¾oz) grated provolone di Monaco, plus extra to finish

extra virgin olive oil

dried oregano

neutral frying oil

sea salt and black pepper

Thinly slice and boil three-quarters of the courgette until tender. Drain, then season with salt and pepper, the provolone, a glug of olive oil and a pinch of oregano. Blend until smooth in a food processor.

Finely slice the rest of the courgette and heat your frying oil to 180°C (356°F) in a deep-sided pan. Deep-fry the courgette slices for 4–5 minutes, until crisp, then set aside on kitchen paper to drain.

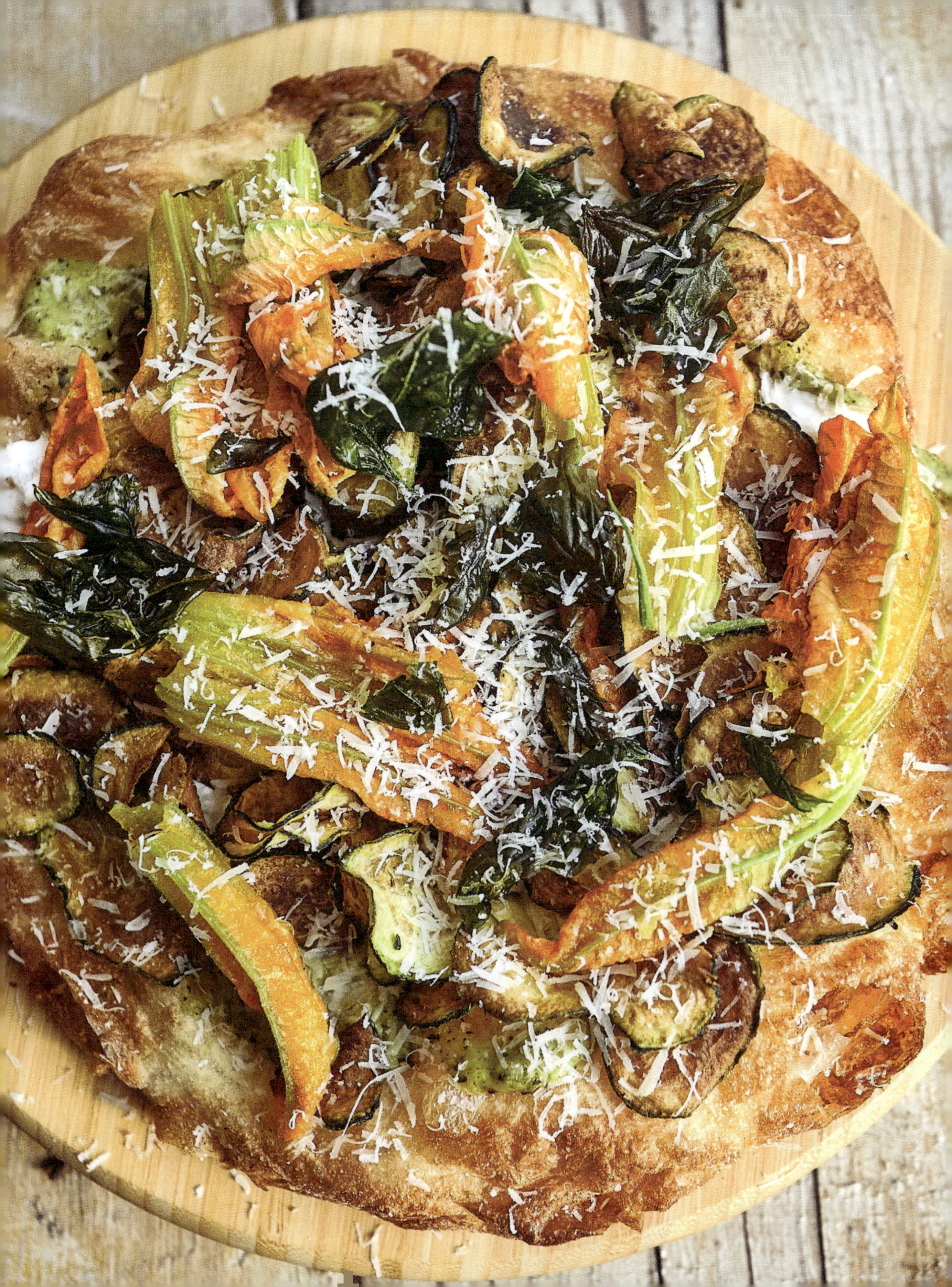

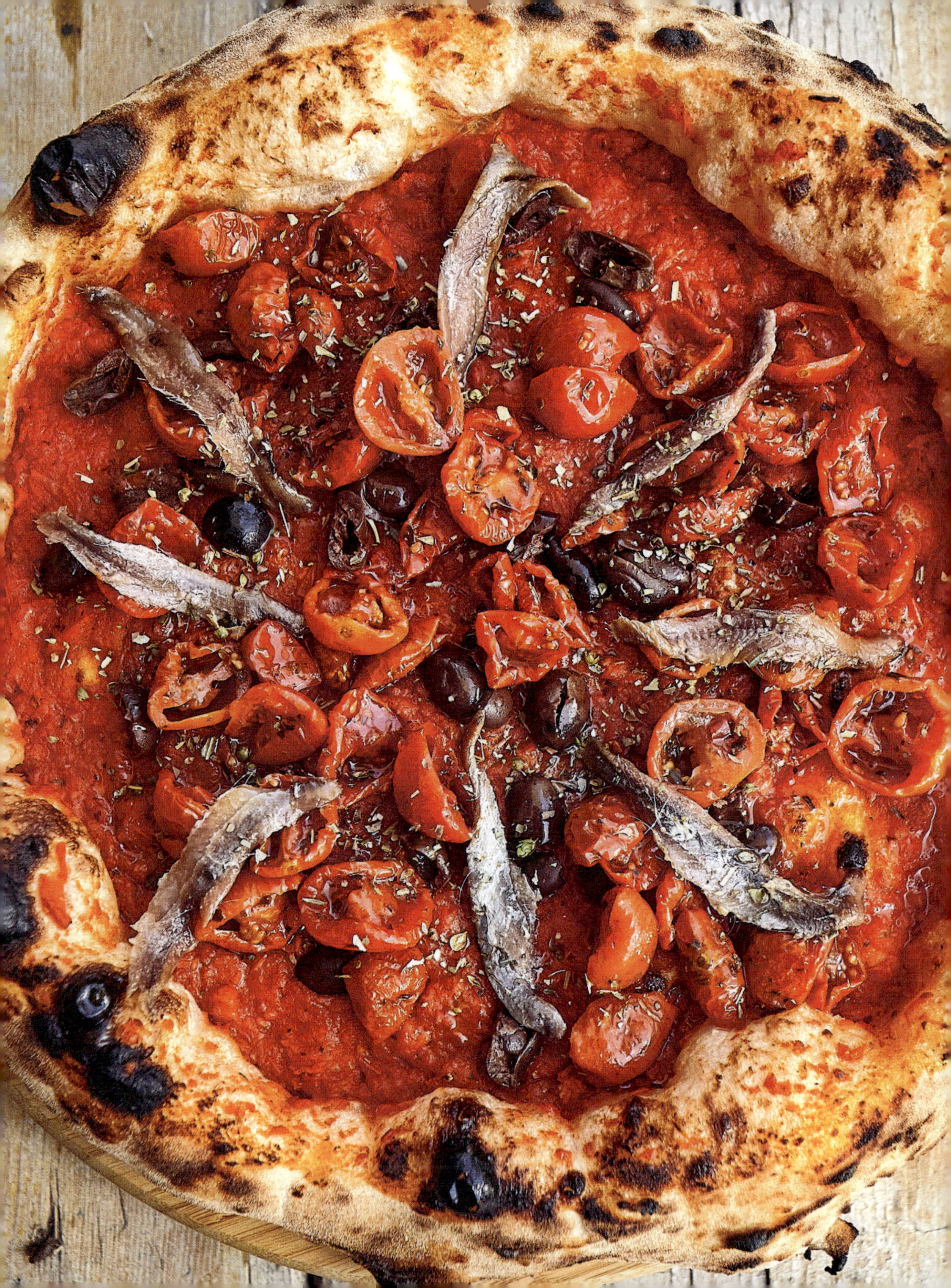

MARINARA DEI SIGNORI

What you need

STG pizza dough (page 92)

tomato sauce (see below)

roasted datterini tomatoes (see below)

Kalamata olives

Cetara anchovies

extra virgin olive oil

How to make it

Stretch a ball of dough out and spread the base with some tomato sauce.

Add some roasted datterini tomatoes, black olives, 8 anchovies and a drizzle of olive oil. Bake in the oven.

For the tomato sauce (makes enough for 4 pizzas)

1 garlic clove, finely chopped

good glug of extra virgin olive oil

400g (14oz) can of tomatoes

healthy pinch of dried oregano

Add the garlic and olive oil to a pan and cook until fragrant, then add the canned tomatoes and oregano and reduce by half.

For the roasted datterini (makes enough for 4 pizzas)

125g (4½oz) datterini tomatoes, halved lengthways

good glug of extra virgin olive oil

sea salt

Toss the halved tomatoes in olive oil and salt and roast for about 20 minutes in an oven set at 160°C fan (350°F) until slightly caramelized and jammy.

GOELDLIN
Salvatore Lioniello
lafiammante
GERLI
Quality Frozen Food

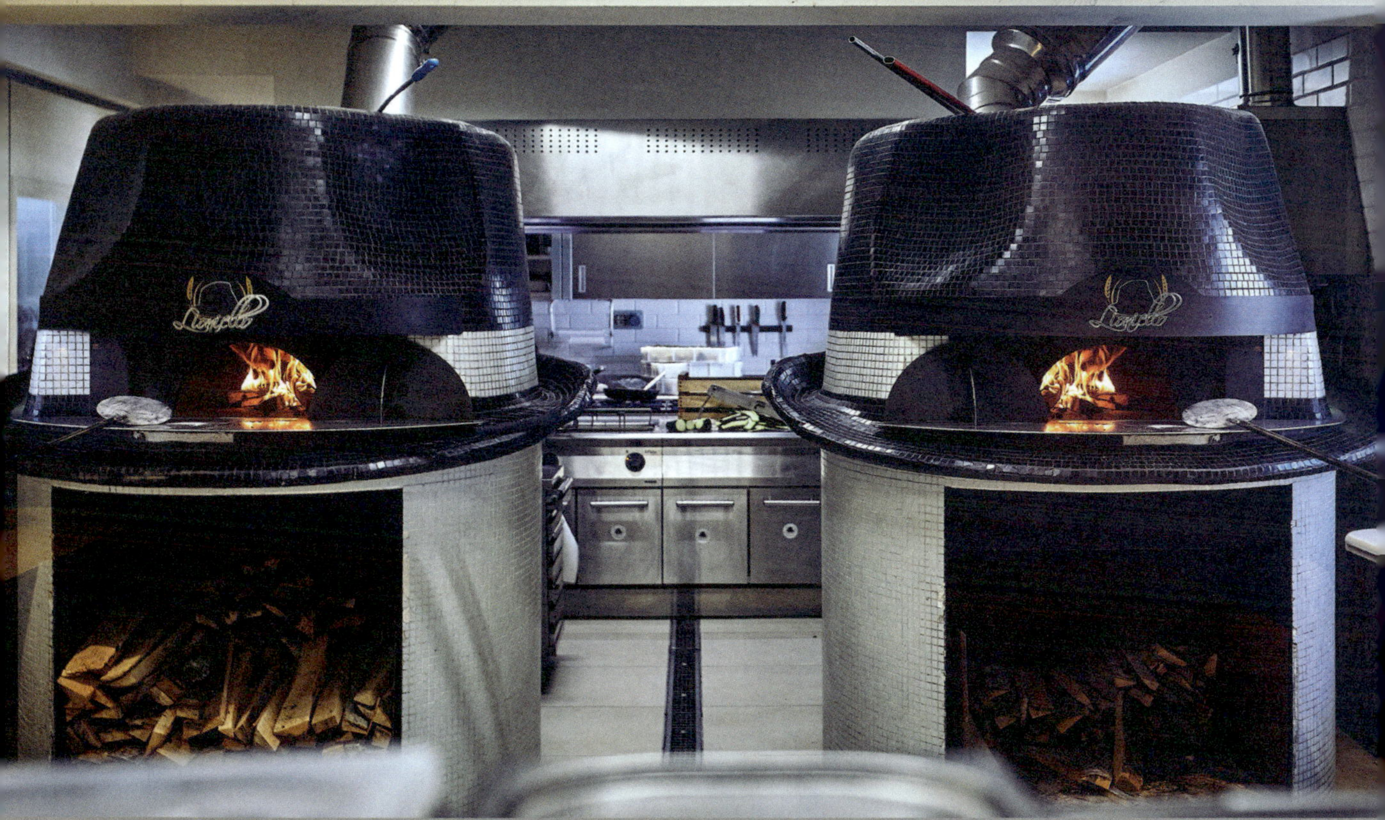

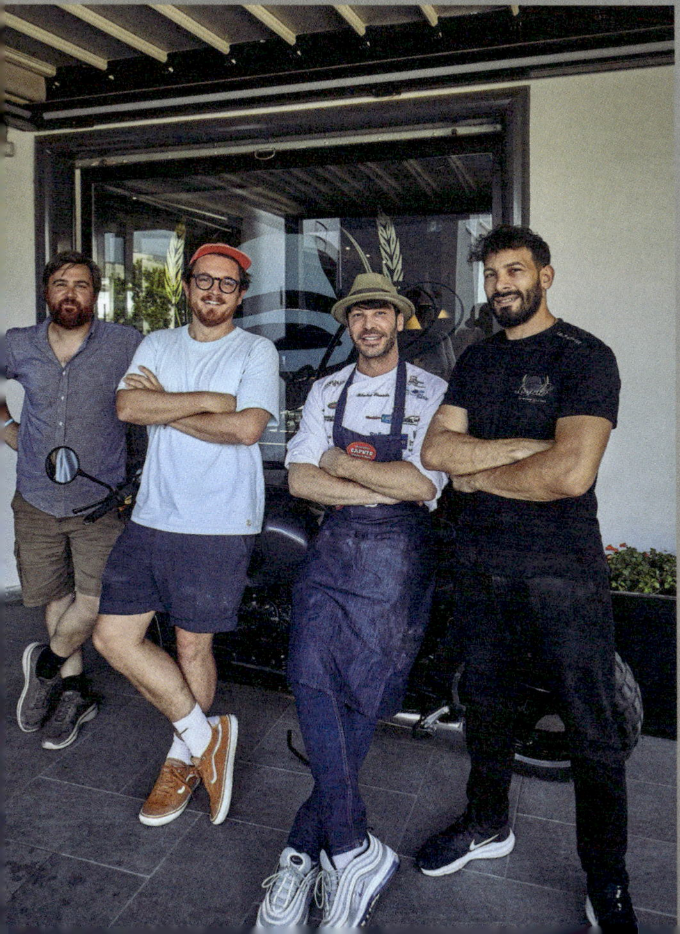

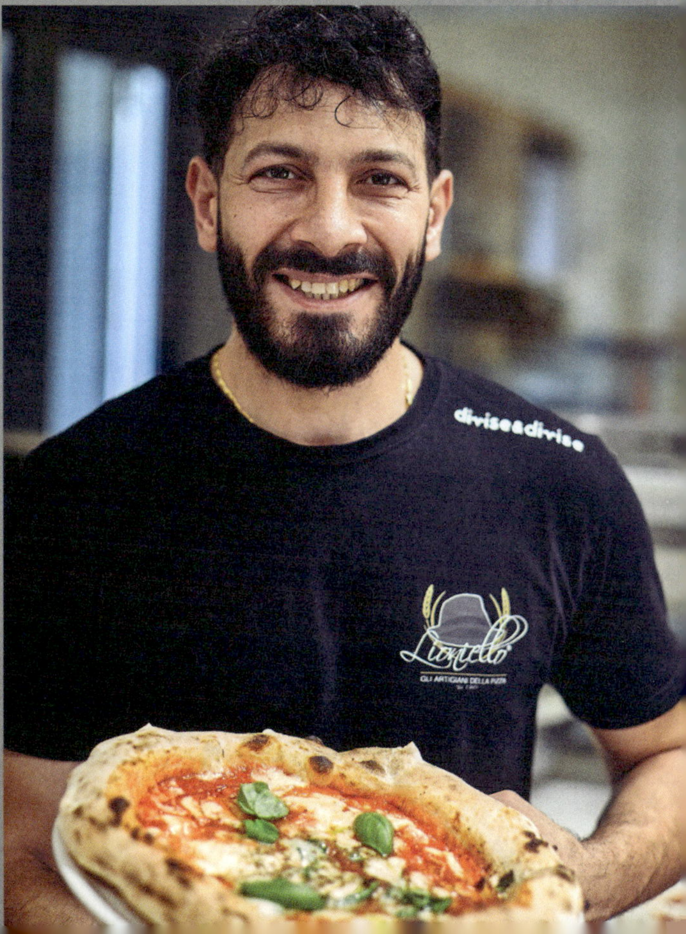
diviseadivise
Lioniello
GLI ARTIGIANI DELLA PIZZA

PARMIGIANA SCOMPOSTA

What you need

STG pizza dough (page 92)

aubergine (eggplant) purée (see below)

roasted tomatoes (see below)

fonduta di Parmigiano, warm (Parmesan fondue – Lioniello makes his own, but you can buy it canned or jarred for ease)

aubergine chips (see below)

deep-fried basil leaves (see below)

How to make it

Stretch a ball of dough out and spread the base with aubergine purée. Top with roasted tomatoes and bake in the oven. Spoon over fonduta di Parmigiano, then top with aubergine chips and deep-fried basil leaves.

For the roasted tomatoes (makes enough for 4 pizzas)

250g (9oz) datterini tomatoes

extra virgin olive oil

sea salt

Toss the tomatoes with olive oil and salt and roast for 20 minutes at 160°C fan (350°F) until concentrated in flavour and colour.

For the aubergine purée, chips and deep-fried basil (makes enough for 4 pizzas)

2 aubergines (eggplants)

50ml (1¾fl oz) extra virgin olive oil

neutral frying oil

handful of basil leaves

sea salt

Roast one of the aubergines whole at 200°C fan (425°F) until the skin has blistered and the flesh is soft. Blend the flesh with olive oil and salt.

Thinly slice the remaining aubergine and heat your frying oil to 180°C (356°F) in a deep-sided pan. Deep-fry the aubergine slices for 4–5 minutes, to create aubergine crisps, then set aside on kitchen paper to drain. Now deep-fry the basil leaves for 1 minute, then drain.

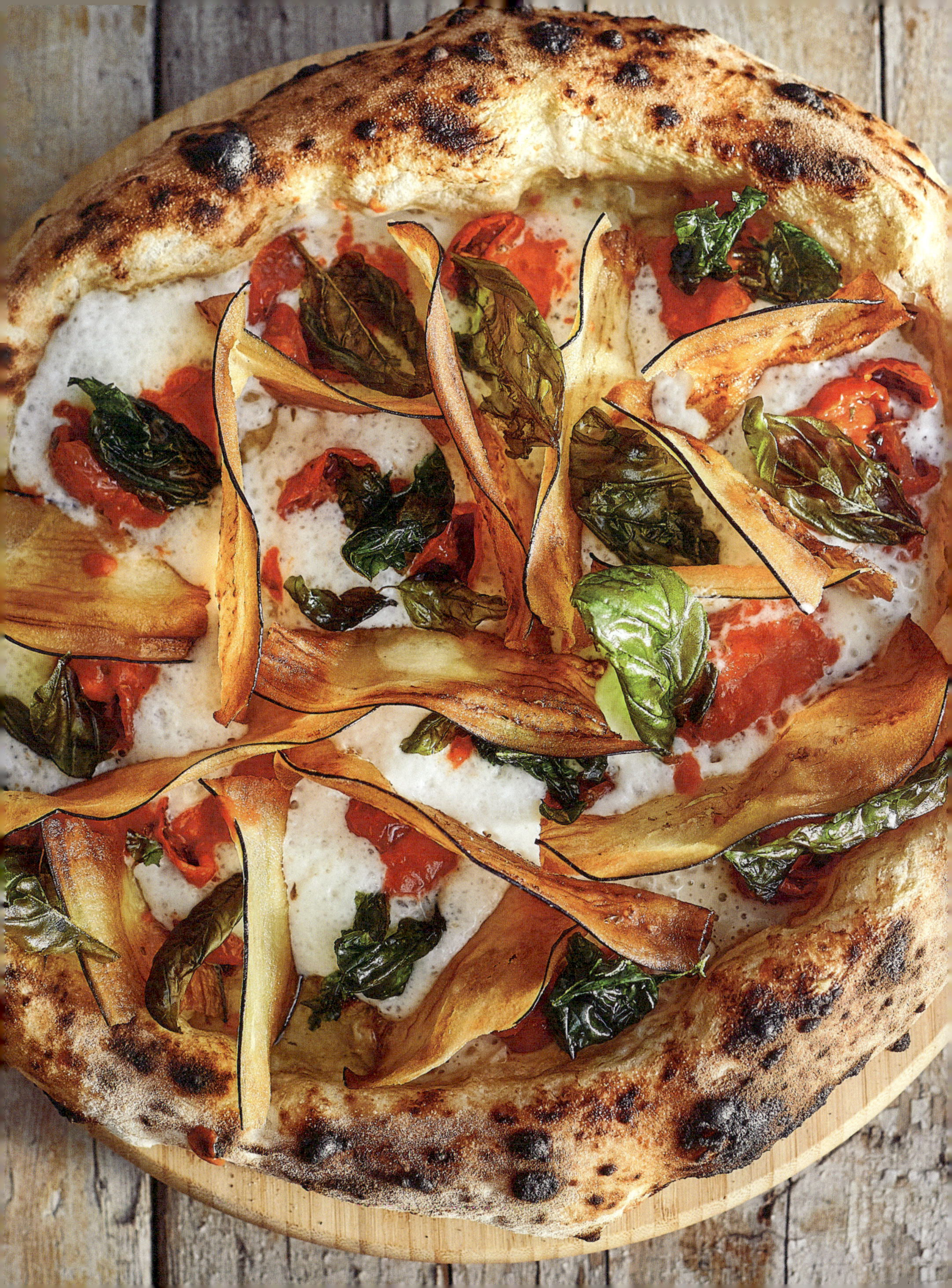

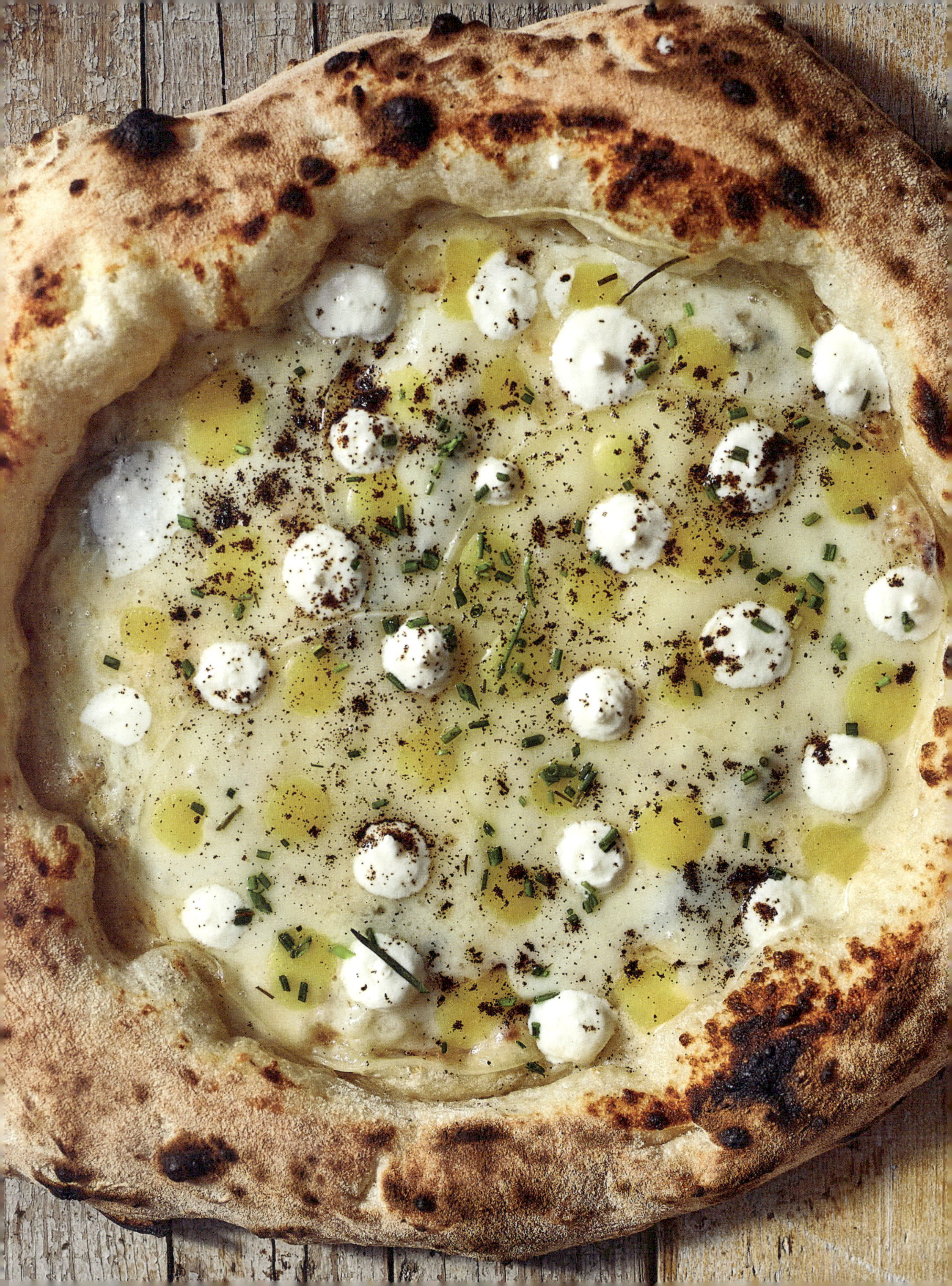

SOGNI DI LATTE

We know, we know – coffee on a pizza?! But trust us, for some reason this just works.

What you need

STG pizza dough (page 92)

caciocavallo cheese

fior di latte mozzarella

Buffalo mozzarella

lemon oil (see below)

sour cream

chives

ground coffee

How to make it

Stretch a ball of dough out and top it with 60g (2¼oz) each of grated caciocavallo, fior di latte and buffalo mozzarella.

Bake in the oven, then dress with lemon oil, dots of sour cream, some finely chopped chives and a sprinkle of ground coffee.

For the lemon oil (makes enough for 30 pizzas and keeps for 7 days)

100ml (3½fl oz) extra virgin olive oil

zest and juice of 1 lemon

sea salt

Whisk the olive oil with the lemon zest and juice. Season with salt to taste.

DAVIDE RUOTOLO

Davide Ruotolo

As we pulled up in the Vespa to the aptly named Palazzo Petrucci, with its high vaulted ceilings and ornate marble floors, head chef Davide was standing in the doorway, waiting. He was dressed like a Michelin-starred chef in crisp whites, and you could tell that he is a serious player. It's no surprise that Davide means business: his pizzeria is unique in Napoli (maybe the world?) as it is the sister restaurant to a fine-dining, Michelin-starred establishment of the same name. Fronted by Lino Scarallo, they focus on incredible locally sourced produce, presented in unique and elaborate ways.

As we head inside the pizzeria, Davide instantly jumps into his pizza philosophy. He first points to a *Juve Merda* ('Juventus are shit') sticker and says that more important than pizza is this sticker and Napoli FC. He goes on to explain he spends a lot of time working with the Michelin chefs to ensure the best produce makes its way into his kitchen and says that his pizza is about 'flavour and texture first, visuals second' (he makes his views on 'instagram' chefs and pizzerias with viral pizzas very clear…).

Davide has been a pizza chef for 17 years and says it was a calling; interestingly, though, he says he doesn't eat pizza that often and he is just passionate about the discipline. He runs a tight ship and often works 7 days a week and crazy hours to deliver his version of the best pizza. His father was a top cardiologist in the city and it does feel like you see that same level of dedication come through in Davide's work.

We asked if he felt Napoli was the best pizza city in the world. He thinks that Napoli has the best ingredients in the world but not the best chefs. 'There is an old belief that if you are Neapolitan, then you are a better pizza chef. That is not true. Some of the best pizza chefs in the world right now are coming out of Asia.'

He then proceeds to roll out these three pizzas: his favourites. Each one delivers on his philosophy of putting flavour at the forefront. They are all beautiful creations, but the depth of flavour combinations absolutely stands out.

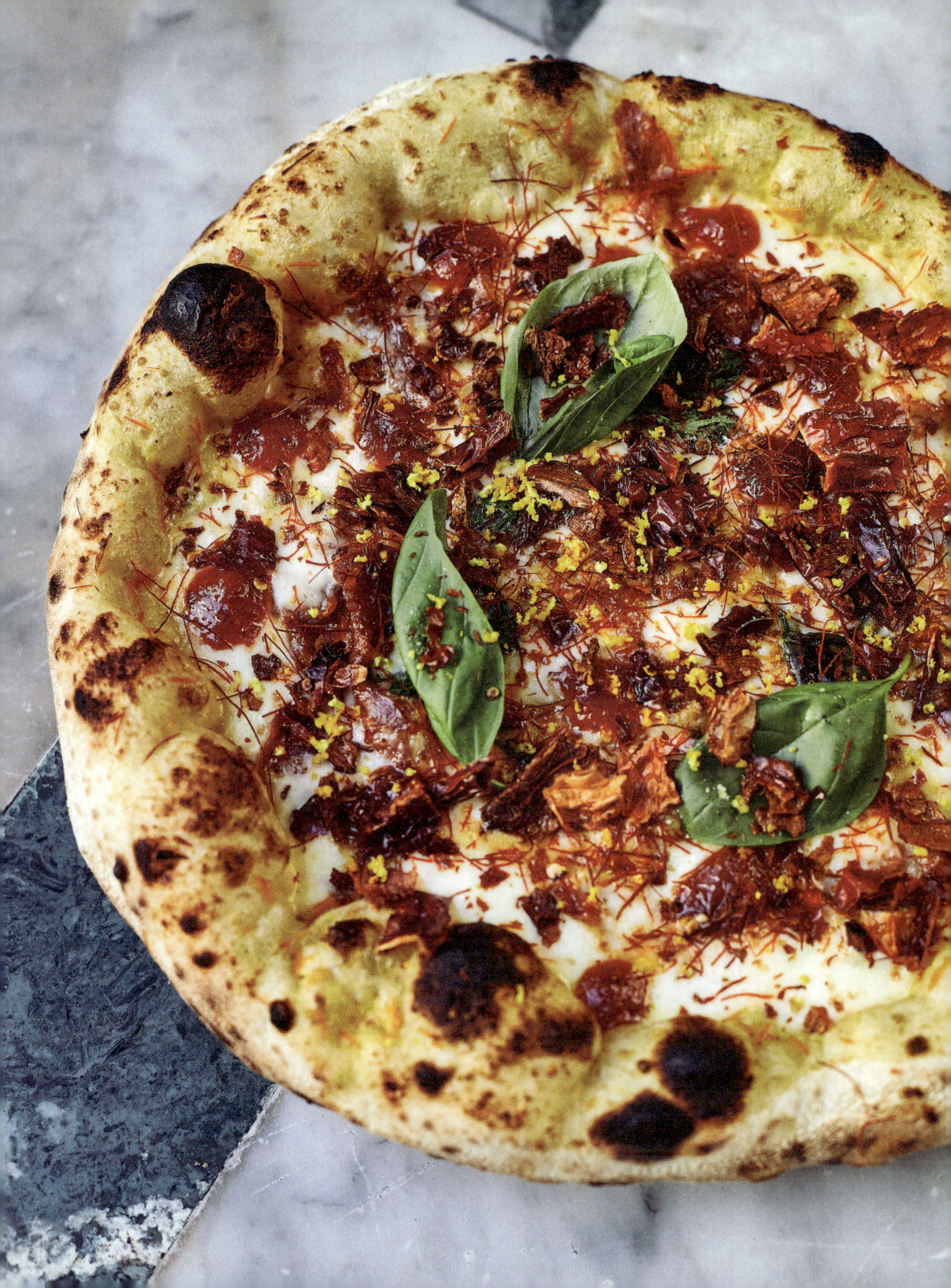

DIAVOLA

What you need

contemporanea pizza dough (page 93)

yellow Piennolo tomatoes

fior di latte mozzarella

sliced spianata salami

chilli jam

crusco pepper strands (or use dried chilli flakes)

orange zest

How to make it

Stretch a ball of dough out and top it with some yellow Piennolo tomatoes and fior di latte mozzarella.

Top with slices of spianata salami then bake in the oven.

Top with dollops of chilli jam and some strands of crusco pepper, then finish with a little grated orange zest.

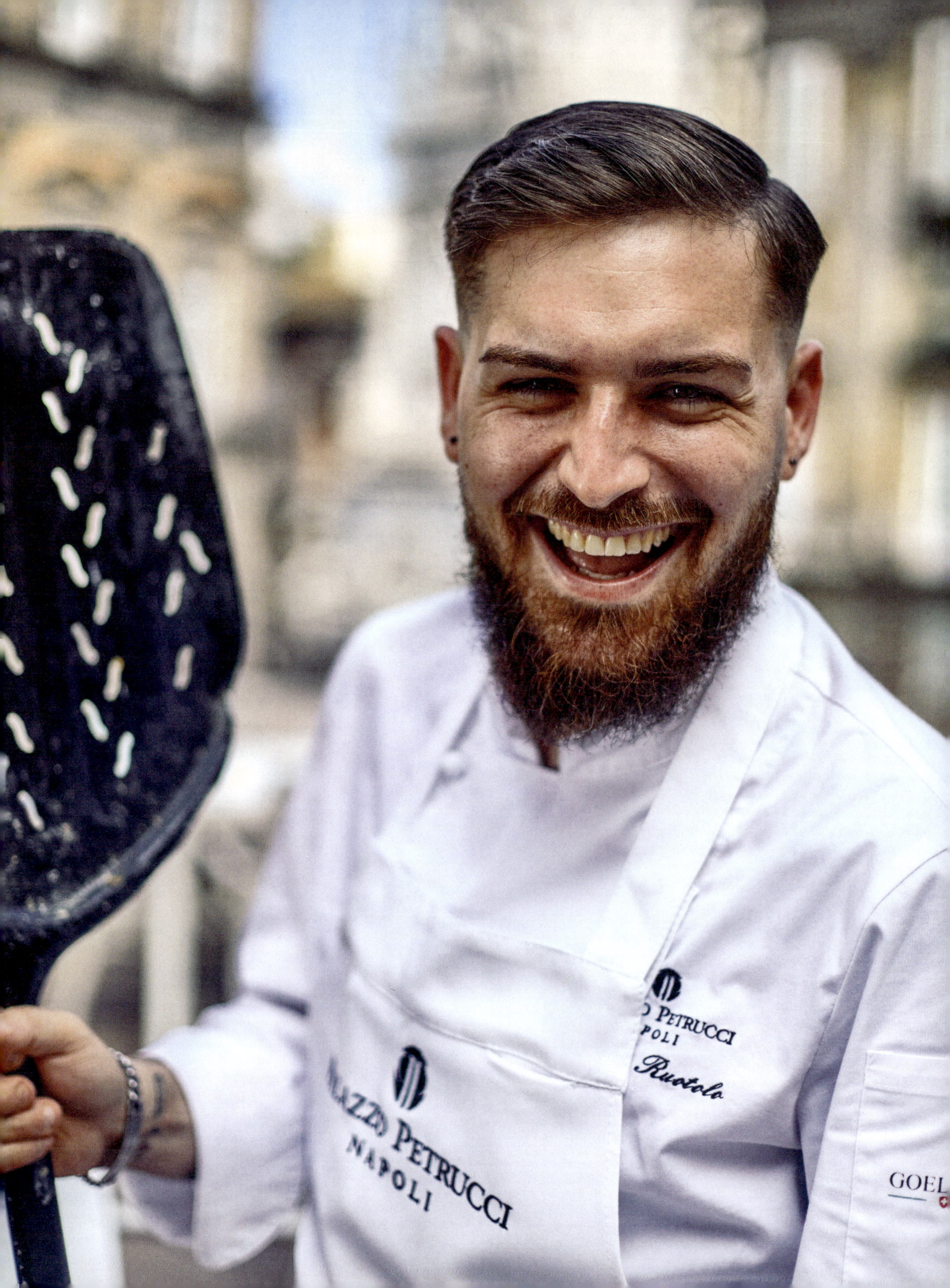
PETRUCCI
POLI
Ruotolo
PETRUCCI
NAPOLI

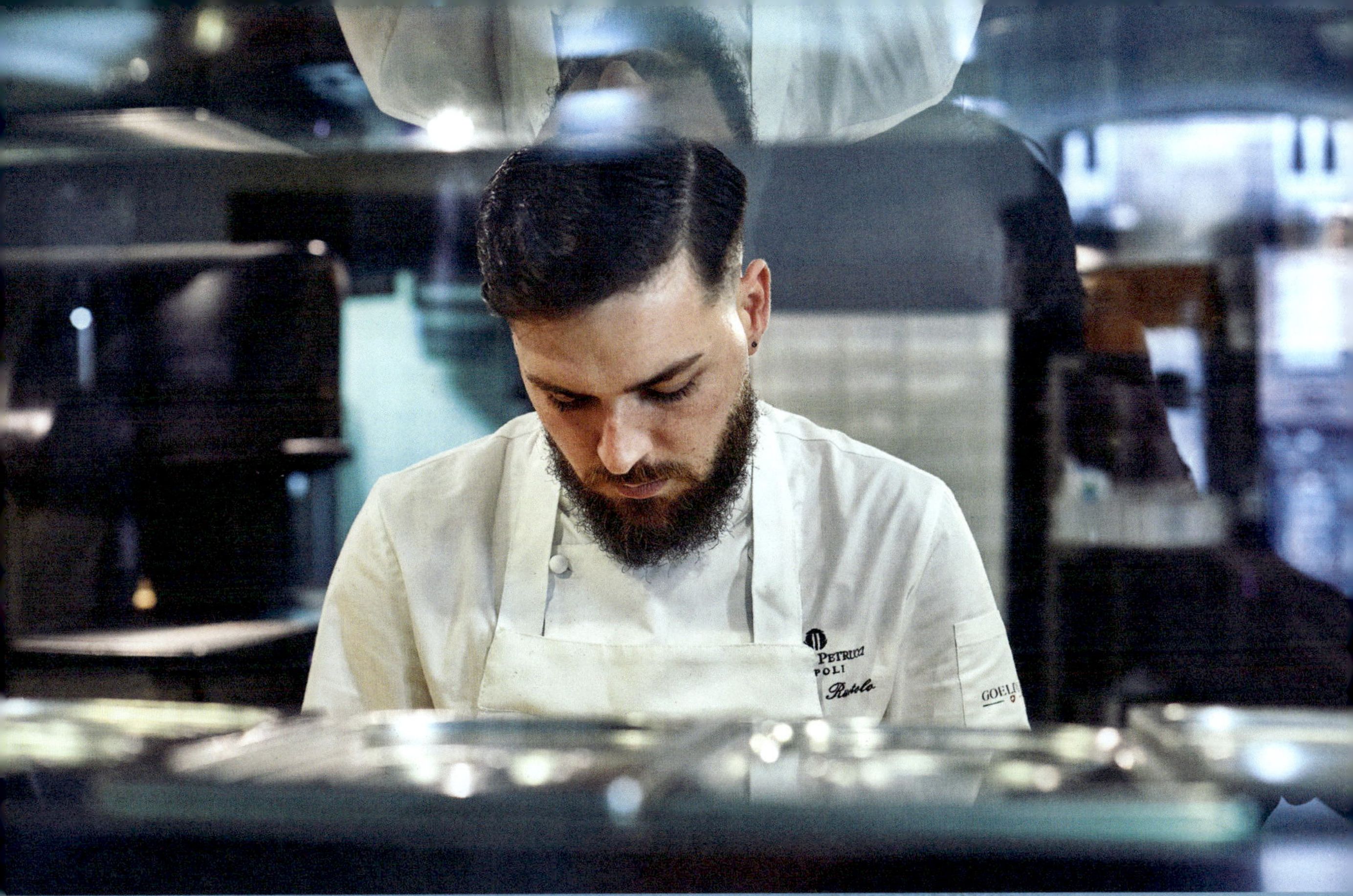

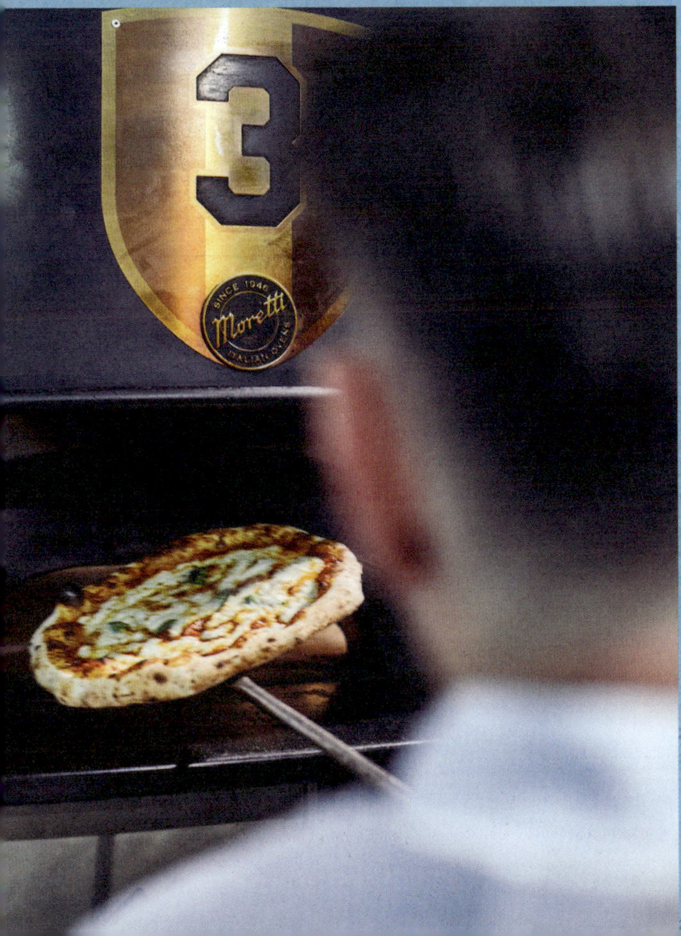
3
SINCE 1946
Moretti
ITALIAN OVEN

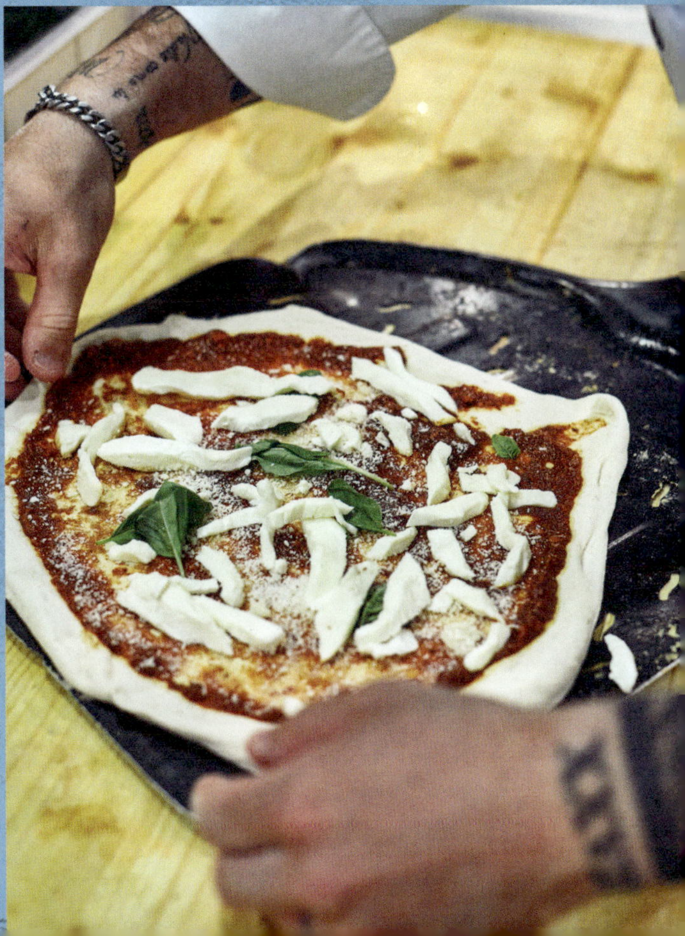

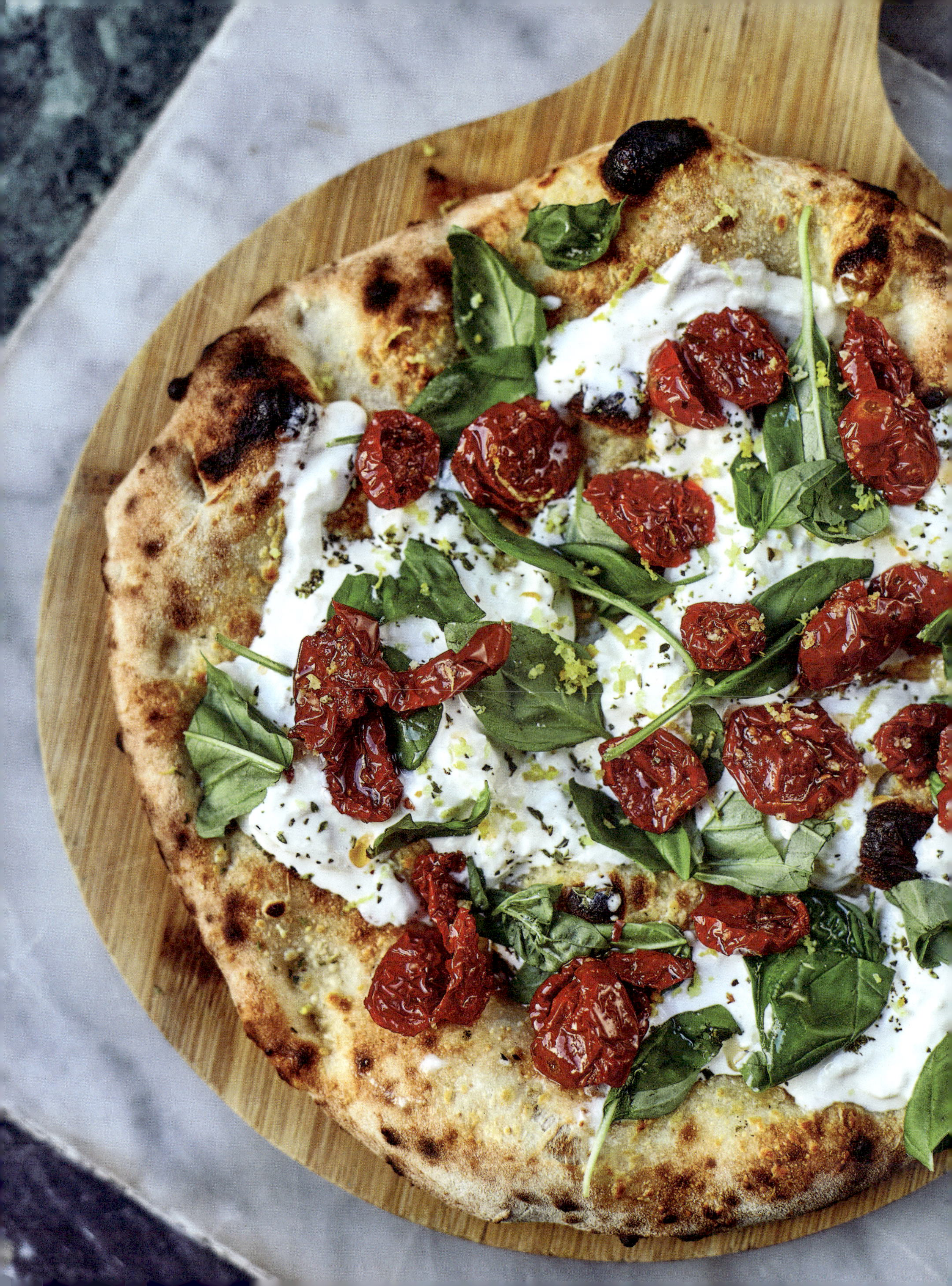

CONTEMPORANEA 2.0

What you need

contemporanea pizza dough (page 93)

extra virgin olive oil

Parmesan

buffalo stracciatella (or use normal stracciatella or burrata)

semi-dried tomatoes

basil

lemon zest

How to make it

Stretch a ball of dough out evenly (without a thinner middle) and brush it with olive oil. Grate over some Parmesan, then bake in the oven.

Top with buffalo stracciatella, semi-dried tomatoes, basil, lemon zest and then finish with a drizzle of olive oil.

PIZZA

FRITTA

#PIZZAFRITTA
Alessandro Baraschino

ALESSANDRO BARASCHINO

Alessandro was one of the first pizza chefs to join us at Pizza Pilgrims back in 2013, and he was a huge part of helping us develop our pizza style and generally getting our head around the madness of running a pizzeria. After four years, Alessandro headed home to the area of Miano in Napoli to follow his true passion, pizza fritta. We arrived at his shop just before lunch service and were met by his whole family: dad, mum, and his girlfriend Giusi who works with him and often runs the fryer. As we walk in we can feel that this is a local shop for local people. Pizza fritta doesn't seem to have made it that far outside of Italy, or even Napoli. People often think it's going to be heavy and greasy (we mean, we get it, that's exactly what it sounds like), but pizza fritta can be incredibly light and delicate. Alessandro says it's all about the dough and the temperature you cook it at. The dough needs to be well proved and not over mixed, to give a light crust. It then needs to be cooked in clean, hot oil. You want the dough to seal instantly as it hits the oil, meaning that no oil is absorbed by the pizza. The flavour of a pizza fritta can also be very refined and subtle. The fried dough takes on a kind of beignet flavour and a sweetness from the caramelized starches. The ingredients actually steam inside the dough, meaning that the mozzarella stays incredibly milky and the flavours don't char as they would in a wood-fired oven.

Alessandro runs us through all the basics of making great pizza fritta and its three main styles: calzone, montenara and dolce. Here are his recipes.

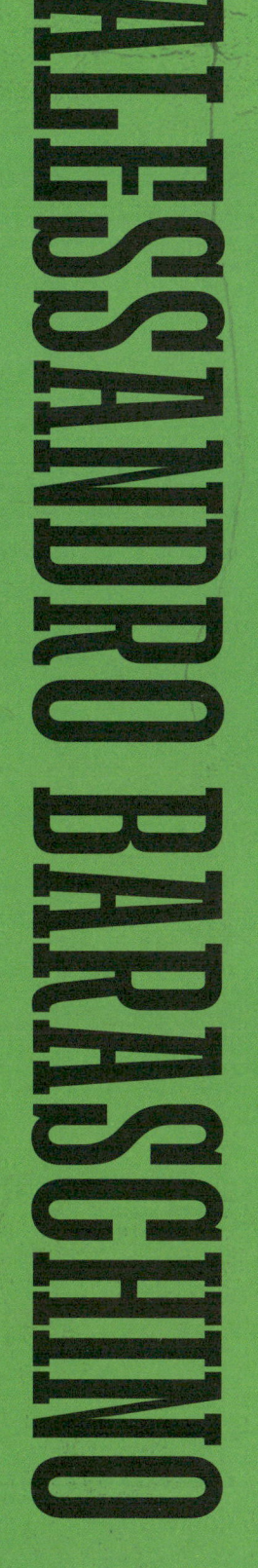

#PIZZAFRITTA
Alessandro Baraschino

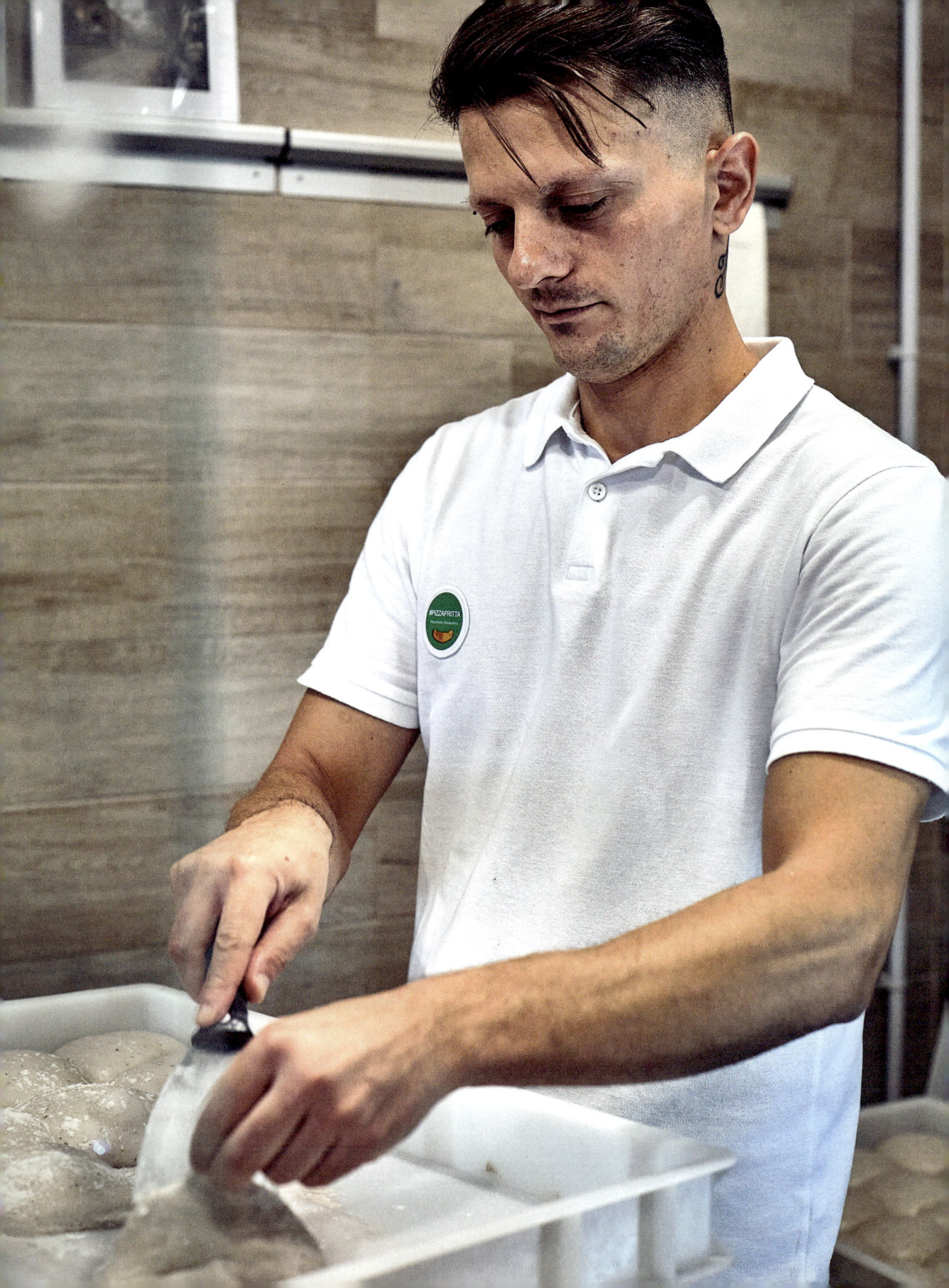
#PIZZAFRITTA

What you need (makes enough for 10 pizza frittas)

1kg (2¼lb) 00 flour (he uses a mixture of Caputo 70% blue, 25% red and 5% tipo 1 – but 100% 00 flour will work well too)

2g (⅟₁₆oz) fresh yeast

630ml (21½fl oz) cold water

20g (¾oz) sea salt

How to make it

First mix the dry flour in the mixer to remove any lumps. Dissolve the yeast in the water, then slowly add this to the flour as you mix. Finally, add the salt and mix for 12 minutes until the dough is smooth and elastic. Remove to the worktop, cover and rest for 1 hour.

Divide the dough into 10 balls, each weighing 160g (5½oz) and prove at room temperature in airtight containers (or one large container) for 6–8 hours until the dough balls have doubled in size.

PIZZA FRITTA PIZZA DOUGH

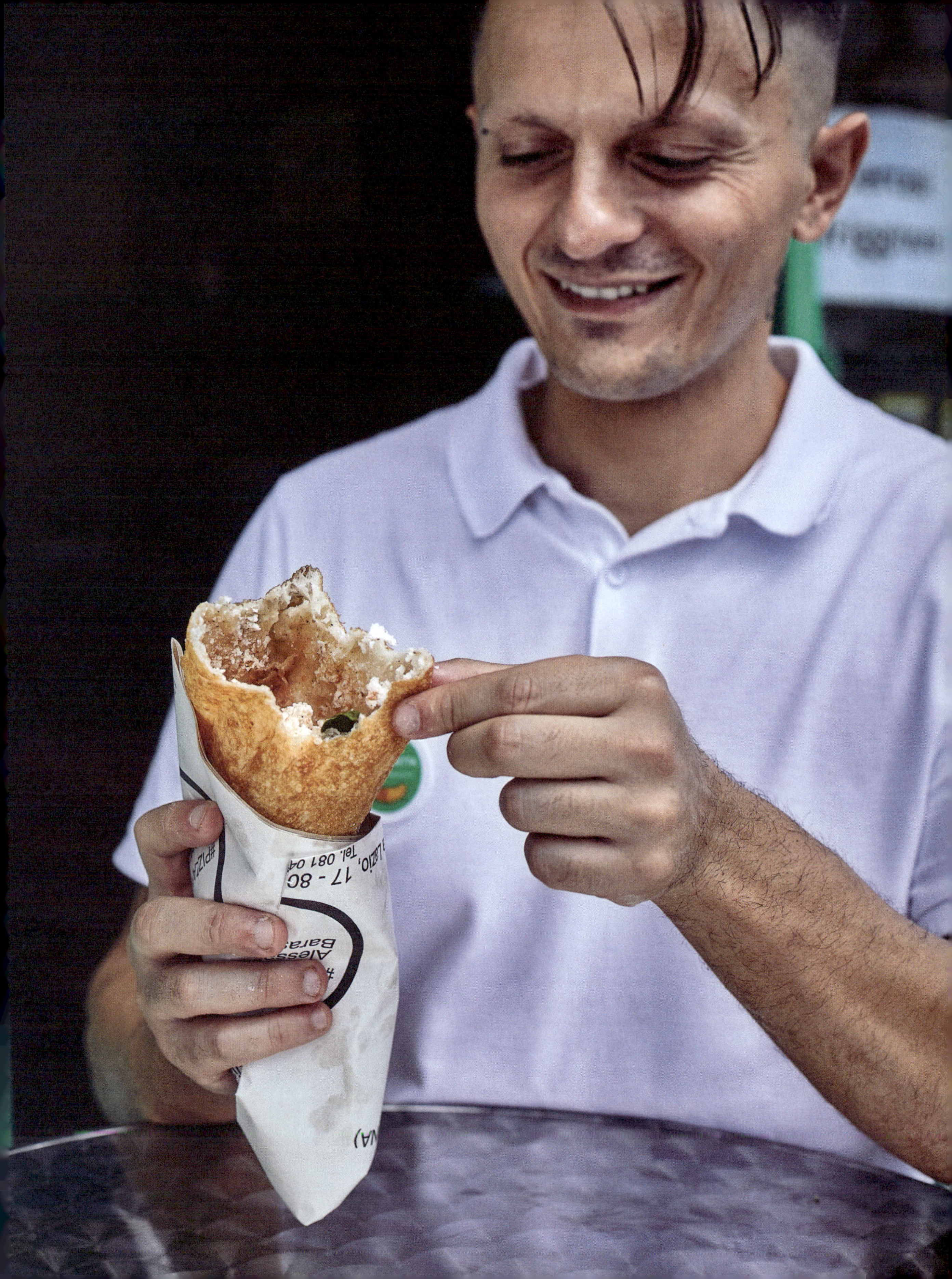

This is a street-food classic and is often eaten on the move. It stars an incredible product called cigoli, a Neapolitan pressed pork belly that has a high fat content and a very meaty flavour. The combination of flavours here is incredible, so we would urge you to try this style of pizza fritta first! You can also leave the dough unfilled, then fold and fry as below, to create a deep-fried pizza dough horn that you can then stuff with your favourite ingredients – try using this for Pepe's Ananascosta on page 166.

What you need

pizza fritta dough (page 229)

ricotta

cigoli (see recipe intro)

provola (smoked) mozzarella

tomato sauce (page 190 or 209)

basil

black pepper

neutral frying oil

How to make it

First stretch your dough ball to a 20–25cm (8–10 inch) flat, even round.

Spread a spoonful of ricotta over the middle of the dough. Top with a handful of finely sliced cigoli, some provola, a spoonful of tomato sauce, a basil leaf and a crack of black pepper.

Fold the dough over to create a half-moon (like a calzone), ensuring you don't trap any air in the pizza as it will burst in the fryer. Use the side of your hand to hammer the seam closed (if there are any holes, then oil will seep in and ruin it).

Heat your neutral frying oil in a deep-sided pan to 180°C (356°F). It should be deep enough to cover one pizza fritta at a time. Pick up the pizza fritta at both ends and lower the middle into the hot oil, gently pulling the ends of the pizza longer, allowing the middle to fry for a few seconds before releasing the whole thing into the oil. This will help set a long, elegant shape to your pizza. Fry for 2–3 minutes, using a pair of spatulas to move it around and douse the top of the dough with the hot oil, then flip the pizza in the oil and ensure the dough cooks to an even golden brown all over. Transfer the pizza fritta to kitchen paper and dab generously to remove excess oil.

To eat 'street style', wrap the bottom half in a piece of greaseproof paper, pick it up and rip off the top of the calzone to allow the steam to release. Then slowly eat your way down like an ice cream cone, being *extremely* careful not to burn yourself, as the inside will be molten lava.

MONTENARA AL RAGÙ

Montenara is probably the oldest style of pizza fritta and dates back to the 1700s when Napoli vendors would fry scraps of dough left over from the bakeries and smear them with pork fat as a quick snack. This version uses Alessandro's traditional Neapolitan ragù, which is incredible and should become your go-to ragù recipe from now on!

What you need

pizza fritta dough (page 229)
neutral frying oil
ragù (see right)
Parmesan
basil

For Ale's Neapolitan ragù (makes enough for about 15 pizzas)

extra virgin olive oil
500g (1lb 2oz) beef shoulder (chuck), cubed
1 large onion, chopped
1 large garlic clove, peeled and smashed
1 glass of white wine
600g (1lb 5oz) passata (strained tomatoes)
2 x 400g (14oz) cans of San Marzano tomatoes
handful of basil
sea salt and black pepper

How to make it

First, make the ragù. Heat some olive oil in a large pan and fry off the beef until golden. Remove the beef, then add the onion and garlic to the pan.

Sauté for 5 minutes until the onion has softened and slightly caramelized, then deglaze the pan with the wine and add the beef back in with both the tomatoes and a good pinch each of salt and black pepper. Cover, turn down the heat to the lowest simmer and cook for 6–7 hours, stirring often to ensure it is not burning on the bottom (add some water if needed).

When cooked, finish the ragù with a handful of basil and extra salt to taste.

For the pizza fritta, stretch your dough ball into a flat, even round (no puffy crust). Using your pizza scraper or a metal spoon, tap lots of small holes in the dough to ensure it cooks evenly and doesn't puff up.

Heat your neutral frying oil in a deep-sided pan to 180°C (356°F). It should be deep enough to cover one pizza fritta at a time. Slide the dough into the oil. (Ale gives the dough a quick spin as it hits the oil to help set a round shape. Give it a try but PLEASE don't burn yourself!)

Use 2 spatulas to keep the dough flat and as round as possible and fry on each side for 2–3 minutes to achieve a beautiful golden crust.

Remove from the pan and dab with kitchen paper to remove excess oil.

Heat a portion of the ragù in a pan until warm, then spoon it over the pizza. Finish with a generous grating of Parmesan and some fresh basil leaves.

#PIZZAFRITTA
Alessandro
Baraschino
17 - 80145 Miano (NA)
081 040 26 88
Via Lazio

STRACCIETTA DI PIZZA AL NUTELLA

A really fun dessert to make, these little deep-fried dough sticks are also covered in sugar and Nutella. Not the picture of health but so delicious and a massive hit with kids (including Alessandro's neighbours).

What you need

pizza fritta dough (page 229)
flour, for dusting
neutral frying oil
Nutella
icing (confectioner's) sugar

How to make it

Stretch a dough ball lengthways between your hands so it is 1cm (½ inch) thick. Using your pizza scraper or a knife, chop the dough into little fingers, then dust with flour to prevent them sticking together.

Heat your neutral frying oil to 180°C (356°F) in a deep-sided pan, then drop the dough fingers into the hot oil and fry while continuously stirring until golden brown, crispy on the outside and soft on the inside.

Remove from the pan and dab with kitchen paper to remove excess oil.

Pile the pizza fritta fingers into a bowl, drizzle them with Nutella and finish with a dusting of icing sugar.

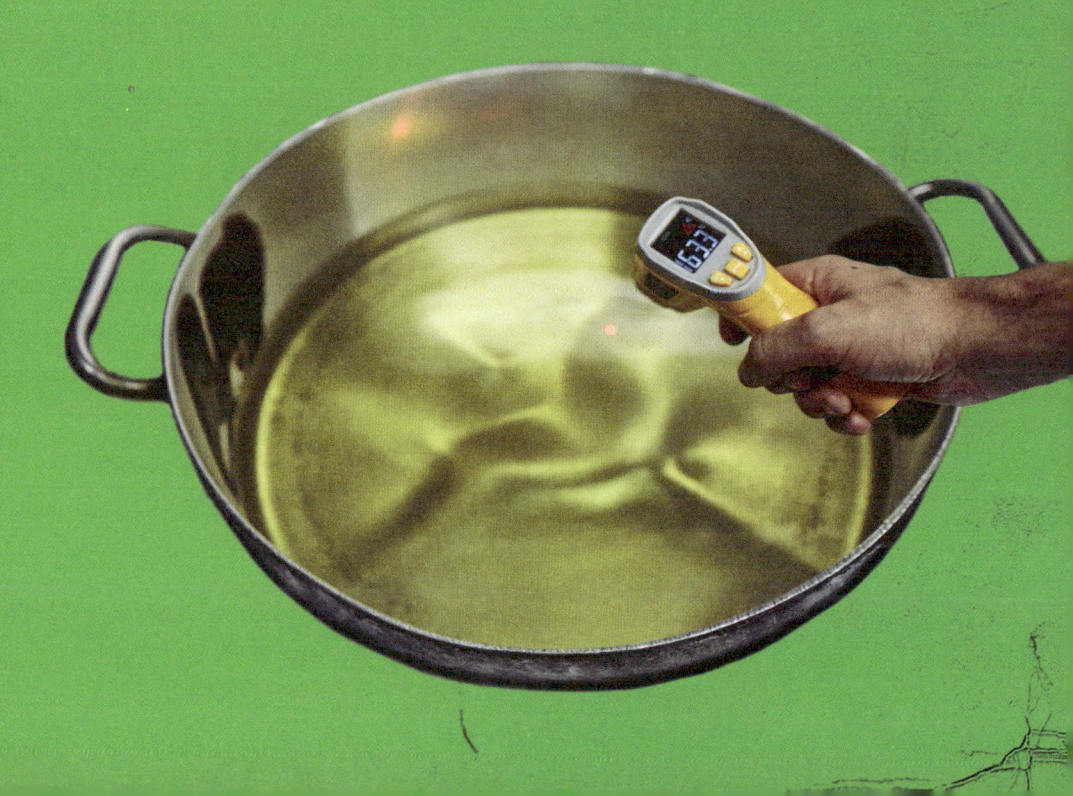

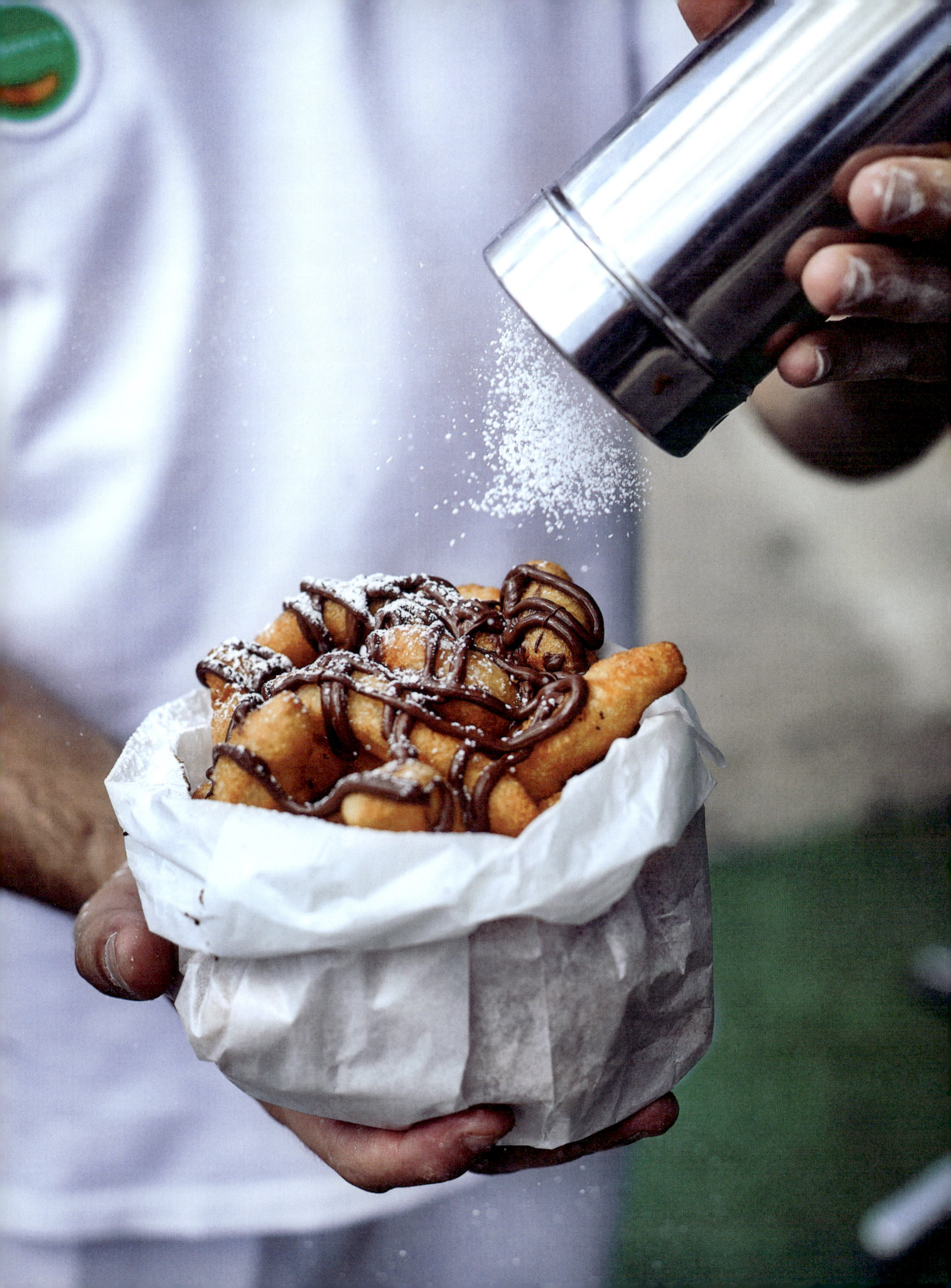

Isabella De Cham
PIZZA FRITTA
STREET FOOD 2023
PIZZERIE D'ITALIA 2023
50 TOP PIZZA 2023
50 TOP PIZZA 2022
BENVENUTI
FRITTA
Napoletana
FRIED

ISABELLA DE CHAM

Alessandro sent us off to see his friend Isabella, who runs a more contemporary pizza fritta restaurant, focusing on locally sourced and sophisticated flavour combinations. Now, in classic Napoli style, as we arrived, Isabella had made a run for the beach after a very hot and busy lunch service. We got hold of her on FaceTime and she said she had left us in the very capable hands of her head chef Alessandra. Isabella runs her pizzeria with a full female crew, which is quite common in the pizza fritta world – wood-fired pizza seems to be very male dominated, whereas pizza fritta is championed by women, and has been for decades. As we get chatting to Alessandra, she tells us that pizza fritta became a popular job for women during and after World War II, when a lot of the men went to war and more women entered the workforce. She also says that Sofia Loren starred in a movie called *L'Oro di Napoli*, where she made pizza fritta, and so it became and 'en vogue' job. She also says (with a smile) that men don't have the patience to make truly great pizza fritta.

Alessandra's passion for pizza fritta is clear. She was born and raised in the area of Sanità, where the pizzeria is located, and is very proud to be cooking for her people and offering delicious, affordable food. Here are the two signature pizzas that celebrate her pizza ethos.

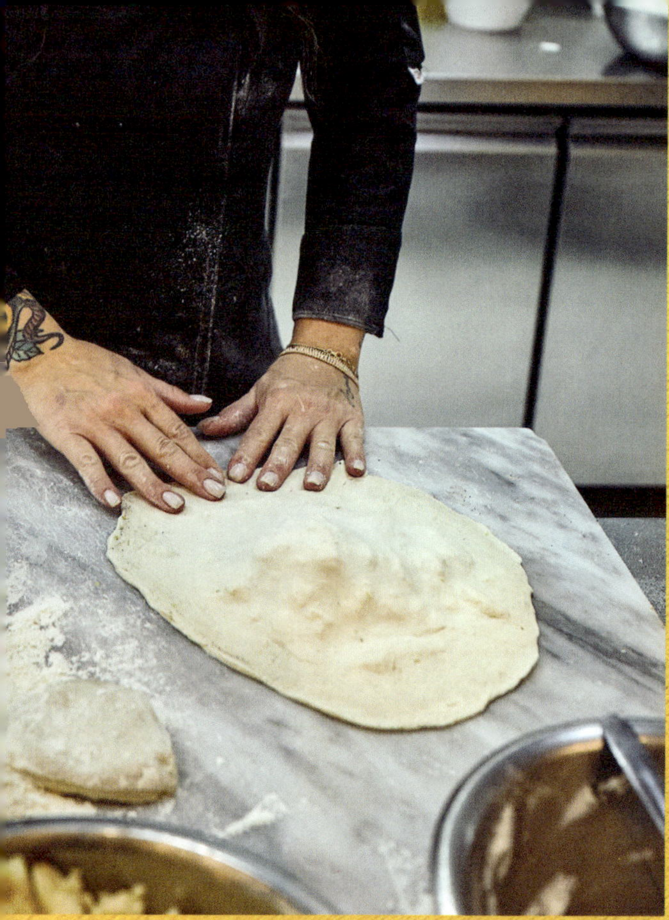
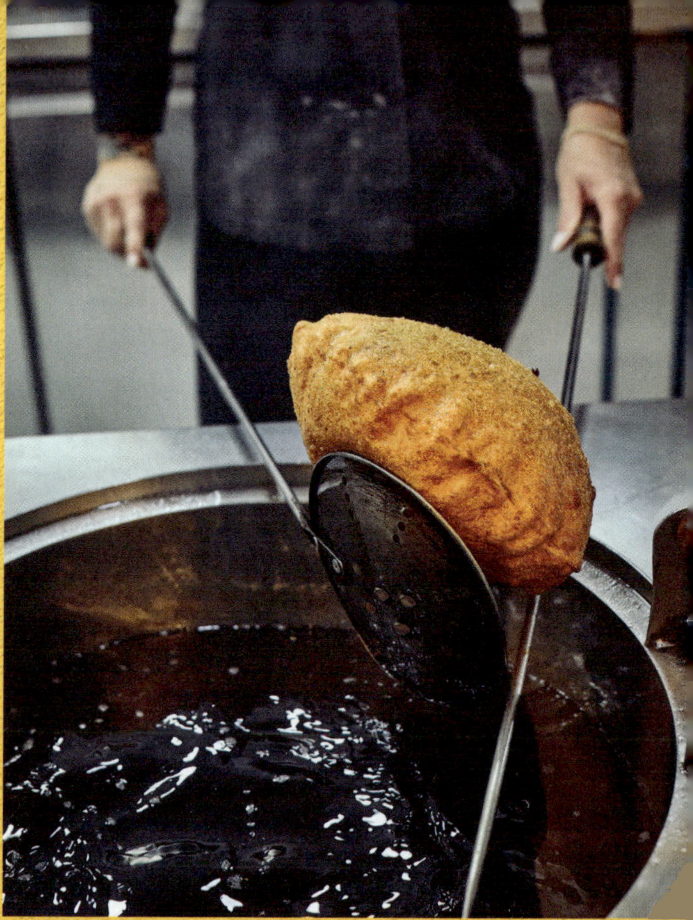
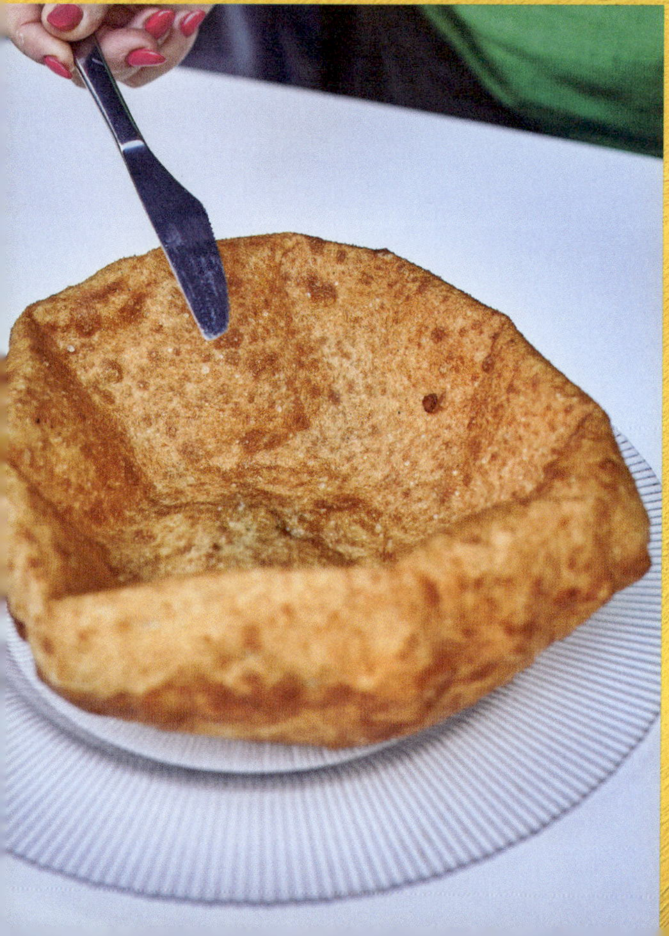
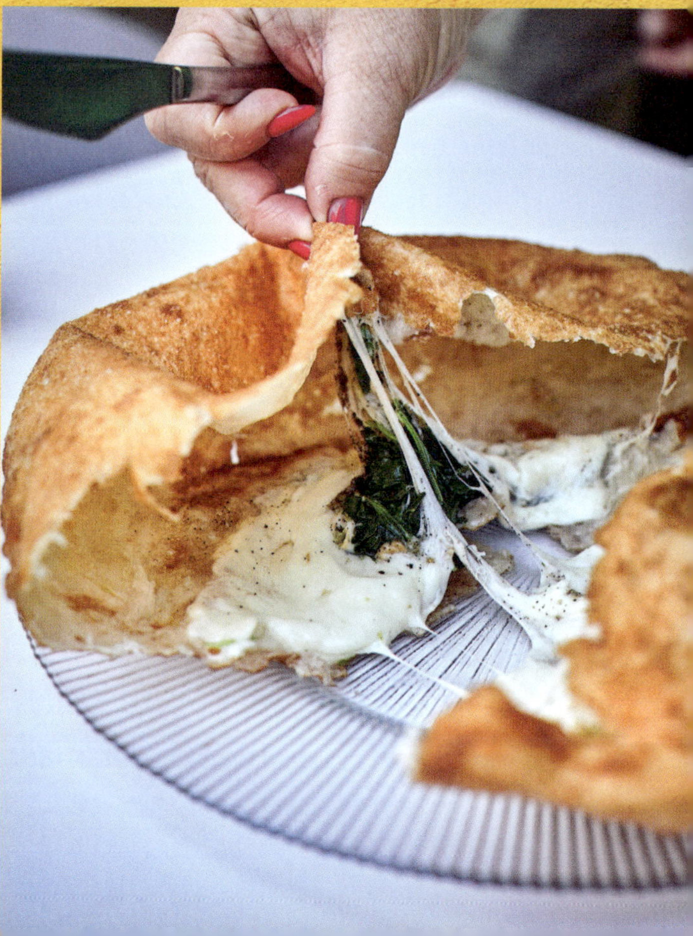

What you need

pizza fritta dough (page 229)

provola (smoked) mozzarella

rocket (arugula) leaves

lemon zest

caciocavallo cheese

basil

neutral frying oil

How to make it

Stretch out a ball of pizza fritta dough into a flat, even round (no puffy crust) and scatter the base with provola. Top with a handful of rocket, the zest of ½ lemon, a generous grating of caciocavallo cheese and a few basil leaves.

Stretch a second dough ball in the same way, and lay it on top of the fillings. Using the palm of your hand, press the outside edges of the pizza together to create a stuffed, round pizza.

Heat your neutral frying oil in a deep-sided pan to 180°C (356°F). It should be deep enough to cover one pizza fritta at a time. Add the pizza, using a metal spoon to move the pizza and douse it with hot oil; it will puff up like a balloon. Continue to nap with oil until the whole pizza is golden brown, then remove from the pan and dab with kitchen paper to remove excess oil.

Stab with a fork to deflate the balloon and create a flat pizza again. Then slice and eat.

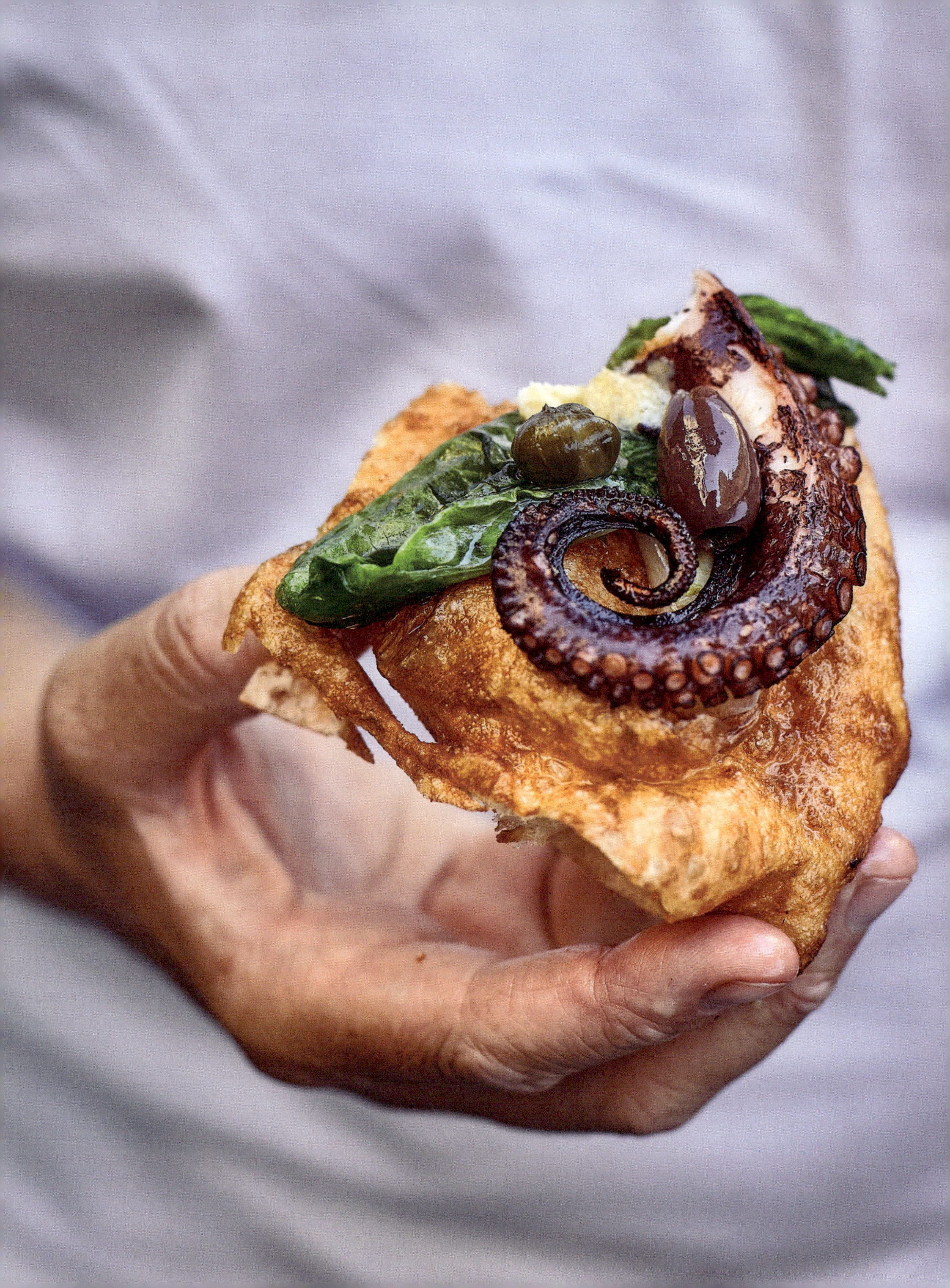

POLPO SANTÀ

What you need

pizza fritta dough (page 229)
neutral frying oil
scarola (see below)
octopus tentacles (see below)
Stilton cheese
black olives
capers

How to make it

Stretch out a ball of pizza fritta dough into an even round (no puffy crust). Using your pizza stecca (spatula) or a metal spoon, tap lots of small holes in the dough to ensure it cooks evenly and doesn't puff up.

Heat your neutral frying oil in a deep-sided pan to 180°C (356°F). It should be deep enough to cover one pizza fritta at a time. Drop the dough into the oil, using 2 spatulas to keep the dough as flat and round as possible. Fry on each side for 2–3 minutes to achieve a beautiful golden crust. Remove from the pan and dab with kitchen paper to remove excess oil.

Cut the pizza into 4 and top each slice with a spoonful of scarola, an octopus tentacle, a crumb of Stilton, an olive and a caper.

For the scarola (makes enough for 4 pizzas)

extra virgin olive oil

1 garlic clove, crushed

240g (8½oz) scarola (a bitter salad leaf from Napoli; endive/chicory will also work well)

sea salt and black pepper

Heat some olive oil in a sauté pan and add the crushed garlic. Add the scarola, season with salt and pepper and sauté for 5 minutes until it has softened and taken on some colour.

For the octopus tentacles (makes enough for 4 pizzas)

½ lemon

600g (1lb 5oz) octopus tentacles

Bring a pan of salted water, with the lemon half added, to the boil. Reduce the heat and drop in the octopus tentacles. Cook low and slow for around an hour until tender, then drain and set aside.

NAPOLI

CUCINA

THE HOLY TRINITY OF FRIGGITORIA

Outside every discerning pizzeria in Napoli you will find what we describe as a 'glass cabinet of joy'. These are wheeled out onto the street, filled with a selection of snacks and treats, often costing no more than a euro, to be eaten immediately on the street. Everyone has their own specialities and creations, but each pizzeria will, without fail, sell these three fritti. Which pizzeria makes the best arancini or who can fry the crunchiest crocchè is the source of infinite debate between locals. It's like supporting a football team – once you've committed, you are staunchly loyal.

TOMATO & MOZZARELLA ARANCINI

Every region of Italy has its variation on this dish, but the Sicilians and Neapolitans are the true champions. There are two main types in Napoli, a beef ragù variation and then our favourite: tomato and mozzarella.

Makes 10

4 tbsp extra virgin olive oil

1 medium onion, finely chopped

2 garlic cloves, minced

300g (10½oz) risotto rice

100ml (scant ½ cup) white wine

750ml (3¼ cups) vegetable stock

400g (14oz) passata (strained tomatoes)

30g (1oz) Parmesan, grated

125g (4½oz) mozzarella, cut into 10 pieces

2 litres (2 quarts) neutral frying oil

200g (7oz) plain (all-purpose) flour

200g (7oz) breadcrumbs

sea salt

Add 2 tablespoons of the olive oil to a large saucepan set over a medium heat. Add the onion and fry for 6–8 minutes until soft, then add the garlic and fry for a further 30 seconds.

Stir in the rice and remaining olive oil, ensuring every grain is coated in the oil, and continue to cook for 3–4 minutes until the edges of the rice begin to go translucent. Pour in the wine and deglaze the pan.

In another pan, combine the stock and passata and warm over a medium heat until hot but not boiling.

Begin adding the tomato stock to the pan of rice, a ladleful at a time, allowing the rice to absorb all the liquid before adding the next. Stir the rice gently throughout this process until the rice is al dente and the consistency is fairly firm (it shouldn't be as loose as a normal risotto).

Recipe continued overleaf

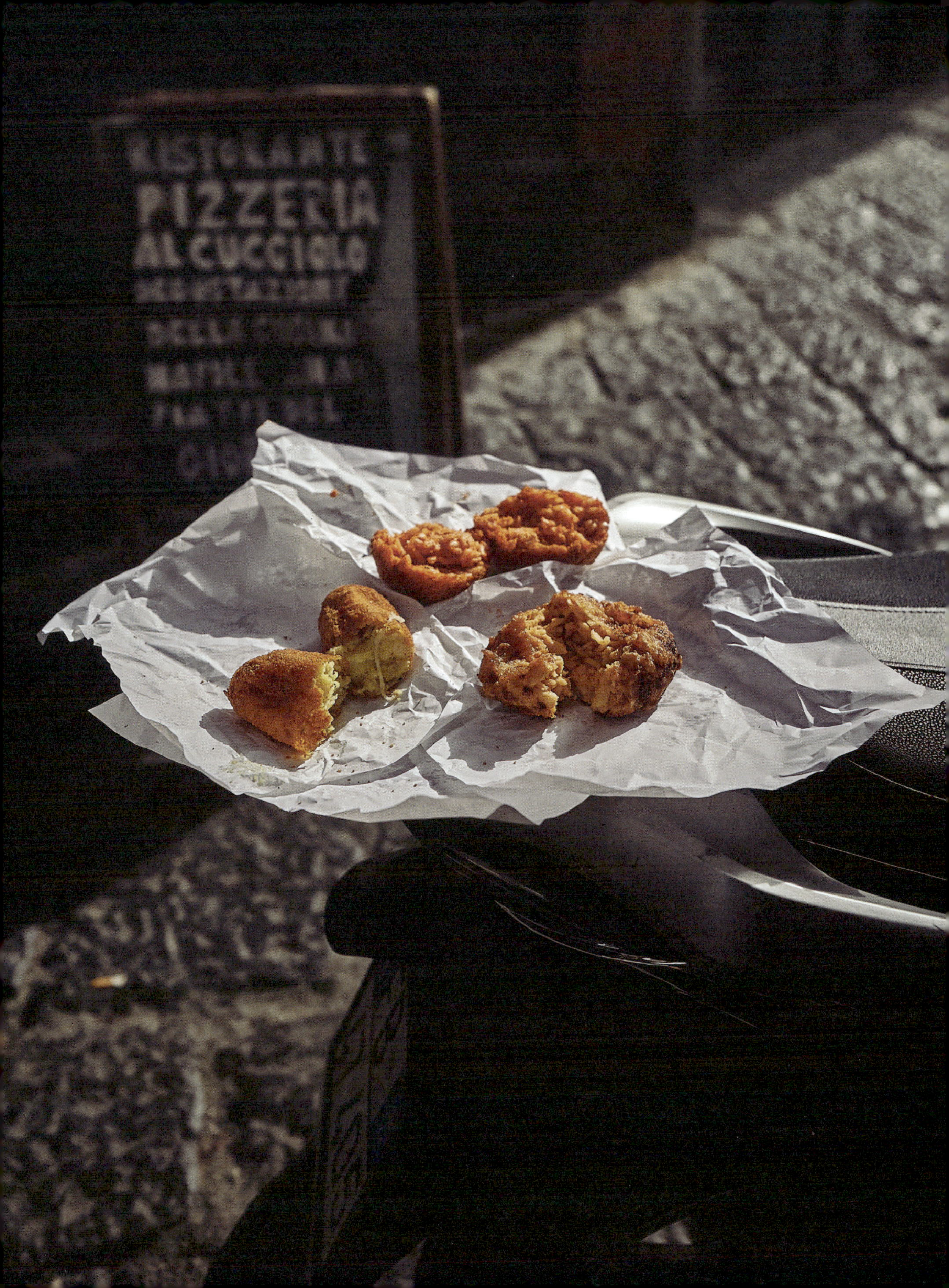
PIZZERIA
AL CUCCIOLO

Stir in the Parmesan, then spread the risotto onto a tray and refrigerate for about 1 hour until cool.

Divide the cooled risotto into 10 equal portions and roll each into a ball. Flatten each ball a little in your hand, then place a piece of mozzarella in the middle and close the rice mix around it, creating a ball again.

Heat your neutral frying oil in a deep-sided pan to 180°C (356°F).

Place the flour a medium bowl and slowly whisk in cold water until it is the consistency of double (heavy) cream. Season with a little salt. Place the breadcrumbs in another medium bowl. One at a time, drop an arancini ball into the flour mixture, ensuring it is totally covered. Allow the excess to drip off, then place it in the breadcrumbs and gently toss to fully coat.

Gently drop the arancini into the hot oil (you may need to do this in 2 or 3 batches to avoid overcrowding the pan) and cook for 6–8 minutes until the arancini are golden brown. Remove from the oil with a slotted spoon, allow to drain briefly on kitchen paper, then serve immediately.

FRITTATINE DI PASTA

A friggitoria shop lives and dies by how well loved its frittatine is. Deep-fried pucks of pasta in *besciamella* (bechamel) and ragù sauce, frittatine are crispy on the outside and gooey and luxurious in the middle. The result is so moreish – if it's made right it should be falling apart as you eat it. It's also the only situation in which is it acceptable to break pasta in half, which is fun!

Makes 8

3 tbsp extra virgin olive oil

250g (9oz) minced (ground) beef

1 medium onion, finely chopped

250g (9oz) peas (frozen or fresh)

250g (9oz) dried bucatini pasta, snapped into thirds

250g (9oz) mozzarella, cut into 1cm (½in) cubes

2 litres (2 quarts) neutral frying oil

For the besciamella

50g (1¾oz) butter

50g (1¾oz) plain (all-purpose) flour

500ml (2 cups) milk

pinch of ground nutmeg

30g (1oz) Parmesan, grated

sea salt and black pepper

For the pastella

200g (7oz) plain (all-purpose) flour

200ml (generous ¾ cup) cold water

pinch of sea salt

Heat the olive oil in a large saucepan set over a medium heat, then add the beef. Fry for about 5 minutes until the beef is browned, then add the onion and continue to cook for 2–3 minutes until a little softened. Next stir in the peas and cook for 2 more minutes. Set the pan to one side.

Bring another large pan of water to the boil, season with salt, then cook the snapped bucatini pasta until al dente. Drain and set aside to cool.

Now make the besciamella. Melt the butter in a saucepan set over a medium heat, then whisk in the flour until smooth and lightly golden brown; this will take 3–4 minutes. Pour the milk into the pan in a slow, steady stream, whisking constantly, until the mixture is smooth. Reduce the heat to low and cook until the sauce has thickened, then stir in the nutmeg and Parmesan and season with salt and pepper to taste. Set aside to cool.

In a large mixing bowl, combine the beef and onion mixture, the cooled pasta, the mozzarella and the besciamella. Stir well – the mixture should be gooey and wet.

Line a baking dish with baking paper, then tip in the mixture and press and spread it into the dish (ideally it should be about 5cm/2in thick). Place in the fridge and leave to firm up for 2–3 hours.

Heat your neutral frying oil in a deep-sided pan to 180°C (356°F).

Turn out the firm mixture onto a clean surface and use an 8–10cm (3–4in) cookie cutter to cut out as many 'pucks' as possible.

To make the pastella, whisk together the flour and water until it is the consistency of double (heavy) cream, then add the salt to season.

One at a time, submerge the pasta pucks in the pastella so they are completely covered, then allow the excess to drip off. Gently lower the coated pucks into the hot oil (cook in batches) and fry for 6–8 minutes until golden all over. Remove from the oil with a slotted spoon, allow to drain briefly on kitchen paper, then serve immediately.

CROCCHÈ

Crocchè makes all our Neapolitan pizza chefs go weak at the knees. It's a taste of their childhood – something you would buy a bag of after school from the local friggitoria shop. An absolute pro tip when in Napoli is to buy a Margherita pizza and a bag of crocchè. Break the crocchè over the pizza, fold the pizza into quarters, then eat while walking down the street. *Va bene!*

Makes 10

1kg (2¼lb) potatoes, such as Maris Piper, peeled

100g (3½oz) mozzarella, cut into 1cm (½in) cubes

100g (3½oz) pecorino, grated

10g (⅓oz) sea salt

freshly ground black pepper, to taste

2 litres (2 quarts) neutral frying oil

300g (10½oz) breadcrumbs

For the pastella

200g (7oz) plain (all-purpose) flour

200ml (generous ¾ cup) cold water

pinch of sea salt

Bring a large pan of water to the boil and cook the potatoes until you can easily pierce them with a sharp knife. Drain, then pass through a potato ricer or mash until smooth. Place the mashed potato in a large bowl and allow to cool for 30 minutes.

Once cool, add the mozzarella, pecorino, salt and plenty of black pepper to the mashed potatoes and mix well. Divide the mixture into 10 equal pieces and roll each into a small sausage shape. Place them on a baking sheet and in the fridge for at least 1 hour to firm up.

Heat your neutral frying oil in a deep-sided pan to 180°C (356°F).

To make the pastella, whisk together the flour and water until it is the consistency of double (heavy) cream, then add the salt to season.

Place the breadcrumbs in a shallow bowl.

One at a time, drop the crocchè into the pastella, ensuring they are totally covered. Allow the excess to drip off, then place them in the breadcrumbs and gently toss to fully coat.

Gently drop the crocchè into the hot oil and fry (in batches) for 6–8 minutes until golden all over. Remove from the oil with a slotted spoon, allow to drain briefly on kitchen paper, then serve immediately.

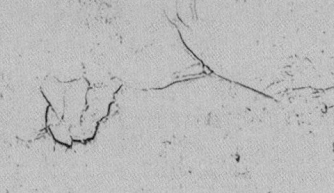

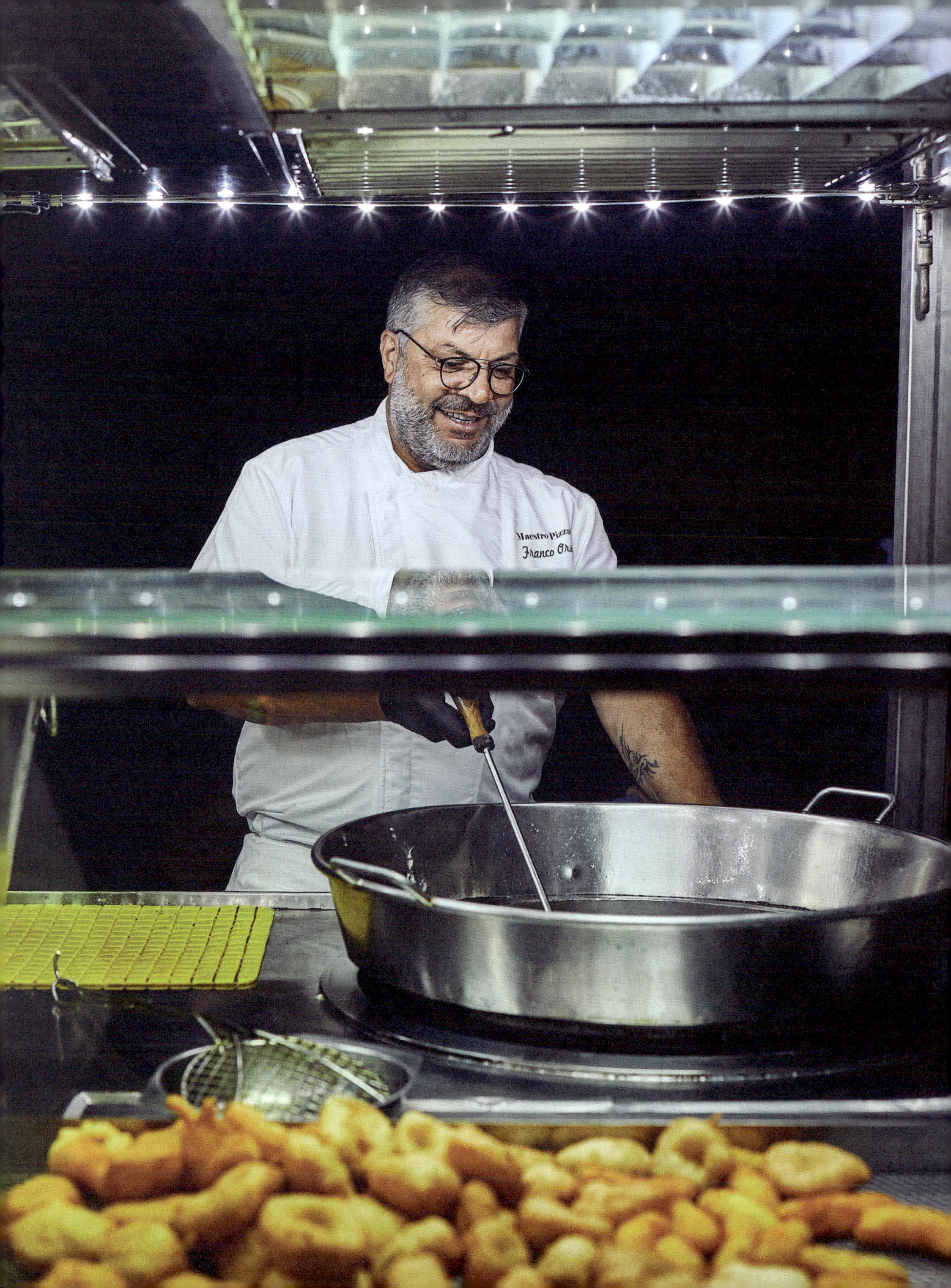

To get a real feel of the old-school friggitoria scene and some of the fried snacks that have been served across Napoli for hundreds of years, we went to visit Francesco and his daughter Ginevra, fourth- and fifth-generation pizza fritta makers who run their business Da Aniello O'Ricciulillo & Figli from their amazing friggitoria van. Every night they take to the streets of Napoli to fry up a dish called zeppole – fried dough balls served in a paper cone. The dough is made in much the same way as pizza fritta dough but the hydration is much higher, at 80%. This creates a dough that is scooped straight from the mixing bowl, shaped and dropped into the hot oil. The fluffy, pillow-like texture inside the zeppole is like nothing else. The dough is traditionally flavoured using local seaweeds, but on the day we visited, they had created a dough using pumpkin flour; it was a very subtle flavour but incredibly moreish.

DA ANIELLO O'RICCIULILLO & FIGLI

ZEPPOLE
PANZEROTTI
SCAGLIUOZZO
LA VERA PIZZA NAPOLETANA
SUMMIT
CUOPPO
FRITTO

FIORDILATTE

ZEPPOLE

What you need (makes 16)

5g (⅕oz) fresh yeast

400ml (14fl oz) water

500g (1lb 2oz) 00 flour

sea salt

neutral frying oil

How to make it

In a large mixing bowl, dissolve the yeast in the water. Add the flour and 1 teaspoon of salt and mix with your hands until you have a thick batter.

Cover the bowl and leave to prove for around 2 hours at room temperature until the batter has doubled in volume.

Heat your frying oil to 180°C (356°F) in a deep-sided pan. You can use a spoon to drop golf-ball-sized pieces of batter into the oil, but to do it like the pros, you rub your hands with oil and, pressing the side of your palm against the side of the bowl, crimp a piece of the batter into your palm. Use your fingers to slightly spread the batter before dropping it into the oil.

Fry in batches for 3–4 minutes, turning them in the oil to ensure they are evenly golden. Drain on kitchen paper and season with a little salt before eating.

FRITTO MISTO

When you spend time in Napoli, you really begin to understand how important the sea is in the day-to-day lives of the people. The classic view looking out from the city across the Bay of Napoli towards Mount Vesuvius, with the tiny fishing day boats bringing in their catch, really sets the scene. Seafood is by far the most prized and celebrated food in the city. And there is no more democratic and delicious way to enjoy seafood in Napoli than fritto misto. You will see the stalls all over the city. The thing you have to look out for is the brown paper cones; if you see an impressive stack of these towering over the counter, you know you are in for some good fritto misto. What goes into a fritto misto varies depending on the season, preference of the chef and your budget. You will always find some prawns and calamari but then it really is dealer's choice. You may get a scallop, a swordfish skewer, tiny squid, some little bianchietti (tiny little whole fish fried) or even a chunk of baccala (salt cod). They are fried in a very simple semolina crust, tossed with sea salt and served up in the cones with a big wedge of lemon and a matador-esque skewer that you can stab your catch with. This way of cooking is so versatile and a lot like Japanese tempura. Feel free to experiment with what's in season as the Neapolitans do – vegetables also work great.

What you need (serves 4)

400–500g (14–18oz) mixed seafood (prawns, salt cod, fresh anchovies, squid, scallops, etc.)

neutral frying oil

400g (14oz) semolina flour

flaky sea salt

lemon wedges

How to make it

Start by preparing the seafood. Peel the prawns, soak the salt cod in fresh cold water for 12 hours in the fridge, de-head the anchovies, clean and remove the skin from the small squid and shell the scallops (or get your fishmonger to do all this for you; or buy prepared seafood from the supermarket).

Pat the seafood dry really well with kitchen paper to ensure it crisps up.

Heat your frying oil to 180°C (356°F) in a deep-sided pan. Add the semolina flour to a large bowl.

Each type of seafood will have a different frying time, so coat and fry in batches, depending on what you are cooking. Toss each type of seafood in the semolina flour, then transfer to the hot oil and fry until golden and crisp (avoid overcooking, otherwise the seafood will be tough).

Drain on kitchen paper to remove any excess oil. Once all your seafood is cooked, toss it in a bowl with some salt and serve it with lemon wedges for squeezing.

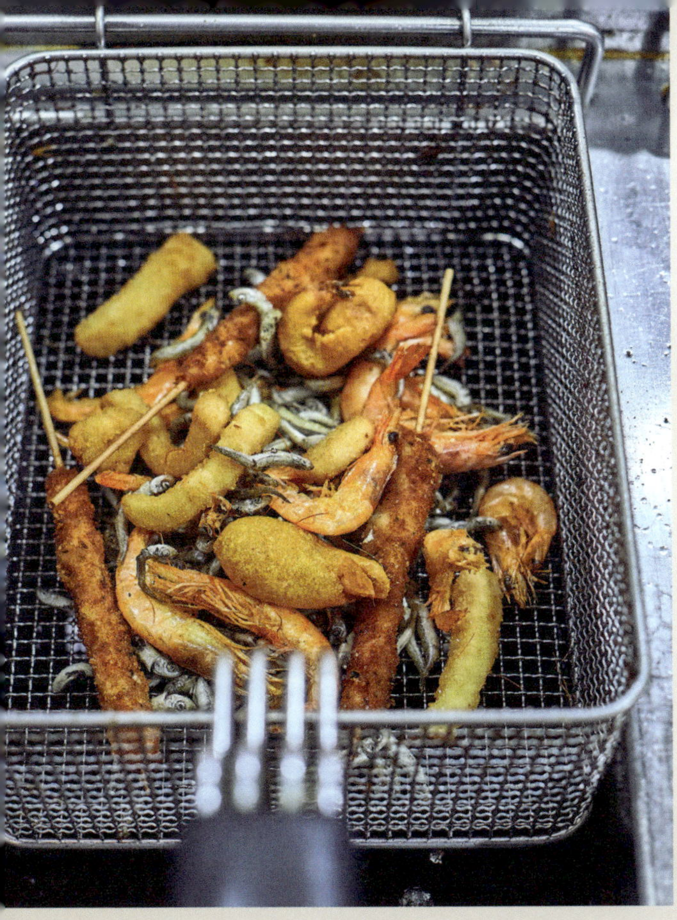

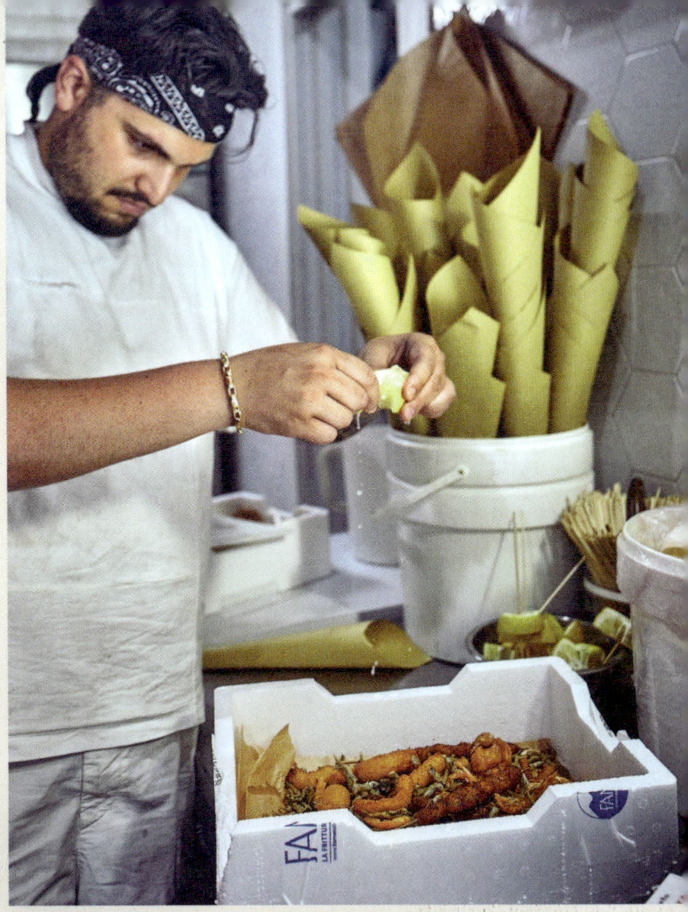

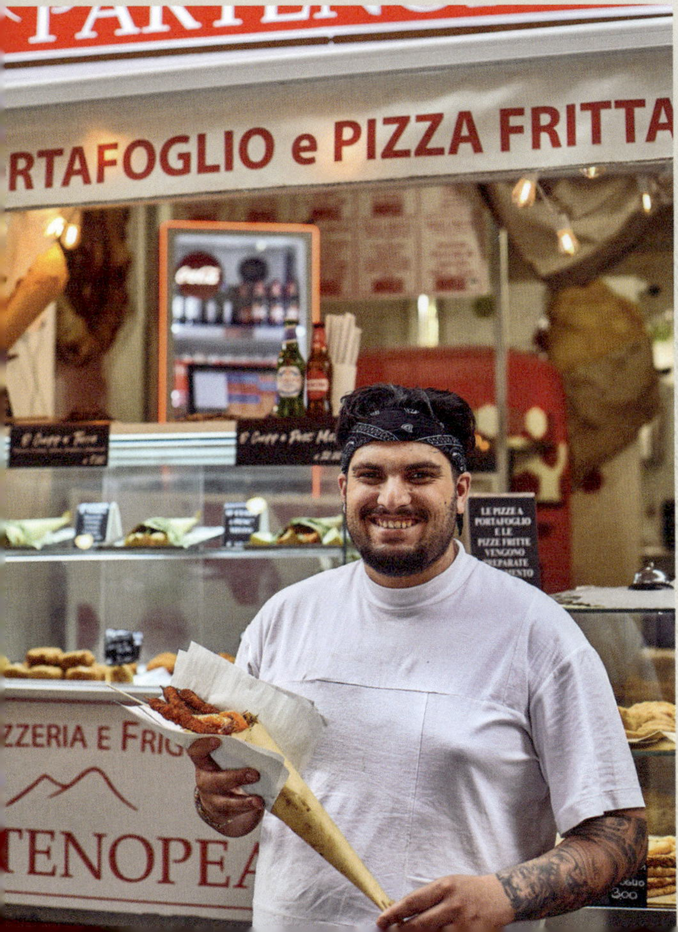
RTAFOGLIO e PIZZA FRITTA
ZZERIA E FRIG
TENOPEA

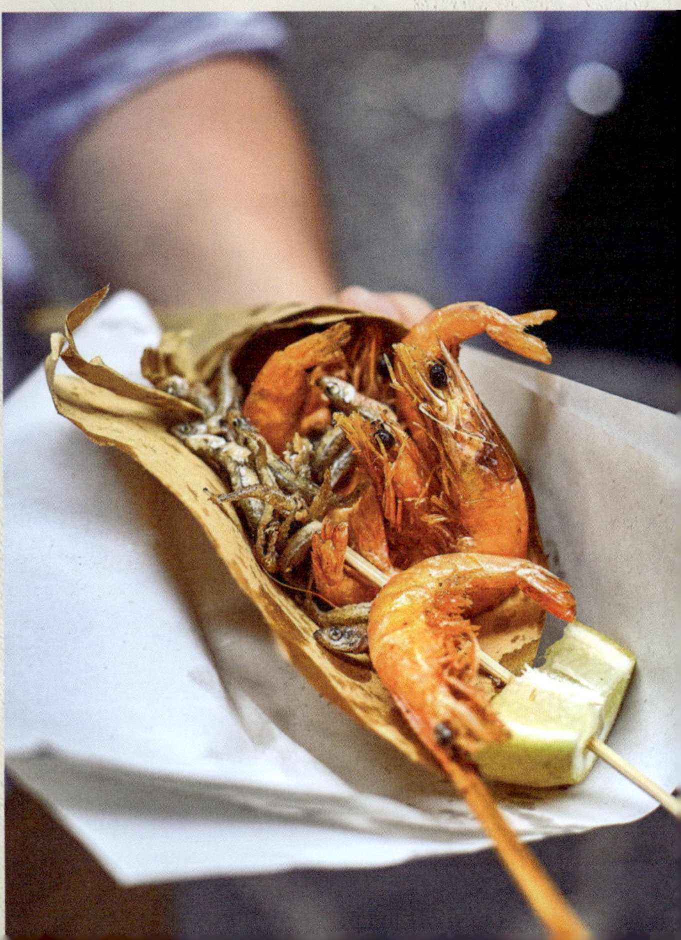

DON VINCE

MEATBALLS

Don Vincenzo. Vincè to his friends. Vincenzo senior to his grandson, Vincenzo Capuano (page 124), and an incredible pizzaiolo and chef in his own right. Vincè has been making pizza since he was 8 years old and claims to have taught his Pizza World Champion grandson everything he knows.

At the age of 82, Vincè knows a few things about traditional Neapolitan cooking. So in 2024 he opened Trattoria Don Vincè down by the Lungo Mare, a shrine to traditional cooking in Napoli. On the night we arrived, Vincè was waiting for us on the steps. He shouted at us down the street and gave us a big hug on arrival. He was kitted out head to toe in Don Vincè merch: hat, jacket, braces and tie. We complimented him on his get-up and he immediately took his tie off and gave it to us (old-school Neapolitan hospitality!). He took us into the kitchen to see his prized meatballs cooking and told us that this was *the* recipe for 'Polpette alla Napoletana'. He grabbed a ladle and fished out a few meatballs onto a plate. He then proceeded to spoon feed us one by one while singing 'Mamma Mia' on repeat. We hope this is giving you a good image of the man. We then sat down and the team brought out all the classics. Salsiccia e friarielli, pasta e patate, pasta fagioli, buffalo mozzarella, bruschetta, frittatine di maccheroni and, last but not least, a pizza fritta topped with his famous meatballs. It was such a great night. Too much food, too many amaro, and all hosted by Vincè, who was working the room like a pro. Do try these meatballs and, if you can, serve them in a white blazer!

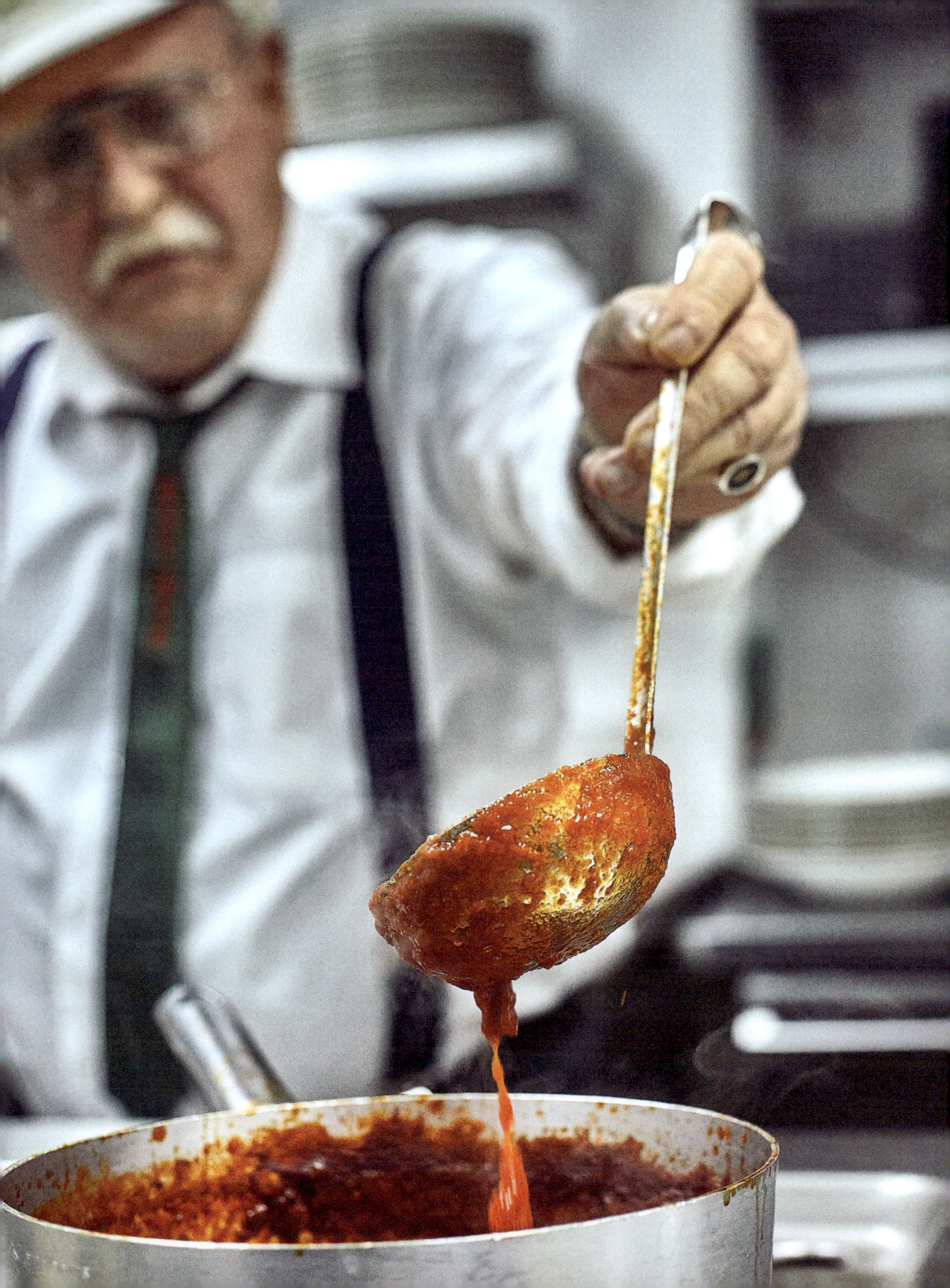

MEATBALLS ALLA VINCÈ

What you need (serves 4)

- 250g (9oz) minced (ground) beef
- 250g (9oz) minced (ground) pork
- 150g (5½oz) breadcrumbs
- 100ml (3½fl oz) milk
- 1 egg
- 50g (2oz) grated Parmesan
- extra virgin olive oil
- 1 medium onion, diced
- 2 garlic cloves, minced
- 800g (1¾lb) San Marzano tomatoes
- basil
- sea salt and black pepper

How to make it

In a large mixing bowl, combine the beef and pork mince with the breadcrumbs, milk, egg, Parmesan and a good pinch each of salt and black pepper. Mix until combined but do not overwork the meat.

Divide the mixture into about sixteen 50g (2oz) meatballs.

In a large wide-bottomed pan, heat a good glug of olive oil. Fry the meatballs until they are browned but not cooked all the way through. Remove from the pan and set aside.

Add the onion and garlic into the pan and cook for 2 minutes until softened. Add the tomatoes, followed by the same weight of water.

Cook over a low heat for 1 hour until the sauce has reduced by a third and the flavours have intensified.

Add your meatballs to the sauce, along with a good handful of basil leaves, and cook together for a further 1 hour until the flavours have combined and the meatballs are tender. During cooking, gently stir the sauce and add a little splash of water if the pan is becoming dry.

Serve with your favourite pasta, crusty bread or greens, or make a pizza fritta alla polpette… (overleaf).

PIZZA FRITTA ALLA POLPETTE

What you need (makes 4)

4 x pizza fritta dough balls (page 229)

2 litres (2 quarts) neutral cooking oil

4 meatballs, including sauce (page 257)

50g (2oz) aged Parmesan, grated

basil

How to make it

Stretch out a ball of pizza fritta dough into an even round (no puffy crust). Using your pizza stecca (spatula) or a metal spoon, tap lots of small holes in the dough to ensure it cooks evenly and doesn't puff up.

Heat your neutral oil in a deep-sided pan to 180°C (356°F). It should be deep enough to cover one pizza fritta at a time. Drop the dough into the oil, using 2 spatulas to keep the dough as flat and round as possible. Fry on each side for 2–3 minutes to achieve a beautiful golden crust. Remove from the pan and dab with kitchen paper to remove excess oil.

Heat the meatballs in a pan with some of the sauce, then top each pizza fritta with one meatball and a few spoonfuls of sauce.

Finish with Parmesan and fresh basil leaves.

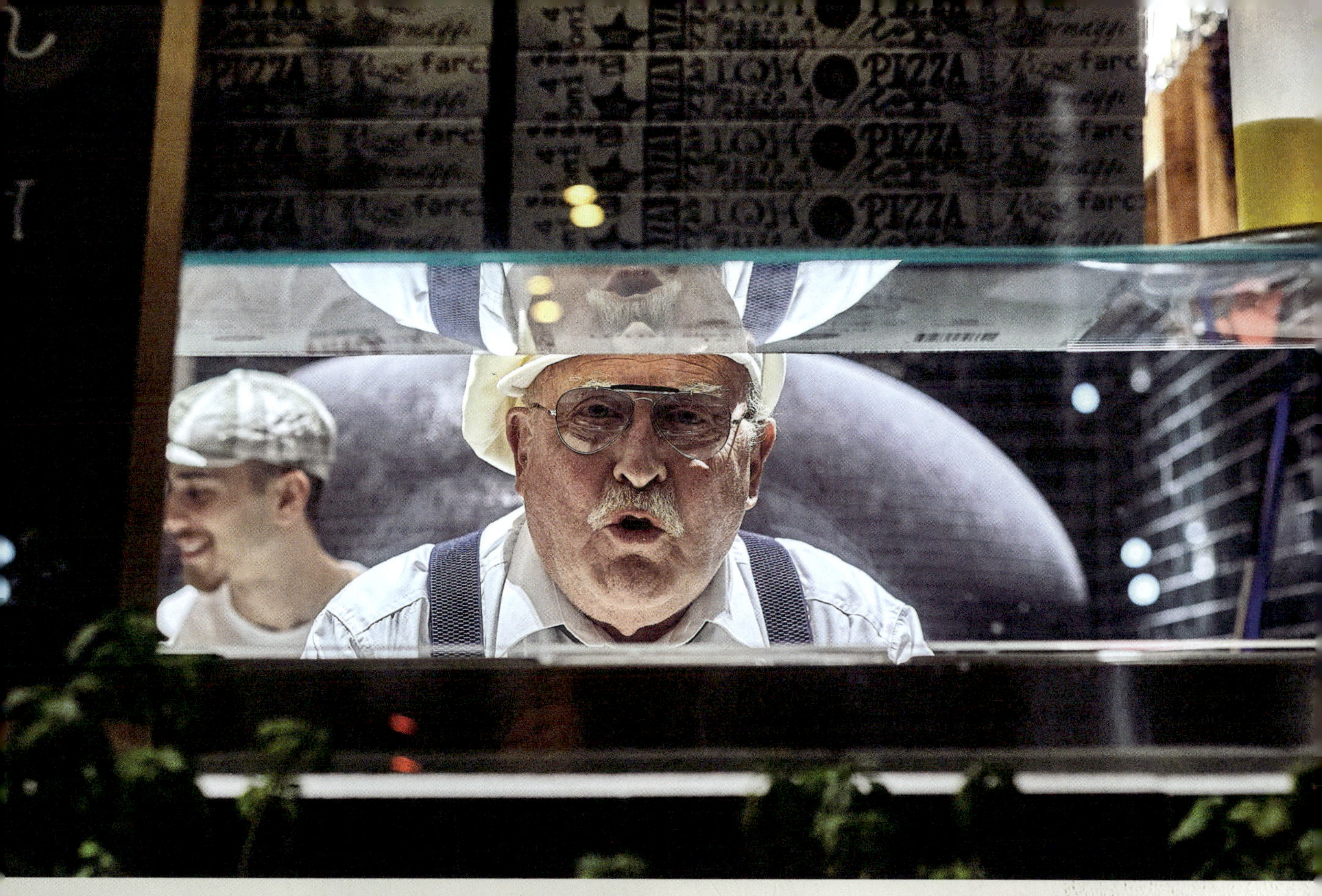
PIZZA

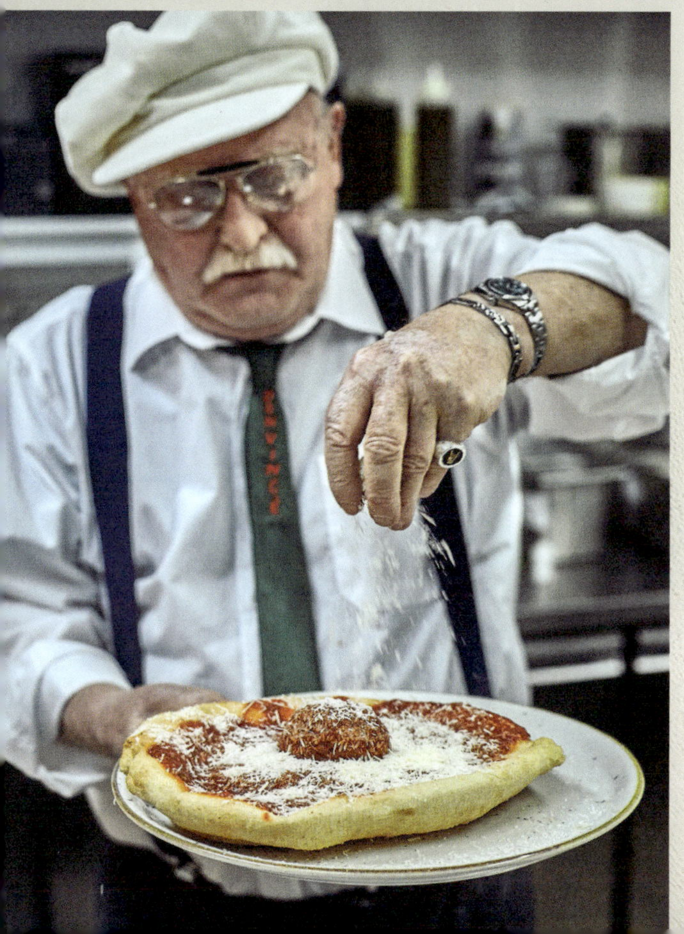

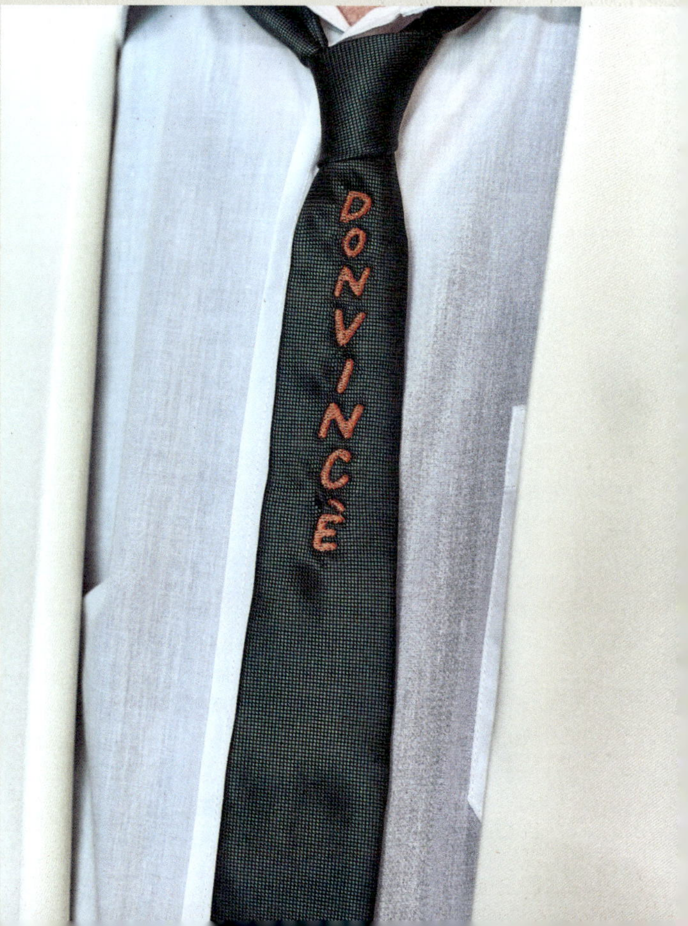
DONVINCÉ

NENNELLA

If you want to taste some good old-fashioned traditional Neapolitan cooking, then you need to go to Trattoria da Nennella. If you also want to be manhandled by your waiter, screamed at for ordering the wrong thing, and all round have the best night ever… you also have to go to Nennella. Every time we are in Napoli with some of our team, we book a big table and it's always the best, most raucous night of the trip.

This little trattoria right in the heart of the Spanish Quarter has been going since 1950 and is a bit of an institution. According to the locals, it's always been this way – waiters dancing on tables, loud accordion music and a classically Neapolitan attitude towards hospitality where they take no bullshit, but all with a smile on their face. We remember one time going there and the owner was hanging from the window bars, air humping to Neapolitan techno and shouting on repeat, *'Juve merda! Juve merda!'*, while pouring a shot of limoncello (we're not sure he was classically trained…).

OK, so go for the experience but also go for the food. The fixed menu for €15 (last time we were there) includes a mixed plate of Italian appetizers with some of the best buffalo mozzarella we've ever eaten. Next you can choose between grilled sausages and friarielli (page 105), seafood paccheri, or their house speciality, pasta e patate. Make sure you get one of everything but make sure you're sitting near the pasta e patate. This is a Napoli classic and something that is cooked more in the home than in restaurants, so tourists don't often get to try it. It's a cheesy, double-carb hit of comfort and probably the best expression of the southern Italian tradition of *cucina povera*, making the most out of not that much.

Once you've finished your food and as many €3 bottles of wine as you can, you are unceremoniously kicked off your table with a small ticket each, which you take outside to a little street stall and exchange for a limoncello, meloncello, amaro or espresso. From there you roll down the hill into the €1 spritz bars of the Spanish Quarter, and the rest of the night gets a little blurry.

TRATTORIA DA
Nennella

PASTA E PATATE

What you need (serves 4)

100ml (3½fl oz) extra virgin olive oil

1 onion, diced

100g (3½oz) smoked pancetta, cubed

½ glass of white wine

600g (1lb 5oz) potatoes, peeled and cut into about 2cm (¾ inch) cubes

8 cherry tomatoes, diced

50g (1¾oz) Parmesan, grated, plus the rind if you have it

400g (14oz) dried mixed pasta shapes (great for using up all your pasta dregs)

150g (5½oz) provola (smoked) mozzarella, cubed

sea salt and black pepper

How to make it

Heat the olive oil in a large pan, add the onion and cook over a medium heat for 2–3 minutes. Add the pancetta and fry until it takes on a little colour and the onions are soft.

Deglaze the pan with the white wine and cook out for a minute.

Add the potatoes and tomatoes, followed by enough water to nearly cover. Add in the Parmesan rind, if using, and simmer over a medium heat until the potatoes are nearly cooked.

Add the pasta and continue to cook over a medium heat, stirring. Add the grated Parmesan and the provola, turn down the heat and stir vigorously. As you stir, the cheese should melt and some of the potato will break down, thickening the sauce to a luxurious, creamy consistency.

Finally, season with salt and pepper to taste and serve up in shallow bowls.

Apparently the sign of a good pasta e patate is you should be able to flip the bowl without losing the contents… good luck with that!

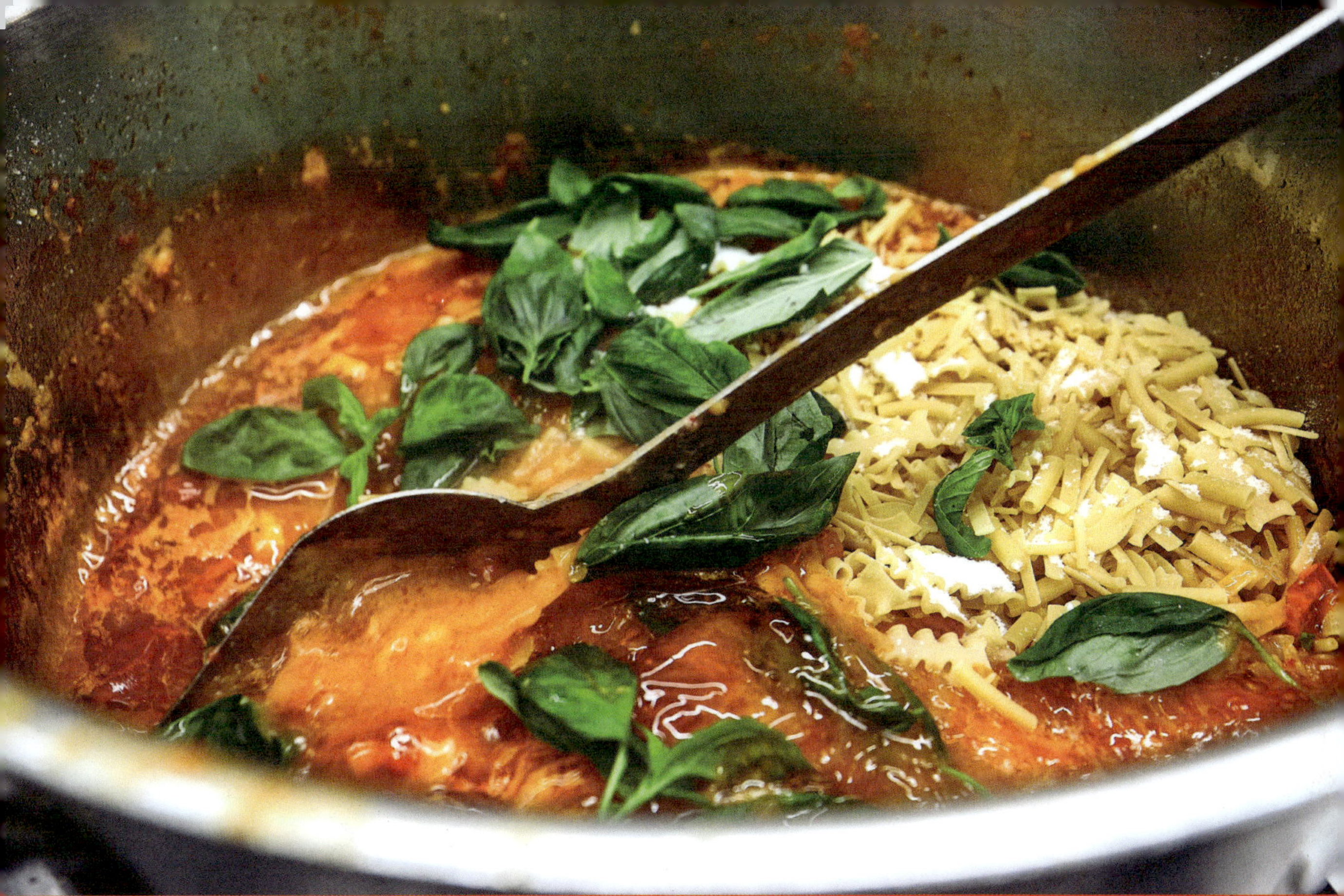

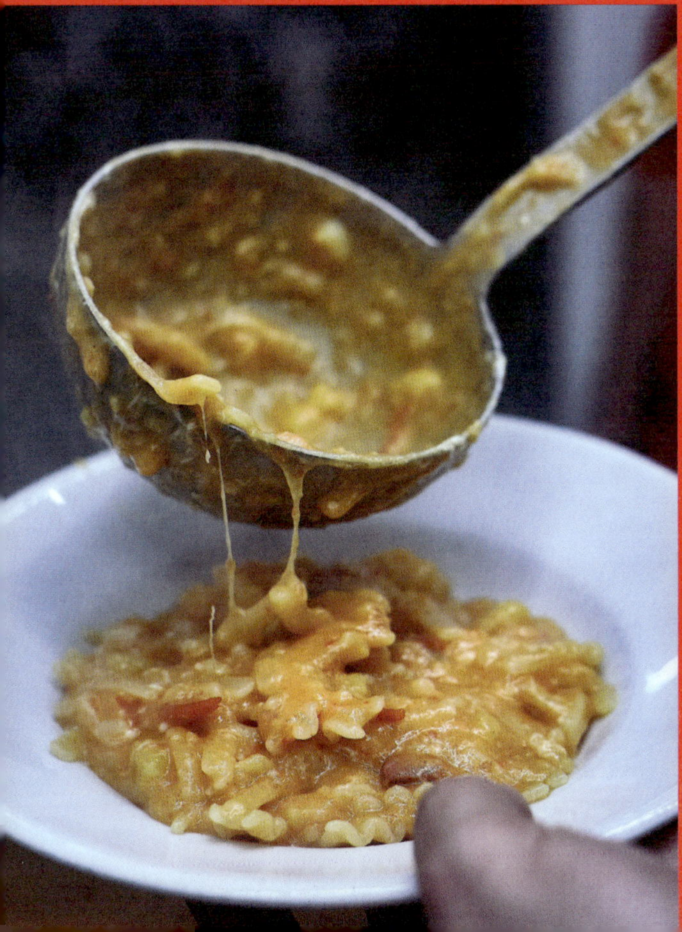

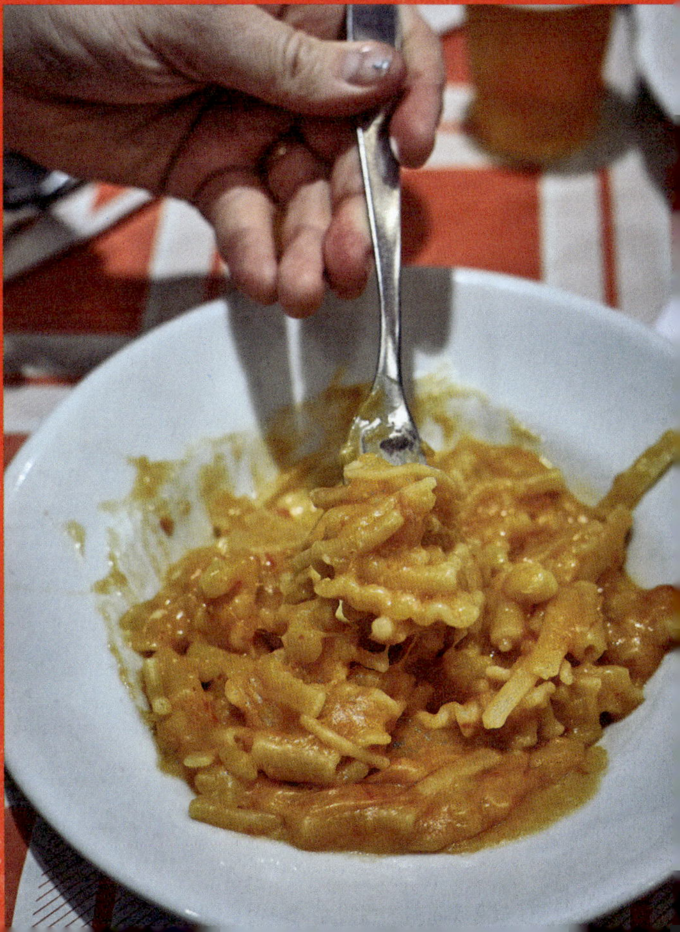

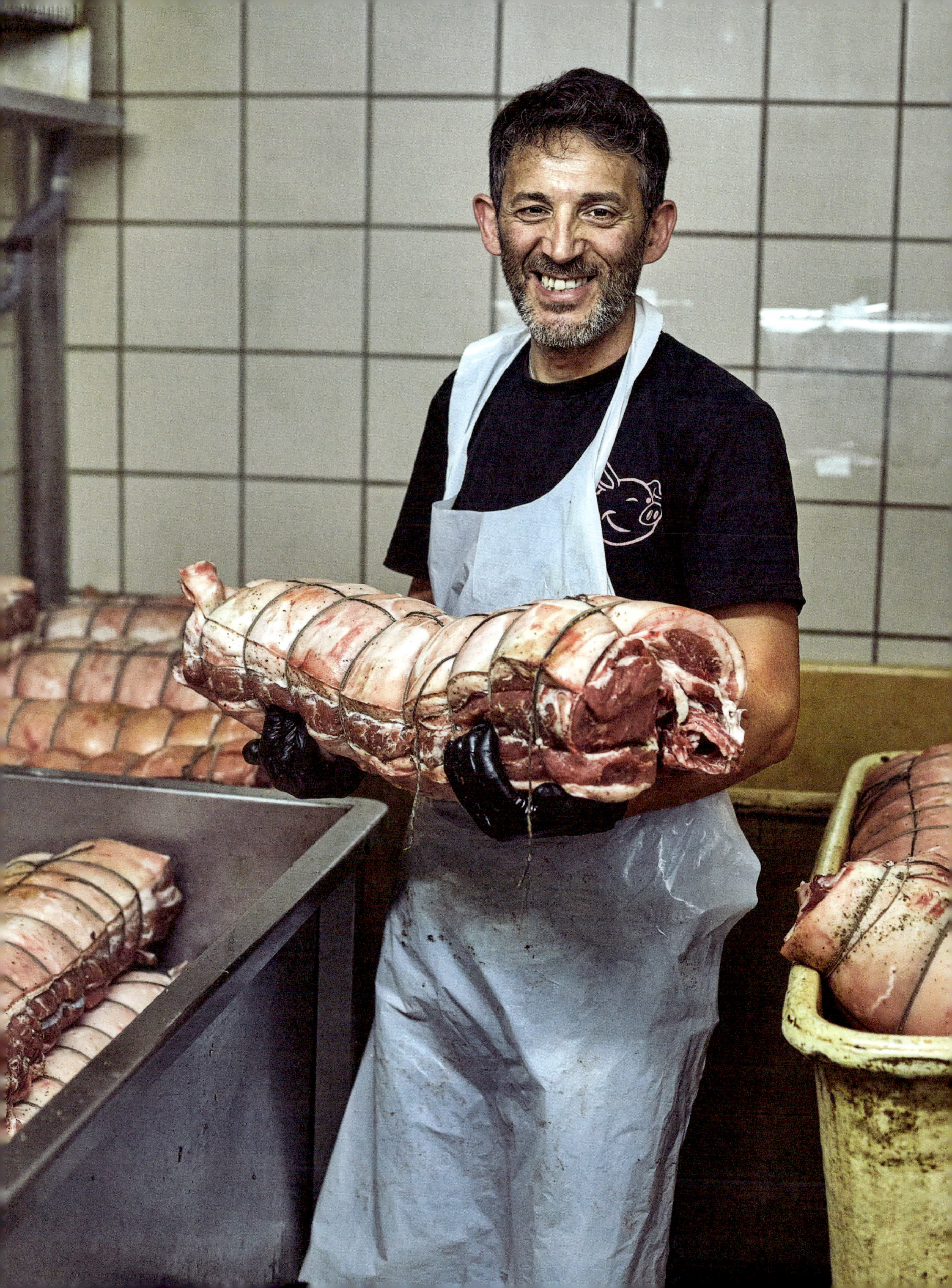

'Porchetta di Napoli? No. Porchetta is Roman!',

says every Italian *ever* when we mention the amazing porchetta coming out of a small unit on the outskirts of Napoli. As we picked flies out of our teeth after a harrowing Vespa motorway stint on the A1 to Caiazzo, passing made him look more like a sailor than butcher. Thirty seconds later and the porchetta was fully tied and ready for roasting. It was transferred to a 'meat gurney' with the others and walked through to the ovens (which are 30-foot deep and take around 20 porchettas at a time!). The doors were closed and the porchetta cooked at 160°C (320°F) for 6–8 hours.

PORCHETTA

Mount Vesuvius behind us, we arrived at a very unassuming production facility on an industrial estate. As we pulled in, Federico came out to greet us. The smell of roasting pork was immediate and he brought us through the plastic curtain to unveil a veritable temple of porchetta.

To the right, Federico's mamma, Giovanna, was wrapping up the day's work, and down the corridor we arrived in the 'porchetta stuffing room'. The speed at which they move is impressive. Federico's colleague Lello fireman-lifted a whole side of Italian pork onto his operating table and set to work deftly deboning the ribs at a rate of about one every two seconds. He then spun the pig, trimmed up some of the fat and made extra incisions so that the flavourings could penetrate deeper. Then the spice mix came out. Federico says it's top secret, but from a little post mortem we detected black pepper, salt, garlic, rosemary, fennel seeds, dried chilli flakes and (maybe) celery salt. The secret mix was liberally applied, and then it was on to the truly magic bit. Lello took out what looked like baler twine and began to make insanely quick and complex loop-and-knot routines that

Federico then opened the other oven next door to reveal the final product emerging from the steam like a contestant on *Stars in Their Eyes* (porchetta in their eyes? I'd watch that show…). The fat had all rendered into the tray below, and was bubbling. The skin was crisp with the most perfect crackling. Federico pushed one of the porchettas with both hands. It cracked off the tray, and incredible juices started running from the meat. He carved off a hunk and we tried it right there, straight from the oven. It was honestly the most delicious roast meat, full of flavour and juiciness.

The porchetta was then left to cool before being wrapped in paper. For the time being, Federico only supplies local restaurants and salumerias, but he is keen to share his produce far and wide. We are in talks to be the first to import it into the UK! Watch this space…

As we 'de-hairnetted', Federico handed us a giant 5kg (11lb) piece of porchetta straight off the line and gave us the number of his good friend Renato Ruggiero, who he said would show us how to cook with it (page 268). Truly what porchetta dreams are made of…

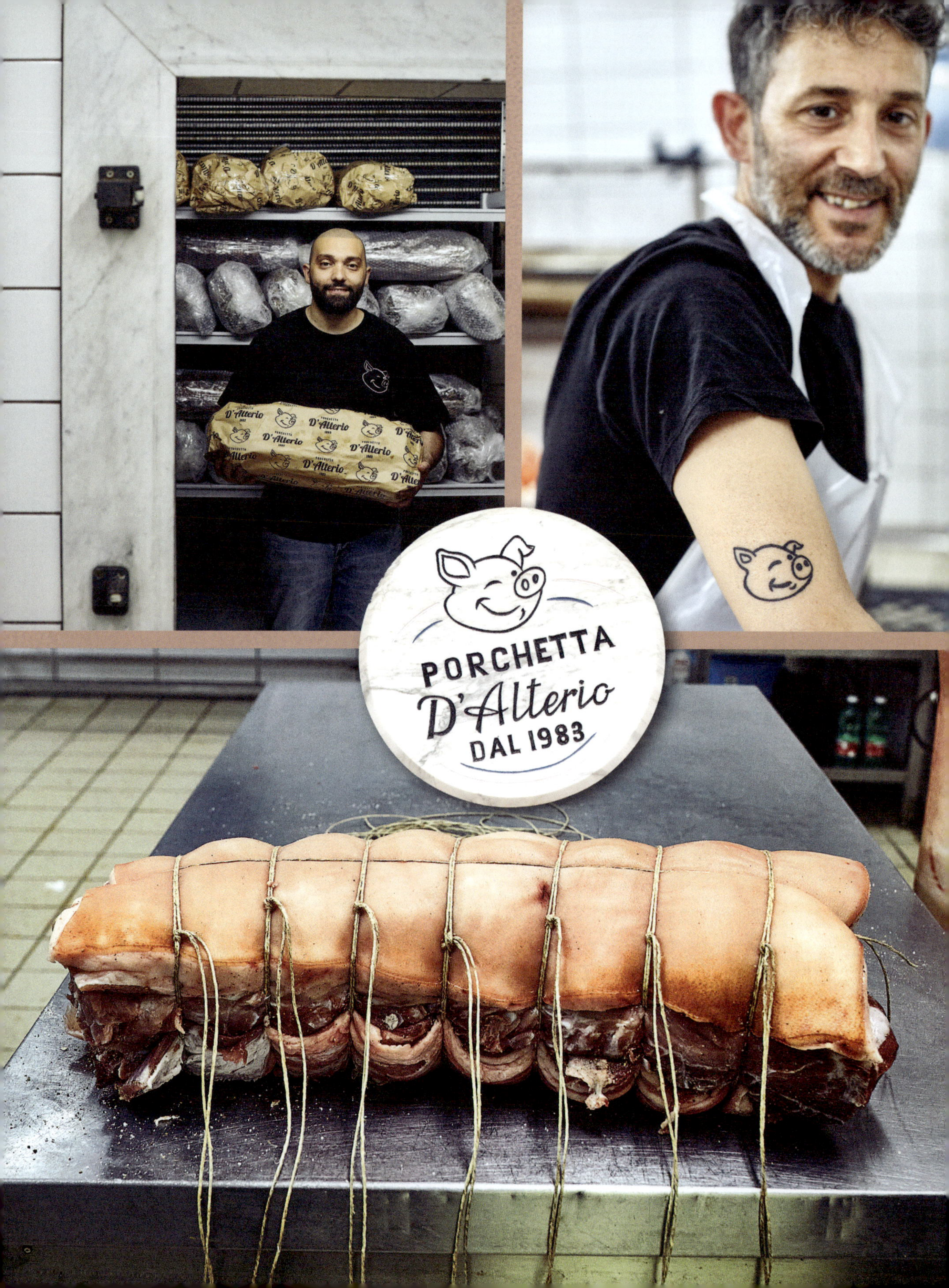
PORCHETTA
D'Alterio
DAL 1983

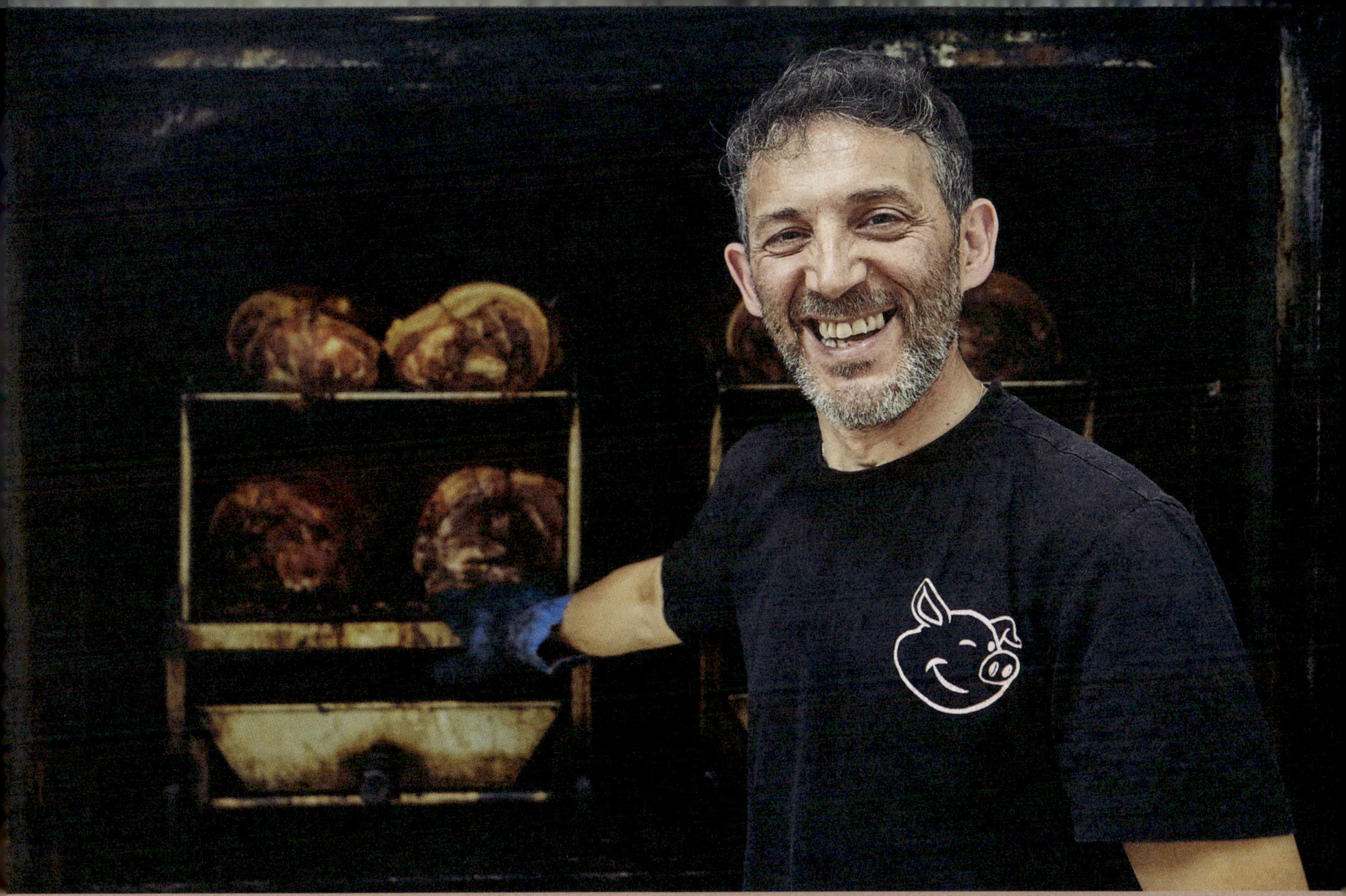
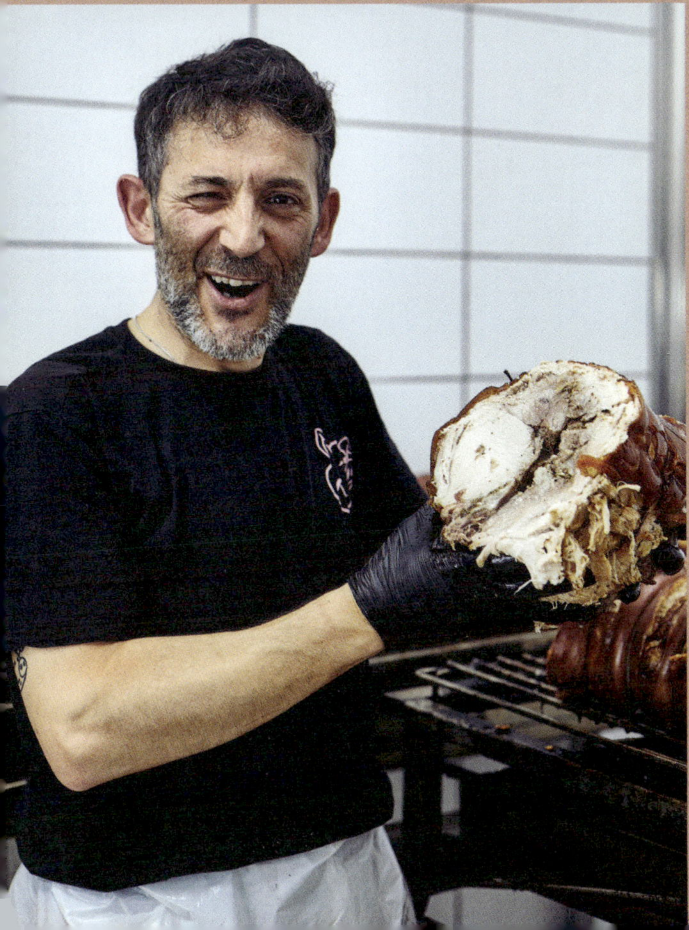
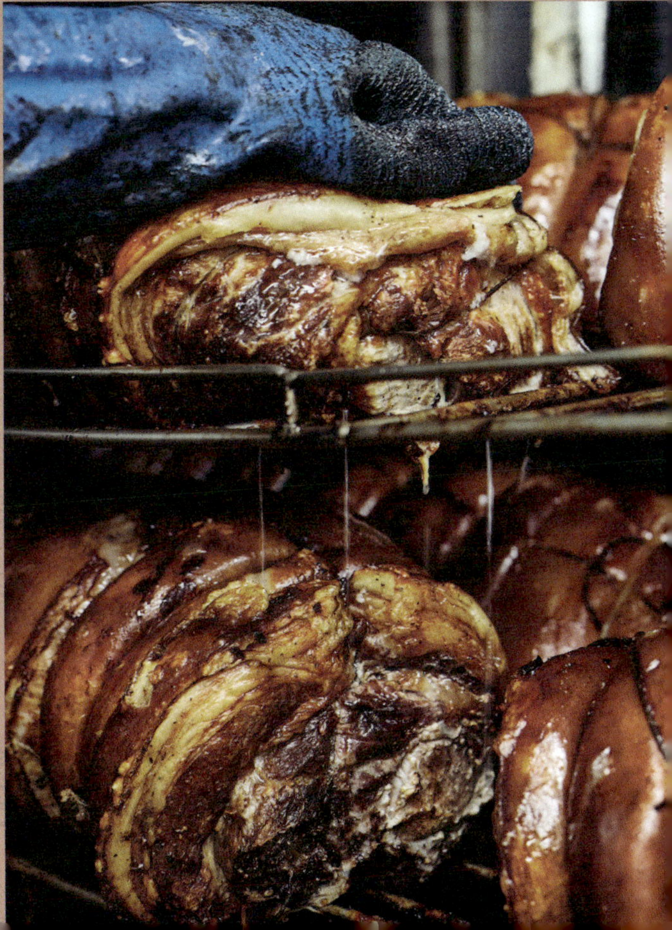

PORCHETTOPELI

What you need

contemporanea pizza dough (page 93)

thinly sliced porchetta

provola (smoked) mozzarella

Parmesan

porchetta crackling

basil

extra virgin olive oil

How to make it

Stretch a ball of dough out and top it with porchetta and provola mozzarella. Grate over some Parmesan, then bake it in the oven.

Finish with come crispy crackling, basil and a drizzle of extra virgin olive oil.

RENATO RUGGIERO

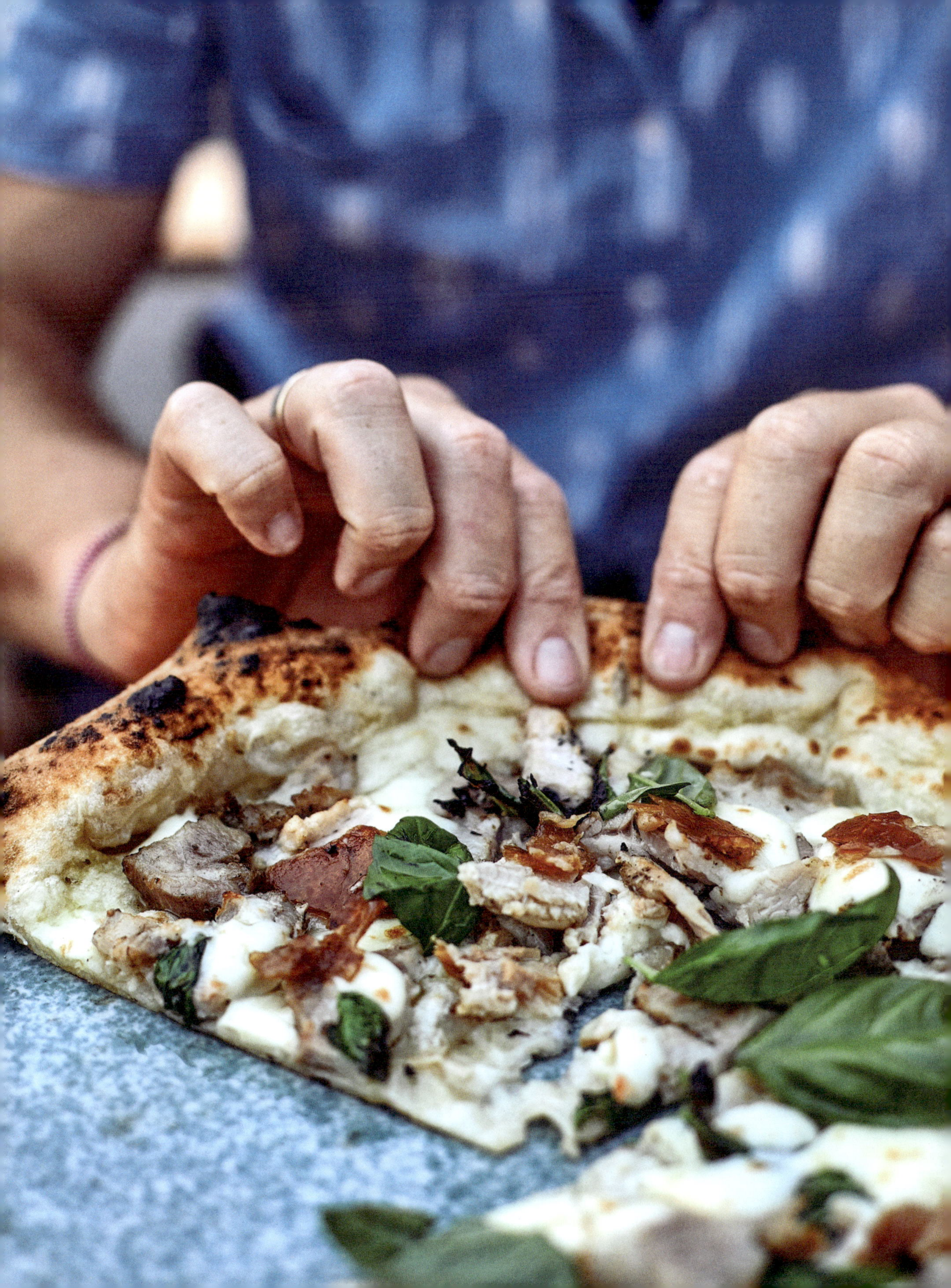

'O PERE E 'O MUSSO

As you walk down Pignasecca market in the Centro Storico, you'll come across a shop with a big glass window proudly displaying boiled pigs' feet and calves' snouts, along with whatever offal is available at the time. The offal is hung from hooks and dressed with lemons as well as a dripping water system to keep the flies away... which only adds to the slightly ominous nature of the shop. What they are selling – *'o pere e 'o musso* – directly translates as 'the foot and the muzzle'. With a giant cleaver, pieces of offal are hacked into bite-sized pieces and tossed into a tray. They are then topped with thin slices of fennel, the juice of half an Amalfi lemon and a seriously good dose of salt, which is usually administered from a cow's horn. A couple of rocket (arugula) leaves and the dish is complete. We remember going for our first bite of foot and face salad and thinking, why? But we were pleasantly surprised. It's tangy, well-seasoned and you couldn't accuse it of being texturally boring... if you can forgive what part of the animal you're eating, tendons have a very satisfying texture. We mean, it's not making it onto the menu any time soon at Pizza Pilgrims, but we do love this dish for how proud the people of Napoli are of it, and how the younger generations embrace it as well. Also, it is delicious with a beer, there's no denying it!

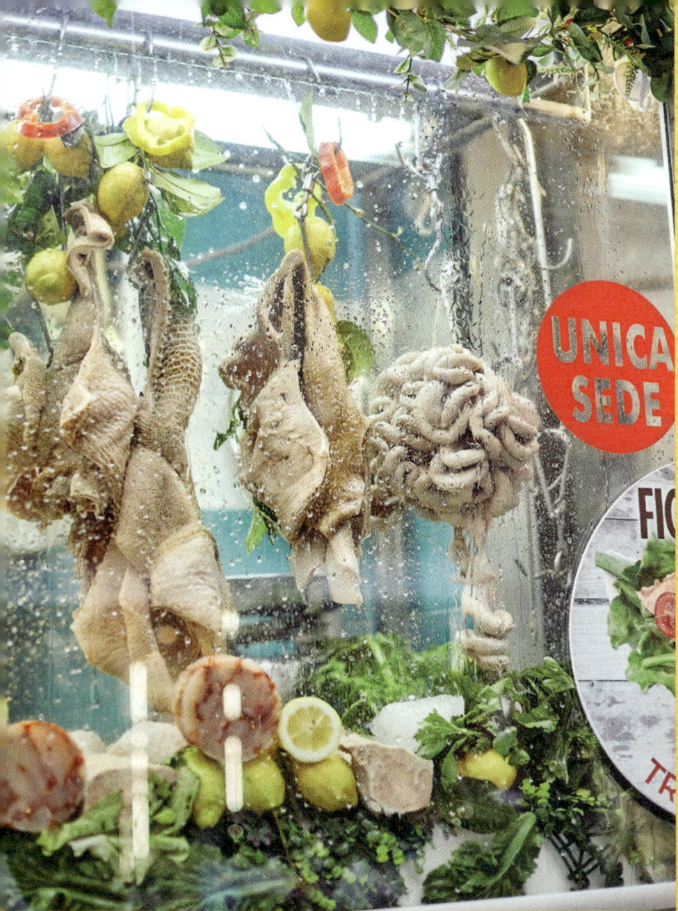
UNICA
SEDE

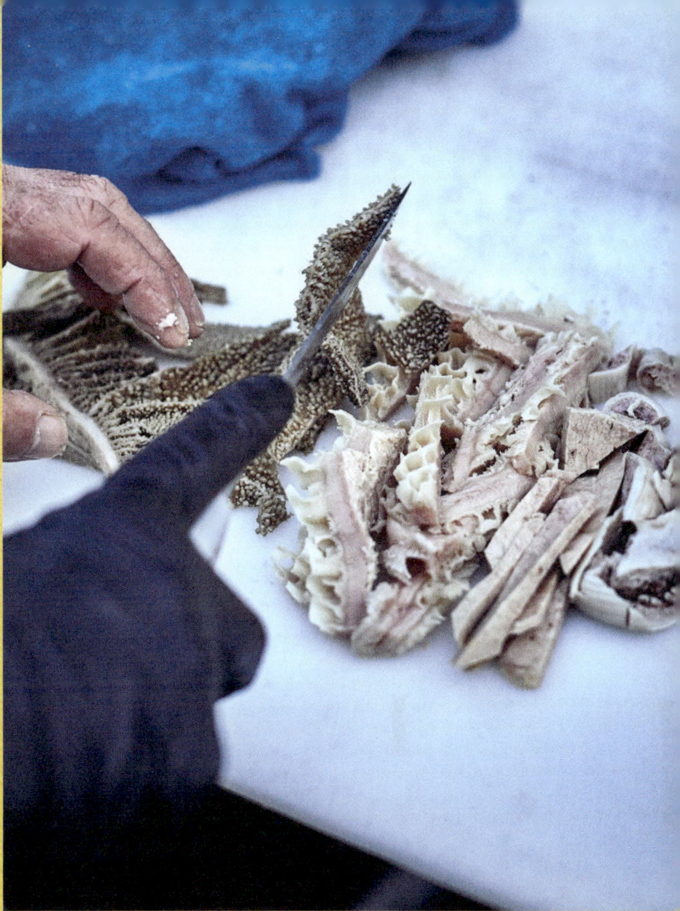

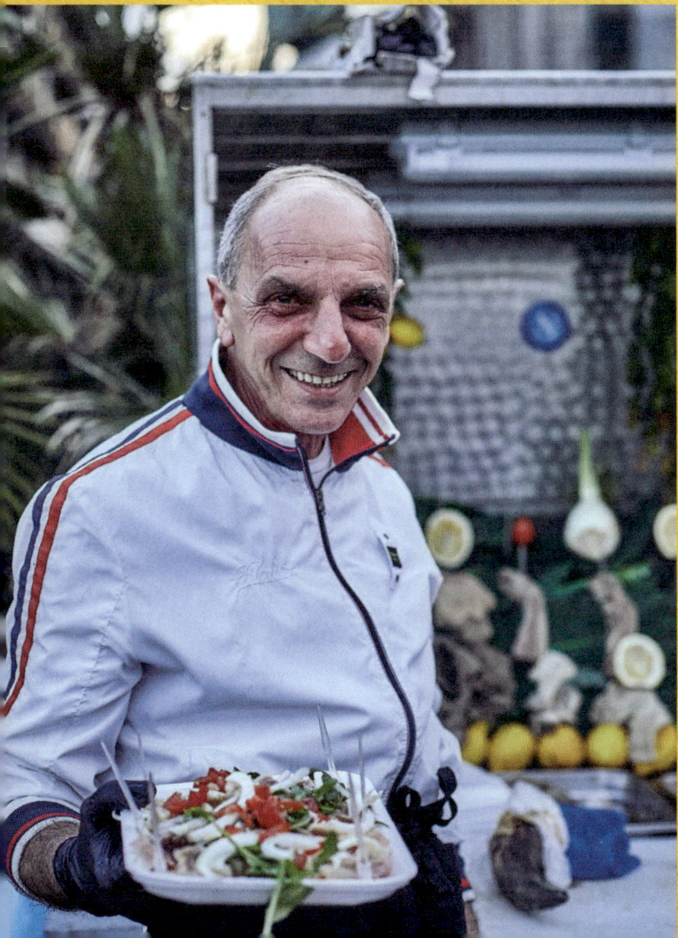

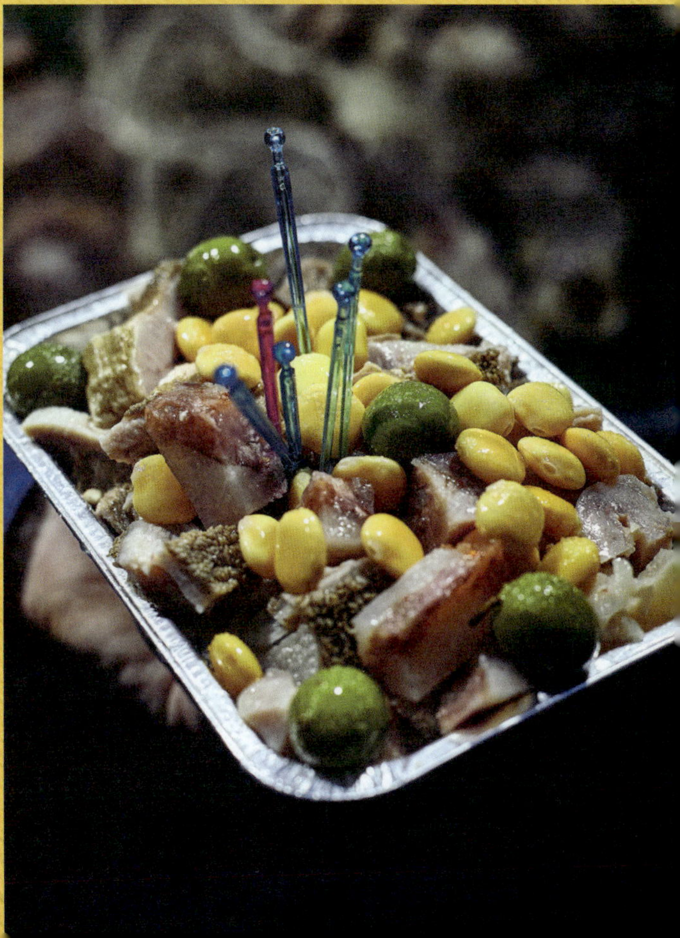

GENOVESE

Genovese: a sauce that literally translates as 'from Genoa' and it's from... Napoli. Go figure. The story goes that it was either brought to Napoli in the 15th century by Genovese sailors arriving in the port of Napoli, or it's named after someone with the surname Genovese (which was very common at the time). Either way, Genovese sauce is the much beloved and lesser known brother to traditional Neapolitan ragù. It's such a simple sauce, in its essence, comprising of mainly sweet onions and beef. When we got to Napoli we asked everyone where to find the best Genovese in the city. Almost all paths led to a man named Alfonso. We arrived at Alfonso's restaurant, Ristorante Europea Mattozzi, which has been open since the '60s, and Alfonso greeted us at the door wearing a sports jacket, cravat, pocket square and incredibly shiny shoes. Alfonso is the real deal. The walls are adorned with photos of him and his wife in the '60s looking unbelievably glamorous – you can tell he has lived a life like one out of the movies. Plus he's an incredible host; he sat us down and started to bring out plate after plate of antipasti. Old-school Neapolitan stuff like anchovy-stuffed courgette flowers, tomato and celery salad, salami, and the freshest buffalo mozzarella you ever tasted. He then invited us back to the kitchen to talk all about Genovese. 'It's about the onions,' he told us. 'You have to reduce and caramelize the onions to release their sweet flavour; low and slow for as long as possible.' He shared with us the recipe he's been using for over 50 years. Make this one rainy Sunday afternoon and raise a glass to Alfonso, The Genovese King. (Recipe overleaf.)

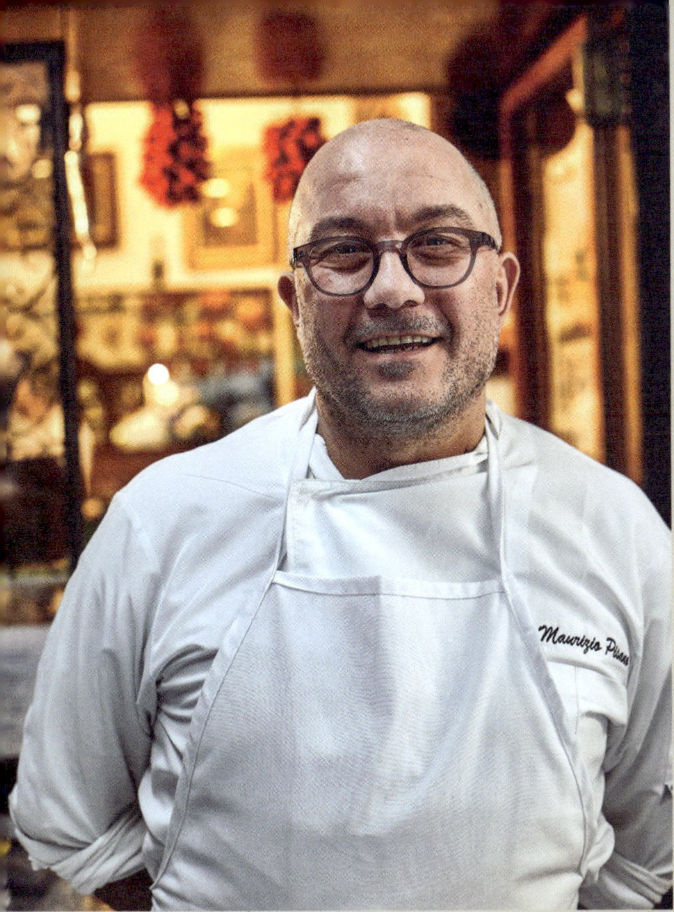
Maurizio

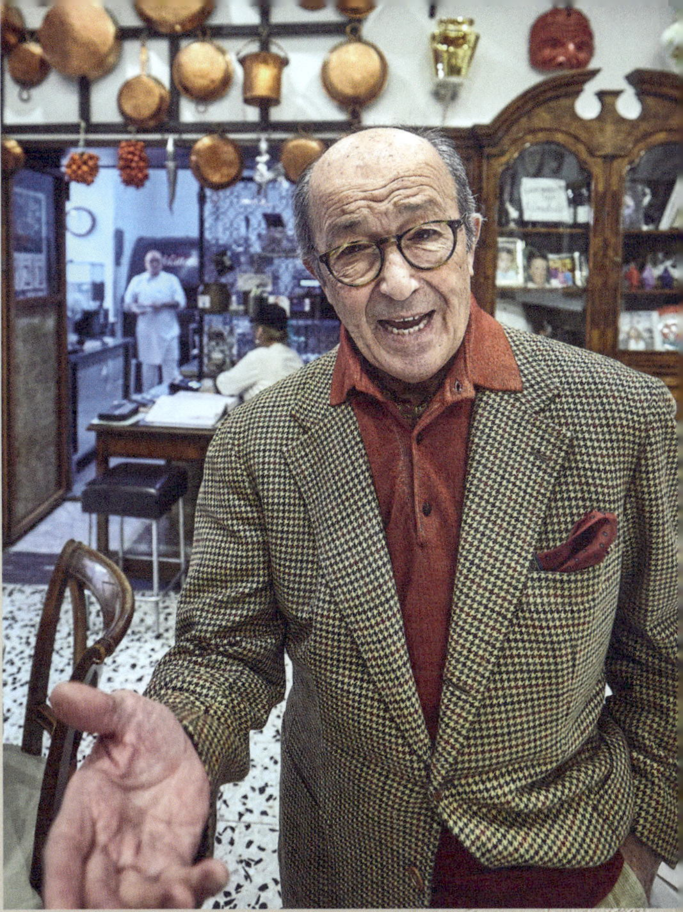

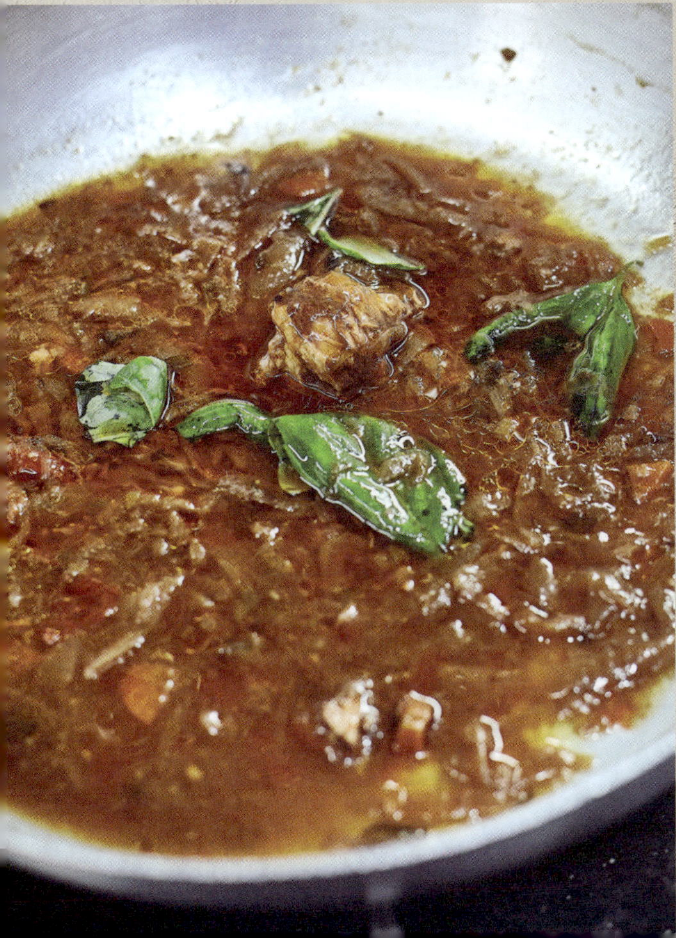

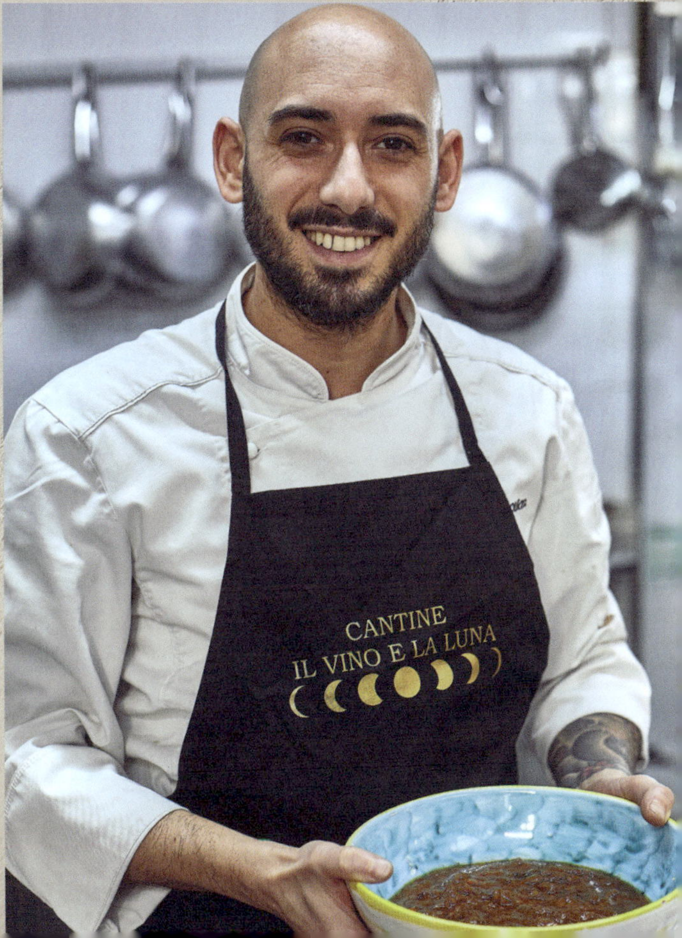
CANTINE
IL VINO E LA LUNA

ZITI ALLA GENOVESE

What you need (serves 6)

extra virgin olive oil

750g (26oz) beef shoulder (chuck), cubed

1.5kg (3½lb) white onions, finely sliced

1 medium carrot, finely diced

2 celery sticks, finely diced

3 bay leaves

250ml (9fl oz) white wine

500g (1lb 2oz) long ziti pasta (rigatoni is also fine)

50g (2oz) Parmesan, grated

basil

sea salt and black pepper

How to make it

Heat a glug of olive oil in a large wide-bottomed pan. Add the beef, season with salt and pepper, and fry until it has taken on some good colour, then add the onions, carrot, celery and bay leaves.

Turn down the heat to low, place a lid on the pan and cook for 2 hours, checking every 30 minutes to ensure it is not burning.

Add the wine and continue to cook for a further 2 hours or until the meat is incredibly tender and the onions have collapsed into a soft, sweet sauce.

Remove the meat from the sauce and use two forks to pull it into strands, then stir it back into the sauce.

Cook the pasta in boiling water until al dente, then drain, reserving some of cooking water.

Add the sauce to the pasta and toss it all together, adding splashes of the pasta cooking water to help the sauce come together.

Top with the grated Parmesan and some basil leaves before serving.

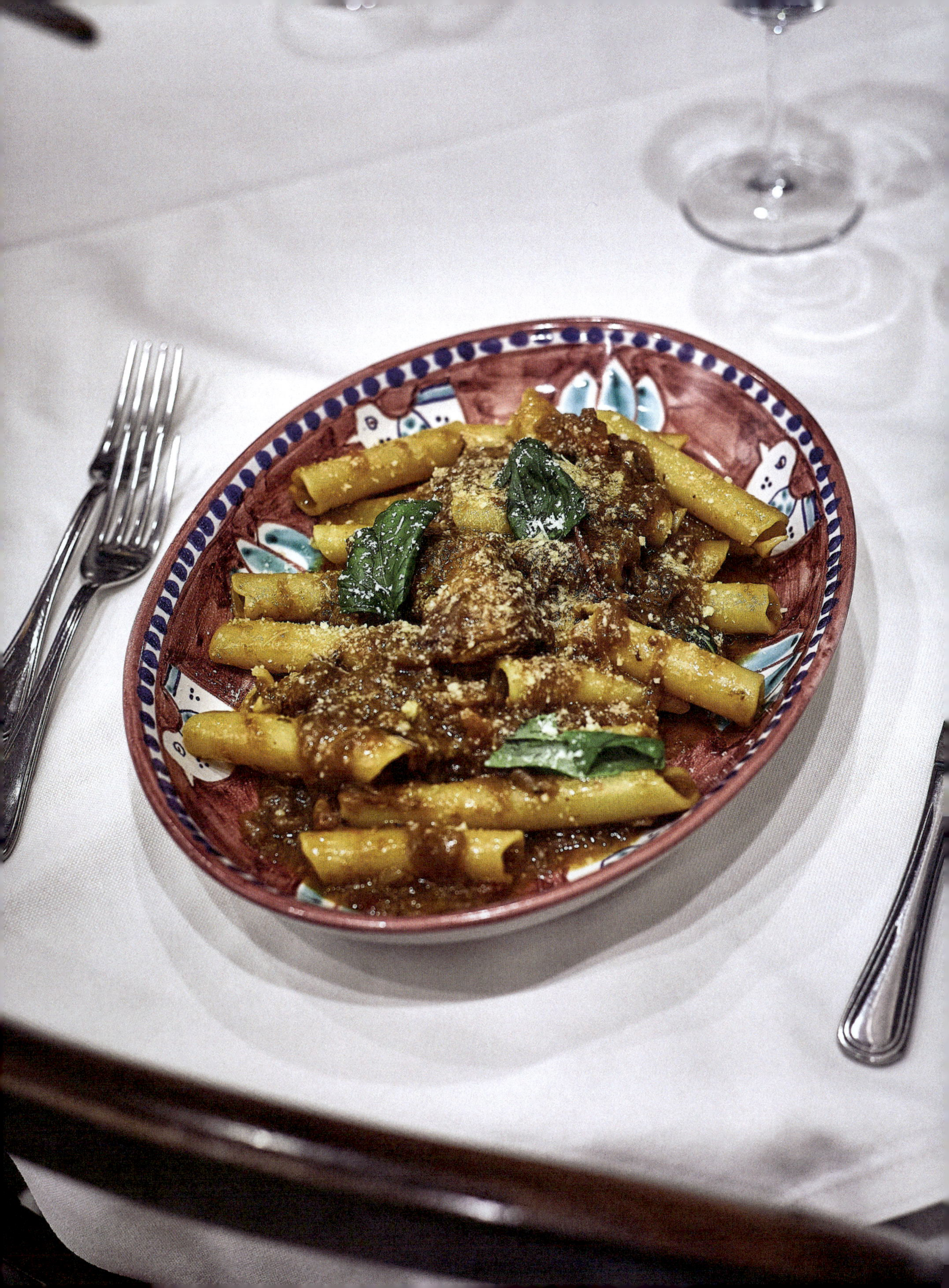

PIZZA GENOVESE

What you need

STG pizza dough (page 92)

Genovese sauce (page 274), cooled

provola (smoked) mozzarella

basil

Parmesan, grated

extra virgin olive oil

How to make it

Stretch a ball of dough out and spread it with some cooled Genovese sauce. Top it with provola mozzarella and some basil leaves, then bake in the oven.

Finish with a some grated Parmesan, a drizzle of extra virgin olive oil, and some more basil.

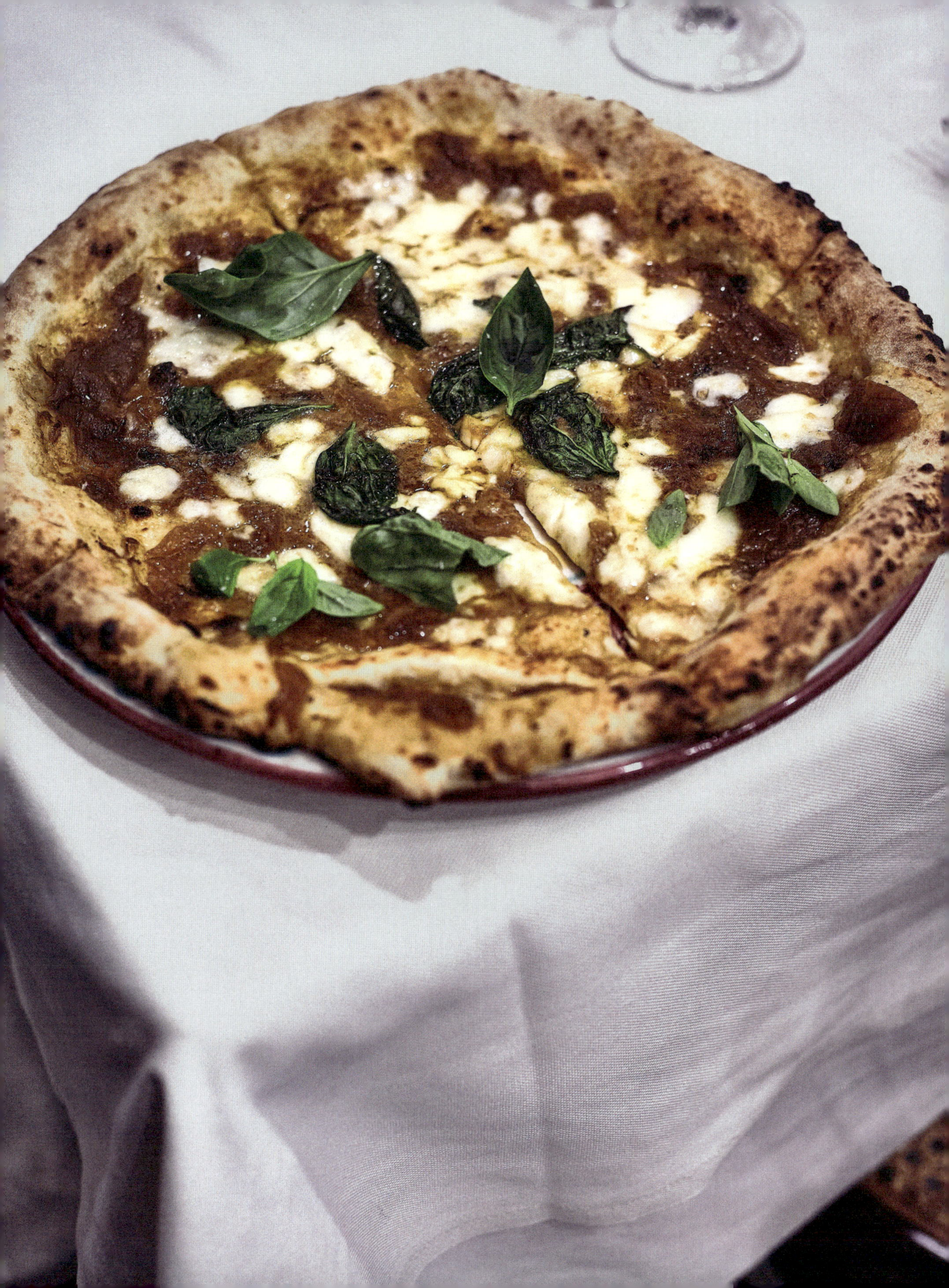

ZINZI
since 1938

SALUMERIAS & PANINI

The truth is, you smell a salumeria before you see it. It's a heady mix of cured hanging hams and salamis; big tanks of that morning's mozzarella sitting in water; huge vats of marinated olives; and bundles of dried herbs strung up over the door. These amazing temples to Neapolitan produce act as central hubs in the community, negating the need for supermarkets and allowing people to shop daily for their food, grab a sandwich at lunch, have a little bitch to the owner about how hot it is, and maybe even get an Amazon parcel delivered.

So here's how it works. You walk in and take a ticket. You then wait 10–15 minutes before you realise that the ticket machine means nothing and you just have to barge your way to the front counter to get served. You talk to the owner about what you want to cook and they will tell you what you should buy: wafer thin pancetta, a big hunk of local Aurichio provolone, some dried pasta and sun-dried tomatoes, and you're set.

Then it's time for the panini. We *love* these panini. They use a bread called sfilatino, which is a foot-long, baguette-style bread that is baked fresh every day, either in the basement or in the bakery around the corner. They cut open the bread and ask '*con mollica o senza?*', which means 'with crumb or without?' You, of course, should say 'without'. They then rip out the soft middle of the loaf, making more room for fillings, and you get to pick anything you like from the counter to fill it.

Here's our order. Start with a base of stracciatella mozzarella, then top this with an embarrassment of wafer-thin (and we mean wafer-thin) mortadella. On the other side of the bread, you want pistachio pesto, then ask them to finish it off by crumbling in whole almond *tarallo* (twisted breadstick snack) to add crunch. The panini is then wrapped up in a huge sheet of paper, chopped in half and bagged up. Grab yourself a little carton of Estathè (Italian peach iced tea) and a Kinder Bueno for good measure and that's lunch sorted.

MOZZARELLA
DI BUFALA
DA VIAGGIO
SOLO ROBBA
E LUSSO
P. De Stefano

COFFEE

& DOLCI

COFFEE CULTURE

If there is one thing more important than pizza in Napoli, it's espresso. Without espresso we don't think anything would happen. It's drunk morning, noon and night, at home, in the street, after meals, after work, before work, to celebrate, to commiserate. Basically, whenever possible.

It arrived on the scene in the 16th century, and following a tricky start after the Catholic Church called it the 'devil's drink', it soon picked up pace. It really took hold first in the port cities that were importing from Africa and the Arab nations, like Trieste and Napoli. Coffee was embraced by the artists, writers and musicians of Napoli, and cafés popped up all over the city, making coffee with great care in cuccumellas or moka pots.

Today, coffee plays a huge role in the city's culture; as you arrive in Piazza Garibaldi you see a vast Hollywood-sized neon sign saying KIMBO, the most famous coffee brand in Napoli.

One of the most special coffee traditions in Napoli is the *caffè sospeso*. Translating as 'suspended coffee', the idea is that you can come to a coffee shop and pay for an extra coffee that someone else less fortunate than you can then come and collect. Somehow this is a perfect analogy for the city. It's a tough place, but people help each other, and the idea that someone can't have their daily coffee because they've fallen on hard times is something that the people felt they needed to fix.

Five rules to drinking espresso in Napoli

Drinking espresso in a bar in Napoli is a ritual, and there are rules. Follow these steps and you'll look like a Neapolitan in no time.

1. Never order a cappuccino after 12pm. Everyone knows that, but to be honest ordering anything but espresso at any time of day is frowned upon. Stick to the strong stuff.

2. You have to pay at the till first, then take your ticket to the counter. You'll show yourself up as a rookie immediately if you try to pay the barista.

3. Always make sure you get the little glass of sparkling water on the side. You take your first sip to cleanse your palate before the espresso.

4. Sugar. Now, we don't drink coffee with sugar normally, but in Napoli it's kind of the done thing. Take a sugar packet, flick it between your fingers, rip it, pour it, stir it. It's all part of their ritual – just go with it.

5. Cups are kept hot to not ruin the espresso. So once you've stirred your coffee, take some of the espresso and spread it around the rim. This will temper the heat and stop you burning your lips.

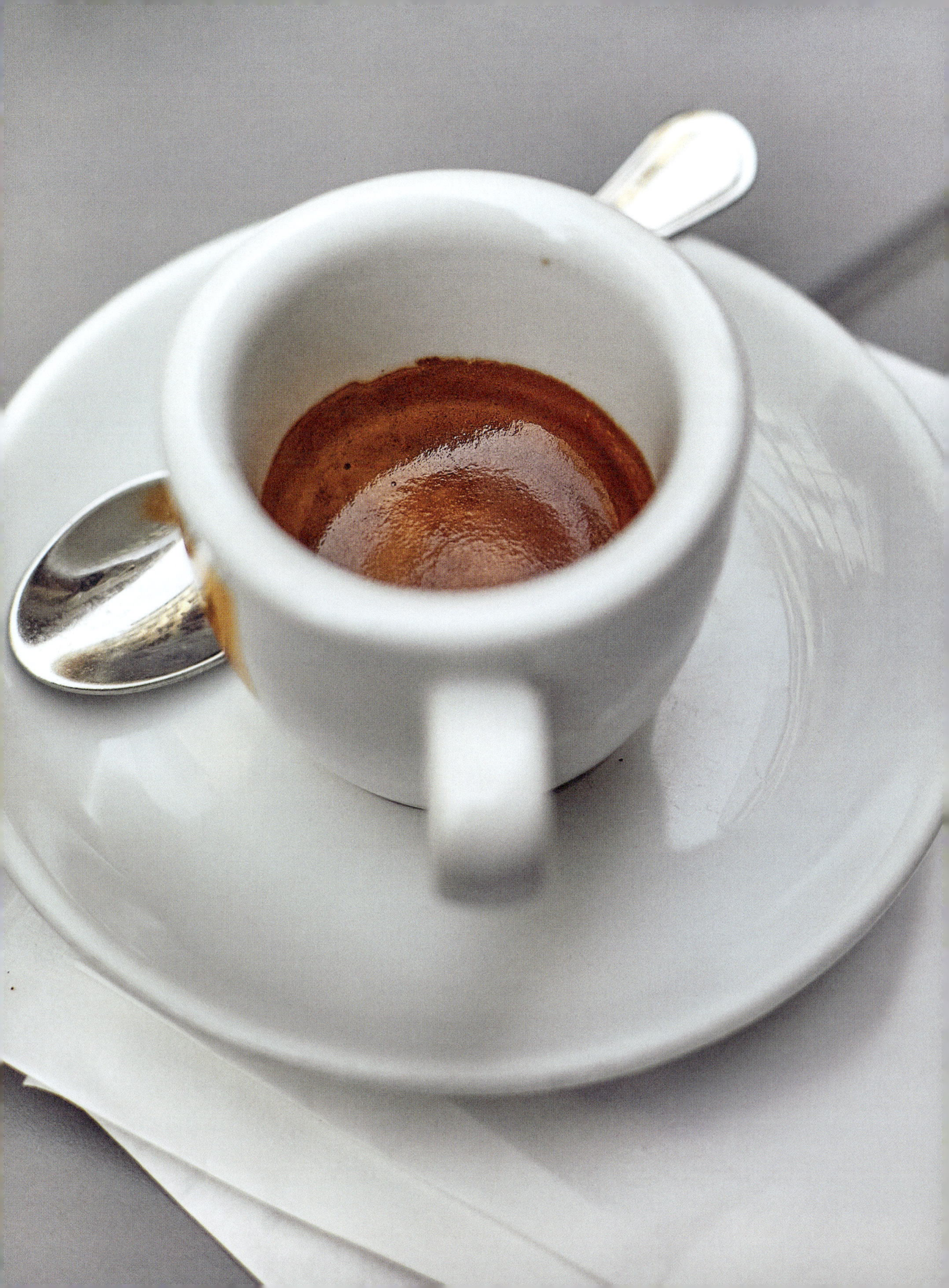

CORNETTI

The most common breakfast in Napoli is espresso and cornetti – cornetti being Italy's answer to the French croissant. If you want to compete with a croissant you have to do something pretty special. And how do the Italians do this? By loading the cornetti with fillings. On the back counter of any bar, you will see three pumps filled with Nutella, pistachio and Amarena sour cherry cream.

They take a cornetto, stab it onto the pump and absolutely cram it full. The result is insanely sweet and indulgent but is somehow the perfect accompaniment to a short, strong espresso. We weren't fans of these to begin with but now we crave ripping open a cornetto first thing and getting pistachio cream everywhere.

CREMA DI CAFFÈ

Making espresso at home in Napoli is serious business. No Nespresso pods here – everyone has a moka pot and we can vouch that it is the easiest, best way to make proper espresso at home. There is one thing they do in Napoli that really elevates this coffee. We never liked using a moka pot because you don't get the crema foam like you do on an espresso, but there's a trick to fix that! In a small bowl, add 2 teaspoons of sugar. Then pour over a little splash of the espresso and stir like hell with a teaspoon. As you keep stirring you will notice the liquid begins to thicken and go pale. Once its turns the colour of caramel, drop a little spoon of it into the bottom of your espresso cup and pour over the hot coffee. It creates a beautiful, thick crema that any barista would be proud of.

COPPA DEL NONNO

When it's summer in Napoli and the city is full, the heat is REAL. The best way to fix that is to duck into a bar and order a coppa del nonno. You'll find it on the back counter in a Slush Puppy-type machine. It's so simple: espresso, sugar and cream, served in a little glass with a spoon, and it is incredible. It's also made at home in Napoli and is easy to make.

What you need

4 shots of espresso

4 tsp sugar

double (heavy) cream

ice cubes

How to make it

Pour the espresso into a jam jar and stir in the sugar. Place in the fridge to cool for 15 minutes.

Fill the jar halfway with cold cream and a few ice cubes. Put the lid on and shake it like a Polaroid… When the cream stops making a sloshing noise and turns to more of a slapping noise, it's ready.

Remove the ice cubes and pour into your favourite cute glasses.

THE ESPRESSO MEN

Another incredible coffee tradition in Napoli, you see The Espresso Men flying around the city (powered by their own wares, no doubt) with lidded trays carrying little paper cups of espresso topped with tin foil. You call your local café and for €1.20 you get a fresh, hot espresso delivered to wherever you are. THAT is the power of espresso in Napoli.

BABA

Salvatore Capparelli

We love the story of the baba. In the 1700s, Tsar Stanislaus of Poland hated a traditional leavened cake called *babka ponczowa*. It was served to him at dinner and he accidentally (yeah, yeah…) dropped a bottle of rum over it. He loved what he tasted and he named it Ali Baba, after *One Thousand and One Nights*. From there, baba made it to Paris, where the recipe was perfected, and then it arrived in Napoli through the French chefs cooking for Neapolitan noble families.

Baba is everywhere in Napoli, and is most popular as a little afternoon pick-me-up eaten on the street or in a bar with a glass of liquor. It's quite an unassuming cake and at first you might think it's going to be a little boring. But when you take a bite it explodes with a physics-defying amount of rum-infused syrup. It really is like nothing else.

We got to spend the afternoon with Baba World Champion Salvatore Capparelli, whose shop in Spaccanapoli is legendary.

Salvatore has been making baba for 41 years and his passion is undeniable. 'You can make emotions with flour, butter, sugar and eggs,' he says as he plunges the freshly baked babas into a bath of rum syrup. He grabs one and wrings it out like a sponge. The yeasted dough is strong and explains why they can hold so much liquid. He hands us a baba each straight from the bath (we strongly suggest adding 'eating a baba straight from the baker' to any self-respecting bucket list).

We toyed with adding the recipe here but we honestly think this is something to leave to the professionals. You can buy the baba cakes dried and then soak them in your own syrup, which is certainly worth doing, but more than that we would suggest getting on a plane, going to Salvatore's shop and trying it direct from the source!

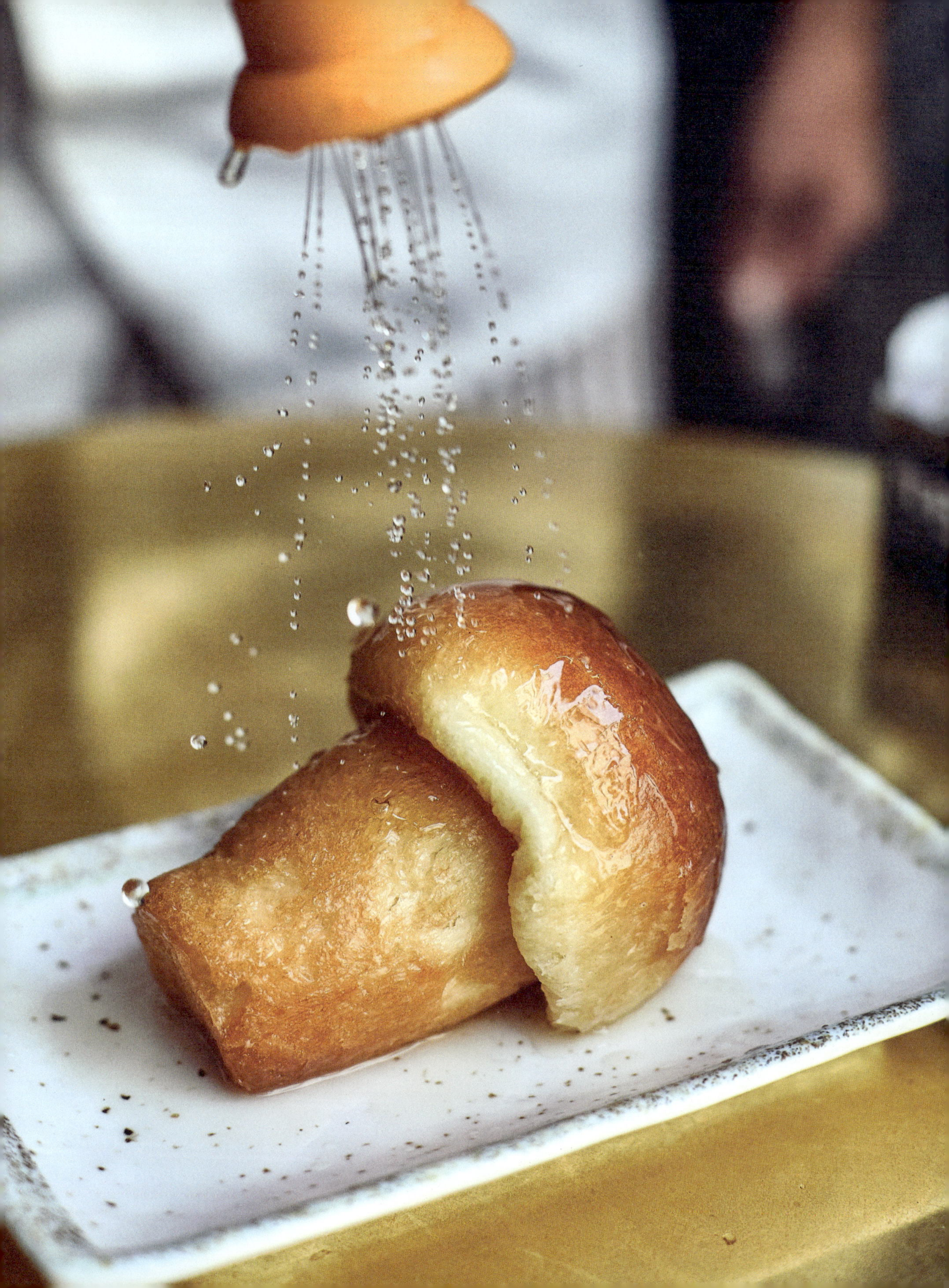

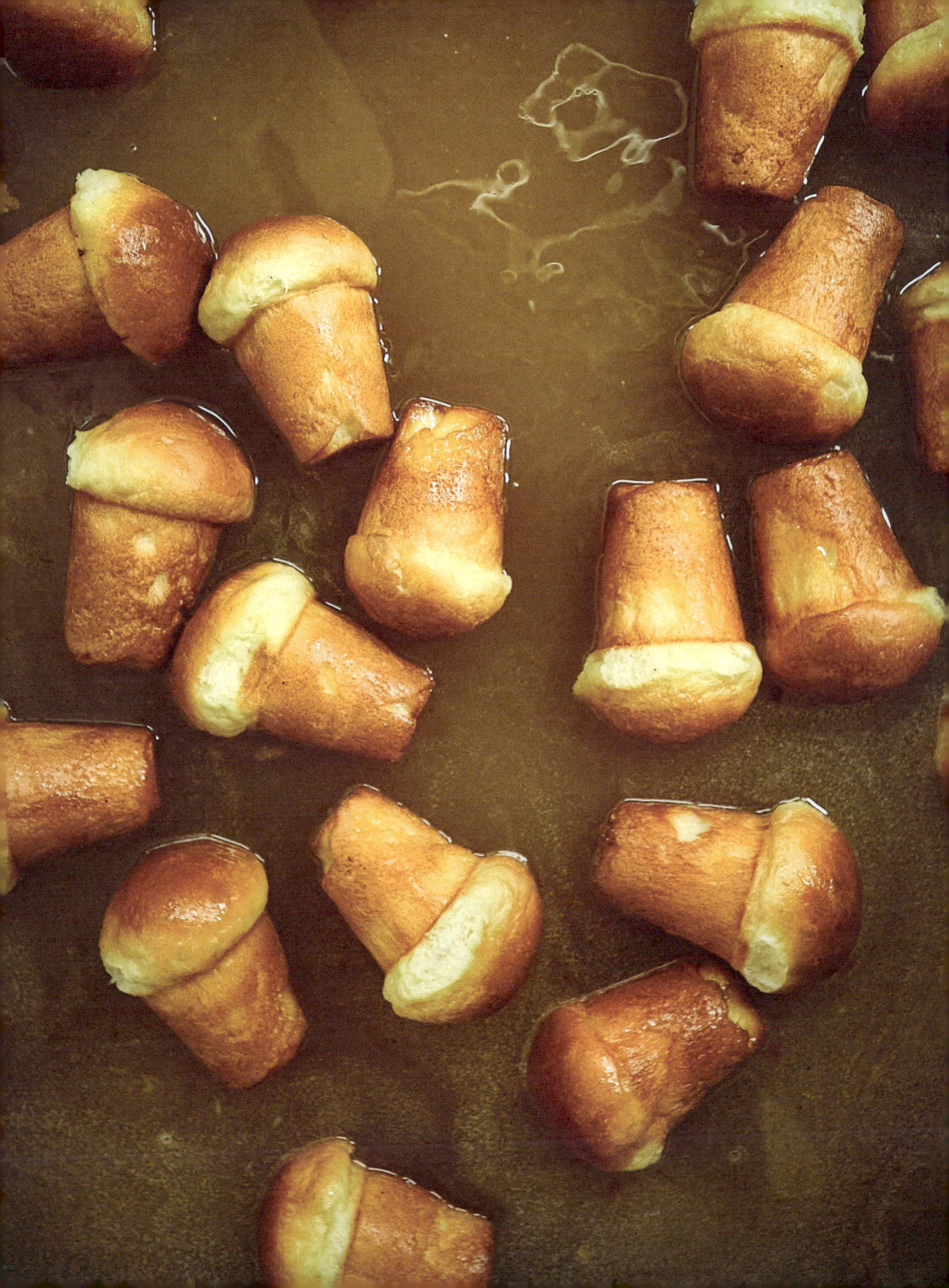

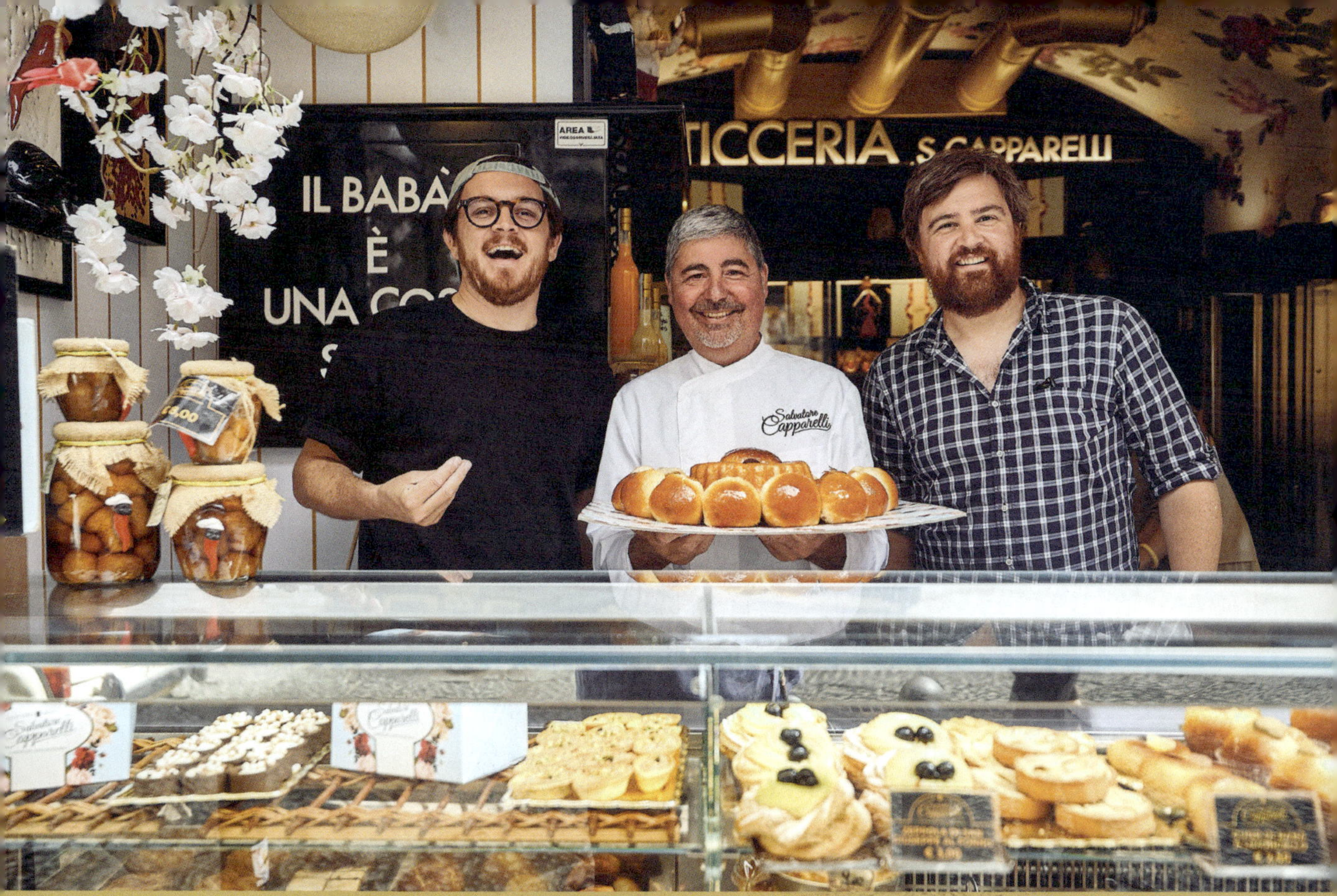
IL BABÀ
È
Salvatore Capparelli

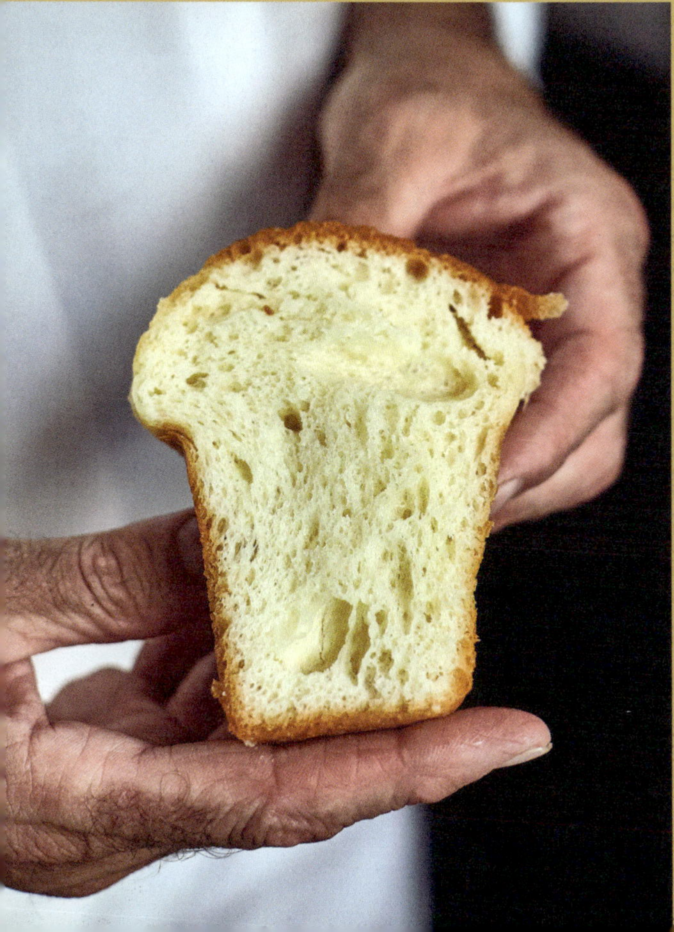

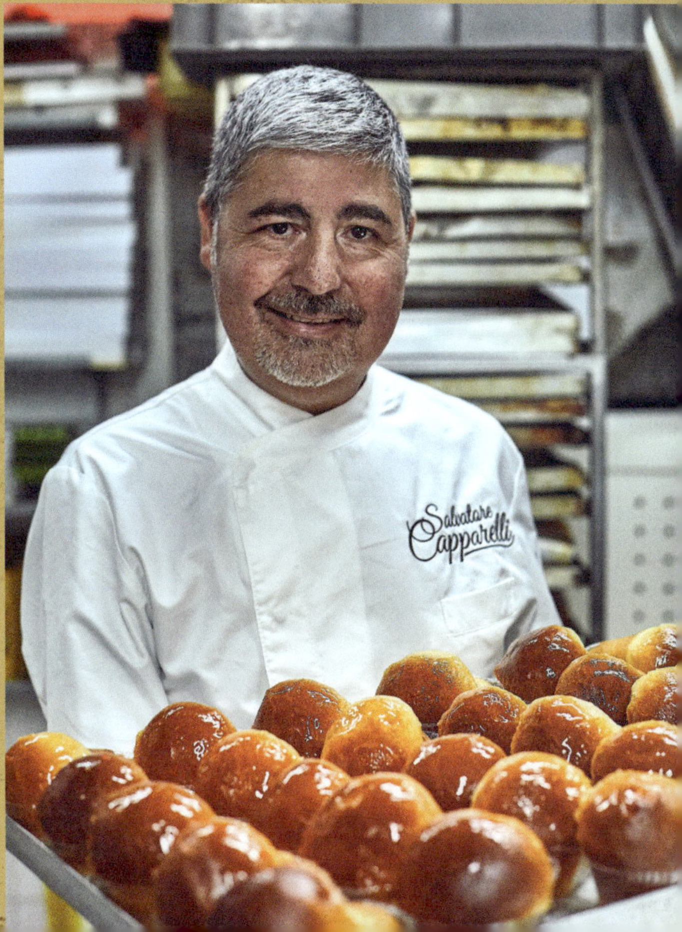
Salvatore Capparelli

CHALET CIRO

We took our Pizza Vespa to Chalet Ciro, a typical seaside chalet on the Bay of Napoli, on a mission to highlight the bringing together of three fantastic Italian passions: espresso, gelato and graffa.

Chalet Ciro is a long-standing establishment where espresso and gelato are celebrated equally; the owner Antonio has been operating from this beautiful location by the sea since 1952. Given they are so well regarded for their fantastic espresso – served in little porcelain cups that are too hot to hold for more than a second or two – and their world-class gelato, it was clearly the perfect place to celebrate the affogato.

Affogato is one of the great one-plus-one-equals-three equations that Napoli has to offer. It is simplicity itself – a shot of hot espresso poured over ice cream – and exactly what you want to eat after a pizza. At once sweet and bitter, it is the perfect post-carb sugar hit.

It is traditionally made with vanilla gelato, but we spent a morning tasting a selection of new flavours and came to the conclusion that it is best with a pistachio gelato – so that is what we now serve in our pizzerias! Try it yourself at home by pouring a shot of espresso over a ball of pistachio gelato.

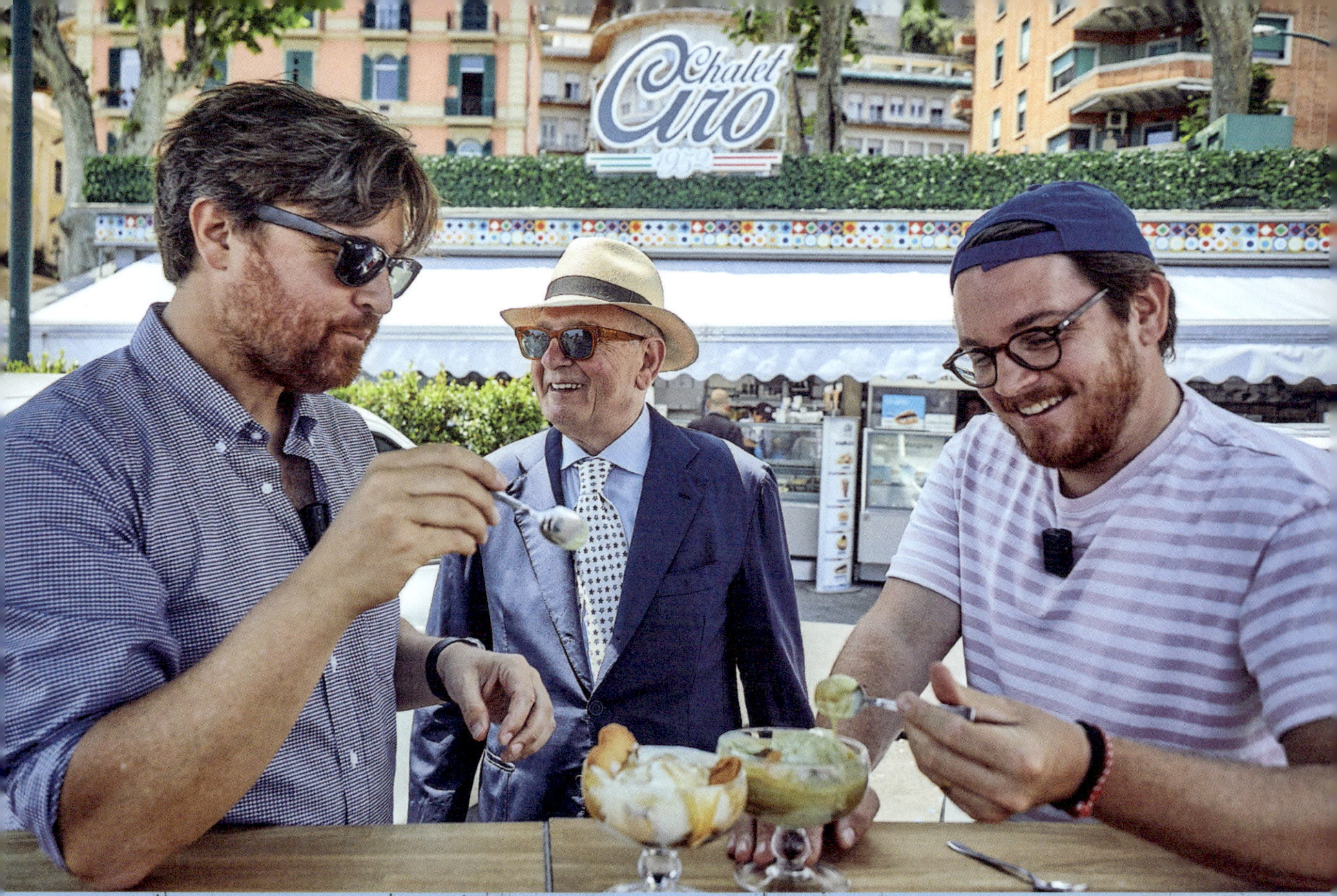
Chalet
Ciro

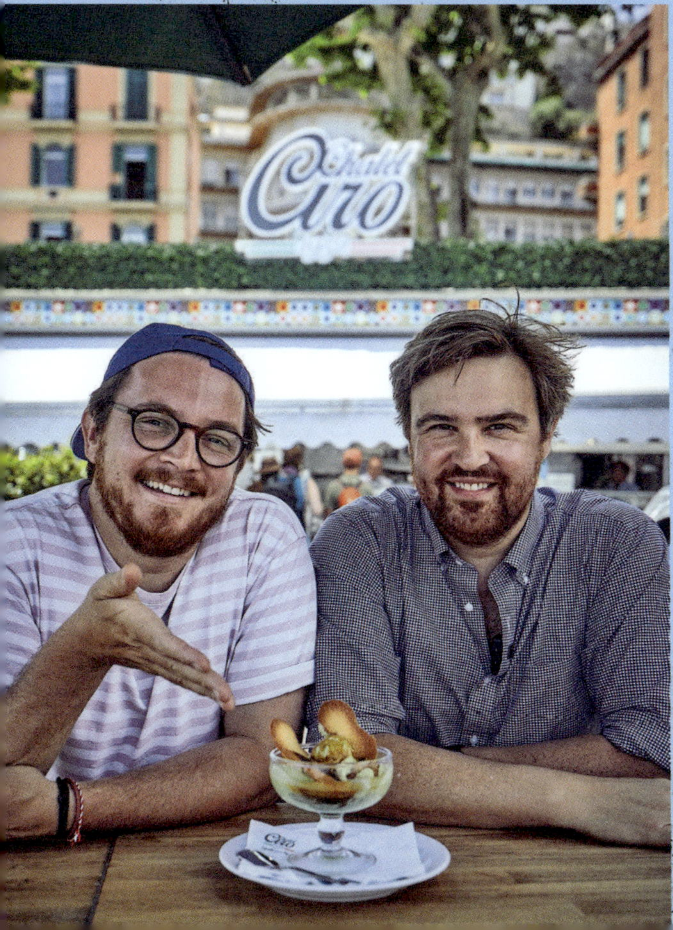
Chalet
Ciro

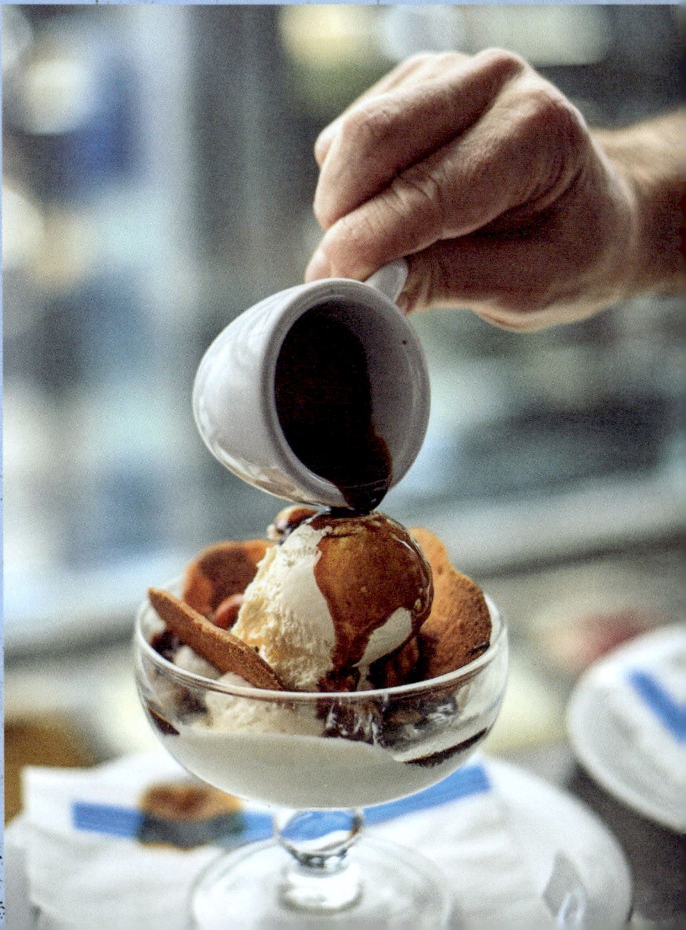

GRAFFA

A graffa is a truly Neapolitan thing... a light and fluffy doughnut that is deep-fried and rolled in sugar, and perfect with – you guessed it – coffee. They were traditionally made for Carnival (and still are around Italy) but in Napoli they took a real shine to them and they can be found in every coffee shop in the city. When you rip open a freshly fried graffa at Chalet Ciro (page 292) you get hit by the steam and the smell. Do you remember funfair doughnuts in a bag? Opening a graffa is like dunking your head in that bag. The secret to the lightness is potatoes; the leavened potato-and-flour dough somehow keeps the doughnut soft and light, but moist. This is a must try.

What you need (makes 8)

300g (10½oz) peeled potatoes

7g (¼oz) dried yeast

100ml (3½fl oz) milk

400g (14oz) plain (all-purpose) flour, plus extra for dusting

2 eggs

50g (1¾oz) butter, at room temperature

50g (1¾oz) caster (superfine) sugar, plus extra for coating

pinch of sea salt

neutral frying oil

How to make it

Boil the potatoes until soft, then drain and mash until smooth. Set aside to cool. Whisk the yeast into the milk to dissolve and set aside while the potato cools.

In a large bowl, combine the flour, eggs, butter, sugar, salt, mashed potato and yeasted milk. Use your hand to bring the dough together but do not over-knead; just mix the dough until smooth. Cover the bowl with a tea (dish) towel and leave for about 2 hours to double in size.

Tip out the dough onto a floured surface and cut into tennis-ball-sized pieces (you should get about 8). Roll each piece to around 25cm (10 inches) long, then pinch the ends slightly and fold the ends over each other to create the classic graffa shape. Leave to rest for 30 minutes on individual pieces of greaseproof paper. Prepare a bowl filled with some sugar.

Heat your frying oil to 180°C (356°F) in a deep-sided pan. Gently drop the graffa into the oil, letting them peel off the greaseproof paper as they go into the pan. Cook (in batches, if needed) for 1–2 minutes on each side, carefully flipping halfway.

Remove from the pan, allowing the excess oil to drip off them, then toss them in the bowl of sugar to coat. Eat immediately!

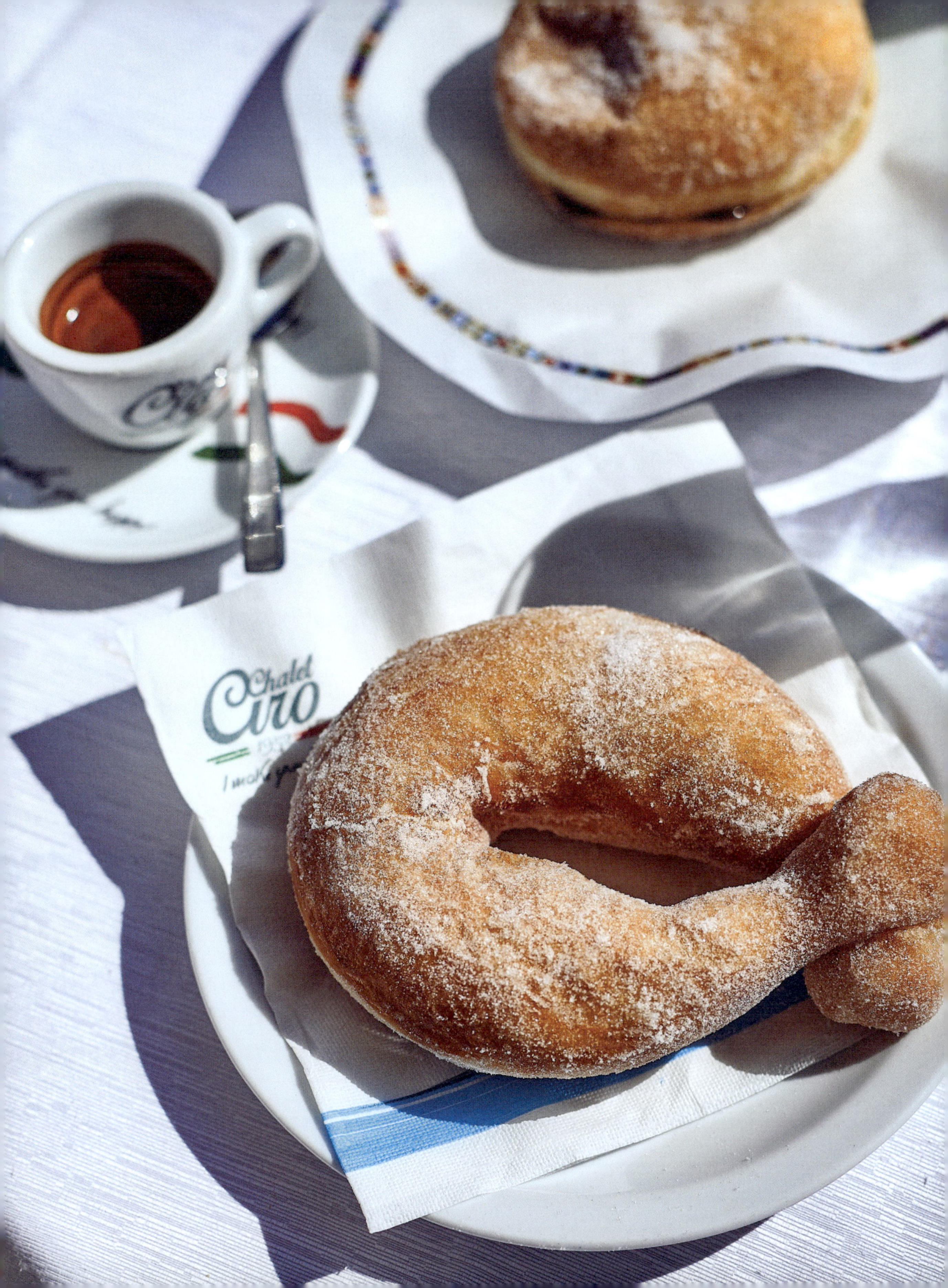
Chalet
Ciro

SFOGLIATELLA ATTANASIO

When we first came to Napoli in 2011, aside from our first true taste of Neapolitan pizza it was the sfogliatella that also captured our hearts. We tasted our first one from a small kiosk at the entrance to the grand Galleria Umberto.

A delicious combination of pastry filled with ricotta that has been sweetened and flavoured with orange and lemon peel, it is usually available in two distinct versions. The *sfogliatella riccia* has a crispy, laminated outer shell with a crazy satisfying crunch, whereas *sfogliatella frolla* has a smoother, shortcrust-style outer shell.

After a few more trips (and many more sfogliatelle) we discovered the true temple to this wonderful product: Attanasio bakery. Nestled just off the Piazza Garibaldi by the main train station in Napoli, it has been trading in that location since 1930, serving sfogliatelle hot from the oven, among other classic Neapolitan pastries. So focused on these baked goods are the team here that they haven't even branched out to serving coffee – if you want a coffee with your pastry (which you do) you need to get it from the café over the road.

We arranged to meet the brothers, Francesco and Mario, who are running the bakery – the third generation of the family to do so. They took us behind the scenes to see the sfogliatelle being made, each one lovingly (but speedily) formed by hand – wrapping the freshly made pastry around the ricotta mix with skill and precision in endless delicious rows. They are then baked and served within minutes. Staying on top of demand on a sunny Neapolitan morning is quite a mission!

> **THERE ARE THREE BEAUTIFUL THINGS IN NAPOLI – VESUVIUS, THE SEA AND SFOGLIATELLE.**

RIPRODUZIONE VIETATA
MARCHIO REGISTRATO
LUNEDI' CHIUSO
www.sfogliatelleattanasio.it

ANTICO FORNO DELLE SFOGLIATELLE CALD
F.lli ATTANASIO
SFOGLIATE
CALDE
ATTANASIO

LEMON SORBET

As you walk through the town of Amalfi, every single holidaymaker is struggling to hold a giant lemon overflowing with a light sorbetto di limone that is melting and dripping down their arm. Now, this could be accused of being Instagram fodder and a bit of marketing genius from the gelateria owner, and in many ways it is, but the truth is there is such a glut of giant Amalfi lemons throughout summer that they don't know what to do with them. The flesh is scooped out to make the sorbetto and the empty lemon makes a perfect, biodegradable cup. Win-win.

What you need (makes about 1.25 litres/5 cups)

500ml (17fl oz) water

250g (9oz) sugar

zest of 3 lemons

500ml (17fl oz) lemon juice

How to make it

In a pan, heat the water and sugar together with the lemon zest. You can add large pieces of zest and remove before freezing, but we like the texture of grating the zest finely and leaving it in the finished sorbet. Your call.

Boil the mixture for a couple of minutes to allow the zest to release its oil, then take off the heat and add the lemon juice.

Pour into a wide dish (removing the zest if in large pieces), cover and place in the freezer.

Remove the dish from the freezer every 30 minutes and mix with a fork to create a slushy texture; do this 4 or 5 times until it is frozen. Remove from the freezer 30 minutes before serving.

LIMONCELLO

Limoncello: the often-free culmination of many millions of Italian meals the world over. Also the creator of some of the great hangovers of the world…

The truth is that this is the experience that most people have with limoncello. They know a sad, see-through, lurid yellow liquid that faintly tastes of artificial lemon. It's a sorry state of affairs.

Proper limoncello is a totally different prospect. It is a thick, almost creamy liquid packed with lemon oil and an intense taste of fresh lemon. It is sweet – that is for sure – but has an amazing intensity of flavour. And as you would expect, it is the quality of the lemons that makes a great limoncello great.

The Amalfi lemon is absolutely perfect for making limoncello, no doubt about it. Back in 2014 when we were embarking on a journey to produce our own, we tested about six or seven different lemon varieties in our quest to make the perfect product. The Amalfi lemon won hands down.

The reason for that is the thick skin, which is packed with lemon oil. If you bite into an Amalfi lemon, this oil coats your lips and actually makes the skin edible! And given limoncello is all about the oil (it contains no juice of the lemon whatsoever), it's a case of the more the merrier.

Other than using great lemons, there is very little expertise needed to making a good limoncello. It is a simple process with a delicious outcome! (Recipe overleaf.)

LIMONE I.G.P.

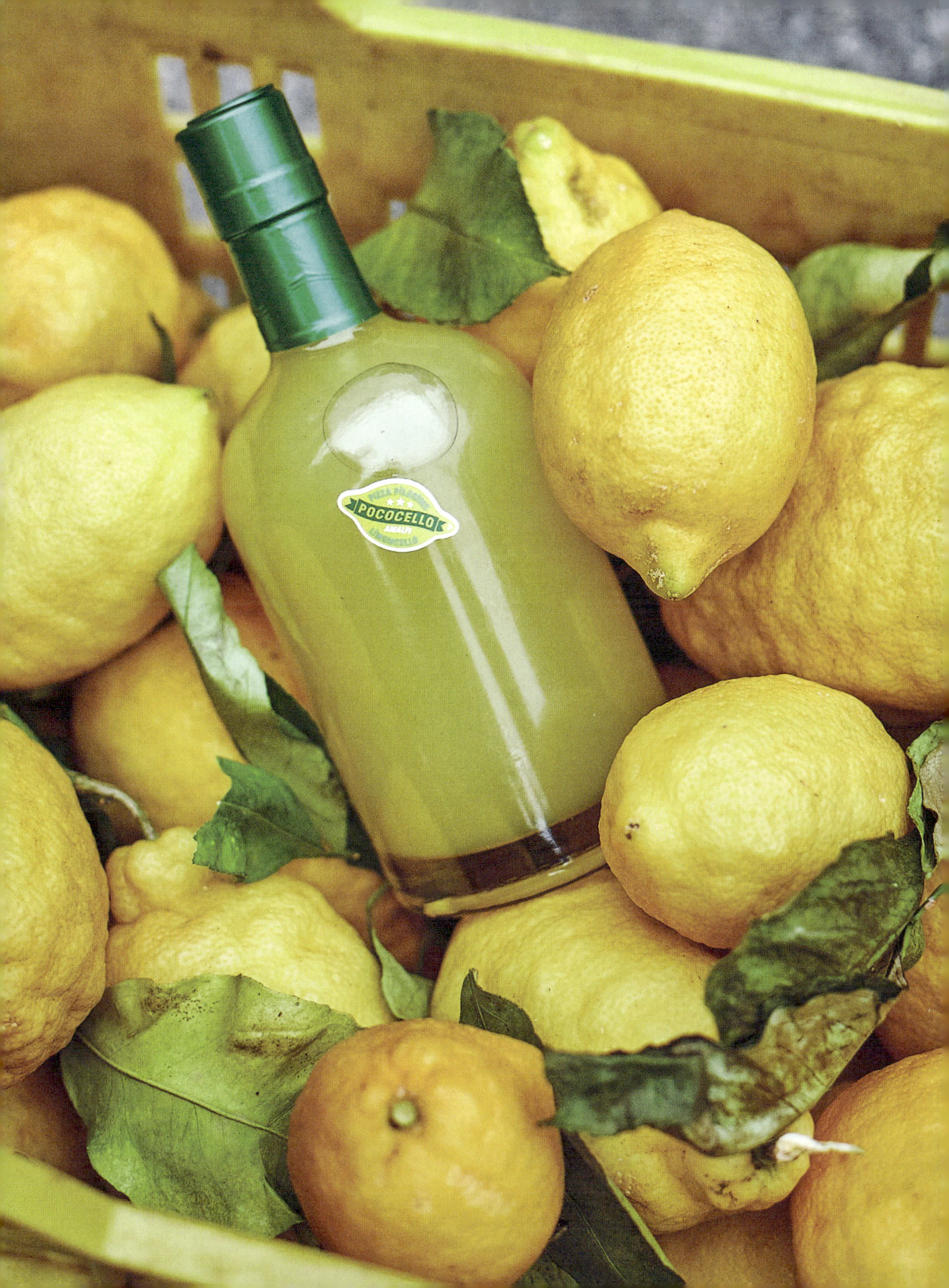
POCOCELLO
AMALFI

Amalfi
Limoni e Limoncello
Production of handcrafted
Lemon Goods

Amalfi
Limoni e Limoncello
Production of handcrafted
Lemon Goods

LIMONCELLO

What you need
(makes 2 bottles)

5 large Amalfi lemons

500ml (17fl oz) full-strength grain alcohol

600ml (20fl oz) mineral water

200g (7oz) caster (superfine) sugar

How to make it

First, use a swivel peeler to pare off the lemon skin, being careful to get as much of the skin/zest as possible without the white pith (which can make your limoncello bitter).

Place the lemon peel in a sealable container and pour over the alcohol. Leave to steep for 1 week until the colour has changed to a dramatic yellow.

Remove the lemon peel and discard. Add the water and sugar to the container and stir to completely combine and dissolve the sugar.

Bottle up your limoncello and place it straight in the freezer to get it ice cold. Serve it neat in a shot glass, or as a replacement (or addition) to the gin in a gin and tonic. Delicious!

A COSCE APERTE

Across Napoli you will find a number of stalls serving what is essentially a Neapolitan version of Gaviscon – albeit much more intense and theatrical, of course.

A cosce aperte literally translates as 'with legs apart'. It involves standing with legs akimbo while the stallholder mixes freshly squeezed lemon juice and soda water with a heaped teaspoon of bicarbonate of soda. This creates a foaming, almost explosive concoction that is handed over, and which you have to attempt to drink down in one go... and standing bent over with your legs apart helps prevent most of it going on your trousers!

It's actually great fun – you usually end up with a small crowd cheering you on. And it is very refreshing after you have just polished off a whole pizza!

We always take the team on day one of our Napoli trips and it never fails to raise a smile.

What you need (makes 1)

juice of 1 lemon

200ml (7fl oz) fizzy water

1 heaped tsp bicarbonate of soda (baking soda)

How to make it

Mix the lemon juice and water in a glass.

Quickly and vigorously stir in the bicarbonate of soda.

Drink the creation as quickly as you can – preferably not inside, as it will go everywhere!

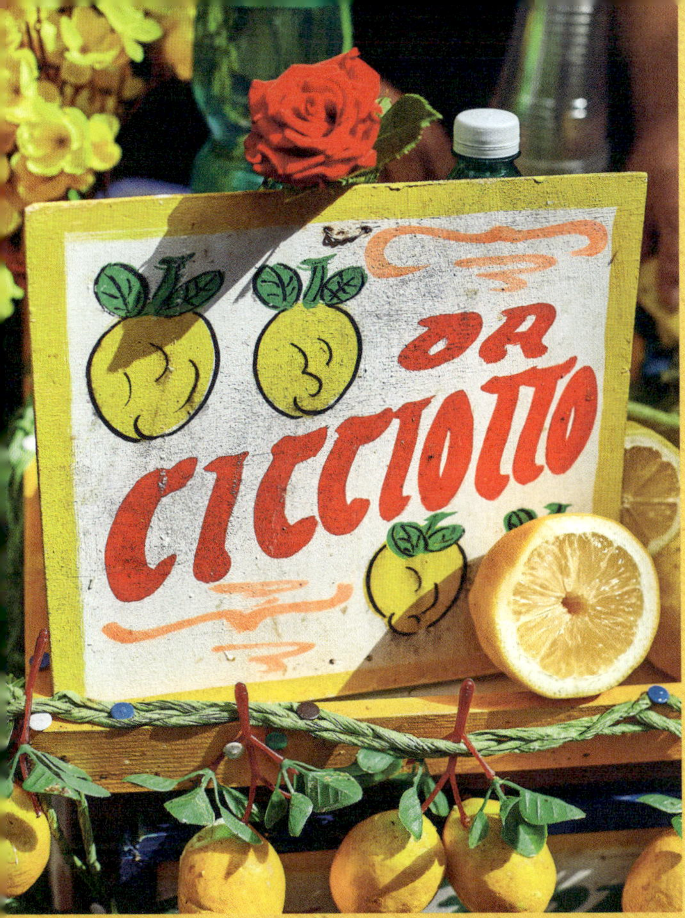
DA
CICCIOTTO

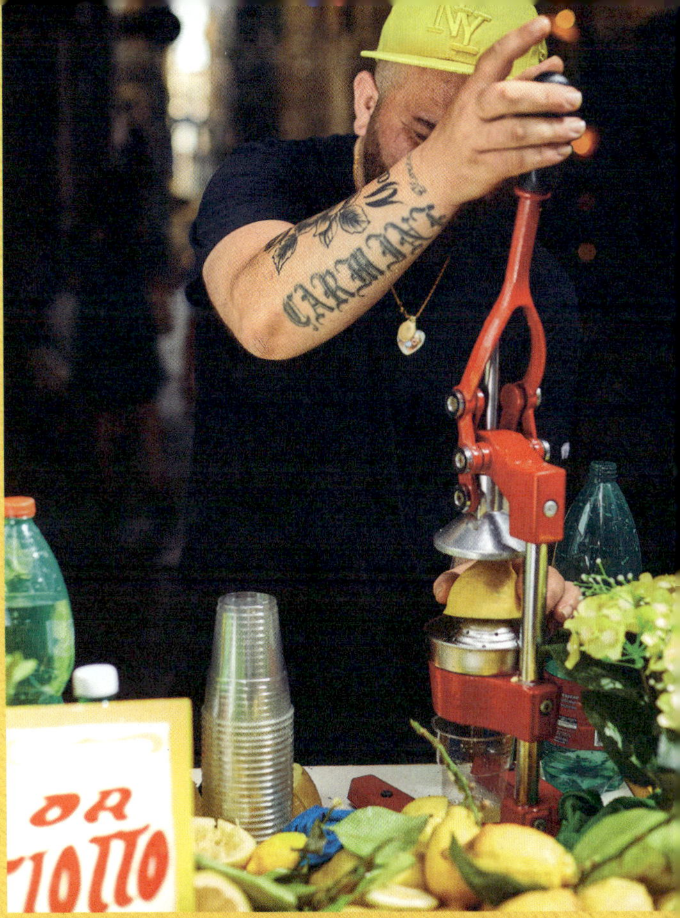
DA

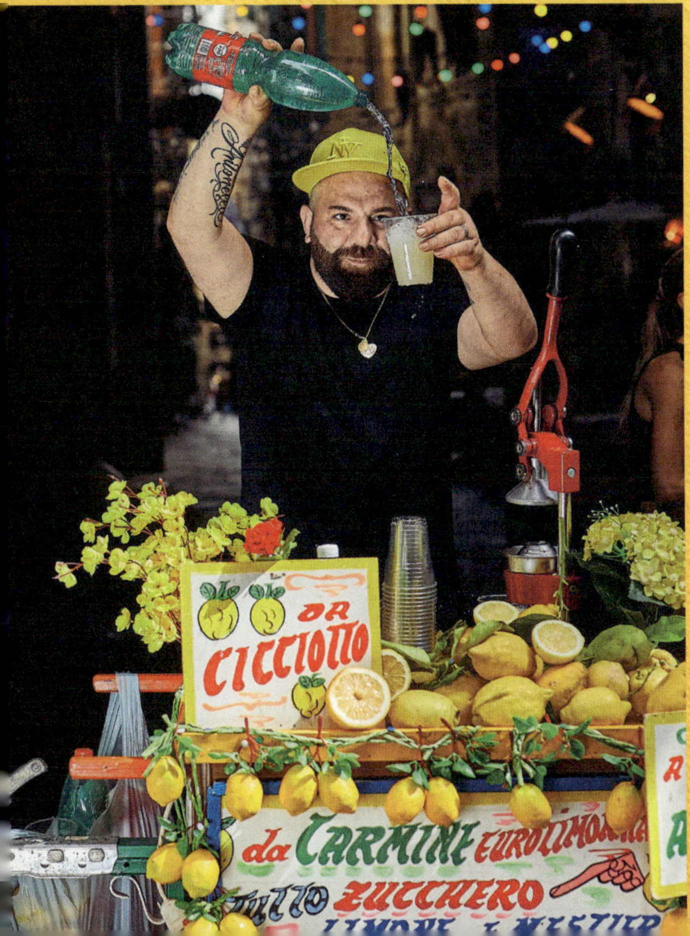
DA
CICCIOTTO
da CARMINE
ZUCCHERO

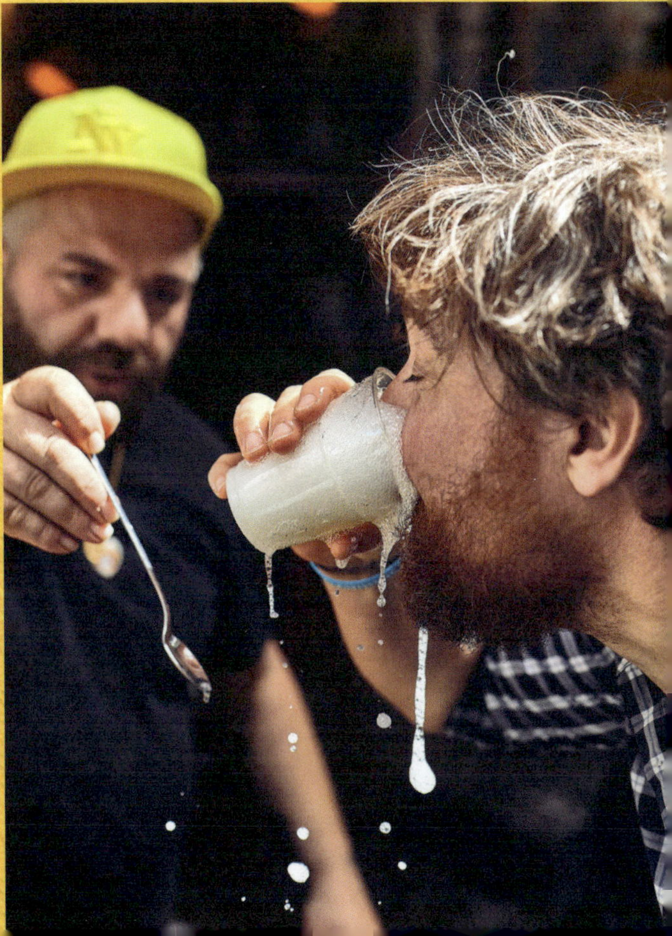

SPRITZ

Spritzes are a big deal in Napoli, and there is no doubt that there is little better way to wind down at the end of a hectic day in the city than with a spritz or two with friends.

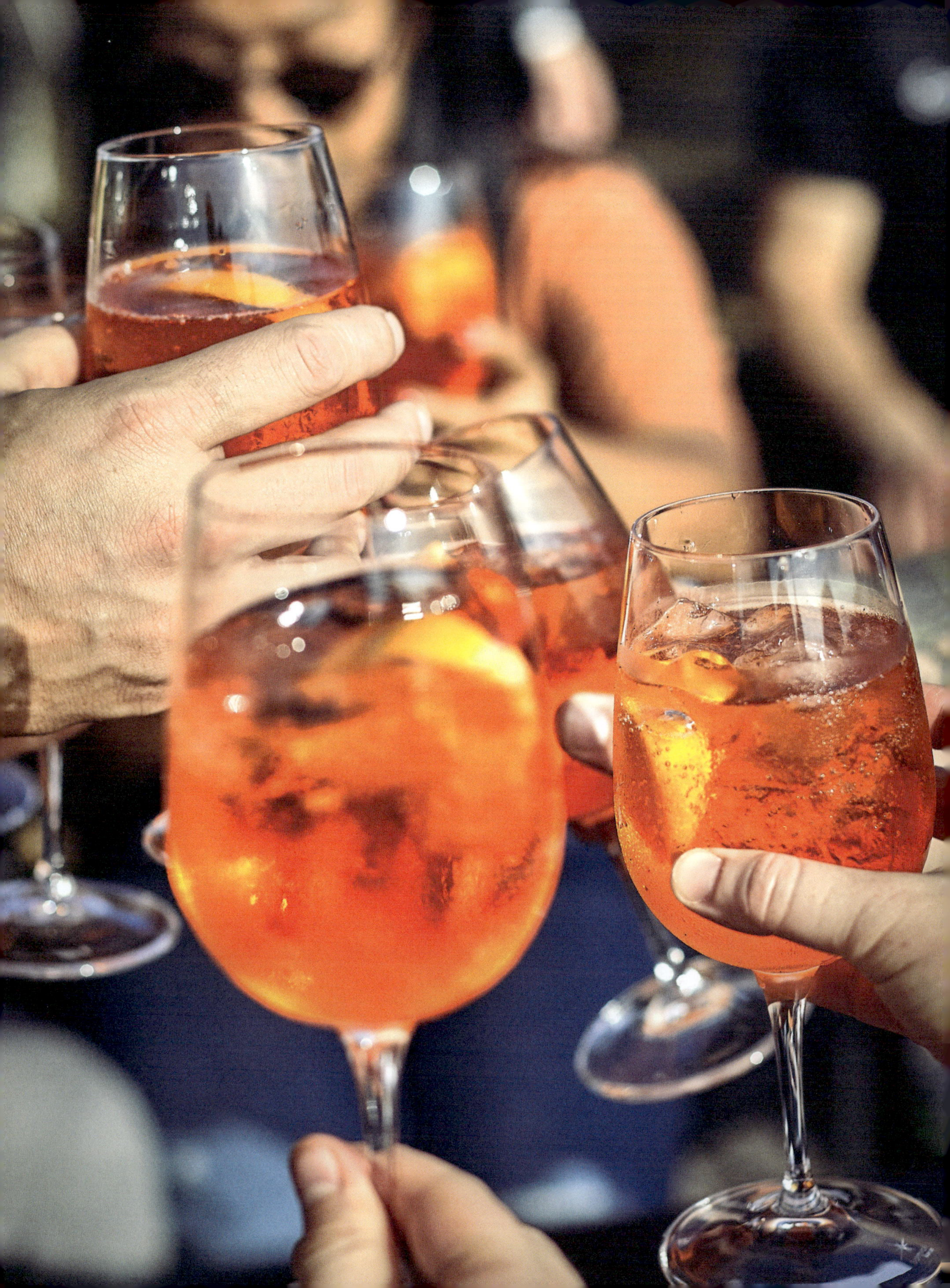

LELLO SPRITZ

We took our Vespa into the heart of the Spanish Quarter to meet Tipo at Lello Spritz, one of the many spritz bars found in this part of town.

We spent the evening testing spritz recipes, and trying all the local favourites as well as his own creations (with the help of his son – who was, like, eight years old, so obviously not drinking!).

Here were some of our favourites from the night that you have to try if you're in Napoli. Twelve varieties: more than an entire football team of spritzes... *Saluti!*

Aperol Spritz
Aperol, prosecco, soda, olive, orange slice

Campari Spritz
Campari, prosecco, soda, orange slice

Cynar Spritz
Cynar, prosecco, soda, orange slice

Limoncello Spritz
Limoncello, prosecco, soda, lemon slice

Maradona Spritz
Blue Curaçao, prosecco, soda, lemon slice

Bellìni Spritz
Peach schnapps, prosecco, soda, lemon slice

Aurora Borealis
Blue Curaçao, orange juice, crème de violette, prosecco

Fiore di Fragola
Strawberry vodka, prosecco, orange juice, soda

Midori Spritz
Midori liqueur, prosecco, elderflower, soda, lemon slice

Tutti Frutti
Peach schnapps, meloncello, prosecco, soda, grenadine

Hugo Spritz
Elderflower liqueur, prosecco, soda, lemon slice

Averna Spritz
Averna, prosecco, soda, lemon slice

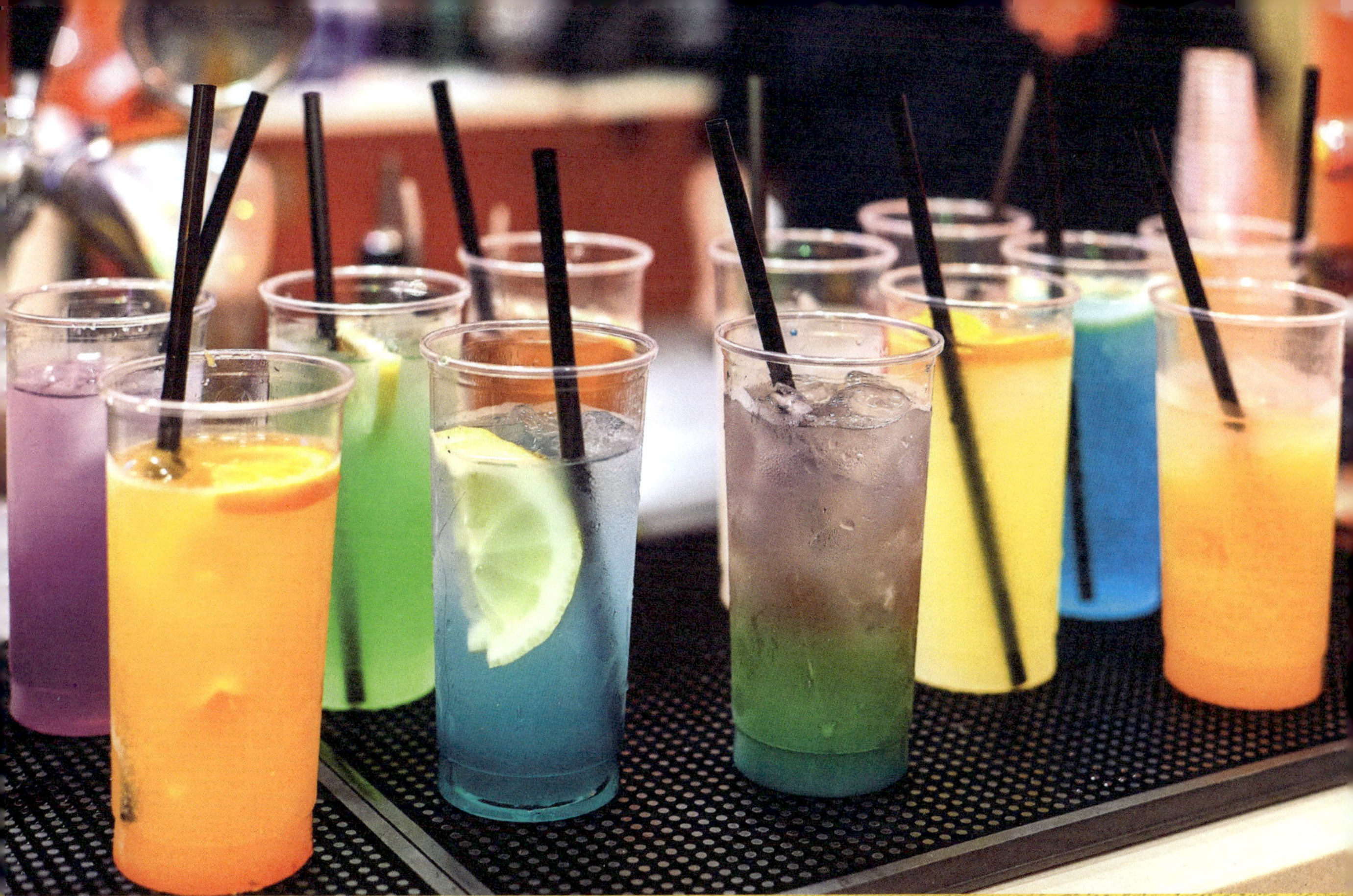

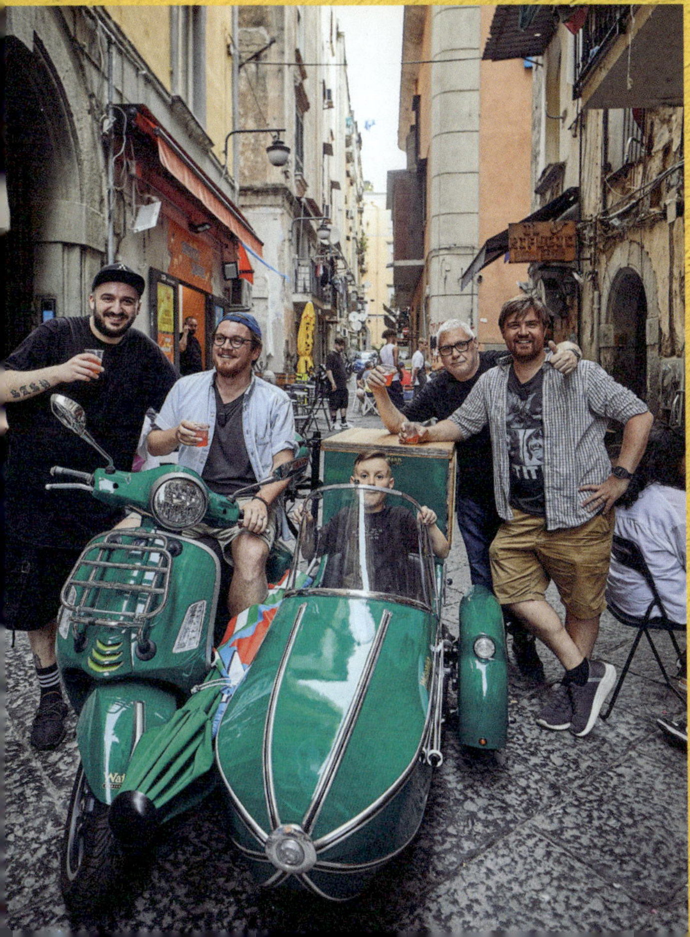

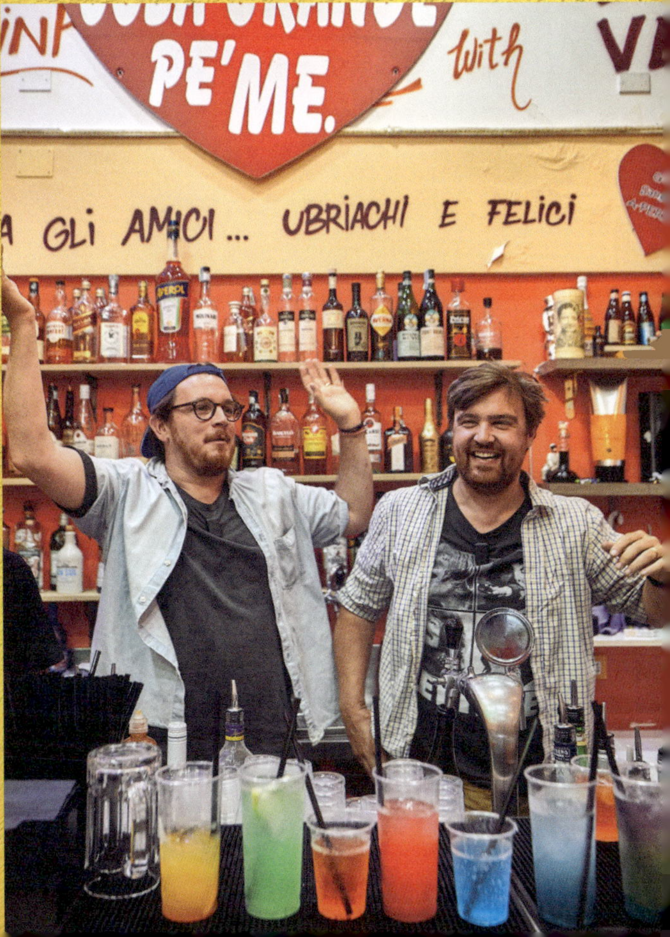
PE'ME.
with
A GLI AMICI ... UBRIACHI E FELICI

GRAZIE

James & Thom

Can you thank a whole city? Is that even allowed? You know what, it's Napoli, and there are no rules. We would like to thank the entire city of Napoli for a) inventing pizza and b) being such a bottomless source of inspiration and joy. Over 12 years and over 65 trips to the city, the people of Napoli have time and time again proven themselves to be the most generous, passionate and hospitable people – you can see it in the hundreds of photos of Napoli locals in this book! We have always felt welcome, and the pizza community have adopted us into their incredible world with open (often floury) arms.

Now, to start at the beginning, we would like to thank Pasquale de Stefano and his daughter Marcella for letting us use his amazing illustrations as the cover of this book. He really is an icon of Napoli and for us to be able to feature his work as our cover is an honour.

Special thanks to the amazing people that make up the pizza community of Napoli. Antimo and Antonella at Caputo who always bend over backwards for us. Giovanni, Marco and Gaetano from Latteria Sorrentina who play a huge role in helping us to bring so many people from Pizza Pilgrims to Napoli. Aniello and Giuseppe from Solania tomatoes: the best in the game! Federico and the guys at Porchetta D'alterio, thank you for setting up a delivery arm to the UK just for us! Salvatore and Marco Aceto who we co-create our wonderful limoncello with: we think your lemon grove is the most beautiful place in the world. Marco from Kimbo coffee for keeping us stocked with proper Neapolitan espresso. The Attanasio brothers for making the best sfogliatella in the city (and never letting us pay!).

And now thank you to the pizzas legends! Alessandro and the team at Da Michele (for the pop up we will never forget!), Francesco Martucci, Vincenzo Capuano, Salvatore Salvo, Gino and Toto Sorbillo, Franco Pepe, Errico Prozio, Carlo Sammarco, Ciro Cascella, Davide Civitiello, Salvatore Lioniello, Davide Ruotolo, Alessandro Baraschino and Isabella De Cham. You are all pizza legends for completely different reasons; some celebrate tradition, some innovation, some are scientists and some are artists. All together you create a wonderful community that has a shared passion that is far reaching. And to all the pizza chefs of Napoli that didn't make it into the book, thank you for doing the hard yards. Making pizza in front of a 500°C wood-fired oven in 35°C Napoli heat with dodgy aircon is no mean feat!

Napoli isn't just about pizza, and neither is this book! Thank you so much to the guys at Trattoria Nenella, Allonso the Genovese King, Don Vince and team, Salvatore the Baba champion, Antonio and team at Chalet Ciro, Tipo, the guys at Lello spritz, our panini pals at Zinzi, Aniello and his daughter who make the most perfect zeppole, and Giuseppe and his fritto misto cones.

Now to thank the people who made this book happen. First and foremost, Dave. You joined up to design a book about pizza 5 years ago; back then I bet you didn't realise how deeply you would fall into the world of pizza. Thank you for all the work you do at Pizza Pilgrims to make everything look slick and thank you for always being ready to strap on a pair of 5Ds and jump on a plane to Napoli to get the shot. We think the book looks amazing and in a style that is uniquely yours. To Sarah and Quadrille, thank you for believing that pizza is a big enough subject to write not just one but two books about! We're up for the third if you guys are... and to Harriet, Sally and Sabina, thank you for bringing it to life and making it a success.

To Dom, our head of pizza at PP and our spiritual (and actual) guide to Napoli. Your passion for pizza and your city is unmatched. Thanks for making every trip to Napoli run so smoothly – that's a tough job! And to Alessandro R, you and Dom make a great team (you may even know more about pizza than him!). Thanks for looking after us in your city.

A huge thank you to all the people who run our pizzerias in the UK, knocking out amazing Neapolitan pizza every day with smiles on their faces and showing people a good time. You are all a team of true hospitality legends! We can't wait to take you all back to Napoli for some Peroni reds, on us, to say thank you properly.

Lastly, and most importantly, thank you to our family: Lena and Jemma for supporting us in this crazy pizza life through thick and thin. We promise we love you more than pizza! Jackson and Sadie for all the taste testing and kids menu ideas. And to Vicky and Shirl for giving us the 'give it a go' gene in the first place...

Dave

I would like to grate lashings of Parmigiano on everything James and Thom have said above, but would also like to say...

A massive thanks to my family, Lou, Vi and Chet, for putting up with me being away in Napoli all the time (and then coming back and talking about pizza and Napoli all the time!).

The biggest of big-ups to James and Thom for inviting me into the Pizza Pilgrims family and allowing me to bring their wonderful ideas to life. I'm honoured to be co-authoring this beautiful beast. In all my years, you are by far the craziest, funniest, most generous and loyal clients I've had.

Thanks to Alessandro, and especially Dom, for translating and fixing and explaining to people why I am pointing a camera in their face. And thanks to all the Neapolitans who allowed me to point a camera in their face. I would also like to thank Pasquale for the inspiration and for allowing me to work with his wonderful brushwork.

Grazie mille to all the Neapolitan chefs and their teams for allowing us into their kitchens and being so generous, welcoming and patient while I got in their way and asked annoying things of them.

A tiny thanks to Alex Pasquini for being my wing man and drone bitch on the Vespa trip.

A large format thanks to Sarah, Laura, Katherine and Quadrille/Penguin and the brilliant Harriet for your trust, help and support. Are we doing Pizza Tokyo, Pizza New York or Pizza São Paulo next?!

A

a cosce aperte 306
affogato 292
Ale's Neapolitan ragù 232
alfonso 272
Amalfi lemons 302
  limoncello 305
the Americana 125, 127
ananas 150
ananascosta 166
anchovies
  marinara dei signori 209
  profumo di costiera 147
  Romana 107
aniello 60, 67
Aperol spritz 310
apricot jam: la crisommola 169
arancini, tomato & mozzarella 244–6
artichoke stem cream: assoluto di carciofo 116
artichokes
  assoluto di carciofo 116
  capricciosa 106
The Associazione Verace Pizza Napoletana (AVPN) 14, 92
assoliuto di pomodoro 120
assoluto di carciofo 116
Attanasio 296–9
aubergines (eggplant): parmigiana scomposta 212
Aurora Borealis 310
autumno 180
Averna spritz 310

B

baba 288
Baraschino, Alessandro 227–35, 237
basil
  the Americana 125, 127
  basil oil 160
  bufala 104
  capricciosa 106
  contemporanea 2.0 223
  cossaca 137, 138
  Margherita 104
  marinara 105
  pizza Genovese 276
  pizza pomodoro 143
  poker 173
  velouté 177
ziti alla Genovese 274
zucca e 'nduja 183
basil leaf powder: scarpetta 163
basil oil 160
  Margherita sbagliata 160
beef
  Ale's Neapolitan ragù 232
  frittatine di pasta 246–7
  meatballs all Vince 257
  oshirase 144
  ziti alla Genovese 274
Bellini spritz 310
bicarbonate of soda (baking soda): a cosce aperte 306
Bonci, Gabriele 137
bottarga: saturnia 122
Brandi 12
breadcrumbs
  crocchè 247
  deep-fried mozzarella bites 82
  tomato & mozzarella arancini 244–6
bufala 104
buffalo mozzarella 76
  ananas 150
  bufala 104
  eccellenza campana 190
  Margherita extra extra 155
  salami Napoli piccante 156
  saturnia 122
  sogni 193
  sogni di latte 215
burrata 85

C

caciocavallo cheese
  donna Isabella 239
  sogni di latte 215
cacioricotta cheese: salami Napoli piccante 156
caffè sospeso 282
calzone
  calzone ripeno 108
  mezza luna calzone 231
Camden Brewery 30
Campari spritz 310
Cannavacciuolo, Antonino 137
capers
  polpo sanità 241
  Romana 107
Capocollo di Martina Franca: autumno 180
Capparelli, Salvatore 288–91
capricciosa 106
Capuano, Vincenzo 14, 255
Caputo 48–55
Caputo, Antimo 18, 50, 52
Caputo, Carmine 52
Caputo, Mauro 50
Caputo Cup 125
Carlo Sammarco Pizzeria 174–83
Cascella, Ciro 184–93
centro Calabria 134
Chalet Ciro 292, 294
cheese 70–87
  the Americana 125, 127
  ananas 150
  ananascosta 166
  assoluto di carciofo 116
  bufala 104
  burrata 85
  calzone ripeno 108
  capricciosa 106
  contemporanea 2.0 223
  cossaca 137, 138
  crocchè 247
  deep-fried mozzarella bites 82
  diavola 106
  diavola (Davide Ruotolo) 219
  donna Isabella 239
  eccellenza campana 190
  frittatine di pasta 246–7
  Margherita 104
  Margherita extra extra 155
  mimosa 107
  mozzarella 74–7
  nerano montenara 206
  oshirase 144
  parmigiana scomposta 212
  pasta e patate 262
  pizza fritta alla polpette 258
  pizza Genovese 276
  poker 173
  polpo sanità 241
  porchettopeli 268
  prawn tartare and stracciatella 128
  profumo di costiera 147
  provola e pepe 108
  provola (smoked) mozzarella 79–83
  Romana 107
  salami Napoli piccante 156
  salsiccia e zucchini 202
  salsiccia e friarielli 105
  saturnia 122
  scarpetta 163
  scugnizzo per sempre 187
  the 7 consistencies of onion 115

314

Index

sogni di latte 215
stracciatella 85
sugni 193
tomato & mozzarella arancini 244–6
velouté 177
ziti alla Genovese 274
zucca e 'nduja 183
see also ricotta
Chieppa, Lorenzo Bianchino 86
chilli jam: diavola 219
chips/fries: the Americana 125, 127
chocolate: stracietta di pizza al Nutella 234
ciccioli: mezza luna calzone 231
ciggoli: scugnizzo per sempre 187
Ciro Casella 3.0 184–93
Civitiello, Davide 194–203
coffee 282–7, 292
coppa del nonno 286
crema di caffè 285
sogni di latte 215
Concettina ai Tre Santi 14
Condurro, Alessandro 24
Condurro, Luigi 19
Condurro, Michele 19
contemporanea pizza dough 52, 55, 93
centro Calabria 134
contemporanea 2.0 223
crocchè e prosciutto 131
diavola 219
eccellenza campana 190
poker 173
porchettopeli 268
prawn tartare and stracciatella 128
scugnizzo per sempre 187
sugni 193
contemporanea 2.0 223
coppa del nonno 286
cornetti 284
cossaca 137, 138
courgette flowers: nerano montenara 206
courgettes (zucchini)
nerano montenara 206
salsiccia e zucchini 202
cream
the Americana 125, 127
coppa del nonno 286
mimosa 107
salami napoli piccante 156
crema di caffè 285
crisco pepper strands: diavola 219

crocchè 247
crocchè e prosciutto 131
Cynar spritz 310

D

Da Aniello O'Ricciulillo & Figli 249
da Cham, Isabella 236–41
Da Michele 14, 17, 18–19, 24, 26
de Stefano, Pasquale 38–43
deep-fried pizza base: la crisommola 169
deep-fried pizza dough horn: ananascosta 166
diavola 106
diavola (Davide Ruotolo) 219
Domenico 88
Don Vince 254–9
donna Isabella 239
dough 90–5
contemporanea 93
pizza fritta 229
ruota di carro 90
SPG 93–4
STG 92
zeppole 249, 251
Doughdown 195
doughnuts: graffa 294
drinks
limoncello 302–5
spritzes 308–11

E

eccellenza campana 190
Esposito, Antonino 18, 93
Esposito, Gennaro 137
Esposito, Raffaele 12
espresso 282, 292
coppa del nonno 286
crema di caffè 285
drinking espresso in Napoli 282
The Espresso Men 287

F

Federico 265
filetti del vesuvio 196
fiore dei fragola 310
fish
marinara dei signori 209
profumo di costiera 147
Romana 107
flour 46–55
gluten 55

hydration 55
pizza flour 52–5
strength ('W index') 55
type 55
football 30–7
fornaio (oven man) 96
Franco Pepe 158–69
frankfurters: the Americana 125, 127
friarielli: salsiccia e friarielli 105
friarielli cream: oshirase 144
friggitoria 242–7
frittatine di pasta 246–7
fritto misto 252

G

Genovese 272
pizza Genovese 276
ziti alla Genovese 274
Gino and Toto Sorbillo 148–57
Giovanni 40
gluten 55
graffa 294
Grana Padano
ananascosta 166
eccellenza Campana 190
sugni 193

H

hazelnuts: la crisommola 169
Hugo spritz 310

I

I Masanielli 112–23
Isabella De Cham Pizza Fritta 236–41

L

la crisommola 169
lardo e papacella 199
Latteria Sorrentina 40
Lello Spritz 310
lemon oil 215
nerano montenara 206
sogni di latte 215
lemons
a cosce aperte 306
contemporanea 2.0 223
donna Isabella 239
lemon and parsley salad 147
lemon oil 215

lemon sorbet 301
limoncello 305
limoncello 302–5
   limoncello spritz 310
Lioniello, Salvatore 204–15
liquorice powder: ananascosta 166
Loren, Sofia 40

M

Maradona, Diego 34–5, 40
Maradona spritz 310
Margherita 12–14, 104
Margherita, Queen of Savoy 12–14
Margherita extra extra 155
Margherita sbagliata 160
marinara 12, 105
marinara dei signori 209
Martucci, Francesco 112–23
meatballs
   meatballs all Vince 257
   pizza fritta alla polpette 258
mezza luna calzone 231
Midori spritz 310
mimosa 107
mint: la crisommola 169
montenara al ragù 232
Mount Vesuvius 9, 12, 68
mozzarella 74–7
   the Americana 125, 127
   ananas 150
   assoluto di carciofo 116
   autumno 180
   bufala 104
   buffalo mozzarella 76
   calzone ripeno 108
   capricciosa 106
   centro Calabria 134
   crocchè 247
   crocchè e prosciutto 131
   deep-fried mozzarella bites 82
   diavola 106
   diavola (Davide Ruotolo) 219
   donna Isabella 239
   eccellenza campana 190
   frittatine di pasta 246–7
   lardo e papacella 199
   Margherita 104
   Margherita extra extra 155
   Margherita sbagliata 160
   mezza luna calzone 231
   mimosa 107
   oshirase 144
   pasta e patate 262
   pizza Genovese 276

poker 173
porchettopeli 268
provola e pepe 108
Romana 107
salami Napoli piccante 156
salsiccia e zucchini 202
salsiccia e friarielli 105
saturnia 122
scarpetta 163
scugnizzo per sempre 187
the 7 consistencies of onion 115
sogni di latte 215
sugni 193
tomato & mozzarella arancini 244–6
velouté 177
zucca e 'nduja 183
Mozzarella di Bufala Campana DOC 76
Mulino Caputo 48–55, 195
mushrooms
   autumno 180
   capricciosa 106
   poker 173

N

Napoli FC 30–7, 40
Napoletana 12, 107
'nduja
   centro Calabria 134
   zucca e 'nduja 183
Neapolitan pizza 88, 92
Nennella 260–3
nerano montenara 206
Nicholas II, Tsar 137
Nutella: straccietta di pizza al Nutella 234
Nuvola (aka The Purple Bag) 52

O

'o pere e 'o musso 270
octopus: polpo sanità 241
offal: 'o pere e 'o musso 270
oils
   basil oil 160
   lemon oil 215
olive powder: la crisommola 169
olives
   capricciosa 106
   marinara dei signori 209
   polpo sanità 241
   Romana 107
onions
   saturnia 122

   the 7 consistencies of onion 115
   ziti alla Genovese 274
oregano
   marinara 105
   San Marzano sandwiches 67
oshirase 144
ovens 96–9

P

Palazzo Petrucci 14, 216–23
pancetta
   pasta e patate 262
   San Marzano sandwiches 67
   scugnizzo per sempre 187
   velouté 177
panini 278
panko breadcrumbs: deep-fried mozzarella bites 82
papacella peppers: lardo e papacella 199
parmesan
   the Americana 125, 127
   bufala 104
   contemporanea 2.0 223
   crocchè e prosciutto 131
   Margherita 104
   montenara al ragù 232
   parmigiana scomposta 212
   pasta e patate 262
   pizza fritta alla polpette 258
   pizza Genovese 276
   prawn tartare and stracciatella 128
   salami Napoli piccante 156
   scarpetta 163
   velouté 177
   ziti alla Genovese 274
parmigiana scomposta 212
parsley: lemon and parsley salad 147
passata (strained tomatoes)
   Ale's Neapolitan ragù 232
   tomato & mozzarella arancini 244–6
pasta
   frittatine di pasta 246–7
   pasta e patate 262
   ziti alla Genovese 274
pastries: sfogliatella attanasio 296
peas: frittatine di pasta 246–7
pecorino
   assoluto di carciofo 116
   cossaca 137, 138
   crocchè 247

profumo di costiera 147
peels 96
Pepe, Franco 14, 158–69
peppers: lardo e papacella 199
Piaggio Ape 18
pickled onions: the 7 consistencies of onion 115
Piennolo tomatoes 58, 68–9
Pilgrims Pizza Summit 94
pineapple
  ananas 150
  ananascosta 166
pizza
  the Americana 125, 127
  ananas 150
  ananascosta 166
  assoliuto di pomodoro 120
  assoluto di carciofo 116
  autumno 180
  bufala 104
  calzone ripeno 108
  capricciosa 106
  centro Calabria 134
  cossaca 137, 138
  crocchè e prosciutto 131
  diavola 106
  diavola (Davide Ruotolo) 219
  eccellenza campana 190
  filetti del vesuvio 196
  la crisommola 169
  lardo e papacella 199
  Margherita 12–14, 104
  Margherita extra extra 155
  Margherita sbagliata 160
  marinara 12, 105
  marinara dei signori 209
  mimosa 107
  Napoletana 12
  Napoli pizza classics 102–9
  Neapolitan pizza 88, 92
  nerano montenara 206
  oshirase 144
  parmigiana scomposta 212
  pizza and Napoli 12–15
  pizza Genovese 276
  pizza pomodoro 143
  poker 173
  porchettopeli 268
  prawn tartare and stracciatella 128
  provola e pepe 108
  Romana 107
  salami Napoli piccante 156
  salsiccia e zucchini 202
  salsiccia e friarielli 105

  saturnia 122
  scarpetta 163
  scugnizzo per sempre 187
  the 7 consistencies of onion 115
  sogni di latte 215
  sugni 193
  velouté 177
  zucca e 'nduja 183
pizza bases 90–5
  contemporanea 93
  ruota di carro 90
  SPG 93–4
  STG 92
pizza flour 52–5
pizza fritta 224–41
  donna Isabella 239
  messa luna calzone 231
  montenara al ragù 232
  pizza fritta alla polpette 258
  pizza fritta dough 229
  polpo sanità 241
  straccietta di pizza al Nutella 234
pizza fritta dough 229
  donna Isabella 239
  mezza luna calzone 231
  montenara al ragù 232
  nerano montenara 206
  polpo sanità 241
  straccietta di pizza al Nutella 234
Pizza Pilgrims 17, 18, 93
  Pilgrims Pizza Summit 94
  Pizza Pilgrimages 18–19, 20–30
  Pizza Vespa 20–30, 50
pizza portafoglio 101
Pizza World 255
Pizzeria (aka The Blue Bag) 52
Pizzeria Di Matteo 74
Pizzeria Enrico Porzio 170–3
Pizzeria Vincenzo Capuano 124–35
poker 173
polpo sanità 241
Pomodorino del Piennolo 58, 68–9
porchetta 265
  porchettopeli 268
pork: meatballs all Vince 257
Porzio, Errico 170–3
potato crocchè 247
  crocchè e prosciutto 131
potatoes
  crocchè 247
  graffa 294
  pasta e patate 262
  velouté 177
prawns (shrimp)
  fritto misto 252

  prawn tartare and stracciatella 128
  profumo di costiera 147
prosciutto: ananascosta 166
prosciutto cotto
  capricciosa 106
  crocchè e prosciutto 131
  mimosa 107
prosciutto di Parma: poker 173
provola e pepe 108
provola (smoked) mozzarella 79–83
  ananas 150
  assoluto di carciofo 116
  autumno 180
  centro Calabria 134
  deep-fried mozzarella bites 82
  donna Isabella 239
  lardo e papacella 199
  mezza luna calzone 231
  pasta e patate 262
  pizza Genovese 276
  poker 173
  porchettopeli 268
  provola e pepe 108
  salsiccia e zucchini 202
  salsiccia e friarielli 105
  scugnizzo per sempre 187
  sugni 193
  zucca e 'nduja 183
provolone 79
pumpkin purée: zucca e 'nduja 183

R

ragù
  Ale's Neapolitan ragù 232
  montenara al ragù 232
rice: tomato & mozzarella arancini 244–6
ricotta 84
  calzone ripeno 108
  crocchè e prosciutto 131
  la crisommola 169
  mezza luna calzone 231
  poker 173
risotto rice: tomato & mozzarella arancini 244–6
rocket (arugula): poker 173
Romana 107
Ruggiero, Renato 265
ruota di carro pizza dough 90, 149
  ananas 150
  filetti del vesuvio 196
  lardo e papacella 199

Margherita extra extra 155
salami Napoli piccante 156
salsiccia e zucchini 202
Ruotolo, Davide 216–23

S

Saccorossa (aka The Red Bag) 52
salad, lemon and parsley 147
salami
  calzone ripeno 108
  diavola 219
  poker 173
  salami Napoli piccante 156
salsiccia e zucchini 202
salsiccia: zucca e 'nduja 183
salsiccia e friarielli 105
salumerias 278
Salvatore, Lionello 96
Salvo 136–47
Salvo, Francesco 137
Salvo, Salvatore 136–47
Sammarco, Carlo 174–83
San Marzano tomatoes 58, 60–7
  San Marzano sandwiches 67
saturnia 122
sausages
  the Americana 125, 127
  centro Calabria 134
  salsiccia e zucchini 202
  salsiccia e friarielli 105
Scarallo, Lino 217
scamorza 79
scarola
  polpo sanità 241
  sugni 193
scarpetta 163
scugnizzo per sempre 187
seafood
  fritto misto 252
  polpo sanità 241
  prawn tartare and stracciatella 128
semolina flour: fritto misto 252
the 7 consistencies of onion 115
sfogliatella attanasio 296
sogni di latte 215
Solania 60
sorbet, lemon 301
Sorbillo, Gino and Toto 148–57
sour cream: sogni di latte 215
soy sauce: oshirase 144
Spanish conquistadors 58
SPG (Speciality Pilgrims Guaranteed) pizza dough 93–4

spianata: diavola 106
spritzes 308–11
Stanislaus, Tsar of Poland 288
STG (Specialità Tradizionale Garantita) pizza dough 92
  the Americana 125, 127
  autumno 180
  cossaca 137, 138
  Margherita sbagliata 160
  marinara dei signori 209
  oshirase 144
  parmigiana scomposta 212
  pizza Genovese 276
  pizza pomodoro 143
  profumo di costiera 147
  scarpetta 163
  sogni di latte 215
  velouté 177
  zucca e 'nduja 183
Stilton cheese: polpo sanità 241
stracciatella 85
  contemporanea 2.0 223
  nerano montenara 206
  prawn tartare and stracciatella 128
stracciatta di pizza al Nutella 234
sugni 193
sun-dried tomatoes: pizza pomodoro 143
sweetcorn: mimosa 107

T

tartare, prawn 128
Tipo 1 (aka The Green Bag) 52
tomato compote: scarpetta 163
tomato cream
  assoliuto di pomodoro 120
  saturnia 122
tomato sauce 190, 209
  bufala 104
  calzone ripeno 108
  capricciosa 106
  centro Calabria 134
  diavola 106
  eccellenza campana 190
  Margherita 104
  Margherita extra extra 155
  Margherita sbagliata 160
  marinara 105
  marinara dei signori 209
  mezza luna calzone 231
  poker 173
  provola e pepe 108

  Romana 107
  salami Napoli piccante 156
  scugnizzo per sempre 187
tomatoes 56–69
  Ale's Neapolitan ragù 232
  assoliuto di pomodoro 120
  contemporanea 2.0 223
  cossaca 137, 138
  diavola 219
  filetti del vesuvio 196
  Margherita extra extra 155
  marinara dei signori 209
  meatballs all Vince 257
  parmigiana scomposta 212
  pasta e patate 262
  Piennolo tomatoes 58, 68–9
  pizza pomodoro 143
  San Marzano sandwiches 67
  San Marzano tomatoes 58, 60–7
  sugni 193
  tomato & mozzarella arancini 244–6
  tomato sauce 190, 209
Trattoria da Nennella 260–3
Trattoria Don Vince 255
Tutti Frutti 310

U

UNESCO 14

V

velouté 177
Vesuvius, Mount 9, 12, 68

W

Watsonian 21
white wine: ziti alla Genovese 274
wood-fired ovens 96

Z

zeppole 249, 251
ziti alla Genovese 274
zucca e 'nduja 183

Quadrille, Penguin Random House UK, One Embassy Gardens, 8 Viaduct Gardens, London SW11 7BW

Quadrille Publishing Limited is part of the Penguin Random House group of companies whose addresses can be found at global.penguinrandomhouse.com

Penguin Random House UK

Copyright © Pizza Pilgrims and Dave Brown 2025

Cover Artwork © Pasquale de Stefano 2025

Pizza Pilgrims and Dave Brown have asserted their right to be identified as the authors of this Work in accordance with the Copyright, Designs and Patents Act 1988

Penguin Random House values and supports copyright. Copyright fuels creativity, encourages diverse voices, promotes freedom of expression and supports a vibrant culture. Thank you for purchasing an authorized edition of this book and for respecting intellectual property laws by not reproducing, scanning or distributing any part of it by any means without permission. You are supporting authors and enabling Penguin Random House to continue to publish books for everyone. No part of this book may be used or reproduced in any manner for the purpose of training artificial intelligence technologies or systems. In accordance with Article 4(3) of the DSM Directive 2019/790, Penguin Random House expressly reserves this work from the text and data mining exception.

Published by Quadrille in 2025

www.penguin.co.uk

A CIP catalogue record for this book is available from the British Library

ISBN 978 1 83783 296 5

10 9 8 7 6 5 4 3 2 1

Managing Director Sarah Lavelle
Project Editor Harriet Webster
Copy Editors Sally Somers and Harriet Webster
Designer and Art Director Dave Brown
Cover Artist Pasquale de Stefano
Photographer Dave Brown
Production Director Stephen Lang
Production Controller Martina Georgieva
Colour Reproduction by F1

Printed in China by C&C Offset Printing Co., Ltd.

The authorised representative in the EEA is Penguin Random House Ireland, Morrison Chambers, 32 Nassau Street, Dublin D02 YH68.

MIX
Paper | Supporting responsible forestry
FSC® C018179

Penguin Random House is committed to a sustainable future for our business, our readers and our planet. This book is made from Forest Stewardship Council® certified paper.

ROME
SCAN CODE TO SEE THE VESPA IN ACTION
CAIAZZO
SALVATORE LIONIELLO P.204
BAGNO
CARLO SAMMARCO P.175
NAPOLI
P.46 CAPUTO FLOUR
CAPUTO
ISOLA D'ISCHIA
PROCIDA
CAPRI